MENGELE
THE COMPLETE STORY
Gerald L. Posner and John Ware

MENGELE

The Complete Story

Gerald L. Posner and
John Ware

A DELL BOOK

Published by
Dell Publishing Co., Inc.
1 Dag Hammarskjold Plaza
New York, New York 10017

Dell ® TM 681510, Dell Publishing Co., Inc.

ISBN: 0-440-15579-7

Reprinted by arrangement with McGraw-Hill Book Company

Printed in the United States of America

June 1987

10 9 8 7 6 5 4 3 2 1

WFH

This book is dedicated to all of Josef Mengele's victims

Contents

———

———

Acknowledgments

———

———

Writing about a man who spent more than half his life as a fugitive, resolved to escape recognition and retribution, was a singularly difficult task. This book is the result of five years of research. During that time we have gathered one of the largest documentary archives on Josef Mengele, some 25,000 pages of published and unpublished documents. We have spent months in South America, many days researching in the archives of different countries, and have taped more than ninety hours of interviews with individuals involved in Mengele's life. We are satisfied that we have conducted a diligent and thorough investigation, and we take full responsibility for the accuracy of the facts and the validity of the judgments presented. Much of our research would not have been possible without the help of many people and organizations, in more than a dozen countries, on four continents.

In the development of documentation we were aided by Dr. Robert Wolfe, Dr. John Mendelsohn, and John Taylor of the National Archives and Records Service, Washington, D.C.; by Daniel Simon, director of the Berlin Document Center, West Berlin; Dr. Y. Arad, director of Yad Vashem, Jerusalem; Dr. Graciella Swiderski, director of the National Archives of Argentina, Buenos Aires; Dr. Celina Moreira Franco, director of the National Record Center of Brazil, Rio de Janeiro; Dr. Alfredo Viloa, director of the National Document Archives of Paraguay, Asunción; Charles Palm, archivist at the Hoover

Institution, Stanford University, California; and Dr. Howard B. Gotlieb, director, and Charles Niles, archivist, of the Special Collections, Boston University, Boston, Massachusetts.

We also acknowledge the extensive and rapid research, exceeding the statutory mandates of the Freedom of Information Act, performed by James K. Hall, Federal Bureau of Investigation, Washington, D.C.; Thomas F. Conley, United States Army Intelligence and Security Command, Fort Meade, Maryland; and Larry Strawderman, Central Intelligence Agency, Washington, D.C.

We record with gratitude the constructive help provided by American diplomatic missions in South America, especially the efforts of Robert Minutillo and Larry Estes, public affairs officers of the U.S. embassies in Asunción and Buenos Aires, respectively. Their extensive knowledge of the countries in which they are posted, and their generous assistance, opened many doors which might otherwise have stayed closed.

Helping us through a myriad of difficulties in South America, in addition to many who did not want to be publicly acknowledged, were Evandro Carlos de Andrade, editor-in-chief, *O'Globo*, Rio de Janeiro; Zevi Ghivelder, executive director, *Manchete* magazine, Rio de Janeiro; Roberto Guareschi, political editor, *El Clarín*, Buenos Aires; Roberto Forchiniti, archive director, *Abril*, Buenos Aires; Enrique Jara, Latin American director of Reuters, Buenos Aires; Cesar Sanchez Bonitato, archive director, *La Nación*, Buenos Aires; and Donillo Manzini, political editor, *Tiempo Argentino*, Buenos Aires. These individuals not only provided unrestricted access to the confidential files of their publications, but they also led us to unexpected and useful sources of information.

Also in South America, special acknowledgment should be given to a number of government officials who collectively gave us access to voluminous and hitherto undisclosed government documentation on Josef Mengele: Dr. Adolfo Barreyro, private secretary to the minister of the interior, Buenos Aires; Dr. Carlos Castro, director of press affairs, presidential palace, Buenos Aires; Dr. Carlos Alberto Flores, director of the Federal Police, Buenos Aires; Dr. Albino Gomez, director of press affairs at the ministry of foreign affairs, Buenos Aires; Dr. Emilio Gibaja, secretary of public information, interior ministry, Buenos Aires; and Dr. Jaime Malamud, human rights advisor to the President of the Republic, Buenos Aires.

Two journalists were instrumental in uncovering new information and sources: Ralph Blumenthal of the *New York Times* and John Martin of ABC Television. We owe a special thanks to Elliot Welles of the Anti-Defamation League in New York, whose commitment to the work of bringing Nazi criminals to justice was a constant inspiration to us.

Some researchers gave assistance far beyond their obligations or the call of friendship. We would like to make particular mention here of Alexandra Weissler, archivist of the Wiener Library, London, for whom no task was too great; her wise counsel and scrupulous regard for accuracy prevailed on countless occasions. Also Tony Wells of the Wiener Library, and the Wiener Library itself; Robert Hodges, Major (ret.), U.S. Air Force, who gave so much of himself; and Annette Mills, who went out of her way to help in her spare time.

Dr. Günther Deschner, historian, of Munich, was an invaluable help in deciphering the more cryptic passages of Mengele's 5,000 pages of prose.

A very special acknowledgment, of course, is due to the survivors of Mengele's experiments, especially Eva Kor and Marc Berkowitz and their worldwide organization C.A.N.D.L.E.S. (Children of Auschwitz Nazi Deadly Lab Experiment Survivors). Many members of their group spent harrowing hours retelling their dreadful experiences when they would much rather have forgotten them. It should be said that the photographic memory of Marc Berkowitz, Mengele's camp messenger, was the actual inspiration for this book.

We would like to thank several former anonymous members of Israel's Central Institute for Intelligence and Special Missions who helped us compile what we know to be the most detailed account of the Mossad's role in the hunt for Josef Mengele.

Special thanks are certainly due to Brian Moser, producer-director for Central T.V., England, of the documentary "Mengele," for his generous contribution; and to Ray Fitzwalter, editor of "World in Action," Granada Television, England, who understood when events were at their most critical. The insight of Andrew Stephen and inborn optimism of Paul Greengrass were priceless assets too.

With apologies to those whom we may have inadvertently omitted, we list the following who were most active and instrumental in bringing this project to fruition:

Zvi Aharoni, London/ Wilfried Ahrens, Argnt, West Germany/ Dr. Pedro Alvarez, Encarnación, Paraguay/ Koby Behar, police spokesman, Jerusalem/ Lutz Bergmann, publishing director, *Bunte*, Munich/ Lawrence Birns, director, Hemispheric Resources Council, Washington, D.C./ Jonathan Bush, general counsel, Holocaust Memorial Council, Washington, D.C./ Dr. Francisco Carmargo, *O'Estado do Parana*, Curitiba, Brazil/ Aaron Citinblum, archivist, *El Clarín*, Buenos Aires/ Cynthia Cohen, Buenos Aires

Martin A. Crowe, special agent, FBI, New York/ Dr. David Crown, Fairfax, Virginia/ Commodore Juan Carlos Cuadrado, Buenos Aires/ Elena S. Danielson, archivist, Hoover Institution, Stanford University, California/ Denny Debbaudt, Detroit/ Delegado Priamo Amaral, Santa Catarina, Brazil/ Delegation of Israeli Associations, Buenos Aires/ William G. Dolde, Esq., FBI, Miami/ Joel Filartiga, Asunción/ Francisco Cunha Pereira Filho, editor, *Gazete do Povo*, Curitiba, Brazil

Dr. Carlos F. Valerio Fo, forensic dentist, São Paulo/ Francis Grant, Inter-American Association for Democracy and Freedom, New York/ Paul D. Gray, assistant director of U.S. Military Records, St. Louis, Missouri/ Art Harris, *Washington Post*, Atlanta, Georgia/ Dr. Stanley Hilton, Louisiana State University, Baton Rouge/ Lt. Col. Barry Hussey, Buenos Aires/ Jaime Jariton, Asunción/ Barbara Jentzch, German State Radio, Washington, D.C./ Jewish World Congress, Buenos Aires

Peter Jones, archivist, British Library, London/ Simon Jones, London/ William B. Jones, U.S. Department of Justice, Washington, D.C./ Mattis Kalir, Tel Aviv/ Gregory Katz, Gannett newspapers, Washington, D.C./ Ottmar Katz, Munich/ Beate and Serge Klarsfeld, Paris/ Dr. P. Kossack, Humboldt University, East Berlin/ Felix Kuballa, journalist, Cologne/ Hermann Langbein, Vienna

Carlos A. van Lerberghe, Buenos Aires/ Augusto Juan Lertora, Argentine deputy consul general, New York/ Malcolm Levene, London/ M. J. Levin, National Security Agency, Washington, D.C./ Robert A. Liff, Miami/ Dr. Carlos Perez Llanas, advisor to the minister of the interior, Buenos Aires/ John Loftus, Boston/ Bill Lowthar, Washington, D.C./ Federal

Judge (ret.) Jorge Luque, Buenos Aires/ Eduard R. Malayan, first secretary of bilateral and cultural affairs, U.S.S.R. embassy, Washington, D.C./ Angelo Marfisi, New York

Mac Margolis, *Newsweek*, Rio de Janeiro/ Chaim Margolit, Tel Aviv/ David Marwell, historian, U.S. Department of Justice, Washington, D.C./ Sally Millwood, New York/ Jorge Mirkin, Buenos Aires/ Lt. Col. (ret.) William Orbello, Austin, Texas/ V. Orechovsky, assistant to the military attaché, U.S.S.R. embassy, Washington, D.C./ Jorge Ortiz, New York/ Christina Patel, London/ Russel A. Powell, Immigration and Naturalization Service, Washington, D.C./ Martina Puzyna, London/ Thomas E. Quigley, Office of International Justice and Peace, Washington, D.C.

Kirn Rattan, London/ Philip Reed, archivist, Imperial War Museum, London/ Dr. Klaus Richter, New York/ Ricardo Rivas, Buenos Aires/ L. Jeffrey Ross, U.S. Department of Justice, Washington, D.C./ Dr. Cesar Augusto Sanabria, Asunción/ Juergen J. Schillinger, Frankfurt/ Amy K. Schmidt, Modern Military Field Branch Records, Washington, D.C./ Richard A. Schussler, Esq., FBI, Los Angeles/ Gavin Scott, *Time*, Rio de Janeiro

Gad Shimron, Tel Aviv/ Paul Silveira, Miami/ Dr. Benjamin Socolosky, Asunción/ Dr. Norman Stone, Oxford University/ Eric Stover, National Endowment for the Advancement of Science, Washington, D.C./ Patrick Swaffer, London/ Hans-Hermann Tiedge, managing editor, *Bunte*, Munich/ Jacobo Timmerman, Buenos Aires/ David and Enriqueta Trachter, Buenos Aires/ Dr. Horacio Luis Tulian, Buenos Aires/ Ambassador (ret.) Benjamin Varon, Boston/ Dr. Alfredo Viamoso, Foz de Iguacu, Brazil/ Esa Webb, London/ Rona Weitz, Amnesty International, New York/ Albert Zarca, Paris/ Dr. Zdenek Zofka, historian, Munich.

In the pursuit of this project, a special acknowledgment to Joan Eckerman for her unfailing receptiveness to the original concept of a biography about Josef Mengele. Her enthusiasm and work helped to bring this book to fruition. To Katherine Ness, whose conscientious line editing repeatedly saved us from serious errors. To Susan Mayer, for kind support and devotion to the project. To Tom Quinn, our senior editor, for his valuable criticisms of the drafts of the book. He provided reassurance and encouragement through the most difficult of times, and his judgment was always impeccable. Pam Bernstein, the literary agent for this project, provided a professionalism and drive which assisted us at all stages.

This book would not have been possible without the constant practical help and indomitable optimism of Joseph Ferrara, Esq. His skills, friendship, and incredible patience lifted us over apparently insurmountable obstacles.

Finally, and most important, we thank our wives, Trisha Posner and Helena Ware, who have lived with Josef Mengele for five years, and whose support and positive attitudes contributed to and are a part of every aspect of this book. It was they who stayed the course, especially during the hectic summer of 1985. It was they who deserve the ultimate credit for this record being written.

Preface

———

———

Josef Mengele has become the symbol of the Third Reich's perversion of medicine in pursuit of racist scientific theories. His mocking smile and soft but deadly touch earned him the title "The Angel of Death." The barbarity of his crime is not in doubt. What is still at issue is how he escaped justice.

As a fugitive, Mengele was variously rumored to be involved in experiments on Indian tribes in South America, to have the ear of dictators, and to have had numerous brushes with death. He was portrayed as a ruthless power broker who could call upon the services of armed guards and killer dogs, and who moved among a score of impenetrable fortresses deep in the jungle. According to this legend, the only clue to his whereabouts was a trail of dead Israeli agents and independent Nazi-hunters whose corpses washed up on the banks of the Parana River.

These apparently superhuman powers of evasion were based on myths about Mengele's postwar life and are disproved by more than 5,000 pages of diaries and letters that he wrote. We have had unique and unrestricted access to them as well as to previously unpublished photographs, some of which appear in this book. The Mengele papers include a diary that he kept from May 1960 to within weeks of his death. There are also many extracts from an autobiography that Mengele started during the 1960s, but which omits any discussion of both Auschwitz and a ten-year period in Argentina from 1949 to 1959. We believe that Mengele never wrote about Auschwitz, fearing that any record of it might help identify him. We can offer no rational explanation for the absence of any account of the 1950s. His son, Rolf, has never seen any writing by his father about this period and does not believe that any exists. We also have several hundred pages of letters that Mengele sent to his family and friends in Germany, and their replies, from 1973 on. (Letters written before 1973 were destroyed by the Mengele family.)

Our comprehensive study of Mengele's own thoughts, together with the unique accounts given to us by members of his family and friends, betrays a perverse pride in what he did at Auschwitz. It is the evidence of his unqualified lack of remorse that is so astounding. This is not, however, just a study in the banality of Mengele's evil. We have focused on Mengele's charmed escape from the Allies and on how he managed to successfully stay on the run for thirty-five years.

This book is an attempt to separate fantasy from reality. It is a straightforward chronicle of Josef Mengele's life, from his silverspoon childhood in Bavaria to his pauper's grave in Brazil sixty-eight years later. We examine the efforts, and the lack of them, to bring him to trial. We think we have provided many answers to what we regard as the most important question of all: Why was he never caught?

This endeavor is the result of a joint enterprise. John Ware, a television producer, became involved in the Mengele case in 1977 when he prepared a documentary for the "World in Action" program of England's Granada Television. Gerald Posner, a lawyer, was drawn to the case in 1981 during his pro bono legal effort to obtain compensation for the surviving twins who had been subjects of Mengele's experiments. Ware and Posner joined forces in 1984, a partnership that flourished despite the transatlantic separation.

Our conclusion is a simple one, written more in despair than in anger. It is not just that Mengele was not punished for his crimes. He did serve a sentence of sorts, biding his time in a succession of seedy South American hideouts—a nasty old man consumed with self-pity, lonely, even bitter with his family who shielded him so effectively. Nor is it just that a chance was missed to confront the powerful Mengele family, living in dynastic isolation from the rest of the civilized world. The real travesty is that by their failure to pursue Mengele when he was alive, the governments of West Germany, Israel, and the United States—as well as those of Argentina, Paraguay, and Brazil—robbed the world of a chance to explore the mind of a man who was the very personification of evil.

MENGELE

The Complete Story

CHAPTER
1

———
———

The Formative Years

———
———

October 14, 1977, São Paulo: It was hot for springtime. By midday the temperature had climbed to the high seventies. Josef Mengele's son, Rolf, was soaked in perspiration. Months of planning for this secret mission to visit his fugitive father had frayed his nerves. Now he was about to embark on the final and most tension-filled stage of all.

Rolf Mengele's political outlook had long been stabilized "diametrically from my father's, at the left-of-center mark." Just turned thirty-three, a product of the sixties, an era of campus unrest and anti-establishment attitudes, Rolf, a law graduate, had emerged as the black sheep of a formidable family dynasty. The wealth and power of his cousins, aunts, and uncles, whose engineering factory had dominated the small town of Günzburg since the First World War, never much appealed to Rolf. For him the Mengeles of Günzburg personified the unacceptable face of capitalism: they were affluent, yet they were bourgeois, petty, and mean; they enjoyed local patronage, yet they took their power for granted. The suspicion and mistrust was mutual. The Günzburgers, as

Rolf called them, at one time viewed him as a left-wing radical.

Politics aside, Rolf and the rest of the Mengele clan shared one common indestructible bond: all were blood relatives of the most hated and sought-after man in the world. Rolf was his only son; the Günzburgers were his nieces and nephews. Nothing could ever change that fact. On this subject, the two Mengele factions found common cause. Rolf despised what his father had done, but he could never bring himself to betray his own flesh and blood: "In the end he was my father." The Günzburgers were rather more ambivalent about Josef's wartime record. They were then, and remain today, skeptical of many of the allegations against him.

Ever since these allegations first surfaced forty years ago, an impenetrable wall of silence had surrounded Josef Mengele's movements. Even Rolf was not informed of all of them. But now, on this warm October day, Rolf wanted to know everything. And he wanted to hear it directly from his father. "I was fed up with the written arguments. I wanted to confront him."

Twenty-one years had passed since Rolf had first met his father, in the Swiss Alps. Then twelve years old, the boy had been introduced to his long lost "Uncle Fritz," who was visiting the family from South America. Little Rolf was spellbound as his uncle regaled him with tales about daring wartime exploits. Four years later Rolf learned who "Uncle Fritz" really was.

Josef Mengele had become the surviving symbol of Hitler's "Final Solution," the incarnation of its monstrosity—cool, detached, and always immaculately prepared for the long-drawn-out rituals of death, the hellish selections which the young SS doctor so regularly attended during his twenty-one months at the Auschwitz concentration camp.

The memory of this slightly built man, scarcely a hair out of place, his dark green tunic neatly pressed, his face well scrubbed, his Death's Head SS cap tilted rakishly to one side, remains vivid for those who survived his scrutiny when they arrived at the Auschwitz railhead. Polished boots slightly apart, his thumb resting on his pistol belt, he surveyed his prey with those dead gimlet eyes. Death to the left, life to the right. Four hundred thousand souls—babies, small children, young girls, mothers, fathers, and grandparents—are said to have been casually waved to the lefthand side with a flick of the cane clasped in a gloved hand. Mengele was the chief provider for the gas chambers and their crematoria. "He had a look that said 'I am the power,'" said one survivor. At the time, Mengele was only thirty-two years old.

There were moments when his death mask gave way to a more animated expression, when Mengele came alive. There was excitement in his eyes, a tender touch in his hands. This was the moment when Josef Mengele, the geneticist, found a pair of twins.

Under Mengele's strict care, twins were housed in special quarters, cosseted, and treated as priceless objects. To him they were valuable. Within their bodies lay a secret that Mengele had determined Auschwitz would unlock. He would differentiate the replica features of each pair of twins from those that showed some variation. The features that were identical he assumed were inherited; the rest developed and acquired by time and the environment. Thus, he reasoned, could Europe's population be controlled and genetically engineered to perfection. Aryan perfection. In his Auschwitz laboratory, Mengele conducted some of the most heinous experiments of the war. Children, strapped to slabs of marble, had their spines, eyes, and inner organs probed, injected, and cut, often with unknown chemicals and without anesthetic.

To some children Mengele gave comfort and sweets. At these times he is said to have been gentle and soothing, going out of his way not to inflict pain. But often the mask would slip. There were violent rages, summary executions, when his strict disciplinary code was offended. Life at the Dantesque court of Dr. Mengele hung on a whim.

This behavior defies rational explanation, and Mengele acquired a reputation as a kind of demon. But to his son, Rolf, the monster was his father, the man who surely could have been the neighborhood doctor. And yet, could he really have been? Lurking there in the darker dungeons of his mind, might there not have been a severe psychological disorder? This was the mystery that tortured Rolf most of all. On the one hand, his family had spoken of his father's genius before the war, his ambition to become a great scientist. They admired his formidable intellect, his fun-loving ways. He was a ladies' man, erudite and polished, whose mind may have been temporarily corrupted by a political system. On the other hand, the horror of his father's crimes went far beyond anything Rolf had ever read about before.

As the rickety bus carrying Rolf Mengele turned into the pot-holed and dusty street where his father lived, one thing became abundantly clear. However omnipotent Josef Mengele might once have been, his last days were being lived out among the poor and lowly. The bus drew near to a seedy yellow stucco building, more a hut than a house. A swirl of dust blew past to reveal an old man, his gray hair carefully combed, stooped by age, broken by half a lifetime on the run. At that moment Rolf Mengele resolved to explore every stage of the rise and fall of his father, Josef.

Josef Mengele was born on March 16, 1911, the eldest of three sons of Karl and Walburga Mengele, whose first child had been stillborn. The family lived in Günzburg, a small and picturesque town that resembled a fifteenth-century hamlet, nestled on the banks of the river Danube. Josef grew up in a devoutly Catholic home that accumulated considerable wealth in a short time. When Josef was born, his father, an engineer, had just become sole owner of a foundry that manufactured farm equipment for milling, wood sawing, and straw cutting. In 1907 he had gone into partnership repairing farm machinery with a mechanic named Andreas Eisenlauer. That year the foundry burned down, the first of several fires over the next few decades that destroyed the premises. With the insurance proceeds, Karl bought a piece of land just outside the town, where he rebuilt the business from scratch. Two years later, Eisenlauer withdrew from the partnership because of ill health and left Karl in charge, with seven men on the payroll.[1]

The company, "Karl Mengele," prospered. By the time Josef was born, Karl could afford his first Benz motor car. He soon acquired a reputation as a shirt-sleeve boss, prepared to work long hours on the foundry floor and to sell his products by driving from farm to farm in his gleaming new car. When war broke out in 1914, the work force was thirty strong.

As a child, Josef saw little of his father, and not much more of his mother. While Karl went off to fight in the war, Walburga Mengele was left in charge of building up the business. She succeeded by establishing herself as a fearsome disciplinarian, in contrast to her husband's less formal style. Under Walburga's command, the firm procured a lucrative contract with the Kaiser to produce a special army vehicle called the *Fouragewagen*.

At the end of the war, "Karl Mengele" returned to peacetime production of farm machinery. By the 1920s it had become the third largest threshing production company in Germany, Karl having taken full advantage of the country's postwar revival program. The name Mengele has dominated Günzburg ever since, as the town's largest employer and its most powerful family. The mayor has invariably been the family notary. Günzburg, as a German judge once said, *is* the Mengele family.[2]

That dominance survives today, with the name "Mengele" prominently displayed in ten-foot letters on the front of the factory. Karl Mengele Strasse is one of the main thoroughfares. An enormous memorial stone in honor of Karl and Walburga and their two younger sons, Alois and Karl Jr., is adorned with fresh flowers each day. There is a playschool named after Ruth, Alois's wife. Josef's nephew, Dieter Mengele, who has more than a $3 million stake in the firm now named "Karl Mengele & Sons," has the most palatial home in town. In all this patronage, there is only one name conspicuous by its absence—"Josef."

With such luxury and power behind him, young Josef was fully expected to play his part in perpetuating the Mengele family dynasty. As the eldest son, he was destined to succeed his father. But Josef's horizons extended far beyond the small-power politics of Günzburg and a seat in the factory boardroom. From an early age he seemed possessed of a searing ambition. As Julius Diesbach, a school friend, recalled:

> Josef was a very ambitious young man with a great need to succeed. He wanted to establish his own fame separate from that already established by his family. He did not want just to succeed but to stand out from the crowd. It was his passion for fame. He once told me that one day I would read his name in the encyclopedia.[3]

Josef was especially anxious to do better than his two brothers, Karl and Alois—particularly Karl, for whom he admits to
having nurtured a jealous streak. They were born only sixteen
months apart and their rivalry thrived in a house not noted for
its warmth or family affection. "Respect rather than affection
seems to have ruled the household," said Norman Stone, historian and Oxford professor who reviewed Mengele's personal
papers after his death was disclosed in June 1985.[4]
The relationship between his parents did not improve the
emotional austerity of the Mengele home. They were known
as a quarrelsome pair. Josef wrote bitterly of his father as "a
cold figure" and of his mother as "not much better at loving,"
although he came to admire her energy and decisive nature.
For the early part of his life, a nanny called Monika fulfilled
the dominant maternal role, coaxing and at times intimidating Josef into holding fast the Catholic faith. For this parental
legacy at least, Mengele was grateful. In his autobiography he
wrote:

> One could feel flattered that the family tradition go-
> ing back generations was continued with the name of
> the Father of Christ, "Josef."[5]

Despite the sibling rivalry that Josef felt for Karl, the three
Mengele boys gradually grew closer. Josef is remembered as a
"sunny and fun-loving child." His favorite treat was a ride on
horseback, pulling the company transports back from the railway sidings near Günzburg after delivering newly machined
army wagons destined for the front. His autobiography, however, reveals that this genial disposition may have masked a
deep-seated "inner suffering," a dissatisfaction with life, although he does not reveal the cause.[6]
To his family and close friends, young Josef was known as
"Beppo"—a gifted child, brighter than his two younger brothers, always near the top of his class but never actually at the
top. At school Josef developed a great interest in music and
art; as a teenager he wrote a play called "Travels to Lichten-
stein," a fairy tale performed for the benefit of a children's
home. But it was his high-school teacher, Uri, who, he wrote,
"created in me excitement for natural sciences." His favorite
subjects were biology, zoology, physics, and natural philoso-

phy. But most "exciting of all for me," he recorded, was "anthropology."

The strictness of his Catholic upbringing produced in the teenage Josef a cynical contempt for the church and its religious festivals, which he viewed as an opportunity merely to fill its coffers. Nevertheless he displayed an active community spirit by joining the Red Cross and the *Grossdeutscher Jugendbund*, a patriotic youth group.

As a child he also had his share of narrow escapes from illnesses and accidents. At the age of six he fell into a deep rainwater barrel while playing, and nearly drowned. He also once suffered from a bad bout of blood poisoning. In 1926 the family doctor diagnosed osteomyelitis, an inflammation of the bone marrow. This disease can cripple in severe cases, but there was no significant incapacitation, as demonstrated by the fact that Mengele went on to become an accomplished skier.[7]*

In April 1930 he passed his *Abitur*, the high-school exams, with a promising but unexceptional grade. His father had counseled him that what counted was "what one achieved, not what one set out to achieve." Initially Josef considered becoming a dentist, since he was convinced it would be very profitable as "there was not even one dentist in my native town." But after discussions with his school friend Julius Diesbach, young Mengele decided dentistry was too specialized. He opted instead for medicine with an emphasis on "anthropology and human genetics, so I could study the whole range of medicine." Thus Josef pursued his desire for recognition in the encyclopedias of the world. "My family will be very impressed when I become the first Mengele scientist," he boasted to his friend Diesbach with a flourish of adolescent pride. That same year his younger brother, Alois, then sixteen, joined the family firm. The middle brother, Karl, like Josef a more bookish personality, went on to study law.*

In October 1930, a confident and ambitious young man with no evidence of interest in Germany's fast-changing polit-

---

* During the June 1985 forensic examination of the bones unearthed in Embu, Brazil, no evidence of osteomyelitis was found. Some skeptics elevated this minor inconsistency to a degree disproportionate to the weight of other consistent evidence in favor of the skeleton being that of Josef Mengele. Leading forensics experts concluded that a mild case of osteomyelitis in a fifteen-year-old child would not be evident in the skeleton more than fifty years later.

ical times, Josef Mengele left the family home and traveled east to the Bavarian capital of Munich. The city was rapidly becoming intoxicated with the racist doctrines of Adolf Hitler's National Socialist German Workers Party. It was in Munich, with its smoky beer halls, that Hitler found such adulation when he blamed "corrupt" Jewish politicians in Berlin for accepting Germany's humiliating surrender in World War I at Versailles. He fanned the flames of ultra-nationalism, held out the dream of a vast new German empire, and implored the Nazi party to deal with "Jewish vermin" by "exterminating it, root and branch." It was in this hotbed of Nazism, the city that gave birth to the Führer's demonic ambition for a German super-race, that young Josef Mengele took the first steps toward the pseudo-scientific pursuit of that goal. He enrolled as a student in the philosophy and medicine faculties of Munich University.

By the time Mengele joined the university student body, the Nazis had become the second largest party in the German parliament. Like many young men he soon found it difficult to "stand aside during these politically stirring times." In his autobiography Mengele recalls his impressions of the Nazi movement and the strong attraction it held for him:

> The students of the university, those who had already reached the voting age, had contributed to this [Nazi] success. I was not then old enough to vote. My political leanings then were, I think for reasons of family tradition, national conservative. . . . I had not joined any political organization. Though indeed I was strongly attracted by the program and the whole organization of the National Socialists. But for the time being I remained an unorganized private person. But in the long run it was impossible to stand aside in these politically stirring times, should our Fatherland not succumb to the Marxist-Bolshevik attack. This simple political concept finally became the decisive factor in my life.

By March 1931 the impressionable Mengele had joined the youth wing of the *Stahlhelm*, an ex-servicemen's organization whose members marched in field uniforms at public events. Young Josef admired the pomp and circumstance of their paramilitary style. Though fiercely nationalistic and right wing, the *Stahlhelm* was not yet affiliated with the Nazi party, for which Mengele showed growing admiration.

While Josef did not join the Nazi party for another six years, his father had decided by 1931 that membership in the party would be a profitable move. With an eye to the future, Karl Mengele, Sr., had for some time been a drinking companion of Georg Deisenhofer, the *Kreisleiter*, or regional party chief, and a virulent anti-Semite who complained after Günzburg's 300 Jews were driven out that there were "none left that I can insult."[8] Shortly after Hitler was swept to power, Karl paid Deisenhofer a sum of money in exchange for a seat on the Günzburg town council. Karl had prepared the way just the previous year by playing host to Hitler himself when he gave a speech on farming at the Mengele factory.* His corruption paid dividends: by 1936 the factory had an annual revenue of more than 1 million reichsmarks and 350 people were on the payroll.[9]

In Munich, meanwhile, Josef was taking courses in anthropology and paleontology as well as medicine. He soon showed himself to be more interested in the cultural origins and development of man than in curing his disabilities. Medicine at German universities was in any case more complementary to Mengele's real interest in evolution, since it was taught in accordance with the guidelines of the social Darwinist theories that Hitler and a growing number of German academics found so attractive.

Precisely what corrupted Mengele's eager young mind is hard to pin down. Probably it was a combination of the political climate and that his real interest in genetics and evolution happened to coincide with the developing concept that some human beings afflicted by disorders were unfit to reproduce, even to live. Perhaps the real catalyst in this lethal brew was that Mengele, first at Munich and later at Frankfurt, studied under the leading exponents of this "unworthy life" theory. His consummate ambition was to succeed in this fashionable new field of evolutionary research. The notion that some lives were not worth living, soon to become academically respectable, may explain why ten years later Mengele experimented

---

* This was Hitler's second visit to Günzburg, the first having taken place in 1930. Heinrich Himmler, Reichsführer of the SS and a former chicken farmer, also visited the town in 1930 and gave a speech on farming.

on concentration camp inmates as though they were laboratory rats. What none of these influences explain is how Mengele became capable of personal acts of quite unrivaled savagery, for which he later showed not the slightest remorse.
"There was nothing in his personality to suggest that he would
do what he did," said Professor Hans Grebe, a contemporary
of Mengele's in the 1930s.[10]

One of the earliest influences on the student doctor was Dr.
Ernst Rudin, whose lectures Mengele regularly attended. Together with some of the leading members of the medical
profession, such as Dr. Alfred Hioche and Dr. Karl Bindong,
Rudin was a leading proponent of the theory that doctors
should destroy "life devoid of value." Rudin himself was one
of the architects of Hitler's compulsory sterilization laws,
which were enacted in July 1933, seven months after he came
to power.

The Law for the Protection of Hereditary Health established the mental and physical conditions that qualified for
compulsory sterilization: feeblemindedness, schizophrenia,
manic depression, epilepsy, hereditary blindness, deafness,
physical deformities, Huntington's disease, and alcoholism.
Rudin and others had crafted their measures to improve the
"quality" of the German race.[11] In fact, they were the start of
a series of escalating genocidal programs: first, euthanasia or
"mercy" killing for the incurably insane; then the mass kill-
ings of people the Nazis judged to be biologically inferior,
such as Gypsies, Slavs, and Jews; finally *Die Endlösung*, the
Final Solution, Hitler's cover name for his plan to exterminate
all the Jews in Europe.

By early 1934, Mengele's time was increasingly consumed
by his studies. Other students never regarded him as a formidable intellect. He distinguished himself more by hard work
than anything else. "He was essentially more industrious and
ambitious than others," said a fellow student and friend, Dr.
Kurt Lambertz. "The more he became involved with the
study of anthropology, genetics, heredity and such things, the
more his interests grew."

Mengele's searing ambition had driven him to work for a
doctorate in anthropology while at the same time striving to
qualify as a doctor in medicine. In October that year, his part-
time paramilitary activities came to a halt when a kidney

ailment forced him to leave the *Sturmabteilung*, the Brown-shirts, ruffians whose job it was to "protect" Nazi mass rallies. Mengele had been automatically transferred to the Brown-shirts in January 1934, after Hitler ordered them to absorb the *Stahlhelm*.[12] His illness left him weak, and he decided to devote all his energy to studying.

The man who gave Mengele his first real leg up the academic ladder was Professor T. Mollinson of Munich University. His expertise in the field of heredity and "racial hygiene" led Mollinson to claim that he could tell if a person had Jewish forebears simply by looking at a photograph. In 1935 Mollinson awarded Mengele a PhD for his thesis entitled "Racial Morphological Research on the Lower Jaw Section of Four Racial Groups." It was a dry but meticulously illustrated dissertation, and concluded that it was possible to detect different racial groups by studying the jaw. In contrast to Mollinson's unscientific assertions, Mengele's report was cogently argued and contained no anti-Semitic or racist overtones. In the summer of 1936 Mengele took his state medical examination in Munich. He passed and was soon working in his first paid job, in Leipzig at the university's medical clinic.*

For four months he was one of the resident junior doctors, a compulsory period of hospital work required for his full medical practitioner's degree. The work was hard and his stay uneventful, with the notable exception that it was in Leipzig that he met a university professor's daughter, Irene Schoenbein, who became his first wife.

Irene was Mengele's first and only real love. She was just nineteen, dividing her time between the handsome young academic and studying art history in Florence. Mengele was so smitten that he soon cast aside a Norwegian girl named Almuth. As Mengele later told his son, Rolf, Irene was so devoted that even the thought of her suitor having had a previous affair made her angry "even though she had won my heart."[13]

They made a dashing young pair—Irene tall, blonde, and good looking, Mengele handsome in a Mediterranean way, dapper, with a passion for fast cars. He boasted he could drive

---

* It was the recommendation of doctors from the Leipzig clinic that a baby born blind, "an idiot—at least it seemed to be an idiot," with a leg and part of an arm missing, should be killed that finally persuaded Hitler to sign a decree legalizing euthanasia on September 1, 1939.

from Günzburg to Frankfurt in three hours in his 1936 Opel, a special-issue model produced to commemorate the Berlin Olympics.

Away from the high life, Mengele's spell as a young hospital doctor, with its exhausting hours and endless ward rounds, seems not to have suited him. He was anxious to return to his studies in genetics. On January 1, 1937, after a recommendation from Professor Mollinson, Mengele was appointed a research assistant at the prestigious Third Reich Institute for Heredity, Biology and Racial Purity at the University of Frankfurt. The appointment would change Mengele's life. He joined the staff of one of Europe's foremost geneticists, Professor Otmar Freiherr von Verschuer, who was devoting much of his time to twin research.

Von Verschuer was an outspoken admirer of Adolf Hitler, paying tribute to him publicly for "being the first statesman to recognize hereditary biological and race hygiene." Two years earlier von Verschuer had defined the Institute's role as being "responsible for ensuring that the care of genes and race, which Germany is leading worldwide, has such a strong basis that it will withstand any attacks from outside."[14]

Mengele became the professor's favorite student; the two men developed a strong mutual respect. Von Verschuer almost certainly influenced Mengele's subsequent appointment to Auschwitz; and later, as wartime director of the Kaiser Wilhelm Institute for Anthropology, Human Hereditary Teaching and Genetics in Berlin, he secured funds for Mengele's experiments at Auschwitz. (This was the Institute where Mengele sent the results of his barbaric and largely worthless research.)

Mengele was now at the epicenter of Nazi philosophical and scientific thinking, which held that it was possible to select, engineer, refine, and ultimately "purify" their race. From this concept to Hitler's policy of genocide was a short but tragic step.

For Mengele, indoctrinated with Nazi race theories, membership in the Nazi party itself was now a simple formality. In May 1937 he submitted his application and was duly issued membership number 5574974.* As a paid-up party member, and with the support of Baron von Verschuer, a rapid rise within the Nazi academic hierarchy was now assured.

Before long Mengele and von Verschuer were working together, writing judicial reports for specially convened courts which sat in judgment over Jews caught cohabiting with German Aryans. Under the Nuremberg Race Law, passed in September 1935, it was an offense for Germans to marry Jews, the purpose of the law being to prevent racial interbreeding. Proven cases of sexual intercourse in this *Rassenschande,* or race defilement process, carried a jail sentence. In one case advice was sought from both von Verschuer and Mengele when a man whose father was Jewish was charged with having an affair with a German woman. The defendant tried to convince the court that although his mother was married to a Jew, he was in fact born as a result of a liaison she had had with a Christian and therefore had no Jewish blood. Giving evidence for the prosecutor's office, Mengele and von Verschuer, having examined the unfortunate man's family history, ears, nose, and other facial features, pronounced that his father was Jewish. The court did not agree, and the two anthropologists lodged a complaint at the verdict, claiming their expertise had been overlooked.[15]

It was against this background at the Frankfurt Institute that Mengele first embraced the idea that through appropriate selection, the heritage of a race could be "improved." Before long the concept was applied in a much starker way, on the ramps at Auschwitz where SS doctors, Mengele especially, selected able-bodied inmates for work and the frailer ones for death. Mengele showed no qualms about being drawn further into this pseudo-scientific mire. Helmut von Verschuer, son of Mengele's Frankfurt mentor, recalled that his father's young disciple was "a man of happy disposition, known by the secretaries at my father's office as 'Father Mengele' because he liked the girls." Certainly Professor von Verschuer thought highly of Mengele; he soon appointed him as one of his assistant physicians. This appointment effectively

---

* This was the first opportunity for Mengele to join the NSDAP after Hitler lifted his four-year embargo on party membership. The embargo had been intended to counter Hitler's fear that the rush to join the National Socialist Party following its 1933 election victory would swing the party's power base in favor of a more liberal regime.

qualified him as a doctor even though he had yet to receive his degree.[16] Von Verschuer later wrote of his protégé:

> He had a keen interest in medical research and surgery. He was also intelligent and cultured. I remember he was a lover of music, including Bach, Verdi, and of course Strauss and Wagner.[17]

By the time Mengele got to Auschwitz he had developed a love of Puccini, too, as survivors—who heard him casually whistling a few bars while carrying out gas chamber selections—grimly recall.

Mengele was only twenty-seven years old, but he had made powerful contacts with some of the foremost doctors and ideologues of the Third Reich. It was inevitable, therefore, that he should apply to join an organization seen as the guardian of the nation's racial purity; the SS, or *Schutzstaffel*. At this time he also joined the NS *Arztebund*, the physicians' association, an imperative for any aspiring Nazi doctor. In May 1938, after the ritual trawl back through four generations to ensure that the Mengele family was free of Jewish or other non-Aryan blood, he was admitted to the SS.* Vanity prevented him from having his blood group tattooed on his skin, however, as all new SS recruits were obliged to do.

Membership in an elite seems to have been important to Mengele: he chose an academic career in preference to conventional medical practice, he joined the Third Reich Institute and later the Kaiser Wilhelm Institute, both leaders in the exclusive field of eugenics, and he went on to join the Waffen SS, an elite within the SS elite itself.

In July 1938 Frankfurt University awarded Mengele his medical degree. Thus he became a licensed practitioner of medicine. As the war clouds gathered over Europe, Mengele was anxious not to be left out of what he perceived would be an inevitable but glorious battle. Determined to be accepted by an SS unit, that October he began three months of basic

---

* SS Colonel Walter Rauff, who organized the development and production of the mobile gas vans estimated to have killed 97,000 Jews and Russians, at first failed the SS heredity test because his fiancee had been married to a Jewish lawyer. Eventually Himmler's office accepted her submission that her first marriage had been "an oversight" due to the fact that she had "not studied racial biology . . . and was unaware of the consequences of this marriage." Rauff died of lung cancer in Santiago, Chile, in May 1983 after several attempts to secure his extradition had failed.

training with the Wehrmacht, the German regular army, a prerequisite for joining the elite fighting force. To his delight, his first posting, to the Snalfedon-Tirol mountain region, called on his skiing skills. When the training was over, Mengele returned to the Frankfurt Institute to continue his research under Professor von Verschuer. Apart from a short spell at the University Clinic in Bonn, where he also attended indoctrination classes for the SS in his spare time, Mengele stayed at the Institute until June 1940, when he joined the army.[18]

During his stay at Frankfurt, Mengele published a research paper on the inheritance of ear fistules, the tiny folds in the ear for which he claimed to have found a hereditary link with indentations of the chin. Experts who have read the paper found it "dull but scientific," and like his previous paper on the racial identification of the lower jaw, devoid of racist innuendo. However, several reviews written by Mengele at Frankfurt on academic books about race and heredity tell a different story. His comments, in 1940, about one book entitled *Fundamentals in Genetics and Race Care*, emphasize his total conviction of the supremacy of the German race.

> The last chapter explains . . . the biological dangers that threaten the German people . . . when discussing the races it would have been desirable if a clearer analysis of the merits and unfavorable features of all European races had been made. I also missed an adequate description of the relationship between the principal races that are to be found in Germany and the cultural achievements of the German people. Also there could have been more sense in explaining the contents rather than the procedural aspects of the laws for prevention of hereditary-diseased offspring and the protection of the hereditary health of the German nation.[19]

Another review of a book discussing the inheritance of congenital heart defects and their detection by X-ray is an ominous hint of things to come at Auschwitz: "Unfortunately the author did not use subjects where the diagnosis could be verified by an autopsy."[20]

By now Mengele had totally identified with the influence of National Socialism on human genetics as taught in Germany in the 1920s and '30s. Nazi racial doctrines and earlier ideas of social Darwinism had fused into one homogeneous concept that stayed with Mengele for the rest of his life. "He was convinced he served a great cause, an attempt by Hitler to prevent mankind from self-destructing," said Professor Andreas Hillgruber, the West German historian who has read Mengele's autobiographical writings on race. "He became the incarnation of Nazism in its extreme."[21]

In July 1939 Mengele married Irene, then almost twenty-two years old, at Oberstdorf. The wedding itself took place after a hitch that at one stage threatened to damage his career. In Mengele's submission to the *Rasse- und Siedlungshauptampt,* the Central Office for Race and Resettlement, to satisfy the SS that there was no trace of Jewish blood in Irene's family, doubts were raised about her grandfather, who was thought to be illegitimate. An exhaustive check back through her ancestors began after papers relating to her great-grandfather, Harry Lyons Dumler, an American diplomat, could not be found. In the absence of proof that Dumler was the father of his wife's son, the suspicion remained that the real father might be Jewish. Thus Irene might have inherited Jewish blood. A search by the German consul in the United States failed to resolve the crisis. But photographs of Irene and her ancestors and glowing testimonials from friends of her "very Nordic ways" finally won the day, and so the marriage was allowed. Yet since Mengele was unable to provide clinching proof that Irene had "pure Aryan blood," much to his chagrin he failed to qualify for the ultimate accolade of racial purity— a place in the hallowed *Sippenbuch,* or Kinship Book, for those who had been able to prove, chapter and verse, that their ancestors were pure Aryan at least since 1750. Thus was the archdisciple of racial "hygiene" himself deprived of a certificate that his wife and future children would be racially "clean." Irony and ignominy apart, there was also the loss of the coveted *Sippenbuch* mementos—swords and silver spoons from Himmler himself on the birth of each "pure" child.

Five weeks after the wedding, the war broke out. According to Mengele's son, Rolf, his father was "pleased about it. He couldn't wait to be called up." To Mengele, as he later wrote, the war represented the "last desperate fight of the German nation for its endangered existence." But his kidney ailment meant he had to wait until the summer of 1940 for his first posting, as a medical officer in a regular army unit at Kassel. It lasted just one month. In August, with the rank of *Unter-sturmführer*, sub-lieutenant, he joined the Waffen SS, which enjoyed a reputation as Hitler's most fanatical combat troops. Nonetheless, Mengele did not experience battlefield conditions until June 1941, when he was posted to the Ukraine, where within a few days he was awarded the Iron Cross Second Class. His wife wrote to a friend:

> Now he finally has his desired call-up. He is stationed in the Ukraine, I assume in that heat. He received the EK2 [Iron Cross Second Class] already in the first days. The stress must be tremendous. Still their enthusiasm has not yet found an end, now that they are finally in battle and . . . facing the "archenemy." Best regards and Heil Hitler . . .[22]

The months before the Ukraine posting were spent in occupied Poland, attached to the Genealogical Section of the Race and Resettlement Office. Under direct orders from Himmler, teams of SS doctors were assigned to examine the racial suitability of those who would inhabit the newly conquered territories. Himmler's four-point program, in which Mengele played an active role, was as follows:

> (1) The annexed territories were to be thoroughly cleansed of non-Germans; (2) persons claiming any German blood would be classified according to documentary evidence first, and lacking that, by racial examination; those in doubtful categories as well as "renegade" [anti-Nazi or "Polish minded"] Germans would be segregated and subjected to special conditions to ensure "re-education and good behavior"; (3) persons exhibiting Germanic features would also undergo racial examinations to determine if their ancestors had been "Polanized"; positive cases would be removed from Poland for better re-Germanization in the Reich proper; (4) similar procedures would be carried out upon orphans from Polish orphanages as well as children coming under public care.[23]

In January 1942 Mengele joined the medical corps of the
Waffen SS's Viking division. It eventually penetrated farther
into Soviet territory than any other German unit deployed
after the Russian offensive launched the previous June. Most
of Mengele's time was spent back of the front line in a defensive position, perhaps fighting partisans. In July the Viking
division moved up to the front to engage in the battle for
Rostow and Bataisk, a battle lasting five bloody days. It was
during this period that Mengele won his Iron Cross First Class.
Irene recalls, "He got his Iron Cross because he rescued two
wounded soldiers out of a burning tank under enemy fire on
the battlefield and gave them medical first aid." A senior
officer later wrote that Mengele had "proved himself
splendidly in front of the enemy," and the Viking divisional
medical officer wrote at the time that he was "a specially
talented medical officer." He was also awarded the Black
Badge for the Wounded and the Medal for the Care of the
German People.[24]*

Toward the end of 1942 Mengele was posted back to the
Race and Resettlement Office, this time at its headquarters in
Berlin. The fact that Mengele worked under the aegis of the
SS and the Police Doctor's Office, which had a medical super-
visory role in the extermination camps, suggests that he was
entrusted with the secret of the Final Solution at quite an
early stage. Although Hitler had decided in the summer of
1941 to press ahead with the Final Solution, the decision to
adopt it as official policy had been taken only the past January,
by fifteen high-ranking bureaucrats before sitting down to
lunch in a secret conclave in the Berlin suburb of Wannsee. It
is possible that as a result of discovering the vast amount of
"human material" available for experiments at Auschwitz,
Mengele, once in Berlin, did all he could to secure a posting
there. It seems equally likely that he sought this job in collaboration with his former tutor, Professor von Verschuer, whose
guiding hand was certainly behind his transfer from the Russian front to Berlin.

By the summer of 1942 von Verschuer was director of the
Kaiser Wilhelm Institute in Berlin, overseeing research pro-

---

* The official volumes of the Fifth SS Panzer Division, "Viking," lists the names of officers
and field doctors, with only one exception: Josef Mengele. His name was evidently omitted
because of the postwar notoriety attached to it.

grams into racial purity. In June 1942, while Mengele was still serving with the Viking division at the Russian front, von Verschuer told a colleague that he planned "to take with me my co-workers, initially Schade and Grebe, later Mengele and Fromme."[25] In January 1943, von Verschuer wrote to another colleague that "my assistant Mengele has been transferred to a post in Berlin so that in his free time he can work at the Institute."[26]

Dr. Benno Müller-Hill, of Cologne University, who has had access to von Verschuer's private papers, is in little doubt that von Verschuer finally persuaded Mengele to take this next and, for him, disastrous step in his life. "I would almost bet it was von Verschuer who talked him into going to Auschwitz," Müller-Hill said. "He would have said, 'There's a big opportunity for science there. Many races there, many people. Why don't you go? It's in the interest of science.'"

After Mengele's transfer to Berlin, he was promoted to the rank of *Hauptsturmführer,* captain. In May 1943 the posting came. By the end of the month he arrived at a vast barbed-wire enclosure in a swampy valley an hour out of Kraków in southern Poland. This was Auschwitz, or to the Germans, who love to abbreviate everything, "the KZ," shorthand for *Konzentrationslager,* or concentration camp.

C H A P T E R
2

———

———

Auschwitz:
May 1943–January 1945

———

———

The sight that greeted Josef Mengele when his train drew near to Auschwitz was awesome. One landmark especially must have caught his eye, as it did for a fellow doctor, Miklos Nyiszli, when he first arrived:

> . . . an immense square chimney built of red bricks tapering towards the summit. I was especially struck by the enormous tongues of flame rising between the lightning rods. . . . I tried to realize what hellish cooking would require such a tremendous fire. . . . A faint wind brought the smoke towards me. My nose, then my throat were filled with the nauseating odor of burning flesh and scorched hair.[1]

In high summer the sun scorched the earth and the stagnant, heavy, breezeless air pervaded every corner of the camp with its stench of burning flesh. In winter, Auschwitz was ravaged by ice storms sweeping in off the Vistula river.

Most Poles considered this remote corner of their country too inhospitable to live in. Himmler considered it the perfect place for the largest extermination center in the Third Reich's genocide program, as its commandant, Rudolf Hoess, guessed after the Reichsführer's visit in March 1941, when he ordered a vast new expansion program:*

> The numbers envisaged were at this time something entirely new in the history of concentration camps. At that time a camp containing 10,000 persons was considered exceptionally large. The insistence of the Reichsführer SS that the construction work must be pushed on regardless of all present or future difficulties, many of which were and would be well nigh insuperable, gave me much food for thought even then.[2]

By the time Mengele arrived in May 1943, Auschwitz was packed with almost 140,000 prisoners and stretched for miles in all directions. Dr. Nyiszli, a Hungarian Jew who served as an inmate pathologist under Mengele's supervision, was overwhelmed when he discovered how large the camp was:

> I returned to Barracks 12 just in time for Dr. Mengele's arrival. He drove up and . . . sent for me and asked me to join him in his car . . . [and we] started off again along the bumpy road. For about twelve minutes we drove through the labyrinth of barbed wire and entered well-guarded gates, thus passing from one section to another. Only then did I realize how vast the KZ was. Few people had the possibility of verifying that because the majority died at the very place to which they were sent when they first arrived. Later I learned that Auschwitz KZ had at certain periods held more than 100,000 people within its enclosure of electrified barbed wire.[3]

This enormous camp, surrounded by barbed wire and patrolled by SS guard dogs, contained five crematoria and gas chambers. On a clear day, flame and black smoke could be seen for thirty miles, spewing from the chimneys of the crematoria that broke the flat marshland skyline around Ausch-

---

* Himmler had chosen the right man for the job in appointing Hoess. He was convicted of murder before the war.

witz. According to Commandant Hoess, the highest total of Jews gassed in twenty-four hours was 9000:

> This figure was attained in the summer of 1944 during the action against Hungary, using all the installations except number three. On that day, owing to delays on the line, five trains arrived instead of three as expected and in addition the carriages were more crowded than usual.[4]

Although, as Hoess said, Himmler ordered records to be burned, "after every large action," the total number of Jews gassed at Auschwitz is known to be about 2.5 million. According to Hoess, this was the figure supplied by Adolf Eichmann* shortly before Berlin was surrounded:

> Eichmann and his permanent deputy, Gunther, were the only ones who possessed the necessary information on which to calculate the total numbers destroyed.[5]

Mass extermination, then, was the primary purpose of Auschwitz, but it was by no means its only important function. Auschwitz was also a slave labor camp, providing a pool of workers for German companies contributing to the war effort. The strongest of the new prisoners were selected to live solely because they could be made to work until they dropped dead. Those who collapsed were sometimes kicked and beaten to determine if they were still alive. Thirty-four companies— many of them still household names today, like Krupp, AEG Telefunken, Siemens, Bayer, and IG Farben—made fortunes from the tortured labor of Jews, Russians, Poles, some Allied prisoners of war, and German prisoners of conscience. The biggest IG Farben factory was at Monowitz, a subcamp in Auschwitz that made synthetic rubber. In return for providing slave labor, Farben paid the SS a daily rate of 4 reichsmarks for a skilled laborer, 3 reichsmarks for an unskilled laborer, and 1 1/2 reichsmarks for a child. In his evidence against Farben directors† in the postwar trials against Ger-

---

* Adolf Eichmann was *Obersturmbannführer*, lieutenant colonel, in charge of Department IV-B-4, the section of the Reich Central Security Office in Berlin responsible for deporting Jews. He was hanged in Israel on May 31, 1962.

† The IG Farben directors, who regularly visited the camp and received monthly reports on its operation, later testified in their defense at the Nuremberg military tribunal that they

man industrialists, Benjamin B. Ferencz, an American lawyer, told the court that Farben crowded 400 prisoners into a block intended for 162. Each wooden bunk, padded only with a thin layer of filthy straw, was shared by three prisoners. Dysentery and diarrhea added to their misery:

> Inmates were literally being worked to death. They were forced to run while unloading heavy cement bags weighing more than one hundred pounds. Drinking water was contaminated, clothing was sparse and the food was totally inadequate. Many died of freezing or starvation. The conditions for all forced laborers were terrible. But by far the worst were the conditions of the Jews.[6]

In sharp contrast to the squalid conditions for inmates, life for the SS noncommissioned ranks who guarded the camp— participating in the gassings euphemistically known as "special actions," executions, and the rounding up of slave labor— was tolerably comfortable. Any "special action" work attracted extra rations: ten cigarettes a day, one-fifth of a liter of vodka, and four ounces of German sausage. But for SS officers, like Mengele, the rewards were even more generous. One of Mengele's Auschwitz colleagues, Dr. Johann Kremer, kept a diary. While he devoted only a few sentences to his role in the "special actions," he recalled in detail how he savored the good life, especially the food served up by chefs at the Waffen SS club. Five September days were particularly memorable:

> Sept. 6: Today, an excellent Sunday dinner; tomato soup, one half of chicken with potatoes and red cabbage, and magnificent vanilla ice cream. . . . In the evening at 8:00 attended another special action outdoors.* Sept. 9: This morning I received most welcome news from my lawyer . . . that I was divorced from my wife from the 1st of the month. Later was present as the physician at the flogging of eight camp inmates and at one execution by shooting with a small calibre gun. Got soap flakes and 2 cakes of soap . . . Sept. 17: Have ordered a casual

---

never noticed anything was wrong and moreover that they were only doing what was "necessary" and that they were "carrying out orders."

* That day 981 Jews were brought from the camp at Drancy, France, to Auschwitz. Out of this number, 16 men and 38 women were admitted to the camp as prisoners. The rest were gassed.

coat from Berlin. *Sept. 20:* This Sunday afternoon I listened from 3 p.m. 'till 6 p.m. to a concert of the prisoners' band in glorious sunshine; the bandmaster was a conductor of the state opera in Warsaw. Eighty musicians. Roast pork for dinner . . . *Sept. 23:* This night was present at the 6th and 7th special actions.* At 8 o'clock in the evening, supper in the home of Grupenführer Pohl, a truly festive meal. We had baked pike, as much as we wanted, real coffee, excellent beer and sandwiches.[7]

Other trappings of a comfortable life were preserved by camp commandant Hoess, who lived with his wife and five children in a white stucco house surrounded by a white picket fence. The garden that circled the house was filled with red hedges and begonias in blue flower boxes. It was, as Hoess recalled, an idyllic setting for his camp home:

Every wish that my wife or children expressed was granted them. The children could live a free and untrammeled life. My wife's garden was a paradise of flowers. . . . The children were . . . particularly fond of the ones [prisoners] who worked on the garden.

My whole family displayed an intense love of agriculture and particularly for animals of all sorts. Every Sunday, I had to walk them all across the fields and visit the stables, and we might never miss out on the kennels where the dogs were kept. Our two horses and the foal were especially beloved.

The children always kept animals in the garden, creatures the prisoners were forever bringing them. Tortoises, martens, cats, lizards: there was always something new and interesting to be seen there. In summer they splashed in the paddling pool in the garden or in the Sola [river]. But their greatest joy was when daddy bathed with them. He had, however, so little time for all these childish pleasures.[8]

It was this attempt to maintain a normal life in the midst of extraordinary cruelty and inhumanity that made Auschwitz a

---

* Two transports of Jews from Slovakia and Drancy, France, were gassed after selections at the railhead.

place out of Dante's Inferno. At times Auschwitz resembled the theater of the absurd. There were even traffic regulations in the camp, and red and green traffic lights. Infractions brought an investigation by the SS traffic court, as Mengele himself discovered a month after his arrival when he hit an SS armaments truck while speeding on his motorcycle toward Birkenau.* Mengele was "injured† and parts of his uniform as well as the motorcycle were damaged," but the court found that "the SS Hauptsturmführer's guilt could not be established."[9]

There were many other Dantesque aspects to life at Auschwitz. The camp had its own soccer stadium, library, photographic lab, theater, SS swimming pool, and symphony orchestra. There was even a brothel called "The Puff," used by SS men and some favored prisoners.

When Mengele entered the nightmare world of Auschwitz, he immediately set himself apart from the other SS doctors. He was the only camp doctor to have served on the eastern front and to have been awarded the Iron Cross and other decorations. Dr. Hans Münch, an SS doctor who served in a bacteriological laboratory in a subcamp of Auschwitz and who became a close friend of Mengele's, remembers that Mengele was enormously proud of his medals and wore them prominently displayed on his uniform. Mengele frequently referred to his combat experience, and he quickly developed a special aura in the camp because of his front-line fighting, which contrasted sharply with the desk careers of the other camp doctors.

Mengele coupled his combat status with workaholic devotion to his duties. While other Auschwitz doctors did no more than was required of them, Mengele was always undertaking new projects and extra responsibility. He flourished in Auschwitz—so much so that even today some survivors still mistak-

---

* Auschwitz was originally a military barracks for the Polish army. Himmler built another camp nearby at Birkenau in 1941. Thereafter it was known as Auschwitz-Birkenau.

† During the forensic examination in Brazil in June 1985, the doctors determined that the skeleton had suffered a hip fracture which was compatible with the type of fracture that could result from a motorcycle accident. Simon Wiesenthal, the Vienna-based Nazi-hunter, speculated that Mengele's Auschwitz accident might have caused a broken hip. The SS files, normally meticulous in reporting details of accidents, omit any mention of this. Irene Mengele does not recall her husband ever talking about a broken hip. The injury discovered in the 1985 examination must therefore have resulted from a postwar accident which none of Mengele's friends know about.

enly refer to him as the chief physician of the camp, a post in
fact held by Dr. Eduard Wirths, who appointed Mengele senior doctor in the women's camp in Birkenau.

Within days after his arrival, while Auschwitz was in the
throes of one of its many typhoid epidemics, Mengele established a reputation for radical and ruthless efficiency. The
nearby marshland made clean water difficult to obtain and
posed a constant threat from mosquitoes.* Other SS doctors
had failed in their efforts to curb typhus in the close quarters
of the camp barracks. Mengele's solution to the epidemic was
set out in one of seventy-eight indictments drawn up in 1981
by the West German Prosecutor's Office, when the authorities
thought he was still alive. In terms of detailed evidence, this
arrest warrant is the most damning and complete document
that was ever compiled against him. According to the warrant, on May 25, 1943, "Mengele sent 507 Gypsies and 528
Gypsy women suspected of typhus to the gas chamber." It also
charged that on "May 25 or 26 he spared those Gypsies who
were German while he sent approximately 600 others to be
gassed."[10]

Such contempt for these lives is explained by Mengele's
view that Gypsies were a subspecies. The irony was that Mengele himself was sometimes known to remark on his own
distinctly un-Aryan looks, which more closely resembled
those of a Gypsy than of a perfect Nordic specimen. Indeed,
Mengele's own racial classification by the SS had put him in
the *Dynarisch-Ostisch* category, which meant that his pre-
dominant features were of "Eastern" origin.[11] Since childhood he had been self-conscious about his slightly tawny skin,
his penetrating brown-green eyes, and his dark brown hair. At
school he had endured mild taunts from his classmates about
his Gypsy looks. And in Bavaria, where Mengele grew up, the
word for "Gypsy" had a derogatory meaning denoting an
unstable and unsettled person. His home town of Günzburg,
especially, was full of folklore about Gypsies coming to kidnap
children who misbehaved.

In late 1943 a severe outbreak of typhus struck the women's
camp in Birkenau, which was then under Mengele's control.
Out of some 20,000 half-starved women, about 7000 were

---

* Mengele himself contracted malaria in June 1943.

seriously ill. According to Dr. Ella Lingens, an Austrian doctor
sent to Auschwitz for trying to help some Jewish friends escape from Vienna, Mengele proposed another of his radical
solutions:

> He sent one entire Jewish block of 600 women to the gas
> chamber and cleared the block. He then had it disin-
> fected from top to bottom. Then he put bathtubs be-
> tween this block and the next, and the women from the
> next block came out to be disinfected and then trans-
> ferred to the clean block. Here they were given a clean
> new nightshirt. The next block was cleaned in this way
> and so on until all the blocks were disinfected. End of
> typhus! The awful thing was that he could not put those
> first 600 somewhere.[12]

Mengele's techniques for eradicating typhus were greatly
admired by the garrison physician, Dr. Wirths. In February
1944, Wirths cited them as one of several reasons why Mengele should be awarded the *Kriegsverdienstkreuz* or War Service Medal, noting that "in combating a severe typhoid epidemic . . . he was infected himself with a very heavy
typhus."[13]*

Mengele's anti-typhus measures were but samples of the
cynical disregard for life that he so quickly developed at
Auschwitz. Toward the end of 1944 there was a shortage of
food. There was not enough even to sustain the meager 700-
calorie-a-day diet for the 40,000 women of C Camp, Birkenau.
Mengele was heard to tell SS colleagues that he could no
longer feed the debilitated prisoners. He would therefore
have them liquidated. During the following ten nights, convoys of trucks carried the women, 4000 a day, to the gas
chamber—"a horrible sight this caravan of trucks, their head-
lights stabbing the darkness, each bearing a human cargo of
eighty women who either filled the air with their screams or
sat mute, paralyzed with fear."[14]

But it was at the railhead selections, when new arrivals
stepped down from their squalid boxcars to meet their fate,
that Mengele established his reputation, even among fellow
SS doctors, as a ruthless cynic. According to an inmate doctor,

---

* Mengele's illness was so severe that he temporarily left Auschwitz to convalesce.

Olga Lengyel, Mengele was "by far and away the chief provider for the gas chamber and the crematory ovens."[15] Two SS doctors were assigned duty at the railhead to examine each new transport. Their capricious powers of life and death as the prisoners filed obediently past were graphically described by Dr. Miklos Nyiszli, who became Mengele's pathologist:

> Any person who had entered the gates of the KZ was a candidate for death. He whose destiny had directed him into the left-hand column was transformed by the gas chamber into a corpse within an hour. Less fortunate was he whom adversity had singled out for the right-hand column. He was still a candidate for death but with this difference—that for three months, or as long as he could endure, he had to submit to all the horrors that the KZ had to offer 'til he dropped from utter exhaustion.[16]

Most SS doctors considered the selections the most stressful of all their camp duties. Dr. Ella Lingens said:

> Some like Werner Rhöde who hated his work, and Hans König who was deeply disgusted by the job, had to get drunk before they appeared on the ramp. Only two doctors performed the selections without any stimulants of any kind: Dr. Josef Mengele and Dr. Fritz Klein. Dr. Mengele was particularly cold and cynical.[17]

Klein's impassive approach stemmed from the fact that he was a virulent anti-Semite. He had hated all Jews since one seduced his fiancée while they were undergraduates, and he was once overheard saying that he even "liked the smell of the crematoria." In Mengele's view the biggest threat to the superiority of the German race was posed by the Jews. "He once told me there are only two gifted people in the world, Germans and Jews, and it's a question of who will be superior," said Dr. Lingens. "So he decided that they had to be destroyed."[18]

For tens of thousands of inmates Mengele was one of the first people they saw at Auschwitz. Many have testified to his immaculate and well-manicured appearance as he exercised his power of life and death. Some women, whom he was not adverse to humiliating by having them parade naked while he carried out his selections, found him a handsome man, though a gap between his upper two front teeth rather spoiled the effect. Survivors remarked on the impression made by his tight-fitting SS uniform with glistening black boots, white gloves, and polished cane as he surveyed his prey with a sure eye, smiling sometimes and whistling an operatic air. "How we hated this charlatan," said Dr. Lengyel. "He profaned the very word 'science.' How we despised his detached, haughty air, his continual whistling, his absurd orders, his frigid cruelty."[19]

> Day after day he was at his post, watching the pitiful crowd of men and women and children go struggling past, all in the last stages of exhaustion from the inhuman journey in cattle trucks. He would point with his cane at each person and direct them with one word: "right" or "left.". . . . He seemed to enjoy his grisly task.[20]

Mengele's sick-bay selections were notorious too, perversely playing on the emotions of prison doctors and their attempts by whatever means possible to save their patients from the gas chamber. Dr. Lingens said:

> The cynical Dr. Mengele made things easy for himself. He ordered us, the prison doctors, to write out meticulous lists of our patients, complete with diagnoses and prognoses. We were to state an approximate date by which the patient would be fit for release from the hospital and for resumption of work.
> It was difficult to refuse writing such a list, as we were told nothing of its purpose, although we guessed it only too well. If we put down that a patient had to remain in the hospital for over three or four weeks, she was condemned. If we put down a shorter term, the doctor would send for the patient and shout at us: "What, you say you're a doctor and you mean to send this half-dead, wretched creature out of the hospital in under four weeks?" This made it seem as if we were ruthlessly cheating the patients of their due time for recovery. Or, if Dr. Mengele accepted the short-term prognosis, he would insist on the release of the patient at the stated

date; in the case of those enfeebled women, a release was sometimes nothing short of murder. It was often impossible to find a way out.[21]

Out of sight of Aryan colleagues like Dr. Lingens who, unlike Jewish doctors, could risk challenging his excesses, Mengele resorted to a variety of cruel methods of execution. The West German indictment lists a monstrous catalogue:

Josef Mengele is accused of having actively and decisively taken part in selections in the prisoners' sick blocks, of such prisoners who through hunger, deprivation, exhaustion, sickness, disease, abuse or other reasons were unfit for work in the camp and whose speedy recovery was not envisaged, and also of those who had contagious or singularly unsightly illnesses, such as a skin outbreak.

Those selected were killed either through injections or firing squads or by painful suffocation to death through prussic acid in the gas chambers in order to make room in the camp for the "fit" prisoners, selected by him or other SS doctors in the aforementioned fashion. The injections that killed were made with phenol, petrol, Evipal, chloroform or air into the circulation, especially into the heart chamber, either with his own hands or he ordered the SS sanitary worker to do it while he watched. He is alleged also to have supervised, in cases of camp and hospital block selections, when SS sanitary workers threw granules of prussic acid formula Zyklon B into the inlet pipes of the rooms with people condemned to die hemmed together, or he threw it himself.[22]

In late August 1943, Mengele's wife, Irene, traveled from Freiburg in Germany, where she had chosen to spend the war, to visit him at Auschwitz. Typhus quarantine restrictions nearly kept her there longer than she had planned. "What's this stench?" Irene is reported to have asked her husband, looking skyward to the chimney and the smoke clouds beyond. "Don't ask me about this," Mengele is said to have casually replied. According to Mengele's son, Rolf, his mother later told him this was the moment when she began to have her doubts, when the marriage first faltered before it finally died six years later. "Because of the war they never had a proper marriage," said Rolf. "My mother was happy, cheerful, full of life, an emotional person."[23] Those of Mengele's SS colleagues who got to know him well remark that he never discussed his personal life. They do not remember him even mentioning the birth of his son in 1944.[24]

There were times, however, when Mengele's icy composure slipped, when he became agitated and excited. These occasions usually occurred when he was searching for twins from the rail transports that had just arrived. " 'Zwillinge, Zwillinge, Zwillinge, twins, twins, twins,' was what he shouted," said Horst von Glasenapp, the West German judge who took scores of affidavits during the 1970s from surviving Mengele victims. One, Irene Slotkin, who was five when she went to Auschwitz, recalled:

> I remember the first time I saw him: he was wearing green, dark green. And I remember his boots; that was probably the level of my eyes. Black shiny boots.
>
> He was asking for "Zwillinge, Zwillinge." He sounded angry. I don't know that I understood if it applied to me. We knew that whatever we had to do, we'd better do it fast and right.[25]

Her brother, René, remembered being saved by Mengele because he was a twin:

> At one point toward the end of the war I was scheduled to go to the chambers. I knew I was going to lose my life. We were being loaded onto trucks when this car comes up. A convertible. That's when I saw Mengele. We were taken off the truck. He stopped the whole procession because they were going to kill his twins.[26]

Another witness, Dr. Martina Puzyna, whom Mengele employed as his anthropologist to measure the external features of twins, once saw him "shrieking in a loud voice, 'Twins, out, twins out,' " while running alongside a procession of Hungarian Jews as they streamed off the train: "There were women walking with the children, going away, and he was giving orders that they should stay behind and would be taken care of."[27]

At other times Mengele would cynically adopt a more soothing tone, as this unnamed witness said in a deposition to the U.S. Army:

> Several times we noticed the hypocritical manner in which the grim doctor Mengele treated women and children alighting from the train. "Madam, take care, your child will catch cold. . . . Madam, you are ill and tired after a long journey; give your child to this lady and you will find it later in the children's nursery." On these days he was in a good mood, treating in a friendly manner the people whom he sent to death and who were very often reduced to smoke five or six hours after their arrival.[28]

But whatever his demeanor, it was Mengele above all others, whom the survivors watching the selections most vividly recall. In the 1964 trial of twenty-two Auschwitz defendants, one witness, Arie Fuks, said that while he worked near the arrival ramps he constantly saw Mengele perform the selections. "But Mengele cannot have been there all of the time?" asked the incredulous judge. "In my opinion, always," responded Fuks. "Night and day."[29]

More than thirty years after the end of the war, Mengele defended the camp selections in nightlong arguments with his son during their meeting in Brazil. Rolf recalls his father's "defense":

> He told me he did not "invent" Auschwitz and that he was not personally responsible for the incidents there. Auschwitz already existed. He wanted to help but that was very limited. He couldn't help everyone. For instance, on the platforms, he asked me what was he to do when the half-dead and infected people arrived? It was beyond one's imagination to describe the circumstances there. He said his job was to clarify only "able to work" and "unable to work." He tried to grade the people as "able to work" as often as possible. He thinks he saved the lives of several thousand people in that way. He didn't order the extermination and he was not responsible.
>
> He said the twins owe their lives to him. He said he

never harmed anybody personally, and he got very excited at this point. He asked me if I—his son—believe the lies in the newspapers.[30]

But Mengele's "defense" is not supported by dozens of sworn statements from inmates as well as fellow doctors and SS men. Mengele did not grade people "able to work" for humanitarian reasons but rather because he viewed Auschwitz as the ultimate human laboratory with a limitless supply of material to pursue his research, which the war had inconveniently interrupted. So obsessed was he with finding vast numbers of twins that he attended railhead selections even when it was not his turn; he could be seen bargaining with the SS doctors on duty to set the twins aside for him.

Mengele's claim that he "never harmed" anyone is also contradicted by the voluminous evidence of his experiments with twins. Mengele's research gathered momentum in the spring of 1944, when the transports carrying Hungarian Jews began to arrive. The West German indictment against Mengele lists witnesses to at least thirty-nine separate selections that he is alleged to have performed between April and August, involving tens of thousands of Jews. The actual figure is probably twice that, since on many occasions no witnesses would have survived.

Although many of Mengele's experiments covered a range of studies, from bacteriology to bone marrow transplants, their principal purpose seems to have been to unlock the secret of creating multiple births with genetically engineered Aryan features. As the West German indictment noted:

> The research into twins occupied a large part of the pseudo experiments of the accused according to the Court's preliminary investigations. This was especially interesting to the Nazi regime, in particular with regard to a desired increase in the birth rate through medically manipulated increase in the number of births of twins.[31]

But the challenge was not just how to improve the fertility of German women, though Mengele showed a passing interest in that with a series of weird sexual experiments. It was really about perfecting and preserving the best features of this mythical Aryan super-race, even down to blue eyes, blond hair, strong and healthy bodies. Quality could not be sacrificed in pursuit of quantity. There could be no weakening of the Aryan strain.

Various other experiments, notably sterilization, were already under way at Auschwitz when Mengele arrived. The purpose of these experiments was to unlock an efficient and easy means of mass sterilization for the recently conquered "inferior races." In addition, Colonel Victor Brack, chief administrative officer at the Reich chancellory, had suggested to Himmler that instead of liquidating Jews it might be more productive to the war effort to put some of them to work, provided a fast and efficient method of birth control could be found. Dr. Horst Schumann and his staff had thus embarked on a series of experimental castrations by X-ray which proved to be extremely painful for the victims. One surviving record shows that Schumann and his doctors performed ninety castrations in one day.*

Women, too, were subjected to massive doses of radiation, and their ovaries were then removed to establish the exact dosage required for sterilization. Mengele's ambition went far beyond finding a method of containing the reproductive capacity of the Jewish race. He was more concerned with guaranteeing the racial purity of future generations of Germans, a research program calculated to catch the imagination of the Nazi hierarchy in order to further his career. Mengele had already made it clear that he intended to pursue an academic career after the war, although Dr. Lingens had doubts about his ability. "I would say he was moderately gifted," she said. "I saw two of his publications before the war and there was certainly nothing brilliant about them. I thought he might make a professor in about twenty years." Dr. Hans Münch, who worked at the Hygiene Institute of the Military SS at Rajsko, an Auschwitz subcamp, and who came to know Mengele well, had no doubt about his motivation:

I saw him as a convinced National Socialist who never questioned how the Final Solution was administered in

---

* Like several other Nazi doctors, Schumann was given the benefit of the doubt when in 1970 his lawyers claimed he was too ill to stand trial. The "terminally ill" Schumann survived a further thirteen years in an affluent Hamburg suburb, never having spent a day in jail for his crimes.

the camp. He was an opportunist. During that period ideology had a great influence. Himmler was one of the great Nazi mystics and it is conceivably possible that pseudo-scientific research was done with the purpose of pleasing Himmler. Certainly Mengele's primary goal was to become a university professor after the war.[32]

The theory that Mengele's blind ambition drove him, that his research was so important to him that any inhumanity paled into insignificance, is reinforced by the findings of the West German indictment:

> The accused, Josef Mengele, is charged with having carried out medical experiments on living prisoners for scientific publication out of ambition and personal career progression. He fully intended the victim to die according to the manner of the experiment and valued their lives very cheaply. They often died merely to further his medical knowledge and academic education.[33]

Funds for his genetics research at Auschwitz had been authorized by the *Deutsche Forschungsgemeinschaft,* the German Research Council, in August 1943. It seems that Professor von Verschuer, then director of the Kaiser Wilhelm Institute for Anthropology, Human Heredity and Genetics, actually secured the grant from the Council. In a progress report to the Council, von Verschuer wrote:

> My co-researcher in this research is my assistant the anthropologist and physician Mengele. He is serving as Hauptsturmführer and camp doctor in the concentration camp Auschwitz. With the permission of the Reichsführer SS [Himmler], anthropological research is being undertaken on the various racial groups in the concentration camp and blood samples will be sent to my laboratory for investigation.[34]

This money was used to construct a special pathology laboratory that Mengele had built into Crematorium 2 at Birkenau, where newly gassed victims could be dissected. It was fitted with the most modern equipment available, its red concrete floor dominated by a dissecting table of polished marble with several sinks, one of them plumbed with nickel taps. The

pathologist he chose to perform this task was the Hungarian
Jewish doctor Miklos Nyiszli, who arrived at Auschwitz on
May 29, 1944. That day Mengele went straight to the railhead
and ordered all doctors to one side. A group of fifty gathered.
Mengele asked those who had studied at German universities,
had a thorough knowledge of pathology, and had practiced
forensic medicine to step forward. "Be careful," he warned
them, "you must be equal to the task." Dr. Nyiszli said:

> His menacing gesture left little to the imagination. I
> glanced at my companions. Perhaps they were intimi-
> dated. What did it matter! My mind was already made
> up. I broke ranks and presented myself. Dr. Mengele
> questioned me at length, asking where I had studied,
> the names of my pathology professors, how I had ac-
> quired a knowledge of forensic medicine, how long I
> had practiced, etc. Apparently my answers were satis-
> factory, for he immediately separated me from the oth-
> ers and ordered my colleagues to return to their places.
> For the moment they were spared.[35]

Dr. Nyiszli's first task was to pass an examination in dissection. Several corpses were brought to him for examination in
the presence of SS and prison doctors:

> I extracted all the organs, noted everything that was
> abnormal, and replied without hesitation to all the nu-
> merous questions they fired at me. Their faces showed
> that their curiosity had been satisfied, and from their
> approving nods and glances I surmised that I had passed
> the examination.[36]

Mengele had already made a bizarre start in his attempt to
perfect the ideal German specimen by seeing if he could
change the pigmentation of eyes by injecting different
colored dyes. Thirty-six children from one barrack in Birkenau were used for the eye tests, which resulted in painful
infections and sometimes blindness. After the tests the children served no further use, and so they were gassed. The
results of this research, which began in the summer of 1943
and was supplemented with funds from the German Research
Council in September of that year, were witnessed by a Jewish
inmate doctor, Vexler Jancu:

In June 1943 I went to the Gypsy camp in Birkenau. I saw a wooden table. On it were samples of eyes. They each had a number and a letter. The eyes were very pale yellow to bright blue, green, and violet.[37]

Another witness, Vera Kriegel, said she saw a wall covered with eyes in one of Mengele's laboratories. "They were pinned up like butterflies," she said. "I thought I was dead and already living in hell."[38]

The eyes were dispatched to Professor von Verschuer's institute in Berlin. Coming across a report on eye pigmentation being drafted by one institute researcher toward the end of the war, the co-editor of a medical publication noted that one set of guinea pigs—"grandparents, parents and children—had died at the same time. One could assume they had been killed in the concentration camp."[39]

In order to perfect a method of mass-producing suitable people to populate the new German territories and replace the depleted ranks of the army, Mengele set out to establish which attributes and disabilities were inherited genetically, as distinct from being acquired by lifestyle and environment. This is best achieved by the comparative study of twins, with one child in each pair used as a control. But such a comparison is valid only if a detailed life history is available. In Auschwitz, this was usually not possible. Mengele therefore used a system that was necessarily random and of dubious scientific worth. This raises a challenge to the assessment of some students of the Mengele phenomenon that, but for the corrupting influence of the times, he might have been a leader in the field of genetics and anthropology.

Twins destined for Mengele's experiments were housed in Barrack 14 of Camp F in Birkenau, nicknamed "the Zoo." There, on Mengele's orders, they were given good food, comfortable beds, and hygienic living conditions to build up their health for the most important part of the experimental process, the comparative study of their anatomy and bodily functions.

The purpose of building up their strength was to prevent infections from interfering with the results of the study, other than those illnesses like typhus which were deliberately induced in order to monitor their effects. Many of the children adored Mengele, "Uncle Pepi," as they called him. On some days he brought them sweets, as Vera Alexander, a survivor, explained:

> He brought chocolate for them, the most beautiful clothes, white pants, even aprons, and the girls had ribbons in their hair. One day he shouted at me because one girl had one ribbon lower than the other. He told me, "How did you do it? They are not as I like them."[40]

Following this preliminary health-building phase, the twins were moved to the hospital in Camp B2F for the "in vivo" stage. This involved experiments performed while the children were alive. Camp records show that transfers of Jewish children, together with twin children, adult twins, dwarfs, and cripples from the transports to the hospital began in July 1944. It is impossible to put a figure on the number of twins on whom Mengele experimented, although an idea of the scale was set out in the West German indictment: "At times it is alleged that 200 pairs of boy twins alone were held in readiness for the experiments of the accused Josef Mengele."[41]

In the first step of the in vivo stage precise measurements were taken of their skulls, ears, noses, and other external features. For this process Mengele employed the services of Dr. Martina Puzyna, former assistant to the Polish anthropology professor Jan Czekanowski at the University of Lwów. Czekanowski had perfected a method of statistically measuring different external features in terms of racial groups. As a member of the Polish underground, Dr. Puzyna was sent to Auschwitz, and she soon contracted typhus. As Dr. Puzyna explained, it was while she was in hospital that Mengele discovered who she was and recruited her:

> Mengele walked past me and I heard the Polish doctor tell him that I had been Professor Czekanowski's assistant before the war. He was very excited about this and told the doctor that I should report to him the following day.
>
> I was so weak that I had to be carried there. When I first saw him sitting there at his desk he struck me as being very young. And clean. He was always clean and smart. Mengele was sitting down with Dr. König. Men-

gele asked me what work I had been doing while in the camp and I told him, "Carrying stones." For some reason he laughed and said, "Well, you'd better come and work for me." My impression was that he was completely indifferent to what was going on around him.[42]

Dr. Puzyna was given her own bed in special hospital quarters and her food ration was doubled to speed her recovery. After she had regained her strength, Mengele took her to an office he had had assigned for her work. She was supplied with the latest Swiss precision measuring instruments and began work after the Hungarian Jews arrived, starting in April 1944. "We weren't supposed to see the twins selections," she said, "but my office was quite near the railway track and I remember seeing him walking up and down at selections, shouting. He looked quite mad sometimes."

For the next six months, almost until Auschwitz was liberated by the Red Army in January 1945, Dr. Puzyna measured 250 pairs of twins, carefully noting down every detail—the distance from the nose to the ear, the distance between the ears, the circumference of the head, and so on. From time to time Mengele came to check her work. "He wasn't very talkative. He just used to look at the charts that had been written up," she said. "He never told me what he was applying this work to, but I had an idea. He wanted every detail, especially any difference in twins, and their eyes."[43]

After the measurements the twins were taken to the men's hospital, Block 15 in Camp B2F. There Mengele had the children strip, and he examined them for hours in the minutest detail. No part of their anatomy escaped his attention. When this examination was over, the real torture began.

Crude surgery and other painful tests were performed, often without anesthetics. There were needless amputations, lumbar punctures, typhus injections, and wounds deliberately infected to compare how each twin reacted. In the view of the West German indictment, all were devoid of "any recognizable knowledge being gained from them." Scores of Mengele's guinea pigs died at this stage, many of them from a particularly bizarre experiment in which the blood supplies of different pairs of twins were interchanged. The results of one of these experiments were graphically described by a witness, Vera Alexander:

> One day Mengele brought chocolate and special clothes. The next day, SS men came and took two children away. They were two of my pets, Tito and Nino. One of them was a hunchback. Two or three days later, an SS man brought them back in a terrible state. They had been cut. The hunchback was sewn to the other child, back to back, their wrists back to back too. There was a terrible smell of gangrene. The cuts were dirty and the children cried every night.[44]

One survivor subjected to this kind of experiment with her sister and a group of several other female twins recalled:

> Each woman was given a blood transfusion from another set of twins so that Mengele could observe the reaction. We two each received 350 cc of blood from a pair of male twins, which brought on a reaction of severe headache and high fever.[45]

Mengele also forced the two sisters to have sex with other twins, apparently to discover if twins would reproduce twins:

> For this reason he wouldn't release us to work and tried to find suitable partners for us. When we objected that such an experiment was impermissible he told us that we were prisoners and that we had no say in the matter.[46]

Irene Slotkin and her twin brother, René, survived this in vivo stage of Mengele's work. She said that "somewhere in my head I had a good impression . . . you know, a doctor is a doctor, and so he's not going to hurt me. But of course he did."

These in vivo tests furnished Mengele only with superficial and incomplete information. In his passion to learn everything about the similarities and differences in twins, it was the next and final stage of his experiments that was the most important: the dissection of their bodies so that their organs and general development could be compared. For this simultaneous evaluation of anomalies, Mengele's twins, his most treasured specimens whom he had cosseted and fed, had to die at the same time. Dr. Miklos Nyiszli, who performed the dissections for Mengele, elaborated:

> Where under normal circumstances can one find twin[s] who die at the same place and at the same time? For twins like everyone else are separated by life's varying circumstances. One may die at ten, the other at fifty. In the Auschwitz camp, however, there were several hundred sets of twins and therefore as many possibilities of dissection.[47]

An explanation for Mengele's behavior—demonstrating sincere affection for small children whom he planned to kill and dissect—has been advanced by Professor Yehuda Bauer of the Hebrew University of Jerusalem:

> People who make experiments on mice or apes or rats can do it because they do not identify with the objects of their experiments. If you make experiments on white rats, you know, white rats can be quite nice. So some of these doctors establish a relationship: this is a nice animal, I have to kill it, but while it is still alive, we have some kind of relationship. That is the kind of relationship that is established between the murderers and their victims.[48]

Among the first child guinea pigs that Mengele delivered to Dr. Nyiszli, who was waiting to perform the autopsy at his newly built laboratory, was a pair of two-year-old twins:

> I opened the file and glanced through it. Very detailed clinical examinations, accompanied by X-rays, descriptions and artists' drawings indicated from the scientific viewpoint the different aspects of these two little beings' twinhood. Only the pathology report was missing. It was my job to supply it. The twins had died at the same time and were now lying beside each other on the big dissection table. It was they who had to—or whose tiny bodies had to—resolve the secret of the reproduction of the race.[49]

Among the forty pages of the West German indictment are nine separate allegations involving the deaths of 153 children whom Mengele is alleged to have killed "in order to undertake dissections." One charge alleges that Mengele had 100 children shot in the back of the head for his autopsies. He is also said to have lured some of the more unwilling children to the crematorium from the experimental block by offering them sweets and then shooting them on the way. One of his most common methods of ensuring simultaneous death was to inject chloroform into their hearts, coagulating the blood and causing heart failure. According to an affidavit by Dr. Nyiszli, Mengele once killed fourteen Gypsy twins himself in this way:

> In the work room next to the dissecting room, fourteen Gypsy twins were waiting and crying bitterly. Dr. Mengele didn't say a single word to us, and prepared a 10 cc and 5 cc syringe. From a box he took Evipal and from another box he took chloroform, which was in 20 cc glass containers, and put these on the operating table. After that the first twin was brought in . . . a fourteen-year-old girl. Dr. Mengele ordered me to undress the girl and put her head on the dissecting table. Then he injected the Evipal into her right arm intravenously. After the child had fallen asleep, he felt for the left ventricle of the heart and injected 10 cc of chloroform. After one little twitch the child was dead, whereupon Dr. Mengele had her taken into the corpse chamber. In this manner all fourteen twins were killed during the night.[50]

This method was first noticed by Dr. Nyiszli on a set of four pairs of twins, all under ten years old, who had attracted Mengele's attention because three of the pairs each had different-colored eyes. The eyes and other organs were removed and dispatched to Professor von Verschuer's Kaiser Wilhelm Institute in Berlin, marked "War Materials—Urgent." Dr. Nyiszli, knowing the children had been murdered by chloroform injection, left the "cause of death" section of his dissection report blank. Since medical experiments carried a high security classification, the facade that all Mengele's guinea pigs had died of "natural causes" had to be maintained and he ordered Dr. Nyiszli to fill it in:

The choice of causes was left to my own judgment and discretion. The only stipulation was that each cause be different.[51]

One of Mengele's common techniques was to infect twins to compare how the illness affected them, first while they were alive, then, for more probing results, after they were dead. An inmate doctor, Joahann Cespiva, said:

During my work at the Gypsy camp I came across Mengele and watched his activities. I personally observed him infecting Gypsy twins with typhus, in order to observe whether the twins reacted differently or in the same way. Shortly after they had been infected they were gassed.[52]

This comparative technique became commonplace; if one twin died of natural causes, "the other twin was killed for comparison." If the slightest difference in ability was discerned, otherwise healthy twins were likely to be permanently disabled by Mengele's curiosity. On one occasion the Reichenbergs, two brothers who greatly resembled each other, were mistakenly selected as twins by one of Mengele's colleagues. They did not object when they were placed in the right-hand column at the ramp, unaware that Mengele and the experimental block awaited them. Ephraim Reichenberg said that his brother had "a beautiful voice and sang once for the Germans." But his own voice was very poor and Mengele wanted to know why one "twin" had a melodious voice while the other did not. He conducted crude surgery on the vocal cords of both children that impaired their speech. Eventually Ephraim lost all use of his vocal cords. Not until late 1984 did his speech return, after a special microphone was installed in his neck just below his jaw, making his voice sound as though it came from a computer. "Until I bought this wonderful device I couldn't speak at all," he said. "This too was invented by the Germans—and that is a pity."

Mengele displayed an extraordinary fascination for anything connected with race. After spotting a hunchbacked father standing next to his fifteen-year-old son, who had a deformed right foot, he was impatient to learn if there were further common abnormalities. He selected them from the ramp and gave them a last meal, which they ate ravenously, unaware that they were soon to die. Dr. Nyiszli was ordered to examine them "with exact clinical methods before they died" and then to perform the dissections. Nyiszli felt himself "suddenly spinning close to the edge of madness." Half an hour later, Mengele had them shot and ordered their skeletons to be prepared by boiling their bodies in water so the flesh could be easily stripped from the bones. The skeletons were then immersed in a bath of petrol to make them dry, odorless, and white. Dr. Nyiszli said:

> Dr. Mengele was highly pleased. He had brought several fellow officers with him. They pompously examined parts of the skeletons and launched into high-sounding scientific terms, talking as if the two victims represented an extremely rare medical phenomenon. They abandoned themselves completely to their pseudoscience.[53]

The skeletons were wrapped in strong paper and again forwarded to Professor von Verschuer's Kaiser Wilhelm Institute in Berlin. After the war von Verschuer claimed that he was unaware of Mengele's activities and at one stage even denied that Mengele had been his assistant. Just how much he did know about Mengele's experiments will probably never be proved, since he destroyed all his correspondence with Mengele. What is certain is that Mengele visited von Verschuer in Berlin at least once while he was at Auschwitz, and it seems inconceivable that the two men did not discuss the nature and the results of his experiments. According to von Verschuer's wife, Mengele confided at a dinner party on one of his Berlin visits that he found great difficulty in carrying out his work at Auschwitz. "It's horrific," she claims he said, "I can't talk about it." Von Verschuer's daughter recalls that her father thought Mengele was clinically depressed and possibly suicidal.[54] Depressed he may have been, but his enthusiasm for his work never flagged. Many inmate doctors recall Mengele as a man who had as much compassion and feeling for the prisoners at Auschwitz as a research scientist has for laboratory rats. "This was where he spent all his spare time," said Dr. Nyiszli about Mengele's custom-built dissection laboratory, "here in this man-made hell. . . . Here within these bloodstained walls, Dr. Mengele sat hunched for hours at a time poring over his microscope."[55]

To Mengele's colleagues he came across as a friendly but obsessive man. Dr. Hans Münch got to know him after Mengele sought his advice on how best to preserve specimens for dispatch to the Kaiser Wilhelm Institute. Dr. Münch was the only Auschwitz doctor acquitted by the Supreme National Tribunal in Kraków in December 1947 at a trial of SS men and claims that he knew nothing of the details of Mengele's experiments. In his view, it was the combination of the madness of Auschwitz and Mengele's driving ambition for academic recognition that explained his behavior:

> In comparison to other doctors in the camp he stood out. He did not fit the normal pattern of SS men and colleagues who he thought drank too much.
> In my view he was a gifted scientist, but a combination of scientific knowledge, opportunism and ambition, which Mengele had, can lead to anything.[56]

Obsessive Mengele certainly was. His appetite for experiments was insatiable. He had a habit of suddenly appearing at a barracks if he was short of "human material." Olga Lengyel, an inmate doctor, said he called at "any hour, day or night. During the inspection all the exits in the barracks were closed. He arrived when we least expected him. Sometimes he'd come in whistling operatic airs."[57] Eva Kor, a twin, remembered the sheer terror that gripped the barracks after morning roll call:

> It wasn't because his face was terrifying. His face could look very pleasant. But the atmosphere in the barracks before he came and all the preparation by the supervisors was creating that atmosphere of terror and horror that Mengele was coming. So everybody had to stand still. He would, for example, notice on one of the bunk beds that a twin was dead. He would yell and scream, "What happened? How is it possible that this twin died?" But, of course, I understand it today. An experiment had been spoiled.[58]

There are those like Dr. Münch who, based on their knowledge of the man as a scientist, believe that although Mengele had no thought for the suffering of his victims or justification for his experiments, "there might have been valid short-term results that might be observed." Whatever the merits of this argument in purely scientific terms, Mengele's main aim, as interpreted by Dr. Puzyna, the inmate anthropologist, was wholly unscientific:

> I found Mengele a picture of what can only be described as a maniac. He turned the truth on its head. He believed you could create a new super-race as though you were breeding horses. He thought it was possible to gain absolute control over a whole race. Man is so infinitely complex that the kind of strict control over such a vast population could never exist. He was a racist and a Nazi. He was ambitious up to the point of being completely inhuman. He was mad about genetic engineering. I believe he thought that when he'd finished with the Jewish race he'd start on the Poles, and when he finished with them, he'd start on someone else. Above all, I believe that he was doing this for himself, for his career. In the end, I believed that he would have killed his own mother if it would have helped him.[59]

Apart from twins, Mengele engaged in a wide variety of other experiments. Ernest Michel worked as an orderly in the Auschwitz infirmary and recalled taking eight women into an experimental room:

> I saw Mengele standing there in his uniform, surrounded by three or four others. There was electrical machinery the likes of which I had never seen. As we brought in each girl, an officer would strap her down. We left quickly because we didn't want to be around Mengele very long. After a while the screaming inside stopped. When we took them out, two of the eight were dead, five were in a coma, one was strapped to the cot. Mengele was standing there, discussing it very casually. The only word I could hear was experiment.[60]

According to the West German indictment, the purpose of these electrical experiments, conducted both in Birkenau and in the slave labor camp at Monowitz, was to test the patient's endurance:

A considerable number of prisoners from Birkenau died in these experiments. . . . From a total of seventy to eighty prisoners on whom the accused carried out such experiments in the spring of 1944, twenty to thirty prisoners are said to have died as a result [in Monowitz].[61]

The indictment said Mengele had a permanent supply "in the summer of 1944 [of] about fifty young women, held in preparation for him in the prisoners' sick block of the women's camp in Birkenau." Many of them died from blood "transfusions and extractions"; he is alleged to have subjected a group of Polish nuns "to extreme X-rays for research purposes from which they suffered severe burns"; he is alleged to have conducted bone marrow transplants with the result that one victim had to have her right leg amputated from the knee because it got infected. She was spared from the gas chamber only "due to the proximity of the Red Army and impending evacuation of the camp"; he is alleged to have operated on the sex organs of male prisoners "supposedly to castrate or sterilize them"; he is said to have had "a number of women prisoners . . . taken to the 'Black Wall' between Blocks 10 and 11 of the main camp and shot. Their breasts were cut off and the muscles from the thigh were kept as cultivating material for experiments in Mengele's hygienic laboratory"; he is said to have forced a mother, Ruth Eliaz, to cover her breasts with tape "to see how long the baby could live without food." As the child grew weaker, she mercy-killed it after a compassionate nurse gave her some morphine and a syringe. He is said to have stood on pregnant women's stomachs until the fetuses were expelled; he is even said to have dissected a one-year-old while the child was still alive.

At such times it might seem that Mengele was motivated by sheer sadism, although most witnesses have remarked not at his pleasure at watching or inflicting suffering but at his total detachment from it. Etched in Dr. Puzyna's memory is a moment when she saw Mengele transfixed by music which an orchestra was playing while a work gang filed past, carrying the day's dead. She said:

Every day people died at work because they were so weak. Mengele was standing there, saying nothing, his head in his hand, eyes down, just listening. He was completely rooted to the spot, utterly oblivious of this march of the dead right next to him. There were bodies and there was Mengele, just enraptured by the music. I remember it happened in the hospital too. The orchestra, a very fine orchestra, Hungarian Jews, just turned up to play and there were people terribly ill all round us, just skeletons. Mengele didn't even look at them.[62]

Dr. Tobias Brocher, a Menninger Foundation psychoanalyst who practiced near Mengele's home town of Günzburg and has studied his behavior, said it exhibited the "narcissistic component of sadism" but not sadism itself:

He didn't take pleasure in inflicting pain, but in the power he exerted by being the man who had to decide between life and death within the ideology of a concentration camp doctor. Mengele had the narcissistic pattern of the professional. In the subculture of medicine as a whole, there is a split between what you have to do and any emotion you might have; between doctors who take a strictly scientific approach and the medical doctor who cares for patients. In Germany this split was evident in the euthanasia program for mental patients, which preceded the concentration camps. Doctors in the euthanasia program rationalized that the persons they condemned to death were "better off now" or that they "would die anyway."[63]

Mengele's personal acts of cruelty, examples of which abound in the West German indictment, were usually provoked by fits of wild and uncontrollable temper. He is said to have "taken the newborn child of a Russian woman, grabbed it by the head and [thrown] it onto a pile of corpses"; he is said to have become "so furious at a camp selection when the *Kapo* of a work detail allowed those prisoners already chosen to die to rejoin those fit for work that he shot him with his own pistol"; there is the case of an old man "selected for the gas chamber who wanted to go over to his son who was in the work group, but Mengele hit him over the head with an iron bar so that his skull split open and he fell to the ground dead"; he is said "to have thrown a newborn baby boy onto a stove, angered at the mother's pregnancy which the selection doctors had failed to spot and which would have normally qualified her for the gas chamber"; he is said "to have shot with his service pistol at least one prisoner of unknown nationality because he stopped on the street without being authorized to"; he is said to have shot a sixteen-year-old girl "who had fled onto a roof out of mortal fear of the gas chamber."

Perhaps most gruesome of all is the allegation that Mengele had 300 children burned alive in an open fire, an event witnessed by several inmates including a Russian named Annani Silovich Pet'ko:

> After a while a large group [of SS officers] arrived on motorcycles, Mengele among them. They drove into the yard and got off their motorcycles. Upon arriving they circled the flames; it burned horizontally. We watched to see what would follow. After a while trucks arrived, dump trucks, with children inside. There were about ten of these trucks. After they had entered the yard an officer gave an order and the trucks backed up to the fire and they started throwing those children right into the fire, into the pit. The children started to scream; some of them managed to crawl out of the burning pit; an officer walked around it with sticks and pushed back those who managed to get out. Hoess and Mengele were present and were giving orders.
>
> The first group of children were from Dnepropetrovsk. I was told by the zone commanders that it was difficult to poison the children in the gas chambers, therefore they were burned in the pit. They were all under five years old. I heard that they had brought either an entire kindergarten or an orphanage from Dnepropetrovsk. Later I was told that some of these children that were brought and burned were actually taken from their mothers.[64]

Although some inmates who knew Mengele have testified that they never saw him commit an act of violence, there are witnesses to corroborate every one of these extraordinary allegations listed in the West German indictment. In view of the fact that Mengele was never brought to trial, these statements will never be tested under rigorous cross-examination. But they would not have been included in the indictment had

they not been judged to have stood a good chance of surviving
courtroom scrutiny. Dr. Gisella Perl, who worked under Mengele as a prison doctor in Birkenau, recalled two examples of
his explosive temper. In the first, a woman prisoner named Ibi
was found by Mengele after she had escaped gas chamber
selections six times. She somehow managed to gather enough
strength each time to jump off the truck taking the victims to
their deaths. Mengele was enraged:

> "You are still here?" Dr. Mengele left the head of the
> column, and with a few easy strides caught up with her.
> He grabbed her by the neck and proceeded to beat her
> head to a bloody pulp. He hit her, slapped her, boxed
> her, always her head—screaming at her at the top of his
> voice, "You want to escape, don't you. You can't escape
> now. This is not a truck, you can't jump. You are going to
> burn like the others, you are going to croak, you dirty
> Jew," and he went on hitting the poor unprotected
> head. As I watched, I saw her two beautiful, intelligent
> eyes disappear under a layer of blood. Her ears weren't
> there any longer, maybe he had torn them off. And in a
> few seconds, her straight, pointed nose was a flat, bro-
> ken, bleeding mass. I closed my eyes, unable to bear it
> any longer, and when I opened them up again, Dr.
> Mengele had stopped hitting her. But instead of a hu-
> man head, Ibi's tall, thin body carried a round, blood-
> red object on its bony shoulders, an unrecognizable ob-
> ject, too horrible to look at; he pushed her back into line.
> Half an hour later, Dr. Mengele returned to the hospi-
> tal. He took a piece of perfumed soap out of his bag and,
> whistling gaily with a smile of deep satisfaction on his
> face, he began to wash his hands.[65]

Dr. Perl's account of the second incident in which Mengele
violently lost his temper shows a highly volatile, unpredictable man—and omnipotent, as the senior doctor in the wom-
en's camp. It happened when he made an unexpected visit to
the women's hospital, where Mengele found Dr. Perl and her
colleagues stoking a fire in order to cook some potatoes which
they had stolen:

The silence lasted only a second; the storm, when it broke, was all the more terrible. He ran around like a wild beast, smashing everything in his way. He kicked over the stove, stomped on our potatoes, overturned the operating table, screaming, shouting incessantly: "Yes, this is how I imagined a Jewish hospital. You dirty whores, you unspeakable Jew swine." Suddenly I conceived a desperate plan. I got up from the floor, went to the shelf, and took down a jar containing a fetus and approached Dr. Mengele. "Herr Hauptsturmführer may be interested in this specimen," I stammered. "Only rarely is it possible to bring it out in one piece." He stopped raving and grabbed the jar out of my hand. His face, which the moment before had looked like the face of a raving maniac, assumed a cruel, satisfied smile. "Good, beautiful, take it to crematory number 2 tomorrow. We are sending it to Berlin." And as if he had forgotten what went on, he turned around and left the hospital.[66]

These displays of violent mood change and such total lack of remorse suggest a man in the grip of a complex psychopathic personality disorder. Somehow the ethical side of Mengele's professional personality never developed. Perhaps it was because the horror of the Russian front and Auschwitz came so soon after he qualified as a doctor. In any event, there is little question that Mengele never suffered feelings of guilt at any stage of his life after Auschwitz: "There are no judges, only revenge seekers," he told his son when they met in São Paulo in 1977, two years before he died. Rolf said his father was quite unrepentant and felt no shame. Only rarely did he display his personal feelings. Once it occurred when Dr. Lingens confronted him by comparing the prisoners at Auschwitz to his own family in Bavaria. She challenged Mengele to consider that any one of a group of dying women he was refusing to treat might, like his own mother, have a son whom she wanted to see again. Caught off guard, Mengele responded meekly: "I don't know if I'll see my mother again."

Such sensitivity was notably absent in one of Mengele's more notorious decisions: to send hundreds of entire families to the gas chamber. At Mengele's insistence the entire Gypsy family camp was liquidated between July 31 and August 2, 1944. A total of 2987 Gypsies were dispatched to the crematorium, the remaining 1408 sent on to Buchenwald. While he was carrying out the selections, a four-year-old girl pleaded with Mengele not to be sent away, calling him "Uncle Doctor." With a "wave of his hand," Mengele is alleged to have signaled to a German *Kapo* to deal with her. The West German indictment says the *Kapo* "flung her against the wheel of a lorry so that her skull was shattered." During roll call two boys hid, and the count therefore did not tally. When they were discovered, Mengele is said to have "driven them to the crematorium in his car."

There are several examples of Mengele showing kindness to children, only to have them killed.[67] This confusing duality of affection and cruelty is a process that Robert Jay Lifton, the distinguished professor of psychiatry and psychology at the City University of New York, calls "doubling." Lifton says that there were two parts in Mengele operating at Auschwitz—the Auschwitz self and the prior self:

> With the Auschwitz self, Mengele's potential for evil became actual, even as he maintained elements of his prior self that included affection towards children. In this process, each self part behaved as a functioning whole: the Auschwitz self enabling him to function in that murderous environment and to exploit its human resources with considerable efficiency; the prior self enabling him to maintain a sense of decency. His powerful commitment to Nazi ideology served as a bridge, a necessary connection between the two.[68]

A good example of Mengele's "doubling" involved a group of Jewish children who were suffering from very painful mouth ulcers, a condition known as noma disease, which causes an extreme form of oral decay. Mengele embarked on a series of experimental cures, soothing the children, anxious to relieve their pain. That was the prior self operating. It was only after he succeeded in finding a cure that the Auschwitz self asserted itself. After some of the children had recovered he sent them to the gas chambers. To Mengele the sole importance of the exercise was that he succeeded, not that he had relieved the children's misery. Once cured, the children, as

had the Gypsies, posed a threat to the purity of the Aryan race
and his ideology directed they be destroyed.

Another example of "doubling" was witnessed by Dr. Olga
Lengyel. She remembered Mengele supervising a birth, ad-
hering fastidiously to every medical precaution and procedure for a Jewish mother and baby. Within an hour he had
sent them both to the gas chamber. He displayed the same
perverse duality by calming anxious children condemned to
die. Mengele turned their last walk into a game which he
called "on the way to the chimney." Then he waited with
great anticipation for his pathologist's report. Surviving child
guinea pigs who had their health built up for the in vivo stage
of his experiments remember Mengele giving them sweets.
He even used to play with them in a kindergarten he had
built. But every time it was the calculating act of a man whose
overriding interest was to get the most out of his "material."

Children for whom Mengele had no use—because they
were neither twins, unusual, nor otherwise of interest—lived
in dread of him. A witness named Kleinmann said at the Adolf
Eichmann trial in Jerusalem in 1961 that he would never
forget the day Mengele arrived at a parade ground where
2000 boys had been ordered to gather. It was the eve of Yom
Kippur:

> All of a sudden a tremble passed through the parade
> ground like an electric current. Dr. Mengele appeared
> on his bicycle. He put his hands behind his back; his lips
> as usual were tightly closed. He went to the center of
> the parade ground, lifted his head so he could survey
> the whole scene, and then his eyes landed on a little boy
> around fifteen years old, perhaps only fourteen years
> old. I remember his face very well. He was blond, very
> thin and very sunburnt. His face had freckles. He was
> standing in the first line when Mengele approached him
> and asked him, "How old are you?" The boy shook and
> said, "I'm eighteen years old." I saw immediately that
> Dr. Mengele was furious and he started shouting, "I'll
> show you. Get me a hammer and some nails and a
> plank." A deathly silence prevailed on the parade
> ground. . . . Mengele approached a tall boy . . . in
> the first row. He put the boy near the goalpost and gave

orders to nail the plank above the boy's head so that it was like the letter "L" only in reverse. Then he ordered the first group to pass under the board. The first group of boys started going in single file. . . . We had no explanations. We understood that the little ones who did not reach the board, who were not tall enough, would be taken to their death.

Attorney General: Did he tell you what would happen to you after passing the measure?

Kleinmann: No, but it could have had no other meaning. It was one hundred percent clear to everyone what the purpose of the game was. We all began stretching. Everyone wanted to get another half inch, another centimeter. I also stretched as much as I could but I despaired. I saw that even taller boys than myself did not attain the necessary height. . . . I thought, this is the end of my life, and all of a sudden my brother whispered to me, "You want to live? Do something . . ." All of a sudden I saw some stones near me. . . . I bent down without being noticed; I picked up a few small rocks; I opened my shoelaces and started stuffing my shoes with little stones. I stuffed them with stones under my heel and this added about an inch to my height.

Presiding Judge: Let us hear how you passed this test.

Kleinmann: I stood there for about ten minutes with these shoes full of stones and rags. . . . Then after about ten minutes all the boys would be passing under the board. Two would make it and two wouldn't. I stood there and finally my brother kept looking at me and said, "No, it's not enough yet." . . . I started looking for another device: to escape and hide among all those tall boys who had already gone under the board and passed the selection. I tried to infiltrate into the groups of the big boys [who had passed the test]. But then another boy tried to infiltrate and Dr. Mengele noticed that and he started shouting at the guard men and *Kapos,* "What are you doing? This is sabotage." And he ordered the entire group to be taken and again passed under the board.[69]

On the second time around Kleinmann again escaped to a group of taller boys, but they had not yet gone under Mengele's board. On the third time around he escaped into a group who had passed the test. But 1000 boys did not make the grade and two days later were gassed.

Some researchers attach much significance to the fact that after the war Mengele was never known to denigrate the Jewish race to his South American hosts. There is also a view among some psychologists who have attempted to study his immense capacity for barbarism that his intellect was too sharp for him to believe, as other Nazis did, that Jews were actually an inferior race. However, this view is not shared by those who drew up the West German indictment against him. The indictment refers to Mengele's "contempt" for Jews, which "manifested itself in particular when he made selections on their religious festivals, which was especially painful for them." The charge goes on:

> Thus it is alleged that he selected Jewish children on the Friday before the Jewish New Year festival 1944 from camp section B2D in Birkenau; he sent 328 children to their death in the gas chambers on the Jewish New Year festival 1944 from camp section B2D in Birkenau; on Jewish Yom Kippur 1944 in camp B2E in Birkenau he hung a batten between the goalposts of a football pitch and those approximately 1000 children who were not the required height were sent to the gas chamber.[70]

Mengele's combination of anti-Semitism and sadism is probably the explanation for this desecration of Jewish holidays with his games of death. Mengele's son remembers that in the 1977 meeting with his father, Mengele attempted to convince him that some races, including Jews, were different or inferior when compared with Aryans. Rolf recalls:

> He alleged he had evidence that Jews were different or abnormal. But he couldn't furnish any convincing proof of it. Most of his arguments were sociological, historical, or political.[71]

But one did not have to be Jewish to fear Mengele's arrival in the camp. For those acquainted with Mengele's reputation as a doctor who relished selections as a game of Russian roulette, the first hint of his presence was a spine-chilling moment. One inmate, Dr. Alfred Fiederkiewicz, gave this account of the trauma suffered by a group of patients awaiting their fate:

> When the patients, having taken off their shirts, were standing two deep, he [Dr. Thilo, another SS doctor] surveyed them and asked for particulars. Before he had inspected not more than a few patients there arrived SS Hauptsturmführer Dr. Mengele. We got frightened because he was an officer of higher rank than Thilo. We knew that Mengele was the greatest killer in the camp, that he had experimented on children and grown-up prisoners, whom he not long ago had sent to die in the gas chambers. And a few days ago he had ordered the whole Gypsy camp to be annihilated. He was a man of strong physique, of medium height, fair haired—when talking with Thilo he smiled slyly and looked with gimlet eyes at the ranks of my patients. In a certain moment I heard the question, "What illness do these skeletons suffer from?" When Thilo answered that it was tuberculosis, Mengele winked and with a movement of his head pointed to the chimneys of the crematoria. The sinister wink was noticed not only by me but also by the patients.[72]

Sixteen months after Mengele arrived at Auschwitz his work was evaluated by the Chief Doctor's Office. On August 19, 1944, his garrison commander produced a report in which Mengele's mental state was described as "outstanding." It also referred in glowing terms to his record of sending people to the gas chamber and to his experiments on twins. The report was written in the coded language that the SS coyly reserved for its more bestial acts. Thus was Mengele's decision to exterminate thousands of Gypsies and women suffering from typhus applauded:

> During his employment as camp physician at the concentration camp Auschwitz he has put his knowledge to practical and theoretical use while fighting serious epidemics. With prudence, perseverance, and energy, he has carried out all tasks given him, often under very

difficult conditions, to the complete satisfaction of his superiors and has shown himself able to cope with every situation.

The same coded language commended his "scientific" work for the Fatherland:

> In addition to that, he, as an anthropologist, has most zealously used his little off-time duty to educate himself further and, utilizing the scientific material at his disposal due to his official position, has made a valuable contribution in his work to anthropological science. Therefore, his performance can be called outstanding.

The report went on to lavish praise on Mengele's leadership qualities:

> In his attitude toward his superiors he shows the impeccable demeanor of an SS officer: the very best military deportment, tact, and reserve. His character makes him a favorite with his comrades. Toward his subordinates he knows how to hold his own with absolute justice and the required strictness, but is at the same time popular and respected.[73]

This picture of a hard but fair man is certainly at odds with Mengele's reputation among noncommissioned SS men. According to Dr. Nyiszli, they trembled at the mention of Mengele's name, as he discovered when he was challenged by an SS soldier for being in F camp, away from his zone:

> I answered him in a quiet voice: "I am here because Dr. Mengele sent me." The name "Mengele" worked like magic. My noncom grew tame in less time than it takes to tell. In an almost fawning manner he asked me how long I intended to stay inside the camp.[74]

The garrison commander's report recommended Mengele for promotion, saying that he had demonstrated "to all an absolute firmness and fitness for the job." Still in coded reference to his experimental work, it said:

> In addition to his medical knowledge, Dr. Mengele is especially knowledgeable in anthropology. He appears

entirely suitable for every other employment, also for
employment in the next highest rank.[75]

Since Himmler's authorization was required for medical
experiments at concentration camps, and since he took a close
personal interest in racial research, it is quite likely that
Mengele's desired ambition of being brought to the Reichsführer SS's attention was achieved. To ensure that this was so,
Mengele set up a sideshow of his most treasured set of dwarfs,
all seven of them, before an audience of one visiting senior
bureaucrat and 2000 SS men. The dwarfs belonged to a
Romanian Jewish circus family, the Moskowitzes. When Mengele first set eyes on two of them, a pair of twins named
Elizabeth and Perla, he exclaimed with delight that he had
"work for twenty years." Mengele stripped the family naked
and triumphantly paraded them on stage, complete with a
family tree to illustrate his point that they were the offspring
of "degenerate" Jewish forebears. The Nazi VIP watched the
performance from the front row, spellbound, capturing it on
his own hand-held movie camera.*

Hopes of promotion and a glittering postwar academic career faded as autumn came to Auschwitz in 1944. Dr. Lingens
said that Mengele appreciated sooner than most that Auschwitz would be liberated by the advancing Red Army and that
the Germans would lose the war. "I remember that in about
September he was saying that it was a pity all his work would
fall in the hands of the Russians," she said. "He knew the war
was coming to an end while most others still thought Hitler
would win."

In the closing months of 1944 Mengele grew sullen and
despondent. His wife, Irene, remembers that his correspondence became increasingly melancholy. She decided to make
her second trip to Auschwitz during the fall of 1944, with the
intent of cheering him. Irene's trip and her impressions are
vividly recorded in her diary from that time. She left five-
month-old Rolf with her in-laws and then departed from Freiburg on August 8, 1944. She traveled by train, via Katowice,
Poland, and arrived on August 10 in Auschwitz, where she
settled into the SS barracks situated just outside the main

---

* The two sisters believed the visitor was Himmler but they are mistaken. His last recorded
visit to Auschwitz was in 1942.

camp, a place she described as "a dreary, desolate area with lodgings that are primitive."

According to her diary, Irene's first three weeks with Josef were idyllic. They had servants in their house—"Jehovah Witnesses in striped prison garb"—and their days were spent bathing in the Sola River and picking blackberries, from which she made jam. Although her diary shows that she was aware of the selections ("the incoming trains were clearly visible"), she shows no indication of knowing about the gruesome experiments and conditions inside the camp. She merely thought of Auschwitz as a large camp for political and wartime prisoners. In the diary she noted that the entire area was enclosed in barbed wire, that there were many guards, that movement without proper identity cards was prohibited, and that "sweet stench" she encountered on her first trip in the summer of 1943 was still everywhere. It seems unthinkable that Josef had not given her an explanation for the smell, and Irene's claim of ignorance should, perhaps, be judged in that light.

On September 1, 1944, Irene's diary describes a scientific conference at Auschwitz to commemorate the opening of a new military hospital. The main speaker was Josef Mengele, and the subject was "Examples of the Work in Anthropological and Hereditary Biology in the Concentration Camp." Irene's words reflect only pride in her husband's work and in his leading role in the conference.

However, although she enjoyed her stay in Auschwitz, she noted in numerous diary entries that her husband seemed depressed. When she tried to talk to him about his work he refused. He told her, "I often wonder who is responsible for all of this." According to her account, all Mengele told her was that service in Auschwitz was the equivalent of service on the front line, and therefore he regarded his work as his "duty, to be practiced in soldierlike obedience." Irene recalls:

I loved him very much. He was my first great love. He was always charming, funny, very sociable—vain too, and bothered because in his opinion he was too short. But in Auschwitz I knew he was downhearted and depressed although he didn't betray it.[76]

Irene believed that Mengele was depressed because he was a man trapped between the orders he was given and his inner dissatisfaction with his work. Irene concludes, "His fate was that he was too conscious of his duty, too obedient, and had too much the spirit of the subordinate." However, those who worked with Mengele give a different version. Dr. Hans Münch believes Mengele's depression resulted not from his Auschwitz duties, but rather from his fear that the Nazis were losing the war and that his days as a free man were numbered. In any case, he never revealed to Irene the cause of his growing anxiety in the autumn of 1944.

Irene was set to leave Auschwitz, after a one-month stay, on September 11. Just before her departure, however, she contracted diphtheria, and within days she had the complicating symptom of an inflamed heart muscle. She remained in the camp hospital for more than a month, much of the time delirious from a high fever. Mengele visited her three times daily, reading to her from Balzac's *Le Diamant*. Over the next few weeks, Irene was shuffled from hospital to hospital as air raid warnings sounded. On September 13, 1944, Irene heard the camp's air raid sirens blast for the first time: she was dragged from her bed to an air raid shelter, but no bombs hit the camp. On September 17 she was moved to a smaller hospital that was considered safer in the event of further bombing raids. On October 7 the sirens again screamed across the camp, and this time antiaircraft artillery answered. On October 13 another swarm of Allied planes passed nearby and a couple of stray bombs actually fell into the camp itself.*

Although the Allied bombings had no substantive effect on Auschwitz, there was a psychological effect: they reminded everyone that the war was going badly for Germany and might soon be over. Irene decided to make the best of those hectic last days with her husband. When released from the

---

* The Allied planes were involved in reconnaissance and limited bombing missions against some of the industrial installations outside Auschwitz-Birkenau. The Allies have never satisfactorily answered why they failed to bomb the camp, even though by late 1944 they had conclusive proof of what was going on there and they could easily have used the bright flames from the crematoria as their target sites. Not only could hundreds of thousands of lives have been saved during the final months of the war, but casualties to inmates, who were housed far away from the crematoria, would have been negligible. The Allies never even attempted to bomb the railway lines leading to the camp, which would have cut off the means of bringing inmates to the murdering machine.

hospital on October 18, she moved into a new flat in the doctors' barracks, equipped with both a kitchen and a bath. She remarked in her diary that she felt "once again like a newlywed." As Auschwitz packed the gas chambers with ever-increasing numbers of people from the Hungarian convoys, Irene and Josef Mengele enjoyed a second honeymoon. On October 30 they left Auschwitz together, Mengele having obtained special permission for a leave. They arrived in Günzburg on November 1. Mengele visited his parents for only a day, and then they proceeded to nearby Freiburg where he saw his nearly eight-month-old baby, Rolf, for the first time. He stayed nearly a week, and then on November 6 he left to return to Auschwitz.

The war that Irene had felt firsthand in Auschwitz followed her back to Freiburg. Heavy Allied bombing forced her to move with Rolf on November 23 to Mengele's parents' home in Günzburg. Allied bombs would eventually drop in the garden of the Mengele home, but family members remained unscathed. As for Josef Mengele, upon his return to Auschwitz he became increasingly depressed and anxious over the deteriorating Nazi battle position. Near the end of 1944 he was sometimes seen pacing up and down the SS doctors' office, silent, morose, head in hands, although he continued with his research almost to the end. He is recorded as having taken sixteen female dwarfs from the hospital camp to the women's camp on December 5 and "experimented on them" three days later. Five survived, but it was assumed that the remaining eleven died as "a direct result of the experiments administered by SS Dr. Mengele."[77] Mengele, meanwhile, moved quickly to cover up the fact that experiments had taken place because they were still classified as a "secret Reich matter" even though they were known to a vast number of inmates. He arrived at the Jewish doctors' quarters for the last time to announce that Auschwitz would be destroyed, and ordered that everything movable was to be packed. Even his marble dissecting table was removed and replaced by concrete slabs.

One of the last inmates to see Mengele was Marc Berkowitz, a twelve-year-old whom Mengele had appointed as his special messenger because he was intrigued by his Aryan looks. Berkowitz said he "tended to him personally, to his meals, to cleaning his special kitchen and his boots. I picked his Brussels

sprouts. . . ." That Christmas Eve, a light snow was falling
and Berkowitz was in a washroom when Mengele passed by.
Pausing at the door, he summoned Berkowitz outside. "Mengele was wearing a leather coat with a soft cap," said
Berkowitz. "His face was reddish, his eyes sort of tired, as if he
was sad. He put his hand on my head and said 'Adieu. You
were a good boy.' And then he was gone."

On the night of January 17 Mengele left Auschwitz, salvag-
ing what records he could from his experiments on twins,
cripples, and dwarfs. The SS already had orders to destroy
sickness reports, temperature charts, and all other evidence
of experiments and genocide by blowing up the crematoria
and shooting patients too feeble to march. Mengele also paid a
last call to his anthropologist Dr. Puzyna, at her office, where
the twins had been measured before succumbing to his knife.
"He came into my office without a word," she said. "He took
all my papers, put them into two boxes, and had them taken
outside to a waiting car."

With the sound of the Red Army's artillery echoing ever
closer in his ears, Josef Mengele fled the madness of Auschwitz. From that night on, he never stopped running.

C H A P T E R
3

———
———

Arrested and Freed

———
———

Josef Mengele had a ten-day start ahead of the Red Army when he joined the growing exodus of German soldiers heading west. By the time the first Russian scouts entered the gates of Auschwitz and Birkenau at 3 p.m. on January 27—and discovered corpses of the 650 prisoners killed by looting SS men—Mengele had arrived at another concentration camp two hundred miles to the northwest. This was Gross Rosen, in Silesia, where bacteriological warfare experiments on Soviet prisoners had been conducted since the beginning of 1942.[1]* But Mengele's stay was short-lived. By February 18 he was on the run again to avoid the advancing Russians, who liberated the camp eight days later.

As Mengele fled Gross Rosen, the man who had secured his posting to Auschwitz moved quickly to cover his own tracks. Professor von Verschuer shipped out two truckloads of docu-

———

* Mengele had been transferred to Gross Rosen together with several other Auschwitz doctors, including his friend Dr. Münch. Even during the final spasms of the war, the SS hierarchy attempted to keep its killing machines operating and fully staffed.

ments from his research institute in Berlin, taking care to destroy all of his correspondence with the Auschwitz doctor.[2]

Meanwhile, Mengele fled westward, where he joined a retreating unit of Wehrmacht soldiers. He stayed with them for the next two months, exchanging his SS uniform for a Wehrmacht officer's. Mengele and his newfound unit remained in central Czechoslovakia, hoping that the tide might turn against the Russian onslaught.

But the Red Army was unstoppable. They advanced at such a pace that once more Mengele and his unit began moving farther west. By May 2, Mengele had advanced to Saaz, in the Sudetenland, where he found a motorized German field hospital, *Kriegslazarett* 2/591. To his surprise, Mengele discovered that one of the chief medical officers attached to the *Kriegslazarett* was a prewar friend, Dr. Hans Otto Kahler.

Kahler had been involved in legitimate twin research before the war at Professor von Verschuer's institute in Frankfurt. Kahler, who had a Jewish great-grandparent, was not a Nazi party member. But von Verschuer so respected his work that he resisted considerable pressure from the Nazi hierarchy to remove him from his staff. It was at Verschuer's institute that Mengele and Kahler had forged their close friendship, one that now became a key factor to Mengele's escape from the Allies.

Although Kahler immediately recognized Mengele and knew he was in the SS, he did not comment on his newfound Wehrmacht officer's uniform. Kahler places Mengele's arrival at the field hospital as the same day that Hitler's suicide was announced on the radio: May 2, 1945. He remembers the event clearly because "Mengele made quite a fuss, refusing to believe the report that Hitler was dead." That evening, Mengele approached Kahler and asked him if he could join the field hospital, pleading that he could be useful in the unit's specialty, internal medicine. Kahler went to the unit's commanding officer and vouched for his friend, and as a result of his efforts, Mengele was allowed to stay.

While stationed with his new unit, Mengele struck up an intimate relationship with a young German nurse. Her name is not known and Mengele does not provide it in his autobiography. He trusted her so completely that when the unit started to move west once again and Mengele feared capture by the Allies, he gave her custody of his precious research notes from Auschwitz. The notes, which his Auschwitz anthropologist, Dr. Puzyna, had seen him gather on the eve of his departure from the camp, would immediately betray him as a concentration camp doctor. Giving the notes to the nurse was prudent for several reasons. First, nurses were registered and almost immediately released when captured by Allied forces. Second, even if her eventual captors should take the time to translate a set of scribbled notes, she could always claim they belonged to someone else, thereby not identifying Mengele as the owner. In that case, Mengele would lose only his notes, and not his life before an Allied court.

After several days, the unit began to move farther northwest, by way of Carlsbad, in order to stay ahead of the advancing Russians. On the night of May 8, 1945, the date Field Marshall Keitel signed the unconditional surrender, Mengele crossed the frontier from Czechoslovakia into Saxony, in what is now East Germany,[3] as he recalled in his autobiography:

> On the night of the armistice the Americans stopped our advance, but the Russians pursued us for the time being. This way we were in a kind of no-man's-land. As long as we had provisions we were tortured only by the uncertainty of to whom this area would be allocated.[4]

Mengele and his unit had settled into the narrow strip in central Europe where the Americans and Russians both informally agreed not to enter—less than twenty-five miles separated the two Allied powers. In the Russian and American pincer, some 15,000 German soldiers had become trapped. In the confusion of moving from Czechoslovakia into the no-man's-land, Mengele's motorized hospital unit split into several sections. When he finally settled in the surrounding forest, Mengele realized he was separated from his friend Dr. Kahler. In this new section, without the support of Kahler, Mengele feared his SS identity would be discovered. One senior physician in the unit, Colonel Fritz Ulmann, suspected that Mengele was an SS man in disguise. Ulmann, who would later become the key to Mengele's postwar freedom, found his behavior in the no-man's-land to be almost comical. Ulmann recalls that every day at roll call Mengele gave a different name: "He evidently couldn't remember what name he

had given the day before, so he must have used four or five
additional names. He was secretive and I knew he had to be
SS."

Somehow Mengele sustained the charade for six weeks
while his unit was stuck in the forest. On June 15, American
forces entered the area and took some 10,000 German prisoners. Mengele was not among them; together with his unit, he
made a run for freedom, and it was temporarily successful.
Mengele remembered the breakout in his autobiography:

> In the end there was less and less food and the rumors
> that the Russians would occupy this area became more
> numerous. So then we decided to act. With several vehi-
> cles and a sanitation unit we formed a column, and with
> some deception we succeeded in passing through the
> Americans. We bypassed their subsequent roadblocks
> and reached Bavarian territory.[5]

His freedom was short-lived. American forces were thick on
the ground, and according to Mengele's own account, within
days his unit was captured:

> In the vicinity of the first large town, Weiden, we were
> stopped and brought to an American camp for prison-
> ers. This way we had reached our goal, precisely when
> the stock of petrol was finished. The Americans then
> took us from one camp to another in which the very
> small rations became even smaller and our hopelessness
> grew.[6]

At the first American camp, Mengele was rejoined with
Hans Kahler, who had been captured in the same vicinity the
same day. And, just as he had hoped, Mengele's nurse friend
was released within hours of her capture, his Auschwitz research notes safely in her custody. At this point, Dr. Kahler
and Dr. Ulmann have different recollections of what name
Mengele used to register in the camp. Dr. Ulmann says he
checked in under his real name. Dr. Kahler says he checked in
as "Memling," the name of a famous Bavarian artist. However, Kahler claims he told Mengele it was dishonorable to use
an alias, and for that reason Mengele subsequently told the
American camp authorities his real name. What is indisput-

able is that within several days of his arrival, the Americans had him in their custody, listed under his true name.

Yet although they knew his name, they did not know he was an SS member, a detail that would have subjected him to a more rigorous interrogation and a cross-check of his name with lists of wanted Nazi criminals. For that, Mengele had his vanity to thank. It was Mengele's decision not to have his blood group tattooed on his chest or arm when he joined the SS in 1938 that clinched his freedom. He had managed to convince the SS that the tattoo was unnecessary and that any competent surgeon would make a cross-match of blood types and not rely solely on the tattoo before administering a transfusion. According to Irene, the real reason had more to do with Mengele's self-worship. He had a habit of standing before a full-length mirror and preening himself, admiring the smoothness of his skin. And it was his skin that he had not wanted to mark.[7]

The failure to have the blood-type tattoo meant that the Americans had no way of knowing that Mengele was a member of the SS. Although American authorities required prisoners to fill out questionnaires and to show their pay book, which listed the unit of service, they never learned about his SS service. Not only did Mengele lie on the questionnaire, but he failed to produce any documents that identified his SS affiliation.

At the time, Mengele had no idea of just how lucky he was. By April 1945, two months before the Americans arrested him, Josef Mengele had been identified as a principal war criminal.[8] Those fortunate enough to survive his bloody knife had begun making statements to the Poles, French, Yugoslavs, British, and Czechs. By May, "Dr. Joseph Mengele, Lagerartz, Oswiecim KL" was already listed by the United Nations War Crimes Commission as wanted for "mass murder and other crimes." His name had also been added to the first Central Registry of War Criminals and Security Suspects (CROW-CASS) list compiled by the Allied High Command in Paris for circulation to detention camps throughout Europe. Finally, the U.S. Judge Advocate General's Office had independently gathered evidence against him. Notwithstanding his high profile as a wanted war criminal, a combination of factors helped Mengele, among them the inefficiency and lack of coordination among various arms of the U.S. occupying forces, the near impossibility of weeding war criminals out of millions of detainees, and above all, his own vanity about the tattoo.

During the immediate aftermath of the war, Allied administration was so chaotic that some "wanted" lists did not filter into the detention camps throughout the summer of 1945. The key question is whether either the UN or CROWCASS wanted lists were ever in the hands of the camp authorities holding Mengele. We may never know the answer. The U.S. Office of Special Investigations was unable to find one despite its very detailed 1985 examination. If the authorities did have the lists, they were palpably negligent. But there is a strong possibility the lists never arrived. Moreover, Mengele was fortunate that the Americans had adopted a policy of processing prisoners as rapidly as possible, due to the enormous numbers swamping the detention camps, as well as a desire to get as many able-bodied people into the cities and fields to rebuild Germany. Although there is no evidence of collusion between the American authorities and Mengele, the fact remains that this notorious war criminal was held for two months and never identified as the "principal war criminal" on the "wanted" list.

Mengele, however, was convinced that it was only a matter of time before he was unmasked as the Auschwitz doctor. He was so worried that he became clinically depressed. His friend Dr. Kahler asked Dr. Ulmann, a neurologist, to examine Mengele and to treat his depression. Ulmann consented, and Mengele soon confided to him the source of his anxiety: the possible discovery of his Auschwitz work. Ulmann not only kept Mengele's secret, but he helped obtain a second identification for him, sensing that the Auschwitz doctor would probably need an alias to survive in postwar Germany. Ulmann was uniquely placed to help Mengele. The Americans had assigned him to the prison staff of the main camp administrative office, where release papers were processed. When Ulmann was eventually released from the camp he was able to obtain a second set of release papers in his name. He gave one set to Mengele. Ulmann's plan was for Mengele to leave the camp using the papers issued to Mengele in his real name. Once outside, where Mengele risked being questioned by Allied troops at any time, he could revert to using Fritz Ulmann's name by showing his fake papers.

Ulmann and Mengele were set to be freed after six weeks, near the end of July 1945. But there was a last-minute hitch. The Americans transported prisoners by truck to their postwar homes, but before the trucks heading for Mengele's section of Bavaria left, the camp was closed and dismantled. As a result, Mengele was moved to a second American camp several kilometers away, and again registered under his real name. There he sat for more than two weeks, until the beginning of September. Finally he was again released and was transported to the Bavarian town of Ingolstadt.

Somehow Mengele's luck just kept running.* As soon as he was dropped off, courtesy of the U.S. Army, Mengele decided to walk to the nearby town of Donauwörth, in the hope of finding sanctuary at the home of a prewar school friend, veterinarian Albert Miller. As he strolled toward Donauwörth, he came across a farmer walking two bicycles along the roadway. They struck up a conversation and the farmer, who would be passing through Donauwörth, asked Mengele if he wanted to ride one of the bicycles. Mengele readily agreed. However, he feared he might be stopped by an American patrol and he did not want to be found with two sets of conflicting identification papers, one in his name and one in the name of his friend, Fritz Ulmann. So he hid the Mengele papers inside the hollow handlebar of the bicycle, and he placed the Ulmann papers in his breast pocket. When Mengele reached Donauwörth, he thanked the farmer and the farmer left with both bicycles. Only later did Mengele realize that he had forgotten his Mengele release papers in the handlebar of the bicycle. He had no

---

* In February 1985, Walter Kempthorne, an ex-Army private, claimed he had seen a doctor named Mengele at the American Idar Oberstein camp, about 200 miles from where Mengele was known to have been held. Kempthorne said that fellow soldiers told him they were "getting him in shape to get hung. This here is Mengele, the bastard who sterilized 3000 women in Auschwitz." Also in February 1985 Richard Schwarz, a retired Washington, D.C. labor lawyer who was also an Army private at Idar Oberstein in 1945, claimed he had "exercised to exhaustion" a German doctor who greatly resembled Mengele. Thomas Berchtold, a former SS man, remembers a "Mengele from Bavaria" in a British POW camp in Schleswig-Holstein, about 400 miles from the site of Mengele's actual capture. Mengele was not in any of these camps. Each soldier most likely confused another concentration camp doctor with Mengele.

idea how to reach the farmer. From that moment on, Josef Mengele had no choice but to live only as Fritz Ulmann.*

Mengele went straight to the house of his friend, Dr. Miller. Miller's wife remembers the day he knocked at the door:

> I answered the door and I saw a soldier standing in front of me. He said, "Good day, my name is Mengele." Later my husband came home and we had dinner. I remember him saying, "Don't believe everything you hear about me. It's not true."[9]

Mengele asked Dr. Miller to contact his family in Günzburg and his wife in Autenreid to tell them he was safe. Even though he professed his innocence, Mengele told Dr. Miller he could not risk capture by Allied forces. But before Miller could do anything, he was arrested by American troops on the very evening that Mengele had arrived at his house. As Miller was driven away for questioning about his wartime role in the Nazi party, Mengele hid in a back room of the house.

Miller's arrest scared Mengele. He left Donauwörth in the middle of the night, determined to make the hazardous journey into the Russian zone in order to locate his nurse friend who was holding his research specimens and notes from Auschwitz. His concentration camp work was so important to him that he was willing to risk capture by the Russians from whom he could expect no mercy. As Mengele later wrote, "It was a crazy undertaking to cross the guarded border. It seems an incredible journey. . . ."

The journey to Gera, now in East Germany, took Mengele more than three weeks. Meanwhile Mrs. Miller contacted Karl Mengele, Jr., in Günzburg, to tell him that the doctor was safe. Karl then told Irene and the rest of the family.

Mengele was fortunate to have chosen the Millers as his first contact in the Günzburg area. Not only did they inform his family of his safety, but they also kept his return a secret from the American authorities. The Millers' readiness to help reflected an attitude prevalent in the Günzburg area. There was a widespread readiness to believe that the allegations against Mengele were false. The town had driven out its 309 resident

---

* The release papers in his own name have never been found, even though the United States government conducted a search through hundreds of old bicycles in Bavaria as late as 1985.

Jews after the Nazis came to power. And broadcasts across Germany by the overseas service of the BBC, claiming that the SS had engaged in monstrous acts of carnage, were viewed as Allied victory propaganda. The Mengele family was more hostile toward the Allies than most local residents since their factory had been damaged by an American bombing raid in January 1945, aimed at a nearby plant suspected of producing nose components for the new Messerschmitt 262 jet bomber.[10]

For Irene Mengele, the good news from the Millers broke months of anxious waiting. Irene had not heard from her husband all year and assumed he was "one of the millions now moving as prisoners or dead." And if she really had not known what he was doing in Auschwitz when she twice visited him there, she certainly did by now. Irene noted in her diary that on May 3, 1945, Allied radio reports listed the war crimes charges against her husband. A month later, on June 11, three American military policemen arrived on her doorstep at Autenreid to ask her where he could be found, ironically while Mengele was languishing in no-man's-land in Saxony, caught between American and Soviet troops. Irene told the Americans that she thought her husband was probably dead.

As for the rest of the Mengele family, the American authorities applied no pressure throughout 1945, although Josef's father and brother were subject to interrogation under the denazification proceedings. During the rest of the year, the Americans accepted Irene's doorstep denial as a satisfactory answer in their hunt for a principal war criminal.

While the Americans were floundering in their search for Mengele, he was returning from the Russian zone, having retrieved his treasured Auschwitz specimens and research notes. This time he went to Munich, to the apartment of trusted friends. The husband, a pharmacist, was an ethnic German from Romania who had served with Mengele in 1942 in the Viking division on the eastern front. This couple is still alive, friendly with Irene Mengele, and provided the following story to her son, Rolf, on the condition that they would not be publicly identified.*

At the end of September 1945, the pharmacist answered a

---

* The Munich couple are the only people, outside of a small circle of family conspirators, who knew Mengele was dead prior to the public discovery in 1985. Irene had confided the death to the pharmacist and his wife and, true to their old comrade, they kept the secret.

knock at the door and found a tired and drawn Josef Mengele standing before him. During the next four weeks the pharmacist and his wife tended to Mengele, restored his strength, and counseled him on the best course for his continued safety. The couple remember Mengele vigorously defending himself:

> I don't have anything to hide. Terrible things happened at Auschwitz, and I did my best to help. One could not do everything. There were terrible disasters there. I could only save so many. I never killed anyone or hurt anyone. I can prove I am innocent of what they could say against me. I am building the facts for my defense. I want to turn myself in and be cleared at a trial.[11]

The pharmacist and his wife thought Mengele was not rational. They were also friends of Dr. Victor Capesius, the chief pharmacist at Auschwitz, and from Capesius they knew what had transpired at the camp.* The pharmacist told Mengele:

> You are crazy. It's impossible. You will never get a fair trial. If you turn yourself in, you will either be shot on the spot or you will get a trial and then be hanged. Forget this nonsense about proving your innocence. We must find a place to hide you.[12]

During the next several weeks, as Mengele recuperated in the safety of his Munich friends' home, the opportunity for safe haven appeared in the form of Dr. Fritz Ulmann's brother-in-law, who happened to also be a friend of the pharmacist. In his autobiography, Mengele code-named Ulmann's brother-in-law "Vieland" and his wife as "Annalise." Both were medical doctors, and they lived in the small Bavarian town of Riedering. Vieland and Annalise met Mengele for the first time during a visit to the pharmacist in Munich. They took an immediate liking to him and offered their help in hiding him. The plan was a simple one. The agricultural zones of Germany were desperate for farm employees, many families having lost young men during the war. Vieland proposed that he accompany Mengele to one such area, south of the city of Rosenheim, and help him find a job as a farmhand on an

---

* Capesius was subsequently charged with complicity in joint murder on at least four separate occasions of 2000 deaths each. He was sentenced to nine years at hard labor.

isolated farm with a quiet and simple family. Vieland convinced Mengele that American troops would never undertake a farm-by-farm search throughout Germany for him, and that the farm family never need know his true identity since he still had a good-conduct pass from the Americans in the name of Fritz Ulmann. Mengele readily agreed.

However, Mengele decided to take a further precaution. He made a copy of the release papers and carefully altered the name to "Fritz Hollmann," changing the "U" to an "H," squeezing an "o" between the "U" and the "l," and placing another "l" between the "l" and the "m." Mengele knew that once he settled into a new area, he would have to register his American release card with the local German authorities. He did not want to register under the name "Ulmann" in case American authorities ever started to check the names of prisoners who had been held with him in detention. The authorities would never tie "Hollmann" to Mengele.

The decision to hide Mengele under a cover name was a wise one. It was clear that rehabilitation into postwar life was going to be impossible. Professor von Verschuer, Mengele's mentor, was dismissed from the Kaiser Wilhelm Institute in June 1945. There was no respite in the stream of allegations of genocide, and in August 1945 the London Agreement between Britain, France, the United States, and the Soviet Union announced that charges would be brought against twenty-four Nazi leaders before an international military tribunal at Nuremberg. Whatever sympathy the citizens of Germany, like Vieland, had to offer Mengele, for the moment at least, the outside world was not going to allow him to bury the past.

Vieland became the key to Mengele's early postwar freedom. In his autobiography Mengele recalled:

> When I first met Vieland, he did not one moment hesitate to take me with him to Riedering, from where he sent me to look out for work and a living. Vieland brought me into the Rosenheim area. This friend [Vieland] brought me through all difficulties here.

Vieland became Mengele's main contact and protector for his next few years in Germany. He acted as Mengele's primary source of information about the outside world. In his

autobiography, Mengele's sole discussion regarding the concentration camps takes place in the form of fictional and rhe-
torical conversations with Vieland. Only in this disguised
manner was Mengele even able to discuss the death camps in
his writings.

It is significant that Vieland was not a Nazi. Mengele described him in the autobiography as:

> [a]n honest man who did not lack civic courage. He was
> no member of the Nazi party and had a clean political
> record. This was the reason why he was given the duty
> as general practitioner in Riedering. The postwar au-
> thorities had forbidden the previous doctor to continue
> his work since he had been screened as a member of the
> Nazi party, and he was forced to perform simple manual
> work.[13]

Vieland was representative of many people in postwar Germany who, although unsympathetic to the Nazis, still refused
to believe the horror of the war crimes stories and viewed
them instead as Allied propaganda. Vieland, while politically
opposed to his philosophy, nevertheless became the central
figure in Mengele's early fugitive existence.

Vieland's first task was to find Mengele a job. Together they
approached several farms in the area around Mangolding, a
farming community within the county of Riedering. It is one
of southern Germany's lush agricultural areas, nestled at the
foot of the Alps, dotted with beautiful marsh lakes.

The first two farms Mengele approached did not need help-
ers, but the third, owned by Georg and Maria Fischer,*
needed another worker. On October 30, 1945, "Fritz
Hollmann" signed on at the Fischer farm for ten marks a
week. The farm, dubbed *Lechnerhof* after the original owner,
Lechner, was over twenty acres in size. The Fischers grew
potatoes and wheat and stocked the farm with a dozen milk-
producing cows. It was a typical Bavarian farm, alpine styled,
extremely well cared for, and prettily adorned with flower
boxes full of geraniums. Mengele slept in a spartan room, ten
by fifteen feet, furnished with only a cupboard and a bed.

---

* During the late 1950s and early '60s in Paraguay, Mengele used the name "Fischer" as
one of his aliases.

Georg Fischer died of stomach cancer in 1959, but his wife, Maria, now seventy-six years old, and Georg's brother, Alois, seventy-nine, who sometimes shared a room with Mengele, recall the young man and the decision to hire him.

Maria Fischer remembers that when Mengele, or "Fritz Hollmann," as they knew him, first arrived, he told them he was a refugee soldier from Görlitz and that his wife was still in the Russian zone. Alois Fischer has never forgotten the day when Mengele first joined the family for a meal to discuss working for them:

> Hollmann had a tremendous appetite. He ate every-thing put on the table without ever commenting on whether he liked it or not. He drank milk daily by the liter. I've never before seen a man who drank so much milk. The first time he joined us for a meal he ate as though he didn't get much to eat during the war. He didn't say a word—he just ate an enormous amount of food. My brother told him, "If you work as much as you eat, then you are my man. We will try you."[14]

Mengele probably worked harder during his years with the Fischers than at any other time in his life. Maria Fischer remembers the routine:

> He had to get up at 6:30 in the morning. First thing was to clean out the stable. At 7:00 we would always have breakfast together. He was very strong and able. Only he didn't know how to milk. He didn't handle the animals at all, that the farmer would always do himself. Fritz also worked a lot in the fields; he would pull out the potatoes, sort them and carry them to the courtyard, and he worked in our forests, sowing and cutting the trees, and cleaning the trunks. He also cut and loaded hay—in fact he did everything. He was very obliging, never started a fight and was always in a good mood.[15]

Sometimes after supper at 7:00 P.M., he stayed up to play a card game called "Schafkopfen." But he usually was so tired that he just went up to his room to sleep.

The Fischers may have been simple country folk, but they soon guessed that their lodger had a past to hide. Nothing would disguise the educated Bavarian accent, the smooth

hands, totally unused to hard labor. Alois Fischer guessed he
was a wanted Nazi:

> He was only looking for a place to hide after the war. He
> evidently had to hide. He had dirt to hide. He must have
> been a Nazi, and we thought he must have been high
> brass. [When] he came he had only one gray flannel suit
> which he wore, not bad quality, but not good either.
> Apart from that he had nothing.
>
> Not even things to wash himself. When he came he
> had very fine hands. He had never worked before, cer-
> tainly not on a farm. He didn't know how to milk a cow.
> . . . But he never talked much. About his person, his
> past or the war, he said nothing at all. He also didn't
> want us to ask him questions about it—that was very
> clear to everybody. He was neither friendly nor un-
> friendly, but always very controlled and disciplined.
>
> Hollmann looked very strong, like a male cat. He was
> also intelligent. He spoke with a slight Bavarian accent,
> always very quietly and briefly. He evidently came from
> an upper-class family. He never had visitors, and he
> didn't leave the house, especially in the beginning.[16]

But "Fritz's" past was of no concern to the Fischers. After
only two weeks on the farm, when Georg Fischer was certain
that Hollmann was a good employee, he told him, "Let's go
register your war papers with the *Bürgermeister*. I am satisfied
with you and your work." Fischer took Mengele to a neighboring farm owned by the local magistrate, to whom Mengele
presented his forged document with the name "Hollmann."
Duly impressed the *Bürgermeister* signed for Mengele, who
noted with contempt how much respect German officials had
"for a piece of paper written in English with a U.S. Army
stamp on it."[17] Mengele kept his original "Ulmann" papers,
which he had used to forge the "Hollmann" copy, hidden in
his room at the Fischer farm.

The suspicion that Mengele was a Nazi did not stop the
Fischers from growing fond of him. They were only too willing to help a young German who earned his daily pay. And as
he grew to trust them more, he became less secretive. Maria
Fischer remembers:

At home he began to talk and laugh a lot. Once on St. Nicholas's Day he acted as Santa. He had made a beard and the Santa hat and then he teased us; and then to all of us, at that time we were seven, he chided us. It was very funny and we laughed until the tears were in our eyes.[18]

Alois Fischer said he "felt sorry for the young man who had fought for Germany." Indeed, the Fischers were a most accommodating group. While Mengele was there they gave shelter to two other Germans, one a woman with a dubious background, who was anxious not to fall into Allied hands, and the other a soldier from the east who had lost his family—and for whom Mengele showed distinctly more compassion than he ever had for similarly bereaved inmates at Auschwitz: "He lost everything, his wife has been evacuated to the middle of Germany and he has been looking for her and can't find her."[19]

While the Fischers were willing to overlook Mengele's past because they were satisfied with his work, unknown to them, he hated it. He found this first phase of his fugitive life very difficult. Outwardly Mengele may have seemed more relaxed, but inside he was a deeply unhappy man. The evidence for this comes from Mengele's autobiography, which he wrote when he was in South America. Mengele said he "feels sorry for himself but not for anyone else," that farm work "is quite a lesson" to him, and that he is "even getting used to the potato harvest." He stayed mentally alert by "talking to myself." They are the words of a man embittered by the fortunes of war, of an unrepentant Nazi who has yet to come to terms with being on the losing side. "It is probably hate that dries [my] tears," he wrote, dismissing Auschwitz, with a gloss acquired over nearly thirty years of skulking around South America, as an episode to which "there is nothing to be added. It is natural and understandable that the camps were suffering very bad hunger after all the problems and therefore what I saw was to be expected."

Mengele was also resentful that while he, a medical doctor, was forced to work on a farm picking potatoes, the occupying American troops "plundered" Germany. "The Crusaders," as he called them, "had an unbelievable conscience."

While Mengele worked on the Fischer farm, his bitterness was always simmering. Alois Fischer recalls an incident in which Mengele's frustration boiled to the surface:

> There was only once a small dispute. He, who was supposed to work as a laborer, gave me an order that I should take the hay down from the threshing fork. I told him he should do it himself. Then he got very angry, only for a short moment, but very much so. He looked at me with great fury. I actually thought he would attack me. But then he completely controlled himself again and such a thing never happened again.[20]

Mengele took his mind off matters by playing mental games. In a menacing echo from the past, he revealed in his autobiography how he used to perform "scientific selection" on the potato crop:

> One had to take a scientific approach to sort out the edible, fodder, and seed potatoes. The frequency of the various sizes followed the binomial distribution according to the Gauss Diagram. The medium sizes therefore are the most plentiful, and the very small ones and the very big ones are much less frequent. But since they [the Fischers] wanted more medium-sized potatoes I moved the border of the selection for the potatoes for consumption accordingly and in this way I obtained more potatoes for consumption than usual. In this way my mind was kept active.[21]

The "great selector" of Auschwitz had been reduced to selecting potatoes. Although degrading for the high-minded Mengele, this low profile helped him to stay free. His role as a farmhand avoided attracting any attention. Throughout this time, Mengele's morale was sustained by visits to his doctor friend, Vieland, who lived in nearby Riedering. On his day off, Mengele brought wild flowers for Vieland's wife and received any medical treatment he required from Vieland himself. And Mengele's family, convinced of his innocence, made trips to Rosenheim to bolster his morale. Maria Fischer does not remember any visitors to the farm, but she does remember that Mengele took short walks, with increasing frequency over the years, to "visit his girlfriend."

Irene realized that trips to Rosenheim were fraught with danger—since Mengele was a wanted fugitive she might be tailed—but she weighed the risks in favor of the visits. She concluded that her husband's morale might be very low if he had access to any of the local newspapers and saw what they printed about him. For instance, in her diary entry of October 7, 1945, she wrote:

> In the local newspaper there appears his name, and it said, "With animal-like lust he saw people die." One would like to laugh. . . . What shall he think if he sees such writings.[22]

Irene's early visits to Rosenheim were cloak-and-dagger affairs. She made her first trip in the summer of 1946, but only after a test run had been taken by Karl Jr. in order to ensure that American authorities were not following Mengele family members. Once Karl told Irene the trip could be made safely, she left Rolf with Mengele's parents in Günzburg and took the train to Rosenheim. Mengele, informed by Vieland of her arrival time, walked toward the train station as she walked toward Mangolding. They met near a popular Bavarian holiday resort, the Sinssee Lake. They walked past each other without so much as a nod and kept walking for several hundred extra yards to make sure they were not followed. Once they were convinced that there was no danger of being caught, they met and spent their time at a local inn.

By the end of 1946 Mengele was convinced the Americans had forgotten him, and he became so brazen that he made two one-week trips to Autenreid to visit Rolf and Irene. Vieland was furious with Mengele for using the "Fritz Ulmann" identity card on the two trips to Autenreid. He thought it was too great a gamble. Vieland reprimanded Mengele: "You are being very risky with my brother-in-law's identification." Mengele exploded in a rage. He took the "Ulmann" papers out of his pocket and ripped them up in front of Vieland. "There, are you satisfied? I don't need them," he yelled. But Mengele's temper had cost him dearly. Without a set of genuine release papers, he was forced to rely on the forged set for the remainder of his time in Germany. It added danger to his already precarious situation. It stopped his travels from Ro-

senheim and left Irene's visits as Mengele's only contact with
his family.

Although Irene intended her trips to serve as a calming
influence on her husband, they had almost the opposite effect.
The visits served as a reminder that their marriage was under
a terrible strain. Rolf believes the marriage had suffered even
before the end of the war:

> My parents never really had a real marriage. Mother
> was a happy, joyous person, full of life and very sensi-
> tive. . . . Her pretty head was filled with thoughts that
> really didn't fit with her life in the bourgeois village of
> Günzburg.[23]

Irene was fast losing faith in her marriage. To compensate
for the absence of her husband, she sought male companions.
Rolf says, "Not affairs, but she was on friendly terms with
several men. That also was necessary, since there was no man
in the family and she needed some protection and help." But
when Mengele learned of these friendships, he was furious.
According to Rolf, their secret meetings deteriorated into
bitter fights.

> Father was insanely jealous. During their short meet-
> ings in the forest, he made scenes that embittered her.
> She should separate from her acquaintances, he said,
> and not see her friends. She shouldn't leave the house.
> He did not appreciate the danger she undertook every
> time she visited him.[24]

It was clear that to Irene the man she married before the
war and the fugitive who emerged after it were two different
people:

> I knew Josef Mengele as an absolutely honorable, de-
> cent, conscientious, very charming, elegant, and fun-
> loving person, otherwise I would not have married him.
> I came from a good, wealthy family and I had plenty of
> opportunities to get married. I think his ambition finally
> became his undoing.[25]

Notwithstanding the tension and deepening rift, Irene visited Mengele almost every two months. Mengele, meanwhile,
had patched up his differences with Vieland and Annalise. He

complained increasingly to Vieland about the growing "war crimes hysteria" and the focus on his service at Auschwitz. But any hopes Mengele may have entertained of war crimes retribution being limited to the twenty-two Nazi principals at Nuremberg was short-lived. In December 1945 the Allies announced that other war criminals would also be brought to trial by the governments of those countries that Hitler had ravaged. In early 1946 Mengele asked Fischer to subscribe to the regional daily *Rosenheimer Anzeiger.* Between that local newspaper and updates from Vieland, Mengele stayed abreast of the war crimes trials and the growing indictments, with keen interest, but an anxious eye.

In April 1946 Mengele learned that he had been publicly named in court for the first time.* Rudolf Hoess, the commandant at Auschwitz, had gone on the stand at Nuremberg to give evidence as chief witness in defense of Ernst Kaltenbrunner, who, as chief of the Reich Main Security Office, had been responsible for administering concentration camps and the program for the extermination of the Jews. Since Hoess himself had dutifully implemented his part of that policy at Auschwitz by personally being responsible for the deaths of some 2.5 million Jews, he seemed a strange choice for Kaltenbrunner's defense. It soon became clear that the purpose was to shift much of the responsibility onto Hoess, since he made a virtue of his compulsion to follow orders, having been brought up to believe that anti-Semitism was a form of pest control.[26] A third of the way through Hoess's evidence, Kaltenbrunner's counsel, Dr. Kauffmann, asked him:

> What became known to you about so-called medical experiments on living internees?
>
> *Hoess:* Medical experiments were carried out in several camps. For instance in Auschwitz there were experiments on sterilization carried out by Professor Klaubert and Dr. Schumann; also experiments on twins by SS medical officer Dr. Mengele.[27]

Meanwhile, according to Rolf, Mengele noticed that a cult of silence had enveloped National Socialist involvement in "medical research." The chief architects like Professor von

---

* The year had already begun badly for him with the death of his mother in January.

Verschuer had to perform some fairly smart footwork as the clamor grew, from the Allies in general and the occupied countries in particular, to prosecute those involved in those heinous crimes. The German academic world split into two camps: those who had been tainted by Nazism but whose excuse was that their involvement was purely academic; and those who were unrepentant and beyond the pale. Von Verschuer skillfully maneuvered himself into the former camp, urging a colleague in 1946: "Let us stay silent about the horror. It is behind us."[28] The final rehabilitation for a man who so enthusiastically secured funds for Mengele's futile work and apprised its nonsensical results came in 1949 when a commission of fellow professors judged him fit to resume his teaching career:

> It would be pharisaical for us to regard in hindsight isolated incidents in the life of an otherwise honorable and brave man, who has had a difficult life and frequently displayed his nobility of character, as an unpardonable moral stain.[29]

Just how deeply these learned men probed is open to question, since they even tried to pull an academic veil over Mengele, saying that "from the available evidence it is not clear how much Dr. Mengele himself knew during the times in question." No attempt by the West German authorities was ever made to prosecute von Verschuer.*

Von Verschuer went on to become a distinguished professor of genetics at Münster University, but he never again discussed his involvement with experiments, although his son Helmut raised the issue once or twice:

> I tried to put my point of view to him, but it was clear that politically we were very different. My own impression is that my father only got to know what was going on very late in the day. But he never responded when defamatory statements were made against him.[30]

Unlike von Verschuer, Mengele could not count on the academic establishment to rewrite history and rally 'round.

---

* Von Verschuer died in August 1969 after lying in a coma since September 1968, when he was knocked down by a vehicle while crossing a road in the rain.

Most alarming of all to Mengele, as he lay low on his Bavarian farm, was the spate of trials against Nazi doctors held by the Americans, British, Russians, and Poles. In his autobiography, Mengele showed his bitterness about the trials in a fictional conversation with Vieland. In this passage, Mengele referred to himself as "Andreas," a pseudonym he adopted to hide his identity in case the papers were ever discovered.

Vieland: Did you already hear the last of the news stories from Nuremberg?

Andreas: In the course of the re-education, the German, who is already pathetic as a result of so much deprivation and hunger, hears only about war crimes which he has allegedly done, of the forced laborers, and about the concentration camps and so on and so on. One must realize that this limelight is only intended to make hundreds of thousands of Germans, including mothers of German soldiers as well as little farmer women who lost two boys to hunger in a Russian POW camp, accuse the "Nazis" of these supposed crimes.

Although Mengele viewed the trials as nothing more than Allied propaganda, his earlier jaunty confidence that he could convince their courts of his innocence vanished with the news of death sentences against three Auschwitz colleagues: Dr. Fritz Klein, with whom he shared the distinction of being the only doctor able to carry out the ghastly railhead selections without a drink; Dr. Werner Rhode; and Dr. Eduard Wirths, chief camp physician. Wirths committed suicide before he could be hanged.

The future looked bleaker still when in December 1946 at Nuremberg, the Americans brought twenty-three leading SS physicians and scientists to court in the so-called Doctors Trial. The indictment specified four charges: conspiracy, war crimes, crimes against humanity, and membership in criminal organizations. The accused were alleged to have been responsible for experiments on inmates involving exposure to high altitudes and low temperatures, and ingestion of seawater; experiments with typhus and infectious jaundice; experiments with sulpha drugs, bone grafting, and mustard gas; the collection of skulls of Jews; euthanasia of undesirable racial groups; and mass sterilization.[31]

Mengele followed the proceedings with consuming interest, especially when the seven death and five life-imprisonment sentences were handed down. Among those hanged was Karl Gebhardt, who directed sulpha experiments on women at Ravensbrück concentration camp. Wounds were deliberately inflicted on victims and then stuffed with wood shavings and gauze strips impregnated with bacteria to simulate battlefield conditions; then the effectiveness of sulfanilamide was studied. During an inspection by Reich Physician SS Ernst Grawitz,* Gebhardt was asked how many deaths had occurred as a result of the sulpha experiments. When told that the answer was none, Grawitz said the conditions did not "conform to battlefield conditions." A new series of experiments were then carried out on twenty-four Polish women, in which the circulation of the blood through their muscles was interrupted at the area of infection by tying off the muscles on either end. Very serious infections resulted, and several women died in terrible pain.[32] In May 1943, the Congress of Reich Physicians and the German Orthopedic Society had presented Gebhardt with its highest accolade for his grotesque experiments at Ravensbrück. (Gebhardt was president of the German Red Cross and doctor to much of Germany's prewar social elite. His father was Himmler's personal physician.)

In the dock with Gebhardt was the doctor who actually prepared the wounds, Fritz Fischer. He got only a life sentence. Dr. Karl Brandt, Hitler's personal physician, who also oversaw the euthanasia program, was sentenced to death. At Nuremberg he attempted to minimize the use of human guinea pigs:

> Quite independently of what actually happened, the human being has always been used in some form for experimental purposes. . . . The jump from animal experiments to human experiments was for practical reasons actually needed.[33]

---

* Ernst Grawitz, a boyhood friend of Himmler's, blew up himself and his family with several hand grenades at the end of the war.

The only female defendant, Dr. Herta Oberheuser, was given twenty years for injecting prisoners with lethal doses of typhus and jaundice.

The significance to Mengele of the verdicts against Fischer, Oberheuser, and Gebhardt was that he too had conducted sulpha experiments, had injected many twins, mostly children, with typhus, and held absolutely to Brandt's view that experiments on humans were an article of faith. And there was no more forceful advocate of euthanasia and the concept of "worthless life" than Josef Mengele, as his postwar autobiography shows. One passage justifying to Vieland the existence of concentration camps is especially revealing:

> It is necessary for each country to have an institution in case of war, where it can keep elements who are of any danger to the country, foreigners who are assumed to be saboteurs, worthless people, willing to do espionage, prostitutes, Gypsies and people who are criminals by profession.
>
> They [Jews] belonged to the group of possible enemies of the country who one had to be assured of . . . because of their internationality, their worldwide organization, their connection even to enemy countries and their intelligence service. . . . This fact alone would be enough to take the measure like the *konzentration.*
>
> When the top leaders of this international organization, the Jewish World Congress, officially declares war on the Deutsches Reich, then there is no need to discuss the right to collect and keep the Jews in camps. . . . Hitler warned Jews in his speech in 1939 not to stir up the people with war against Germany, that it could end up badly for them.[34]

In another of his fictional autobiographical conversations with Vieland, Mengele (as "Andreas") even defended the conditions discovered in the concentration camp at the end of the war:

> *Vieland:* Recently I saw in Munich a film about the concentration camps. It seems that there were terrible conditions there. Even if one disregards the scenes which are not authentic and may have come from news-

reels from mass Allied bombings of German towns, the movie shows nevertheless, without leaving any doubts, that people lived and also died there under catastrophic conditions of malnutrition.

Andreas: Yes, that was probably the case. [Andreas really doesn't want to say anything more about the subject but he finally asks Doctor Vieland,] When do you believe these movies were made?

Vieland: I assume after the occupation of the camp by the Allies.

Andreas: Certainly not earlier. And thus you get only information about the conditions that existed at the time the movie was made, or maybe several weeks or months before that, during which the last throes of the war were being staged. Every person who lived through this catastrophe knows the insurmountable difficulties in providing provisions which were prevalent during the last months of the war. The camps necessarily suffered to an extremely great degree under the chaos of the debacle of the collapse. And it was that that led to the conditions as they were shown in this movie.

Although Mengele attempted to justify the imprisonment of Jews and the conditions in the camps, other members of the Mengele family were more realistic, and they knew that his capture would mean certain execution. Faced with the prospect of Josef joining his Auschwitz colleagues on the gallows, his father and his wife, among others, tried to dupe the American authorities into believing that Josef Mengele was dead. Their efforts, combined with a lack of initiative and a general inefficiency on the part of the American occupation forces, ensured Mengele's freedom in postwar Germany.

Mengele's father, Karl, had moved from an early date to bury his son's tracks. As the former *Kreiswirtschaftsbrater,* or economic advisor, to the regional Nazi party covering the Günzburg area, Karl was placed in custody in March 1946, awaiting Allied denazification hearings. The purpose of *Entnazifizierung* was to grade party members into categories so that appropriate action could be taken, ranging from criminal charges to police surveillance or even acquittal, for those who could prove they had resisted Hitler's tyranny. Twice Karl Sr. told the Americans that his son was missing in action. On the third occasion he told them he knew he was dead.

While Karl maintained that facade in Günzburg, Irene did the same in nearby Autenreid. When military police visited Irene in June 1945 she told them her husband was missing in the Russian zone, presumed dead. At that time, that is what she genuinely believed. But even after she knew he was alive and safe, Irene maintained the game with her friends and acquaintances in Autenreid and Günzburg. Afraid that one of them might be an informer to the occupying Americans, she insisted to all that Mengele was missing and probably dead. Letters from Irene to friends at the time state her "firm belief I shall never see my husband alive." She even turned up at the local Catholic church, dressed in black, and asked the priest to pray for the repose of the soul of her deceased husband.

For one important section of the American postwar administration, the Chief Counsel's Office for War Crimes, the efforts of Karl Sr. and Irene contributed to the acceptance of Mengele's death. It certainly explains why no attempts were made to expand the investigation or even to follow Irene or other family members in order to locate the missing camp doctor.

One person who believed Mengele was still alive and desperately wanted him tried was Dr. Gisella Perl, an inmate gynecologist who had worked for Mengele at Auschwitz. She witnessed, firsthand, some of his worst excesses. In January 1947, Dr. Perl wrote to the American authorities offering to give evidence against Mengele after she had read an article in a New York newspaper that claimed he had been captured. The report turned out to be false, and her letter was lost in the bureaucracy and went unanswered. Then in October 1947, she tried again by writing to the War Crimes Branch of the Civil Affairs Division in Washington, saying that Mengele was "the greatest mass murderer" and that she had "many important things to tell . . . to awaken the conscience of the world."[35] The response to Dr. Perl is indicative of the general confusion, disorganization, and lack of cooperation among the various arms of the American occupation forces seeking to bring Nazis to justice. This time, instead of ignoring Dr. Perl, the Americans mistakenly assumed that Mengele was among the forty SS men, including some doctors, then standing trial before the Polish Supreme National Tribunal in Kraków. They replied to Dr. Perl that they had asked Brigadier General Telford Taylor, U.S. Chief of Counsel for War Crimes at Nuremberg, to ascertain the status of the trial from the Polish government representative there.[36] Meanwhile, an official in the Locator and Apprehension Branch in Nuremberg came across an indication in a file to the effect that Mengele was dead. Without cross-checking with any other U.S. government division, Mengele's death was assumed to be established. On January 19, 1948, Telford Taylor replied to Washington: "We wish to advise our records show Dr. Mengerle [sic] is dead as of October 1946."[37]

Telford Taylor's response appears to have been based on the results of Karl Mengele's ability to convince his interrogators that his son was dead, as well as Irene's deception in Autenreid. The fact that Taylor responded to Washington by misspelling Mengele's name is indicative of the postwar chaos engulfing a war crimes section understaffed, overworked, and unable to make the kind of double-checks that might reasonably have been expected in the case of such a monstrous criminal as Mengele. In any event, on February 12, 1948, Dr. Perl was informed of "Dr. Mengele's death" and thanked for her offer to appear as a witness.[38] There the matter rested until the West Germans issued an arrest warrant almost twelve years later.

While Telford Taylor's staff at Nuremberg believed Mengele was dead, another branch of the American administration in Europe thought he was alive.

On April 29, 1947, Special Agent Benjamin J. Gorby of the 970th Counter-Intelligence Corps received information that Mengele had been arrested. His source was one of the many different newspapers circulating at displaced persons camps for refugees. As early as December 1946, press reports indicated that Mengele had been captured by Allied forces. They had begun with reports from Vienna, in the Jewish political prisoners paper.*

Gorby heard that the arrest was reported in a Vienna news-

---

* The source for the report was an Auschwitz survivor, Mordka Danielski. When contacted in 1985, Danielski could not recall ever hearing that Mengele was captured. He had no idea how he was listed in documents as the source of the wrong information.

paper and assumed Mengele had been arrested there. Since the 430th Counter-Intelligence Corps detachment was responsible for the Vienna area, Gorby cabled the 430th CIC in Vienna, asking them to question Mengele "with regard to the fate of a group of approximately 20 Jewish children who were alleged to have been removed by him from the Auschwitz camp in November 1944 and taken to an unknown place." Gorby added:

> The fact of the removal of the Jewish children from Auschwitz by Dr. Mengele was confirmed to this office by the father of one of the children who lives in [illegible]. Other parents of the children among the group are still alive and most eager to have news from or about their children.[39]

There is no evidence that Mengele was arrested in Vienna, according to an inquiry conducted by the Justice Department's Office of Special Investigation (OSI). Almost certainly, Gorby was acting in good faith on the DP camp's erroneous newspaper story, but he made several assumptions without checking the facts. Mengele's diaries mention no arrest. Irene says her husband was not arrested again after his initial detention in mid-1945. Nevertheless, the public disclosure of the Gorby document in January 1985 by the Simon Wiesenthal Center in Los Angeles had an explosive effect even though the document itself had been available since August 1983.* The result was a series of Senate subcommittee hearings which led to a directive that the OSI spearhead a special effort to find Mengele. The Army was also urged to inquire as to whether Mengele had ever been in their custody after the war. It was the largest investigation of its kind ever undertaken by the United States government.[40]

Special Agent Gorby was not the only person who believed Mengele had been captured by American forces during 1946 or 1947. French government documents, obtained in October 1985, state unequivocally that Mengele had been captured by the Americans in late 1946. According to the French, Men-

---

* The documents were declassified to the authors in response to a Freedom of Information Act request following an administrative appeal to the Department of the Army on August 31, 1983. Gerald Posner was called before the Senate to testify on the documents and the question of whether Mengele had been held by American forces.

gele was detained, was known to be the "notorious camp
doctor from Auschwitz," and was released, without explanation, by the Americans on November 29, 1946. The French
claimed that American authorities confirmed the Mengele
arrest and release on February 20, 1947. Again, although the
documents are superficially impressive, they are unsupported
by any evidence in any government file. The French claim
that Americans confirmed a 1946 arrest and release. No
American detention records reflect such an event. There is no
denial that Mengele continued to reside quietly on the farm at
Mangolding until the middle of 1948. If he had been captured
by the Americans at the end of 1946, he is unlikely to have
returned to the U.S. zone of Germany for the next eighteen
months. Although the source of the French documents is not
known, they are mistaken.

American confusion was a match for the French. While
Telford Taylor's War Crimes Branch in Nuremberg believed
Mengele was dead, his name continued to appear for most of
the postwar 1940s on the Central Registry of War Criminals
and Security Suspects (CROWCASS), a list meant to be distributed quarterly to detention camps. Again, this is evidence of
the ineptitude that characterized the postwar efforts to find
missing Nazis. The CROWCASS system was paralyzed by inefficiency. Since May 1946, CROWCASS had been little more
than a mailing center in Berlin, the whole operation having
moved from its British-run headquarters in Paris following a
revolt by the American staff, inept logistical arrangements,
and a boycott by the Russians. Few names, if any, were added
to the lists sent after the move to Berlin. The fact that
Mengele's name remained on them so long after Telford Taylor believed him to be dead is unfortunately typical of the
CROWCASS efforts after the war.

While Mengele resided quietly in Mangolding, the American efforts to find him were halfhearted and ineffective.
Mengele's deep cover as a farmhand may well have been
unnecessary. It is incontestable that after the American authorities mistakenly released Mengele from custody in mid-
1945, they never came close to finding him, even though he
lived in the U.S. occupation zone for another four years.

The closest authorities came to finding Mengele was not the
result of American efforts, but rather a chance inspection by

two German policemen in 1946. In his autobiography, Mengele recalled the moment he had his first face-to-face confrontation with authorities since his release from the American detention camp:

> Two German police came to the farm on a motorbike and a sidecar and asked to talk to the released prisoner of war. Andreas [Mengele] said, "I'm the ex-POW" and was ordered to produce his American release card. Andreas retrieved his card from his room and gave it to one of the control policemen. As they reviewed it, Andreas's alarm abated. After a short look the policeman handed back the card. Again one thought how at that time any German official had the greatest respect for any document that was written in English and stamped by the U.S. Army.

With the exception of that one intrusion by the German police, Mengele's stay on the Fischer farm was uneventful. His major preoccupation was not avoiding his pursuers, but keeping himself entertained.

CHAPTER
4

———
———

Flight from Europe

———
———

While Josef Mengele was residing quietly on the Fischer farm, Karl Sr. had been released from custody after completing the denazification process. Business at the Mengele factory in Günzburg was booming. As Karl observed, "There was so much reconstruction going on, there was money to be made from it." One of the biggest money-makers proved to be wheelbarrows. By the end of the decade, wheelbarrows stamped with the name "MENGELE" were to be seen at thousands of building sites across the new Federal Republic and annual revenue was 5.4 million deutschemarks a year.[1] Nonetheless, Karl complained bitterly to the Allies that they were thwarting his expansion plans because they would not immediately allow his son, Karl, to join him. Like his father, Karl Jr. had joined the Nazi party. During his denazification process, the Allies were reluctant to release him to an active role in the company, arguing that two former active Nazi party members should not have influential positions in a large company so soon after the war. It was not until Alois returned home in 1949, after languishing in a POW camp in Yugoslavia, that Karl Sr. had both his sons working for him.

The rejuvenation of the Mengele firm was fortunate for Josef, because by the fall of 1948 he had decided that there was no future for him in Germany. The prosperity of the family business would allow Mengele to buy his way to freedom, paying for false travel documents as well as guides who would lead him across Europe and onto a boat steaming toward South America.

Mengele made his decision to flee because he was sure his fate would be sealed if he was captured in Germany and placed on trial. It was true that several doctors as culpable as he had somehow managed to wriggle free. Dr. Renno, one of the two chief doctors of the Hartheim Euthanasia Institute, was excused from standing trial because of poor health. (Notwithstanding his apparently imminent demise, Renno went on to live peacefully in the Black Forest for another thirty-five years.) There also had been some remarkable acquittals. Dr. Adolf Pokorny, who had written to Himmler saying, "The enemy must be not only conquered but exterminated," left the "Doctors Trial" a free man, even though he was the architect of the Third Reich's plans to sterilize millions of people in the occupied territories.

But Mengele was not prepared to count on having Pokorny's good fortune, and reluctantly the family agreed. By the fall of 1948, Mengele had made up his mind to leave Germany and build a life elsewhere. Argentina was the preferred choice of sanctuary. Although Karl Mengele's firm had no branches there, several business connections had been made that his father thought Josef might develop. And there was a groundswell of Nazi sympathy in Argentina. But it was still regarded as something of a stopgap measure, as Alois later confided to Mengele's school friend Julius Diesbach: "The family was convinced that Josef would have to stay in Argentina only until the war crimes fever had subsided in Europe."[2]

Karl Sr.'s hope was that when the war crimes "hysteria" had ceased, Josef would be able to return to Günzburg and share in the running of the family business. Preparations for the Mengele brothers to take over the reins were made with the announcement in January 1949 that the firm was to be called "Karl Mengele & Sons."

According to Rolf Mengele, his father returned to the Günzburg area in August 1948, and hid in the nearby forests until the spring of 1949. The Fischers were not surprised when Mengele suddenly left. Alois recalls:

> We always thought that he only wanted to hide and that someday he would disappear. And that's what did happen—suddenly he disappeared. He took only his money and the suit he had come with. Absolutely nothing else. We were not surprised. We thought that he must have found a better hiding place. We never heard anything from him since then.[3]

While in the Günzburg region, Mengele told Irene that he expected her and Rolf to follow once he had established himself in Buenos Aires. But Irene could not agree to go with him. Rolf describes the predicament in which his mother found herself:

> My mother did not want to go into hiding with him. She loved Germany and Europe, the culture was dear to her as she had studied art history, and she was close to her parents. Also, in 1948 she had met Alfons Hackenjos, later to be her second husband. Yet, still it was a very difficult decision for her because she still had feelings for Josef. She made a conscious effort to erase his picture from her mind and terminate her feelings for him.[4]

Spurned by his wife and wanted by the Allies, Mengele fled the smoldering embers of Nazi Germany in the spring of 1949, alone and bitter that his fight to "save his country from destruction by the Jews" had been thus rewarded. Mengele's flight was arranged and paid for by his family through former SS contacts in the Günzburg area. The escape across the Alps involved plenty of cloak-and-dagger but very little of the clockwork precision that mythology has ascribed to the Masonic-like brotherhood of postwar Nazi escape groups.

The journey began by train to Innsbruck. Mengele was questioned on the way by Austrian customs officers, who asked him where he was from. "Brixen, in Germany," he replied, which seemed to satisfy them. They did not ask to see his identity papers, and they did not question him again. From Innsbruck he traveled to an inn at Steinach, at the foot of the

Brenner Pass, arriving on Easter Sunday, April 17. There he spent the night, 400 yards from the Italian border, and met the first of five mystery men who helped him at various stages of his journey and whom Mengele identifies in his diary only by code names.* This man was "Xavier."

The following morning Mengele rose in the early hours to be led by a guide across the Brenner Pass. Forty years later the guide's identity is still a local secret, although Jakob Strickner, a wartime SS sergeant, claims to know. "I'm the only one around here who does know," boasted Strickner, "but I'm not saying." The need for the clandestine crossing arose after the Mengele family's attempt to obtain a false passport failed dismally. With no experience in dealing in the black market, Karl Sr. paid 7000 deutschemarks for a passport,† but it was so amateurishly forged that even the dimmest border guard would have been suspicious.[5]

The Brenner crossing took Mengele only an hour. In his account of the journey, he says there was a full moon and that he saw edelweiss and the basin of the Brenner Pass several thousand feet below. Once on the Italian side, he went to the railway station, waited in the only restaurant, and caught the first workers' train to Vipiteno at 5:45 a.m. On this leg of the journey the first of several hitches occurred. Mengele mistakenly got off at Brennerbad, thinking he had arrived at Vipiteno. Before boarding the next train, he waited for a crowd to build up so he could "walk behind tall people before getting on the train." When he finally got to Vipiteno, before venturing down he hung back in his carriage until the platform had filled up with passengers.

The network providing the escape service had booked Mengele in at the Golden Cross Inn under the name listed on his forged set of American release papers, "Fritz Hollmann." There he was approached by an Italian called "Nino," who said the code word "rosemary" and handed him a German identity card after Mengele gave him a passport-sized photograph. At the Golden Cross, Mengele met a second man

---

* The identities of only two of the five men have been uncovered. One was Hans Sedlmeier, a childhood school friend of Mengele's, and an executive in the Mengele company. Another was Adolf Steiner, brother of Franz Steiner, director of the Italian Karl Mengele subsidiary in Merano, Italy.

† In terms of dollars, 7000 of the brand-new deutschemarks, not very long after the postwar currency reform, was not much—but was a small fortune in Europe.

whom he called "Erwin" and whom his son, Rolf, now assumes was Hans Sedlmeier, a school friend and the family firm's sales manager since 1944. "Erwin" brought Mengele greetings from his father and cash in dollars for the long journey ahead. He also brought him "a small suitcase filled with scientific specimens" from his Auschwitz experiments, which he had retrieved from his girlfriend nurse behind Russian lines in 1945.[6]*

Mengele had a month at the Golden Cross to memorize the travel plan that "Erwin" had given him. From Vipiteno he went on to Bosen, where he arrived by train in mid-May. There he met "Kurt," who was in charge of the final phase of getting Mengele out of Europe. In his account of this stage, Mengele again spoke of himself in the third person as "Andreas," and he described his initial impressions of "Kurt."

> His actions and mannerisms suited his small round body. There was an industriousness in his walk as well as his speech. Perhaps he was preoccupied with getting through the ordeal in a hurry. Andreas didn't notice anxiety, but something like suppressed animosity. Kurt was reserved but always obliging.[7]

"Kurt" told Mengele that passage to Buenos Aires had been booked for him on the *North King,* leaving Genoa in two weeks. The ticket, tourist class, cost 120,000 lira, and there was little time to lose. There was one outstanding matter to resolve—an International Red Cross passport, which "Kurt" confidently said he could acquire from the Swiss consul.† "We can get that done today," he said. "Tomorrow we'll take care of the formalities at the Argentine consulate."[8]

Mengele met no resistance at the Swiss consulate where his

---

* Rolf believes the suitcase may have contained his notes from Auschwitz. In addition, Mengele's autobiography mentions that the package from Sedlmeier contained two glass slides with a blood sample between them—also possibly from Auschwitz. It is known that Josef Mengele had the suitcase with him when he entered South America, because in his autobiography he mentions that Argentine customs officials questioned him about the suitcase and its contents. It is never again mentioned. Its whereabouts are unknown.

† The International Red Cross file on Josef Mengele was shrouded in secrecy for forty years after the war. Only after one of the authors, Gerald Posner, testified before the U.S. Senate that the International Red Cross in Geneva refused to release the file did the United States decide to act. Based upon a written request from Secretary of State George Shultz, the Red Cross finally made the Mengele file public, and the information it contained helped to fill in some of the details of Mengele's final efforts to escape Europe.

application was processed by a woman he described as being "of riper years." "Kurt" introduced his friend as "Helmut Gregor," a "technician" who was requesting a passport for passage to Argentina because he had been "a prisoner of war or internee." As with any effective cover, the identity that "Kurt" created for "Helmut Gregor" had enough similarities to the man who stood before the Swiss official to satisfy her that they were one and the same person, though as Mengele later remarked, judging by her lack of concentration she did not seem to care.

"Gregor" was born on August 6, 1911, just five months after Mengele's real birth date; his religion was Catholic, as was Mengele's; he was a German citizen like Mengele, although his original nationality was Italian. The real deception, apart from the name, was the statement that "Gregor" had been born in the Dolomites, at Alto Adige, and could prove his identity with his identity card, issued on April 4, 1948, at Teremeno in Alto Adige, where he claimed to have lived since 1944. Although Mengele's identity papers were stamped "Authorization to disembark in Argentina," granted as of September 1948, Mengele still needed a current consulate stamp on his Argentine visa.[9]

The following day "Gregor" went to the Argentine consulate, where he made his application. He met their demand for a fourteen-day-old vaccination certificate with a phony pre-dated one supplied by a Croatian doctor. Then the Argentineans raised an objection: The Swiss consulate official had written the issue date for Mengele's passport in the space reserved for the expiration date. It was, therefore, technically out of date. The apologetic Swiss woman reissued his Red Cross passport. This time the Argentineans promised Mengele a visa, provided he passed a medical exam. "Kurt" hurriedly took Mengele to the *North King*'s embarkation building, where he was examined. Commenting on the unhygienic conditions, Mengele noted with disgust:

> They were looking for trachoma cases using the same glass rod and the same unwashed hands. . . . If one did not have a contagious disease before the examination, one most probably had it after the examination.[10]

But there was yet one more obstacle to overcome. Mengele needed an Italian exit visa, and the corrupt official in the immigration department who usually helped "Kurt" was on holiday. "You'll just have to manage by yourself," "Kurt" told Mengele, advising him to try to bribe the official in charge with a 20,000 lira note tucked between his papers.

The *North King* was due to sail in three days, on May 25. Mengele was getting desperate. Taking his guide's advice, he made the approach to the official by paper-clipping the 20,000 lira note to the inside of the folder containing his forged papers. The official glanced inside the file, peeled off the note, returned the file, and then, ominously, exchanged glances with another official. At first Mengele thought the money was "just not enough of a bribe." Then he was ordered up three flights of stairs, led into a room, and the questioning began. A policeman demanded to know where Mengele's Italian visa was, where he came from. As Mengele later wrote, "A thunderstorm [came] over Andreas" as he tried in vain to persuade his interrogator that he was an Italian by birth, from Alto Adige. Mengele recalled: "The policeman yelled in broken German, 'I don't believe that. I will investigate you.' For the moment he is arrested. That word hits Andreas."[11]

Mengele was taken to a cell and ordered to turn out his pockets. "Forty-five dollars are the most interesting part of the contents to the Italian police," Mengele observed. Then he was "locked in an iron-barred cage in the hallway." Like a "wild cat" he paced back and forth. The obscene graffiti adorning his cell walls seemed to bother him more than almost anything else. As Inge Byhan, who examined Mengele's diary for the West German magazine *Bunte* observed: "He was so very upset about this. I wrote, 'What's more obscene— these little things on the wall of the cell or the hills of bones in Auschwitz.' "[12]

Mengele was contemptuous of his cell mates—"these disgusting rural rejects"—particularly a gnomelike crippled street musician and a morphine-addicted doctor whose withdrawal symptoms Mengele attributed to his "constitutional inferiority." Once the addict reacted so badly that he deliberately broke a window in order to cut his arm on the glass. Unmoved to help or intervene, Mengele later cruelly remarked, "The creator of this action sleeps peacefully in the prison hospital under the comfortable blanket of painkillers he received for his self-inflicted injuries, the sleep of the addict." Of his other cell mates, including an Englishman, only an Italian submarine commander, a Fascist like himself, was worth the time of day. "His words," wrote Mengele, "came truly from the soul of a National Socialist, a man who spoke contemptuously of the Communist rabble as the sewerage of the big towns that now controlled Italy."[13]

After spending three weeks in jail, Mengele lost all hope of escaping. The immigration department knew that his papers were false. They began to question him about "Kurt": who was he, where could he be found, and how much had Mengele paid for his help? A 4 a.m. call to the Croatian doctor who had given Mengele his false vaccination certificate seemed to seal his fate: there was nothing more, he said, that he could do. Sleepless, Mengele "sank into a state of depressed lethargy." The game, it seemed, was up. Then, as was to happen so often over the next thirty years, Mengele's fortunes changed dramatically. Kurt's corrupt immigration official returned from holiday and straightened matters out. "Suddenly they discovered their mistake," wrote Mengele, "and the policeman is unusually friendly and asks Andreas if he is a Jew and some more questions." Finally Mengele was freed and granted his exit permit. And to his great relief, the *North King* was still at the dock.

In mid-July 1949, the *North King* finally sailed for Buenos Aires. Mengele was in a buoyant mood. The immigration official who had rescued him from jail had arranged for him to travel second class instead of tourist, at no extra cost. Watching the Italian coastline recede, Mengele made the banal observation, "Waves, all is waves." Then over the loudspeaker came the announcement that the ship had crossed the three-mile zone and was out of Italian territorial waters. Finally assured of his freedom, Josef Mengele retired to his cabin. "So this is how it feels to emigrate," he reflected as he settled in for a long sleep.[14]

C H A P T E R
5

———

Argentina:
Lull before the Storm

———

———

The *North King* crept across the South Atlantic toward Buenos Aires at a steady eight knots, taking more than four weeks for the journey. When the ship finally docked on August 26, 1949, it was springtime in the Argentine capital. But for Josef Mengele the promise of better days ahead was short-lived. From the moment "Helmut Gregor" stepped ashore, things began to go wrong.

Mengele was expecting an acquaintance to greet him at dockside, a doctor he had met once in 1939 and to whom he referred in his diary as "Rolf Nuckert." But the man was nowhere to be seen. As Mengele went through customs, there was another hitch. An inquisitive officer wanted to inspect one of Mengele's suitcases, the one containing his research notes and specimens. The customs agent asked Mengele what was in the suitcase. Mengele matter-of-factly told him "biological notes." There was an awkward moment as the port doctor was called in to examine the documents. Not understanding a word of German, the doctor stared at the documents, shrugged his shoulders, and waved Mengele through.[1]

Friendless and without a place to stay, Mengele decided to take a taxi to the city center to find a place to sleep. Then he realized he had no Argentine pesos, as he had been unable to change his currency at the port. Cursing to himself, he turned to two Italians he had befriended on the voyage. They took him to a run-down hotel called the Palermo, "third class," as he noted, where he shared a room with his two companions and used a toilet and washbasin down the hallway.

Armed with the address of an engineer in the textile business to whom Mengele's diary also gives a fictitious name, "Schott," he went in search of work. On the way to the engineer's office, Mengele passed the *Casa Rosado*, the presidential palace of Argentina's new dictator, Juan Perón. Admiring the smartly dressed soldiers clasping their swords as they guarded the palace gates, Mengele reflected that tradition, "especially military tradition, is still one of the most stabilizing influences in politics" and that it was only the Germans who were "doing their best to destroy tradition in their offering of collective guilt." Unhappily for Mengele, when he eventually arrived at the office he discovered that "Schott" could not give him a managerial job. He did offer him one on the factory floor, however, as a wool comber. As an inducement, "Schott" told Mengele that he would be working alongside the grandson of a notable Argentine statesman. Mengele was not impressed on either count and decided to look elsewhere.[2]

The experience may have had a sobering effect, even on Mengele's overdeveloped estimate of his own worth. As a farmhand in southern Bavaria he had already tumbled a long way from the omnipotent post he had held at Auschwitz. But at least he was never far from Günzburg and his powerful family. Now in his downfall he plumbed new depths, alone, with a shared pensione room for a home, shuffling around the city in search of a menial job. He finally settled for one as a carpenter because it came with a room in the Vicente Lopez district of Buenos Aires. The room had no windows and still he had no privacy, having to share it with an engineer.

His roommate, noticing that Mengele's bags included some medical instruments such as hypodermics, deduced that he was a doctor. At first Mengele denied this, but he relented after the engineer's daughter became quite ill and he pleaded with Mengele to stop lying about his medical past and treat the child. Mengele isolated her in the storehouse and treated her with cold compresses to reduce the fever, prescribing a diet of chamomile tea and sulfonamide tablets. Mengele also swore the engineer to secrecy regarding his true profession.

Mengele's concern about his medical past becoming public knowledge was just one of the strains that weighed upon him during his early months in Buenos Aires. The trauma of fugitive life in a strange city 6000 miles from home must have been severe. Since his arrival in South America, he had begun to keep a daily diary, reflecting in his writings the many crises he faced. But for some unexplained reason his diary stops abruptly in mid-sentence at this point. In a 1975 letter to his son, Rolf, Mengele informed the family that he wrote of his time in Argentina, but the family claims not to know the whereabouts of this part of his diary. The family may have deliberately destroyed it in order to protect the reputations of Karl Sr. and Alois, who, contrary to the family's indignant denials, employed Mengele as a salesman for much of this time. The diary does not resume for another ten years, until May 1960, the month that Adolf Eichmann was kidnapped in Argentina. Significantly, perhaps, it was also at that point that Mengele ceased to work for the Günzburg firm.

Nevertheless, much can be gleaned from the many letters Mengele wrote home to his family. In his early letters, Mengele, although bothered by his fugitive existence, expressed surprise at the ease with which he was settling into Buenos Aires life.* By selecting Argentina as his South American country of exile, Mengele had unwittingly chosen a nation so advanced that the culture shock was greatly reduced. By the end of the 1940s Argentina had become the technological leader of South America, boasting more than half the continent's telephones, televisions, and railway lines. It had enormous natural resources as well as the healthiest and most literate population on the continent. And whatever Argentina

---

* All letters from Josef Mengele to his family and friends before 1973 were later burned by the family, because the letters were handwritten and the family feared that their discovery would identify Mengele as the writer. After 1973, letters from Mengele were typewritten and were kept by the family. The contents of the early letters were attested to by Rolf and Irene Mengele.

was in 1949, Buenos Aires was a microcosm. It was certainly the most culturally advanced and sophisticated city in South America. There were eighteen major daily newspapers, three of them in German. The arts were extensively represented: the Colón theater, which Mengele frequented, was modeled on the elaborate Paris Opera and presented some of the world's finest classical musicians and operatic performers. Mengele proved to be an avid theater-goer. To his delight, he found the city had forty-seven functioning theaters, more than either London or New York. Academically it was flourishing too, with six universities turning out more lawyers and doctors than all the other South American countries combined.

Buenos Aires reminded Mengele of Paris—the sculpted plazas, the iron-gray roofs, the diagonal layout of streets intersecting at sharp angles, the impeccably dressed children, the high ceilings over French windows, and the innumerable outdoor cafés in Art Nouveau style. Mengele also discovered a parochial and elitist attitude amongst Argentineans that was reminiscent of that held by the most fervent German National Socialists. The "primitives" of Paraguay and Peru were held in contempt. Argentineans often said they were "traveling to South America" when visiting Brazil or Chile. Mengele found the Argentine attitude of superiority comforting, certainly not alien.*

But despite its rapid progress, in 1949 Argentina was also a country stricken with serious problems. Just beyond the Parisian-style facades could be seen the *villas miserias,* the shantytowns, crammed with half a million people enduring the most squalid and degrading conditions. The rift between rich and poor was vast. A cattle aristocracy controlled the nation. These Argentine lords of the land held positions comparable with the aristocracy in the feudalistic Austro-Hungarian empire—an oligarchy of some 200 families closely interlocked by matrimonial ties, established over several generations of social primacy and aristocratic tradition. Economic conditions were deteriorating. The budget deficit was enormous, unemployment substantial, government salaries in arrears, and tax

---

* Argentina's attitude of superiority in Latin America is best evidenced by its later refusal to allow the Peace Corps to operate in that country. An Argentine official told an American diplomat, "Why should Argentina have a Peace Corps? Do you send one to France?"

collections haphazardly enforced. The black market was rampant; for fugitives like Mengele, the scope for bribes was unlimited.

The religious climate also was compatible for Mengele. Argentineans were not only passionately parochial, they were religiously conservative, bordering on institutionalized anti-Semitism. The official state religion, Roman Catholicism, was largely represented by an inflexible and intolerant church hierarchy. The Church's influence was such that it was able to sponsor a constitutional amendment limiting the presidency of the republic to Roman Catholics, and its indirect political influence prevented Jews from attaining cabinet-level positions until 1951.

There were other major advantages to Argentina as a sanctuary. Before the war a large and powerful German community had firmly established itself. Some schools in the more fashionable suburbs of Buenos Aires actually taught in German. In all but name these neighborhoods were reminiscent of Germany, and many of their residents held prominent civic and business positions. After Hitler became chancellor in 1933, two of the city's German newspapers adopted a strong pro-Nazi slant. By the time the German Army had blasted its way into Poland, most Germans in Argentina supported Hitler. Nazi sentiment ran so high, in fact, that the Argentine government ordered an investigation into its growth among German Argentineans to determine whether it posed a serious threat. On November 28, 1941, the Investigating Commission on Anti-Argentine Activities concluded that thousands of German immigrants were "controlled by the German Reich" and that many of them received financial help from Nazi Germany in order "to foment a Third Reich in Argentina." The commission noted the new Reich's racial policies toward Jews and said that "anti-Semitism is a fundamental principle of the new immigrants."[3]

The commission provided voluminous evidence to support its allegations: bank transfers from Nazi accounts in Germany and Switzerland to German front organizations and businesses in Argentina; organizational charts which showed the Nazi hierarchy and levels of authority in Argentina and the connection to Europe; dozens of Third Reich pamphlets and periodicals espousing that Argentina be made a southern-hemisphere Nazi state.

By the time the commission issued its report, however, the Argentine government was firmly pro-Axis. Nazi counter-intelligence, the *Abwehr*, had established an active network of agents throughout the country. The proliferation of Allied embassies and business interests made technically neutral Argentina one of the most attractive listening posts outside Europe. During its peak operational period, from 1942 to 1944, the *Abwehr* employed more than 1500 agents and informers in Argentina. Most of these agents returned to normal lives after the war, but they provided a nucleus that allowed Nazi fugitives to move freely about the country. Strong and reliable contacts had been forged with the Argentine police and intelligence service. They were contacts that were to prove indispensable to men like Mengele.

Behind this administrative labyrinth of Nazi sympathies was Argentina's new president, Juan Domingo Perón. He seized power on June 4, 1943, in a military coup, having decided that "Argentina needed saving." Perón had become infatuated with fascism while serving as military attaché to Italy. Mussolini's histrionics and his concept of the Fascist corporate state held a fascination for Perón. Once in power, he instituted radical reforms of his own and did more for the working class than had any of his predecessors. Perón thus became a hero to the *descamisados,* the "shirtless ones." While European Fascists were symbolized by black and brown shirts, Perón, not to be outdone, said Argentina "will be represented by the shirtless ones."[4]

Alarmed by his rise to power and his popularity, rival Argentine leaders had Perón arrested in October 1945. After a short exile on the island of Plata he was released, thanks to the leadership skills of a young blonde radio announcer, Eva Duarte. Despite the best efforts of U.S. Ambassador Spruille Braden, who published a state department "blue book" documenting Perón's wartime pro-Axis activities and his close personal business ties to leading Nazis, he won the popular election easily in June 1946 and was restored to power.

Before his brief exile, Perón had set aside 10,000 blank Argentine passports and identity cards for use by ranking Nazi fugitives. He also dispatched a personal agent, Carlos

Pineyro, to Copenhagen as a member of the Argentine lega-
tion to help channel Nazis into escape routes. Pineyro was not
a great success. On December 6, 1945, the Danes expelled
him, claiming that he was using his diplomatic status to
"smuggle Nazis out of Denmark to South America."⁵

Although Perón continued to believe that a reconstructed
Germany would return to Nazism within a decade to fulfill
Hitler's dream of a thousand-year Reich, his reasons for helping escaping Nazis was not just ideological. There was much
money to be made as well. Perón was strongly suspected of
having benefited from the booty that the Nazi hierarchy had
smuggled out of Europe as a postwar nest egg in the event of
defeat. From August 1942 through 1944, crates with markings
like "Auschwitz" and "Treblinka" were sent directly to the
Reichsbank in Berlin. The bank's senior clerk, Albert Thoms,
said:

> The incoming quantities of gold teeth grew by leaps and
> bounds, as did other valuables. Once we received
> twelve kilos of pearls in a single shipment. I've never
> seen such a mass of sparkling baubles in all my life.⁶

Reichsbank records show that more than 3500 ounces of plati-
num, 550,000 ounces of gold, and 4638 carats of diamonds, as
well as hundreds of works of art, were then packed into special pouches, along with millions of gold marks, pounds ster-
ling, dollars, and Swiss francs. The treasure was shipped by six
German U-boats in an operation code-named *Aktion Feuer-
land*, "Operation Land of Fire."⁷ It was handled on arrival in
Argentina by four German "trustees": Ludwig Freude, a well-
known German Argentine banker with close Nazi ties; Ricardo Staudt, a prominent Argentine businessman listed as
the number-two Nazi in the state department's "blue book"
(he was also a lieutenant in the Argentine naval reserve and
the German ambassador without portfolio); Dr. Heinrich
Dorge, a former aide to Dr. Hjalmar Schacht, the Nazis' financial wizard, who arrived in Argentina in the 1930s as a representative of German banking interests and later became a
consultant to the Argentine central bank; and Ricardo von
Leute, an officer of the Banco Aleman Transatlantico.

These four German representatives turned the incoming
booty into currency and gold and deposited it in vaults in the

Banco Germanico, and the Banco Tourquist. All deposits were made in the name of Perón's then mistress and future wife, Eva Duarte.[8] After Perón married Eva on October 21, 1945, they consolidated their hold over the Nazi hoard and eliminated any possible interference from the four German trustees. First, Freude was "investigated" on a variety of charges including espionage and fraud. Then, as suddenly as it began, the investigation ended. On September 6, 1946, it was announced that the "investigation of Ludwig Freude was terminated by presidential decree." This was Perón's warning to the four Germans that they were in his country and subject to his whims. Over the course of the next seven years they all died violently. Heinrich Dorge's body was found in a Buenos Aires street in 1949; Ricardo von Leute was murdered in the city in December 1950; then Ricardo Staudt died in a hit-and-run accident; finally Ludwig Freude was found slumped over his breakfast table in 1952. He had drunk poisoned coffee.

This then was the country where Josef Mengele arrived in September 1949; a hotbed of Nazi intrigue ruled by a dictator who had lined his pockets with death-camp booty. It was not a country that was going to inquire too deeply into the background of any German bearing a Red Cross passport and claiming to be a war refugee. Nor was its immigration service likely to take an interest in the address in Buenos Aires that the new immigrant gave upon disembarkation. Had they done so, they would have found a spacious colonial-style house at Calle Arenales 2460 in the posh suburb of Florida, the house of a man named Gerard Malbranc, who had been listed by the Investigating Commission on Anti-Argentine Activities as a suspected Nazi sympathizer. Mengele moved in there after spending several grim weeks in the seedy one-room lodging he shared with the engineer in Vicente Lopez.*

At the Malbrancs', Mengele was known as a model tenant, giving no hint of the tantrums and authoritarian behavior he was to inflict on other hosts in years to come. Visitors to the house included survivors of the German battleship *Graf Spee*, scuttled in the River Plate after being crippled by three British warships in the first months of the war. Before long Men-

---

* During his stay at the Malbranc home, Mengele bought a dog, which his wife, Irene, requested that he call "Harry Lyons" in honor of one of her American relatives. Mengele did not think that "Harry" sounded Aryan and therefore dubbed the dog "Heinrich Lyons."

gele joined a circle of prominent Argentineans and Nazis who
had held important jobs in the Third Reich. All in their different ways gave help to Mengele over the next decade and
encouraged him not to lose heart in his darker moments of
despair.

One of the first of these contacts was a former *Abwehr*
officer, Willem Sassen, whose entry to Argentina had been
smoothed by the remnants of the Nazi spy network that had
so efficiently operated there during the war. Sassen was born
in Holland, but he became a member of the SS. His counter-
intelligence work involved him with the *Abwehr's* dis-
information unit, *Skorpion.* Since arriving in South America
in 1948, Sassen's activities had included acting as a spokesman
for Adolf Eichmann. He later gave public-relations advice to
unsavory South American dictators such as Chile's Augusto
Pinochet and Paraguay's Alfredo Stroessner.

Interviewed by Britain's Granada Television in 1978, when
Mengele was still alive, the chain-smoking Sassen spoke up for
his friend, whom he said he first met in 1949. He described
Mengele as a "brilliant man from an intellectual point of view,
a good philosopher, historian, and a very good medical man."
Sassen went on:

> So if you take his case and see the horrible stories they
> are talking about, selecting eyes and I don't know what
> all, there are no means, we have no means at our dis-
> posal, to prove to the contrary. If you take the fact that
> this man, whom I really knew closely I can say, and who
> talked to me about the experiments he had done during
> the war, experiments for example with volunteers, crip-
> pled people and others from the armed forces of Ger-
> many, in order to know how a man reacts under circum-
> stances of duress, such as cold or heat or water—
> experiments which are today continued by the Ameri-
> cans [and] British commandoes as well—so those experi-
> ments were, of course, done on the bodies of those vol-
> unteers. Now there is another question: that it seems
> that those experiments were done with prisoners as
> well, but of course there is no proof of it.[9]

In 1952 Sassen introduced Mengele to Adolf Eichmann,
who was living in Buenos Aires under the alias "Ricardo Kle-

ment." Stripped of his SS colonel's uniform, Eichmann cut a
pathetic figure as he shuffled around Buenos Aires in shabby
civilian clothes. Unlike Mengele, Eichmann was being actively hunted, his role as the logistical organizer of the Final
Solution having been mentioned in the Nuremberg trials numerous times. The two men met from time to time at the ABC
city center café, but they never became close friends. Mengele did not like the downtrodden aura of fear surrounding
Eichmann, whom he regarded as a broken man. Moreover
Eichmann was virtually penniless, whereas Mengele was getting support from the family in Günzburg, as Sassen explained:

> I mean, they are two completely different kinds of peo-
> ple, Eichmann and Mengele. Moreover Mengele does
> dispose, could dispose of, his own means, which Eich-
> mann never had. He [Eichmann] was a tragic figure
> because in reality, that [the Final Solution] was not his
> business. He would have liked to have been a common
> soldier on the front. That was his dream.[10]

Soon after his arrival Mengele also met the man he later
called his "dear, dear friend," who "gave me heart when I
despaired." Of all Mengele's many mentors during this period
of his fugitive life, none was more valued than Frederico
Haase, a distinguished architect who lived in Buenos Aires.
Haase knew everyone who might be important to Mengele.
His wife was the daughter of the man who became Paraguay's
finance minister when President Stroessner seized power in
1954. She and her husband provided an invaluable link to the
influential Paraguayans who smoothed Mengele's path to citizenship there in 1959. Haase also introduced Mengele to another vital contact, Colonel Hans Ulrich Rudel, Hitler's most
decorated *Luftwaffe* ace whose extensive political and commercial network of friends would help Mengele in many important ways.[11]

During the war Rudel sank a cruiser and a battleship, and
he was shot down and captured by the Russians. He escaped
and was shot down again, this time losing a leg. Altogether he
was credited with 2530 operations and 532 tank kills. His feats
were so extraordinary that Hitler created a special award just
for him: The Knight's Cross with Golden Oak Leaves, Swords

and Diamonds. Rudel's name was associated with the escapes
of many wanted Nazis from Europe, organized by a group
informally called *Kameradenwerk*. Far from the clandestine
role that some Nazi hunters have ascribed to men like Rudel,
he was in fact a shameless publicist and like Mengele had a
giant ego. Several glossy books featuring hundreds of photographs of his daring wartime exploits have been published,
and he was especially anxious to be photographed in a variety
of macho pursuits: high diving, hard tennis games, snow- and
water-skiing. Rudel's boundless energy despite the handicap
of an artificial leg was all part of keeping alive the Reich's lost
spirit of German heroism, courage, and discipline.

When Mengele first met Rudel, he was in self-imposed exile
in Argentina on the payroll of the Perón government as an
advisor to the National Institute of Aeronautics in Córdoba.[12]
Rudel was also collaborating with Sassen by giving advice at
the Argentine end of *Kameradenwerk* to newly arrived fugitives on such issues as where to obtain forged papers. Although Rudel was an unrepentant Nazi, attending neo-Nazi
rallies and visiting SS shrines right up to his death in 1982, his
close relationship with dictators Juan Perón and Alfredo
Stroessner, and later Augusto Pinochet, made him attractive
to several major German firms, including Siemens, as a roving
ambassador. It was on one of Rudel's frequent business trips to
Paraguay in the early 1950s that Mengele made the first of
many trips there to explore sales prospects for his father's firm
in Günzburg.

The date of this first visit to Paraguay was "around 1951,
according to three separate reports," recorded one CIA memorandum. "He worked for some time as a salesman [for a]
West German farm machinery firm. . . . During the time
that Mengele was in Paraguay he never tried to hide [his]
identity or use a false name even during trips to Argentina
and Brazil."[13] Cross-checked with Mengele's surviving
friends who remember this period, the report seems to be one
of the few accurate pieces of information that the CIA managed to find on him. To this day, however, Mengele's family
denies any suggestion of financial support from the Günzburg
firm. Dieter Mengele, Josef's nephew—who now jointly runs
the company with Mengele's stepson, Karl Heinz—was
quizzed by John Martin of ABC News as late as March 1985:

Martin: One of the most frequently cited rumors is that your grandfather [Karl Sr.] and the company must, for all these years, have been supporting Josef Mengele. It must be the source of his income. Is that true?

Dieter Mengele: That's absolutely not true. The company . . . my grandfather bought the company in 1911. And then after the Second World War he put his two sons, Alois and Karl, into the company. And when these three died, Karl Heinz and I took over the company. And there's no truth at all that Josef Mengele got money or has any shares of the company. That's absolutely not true.

Martin: Do you have any idea how he has supported himself all these years?

Dieter Mengele: I have no idea. . . . I have no idea. I know that in Argentina, he has a little factory where he makes bolts. But that's the only thing I know about how he survives.[14]

Dieter's recollection is at odds with the facts. One of the first people Mengele met on his early business trips to Paraguay was a fellow Fascist, Werner Jung. Jung was the chief of a German youth group that was effectively the local Nazi party during the war.* He had emigrated to Paraguay in 1936 as an executive of a German company, Ferretaria Alemania, which acted as agent for several German companies and sold light machinery and tools. Although it was Frederico Haase who introduced the Jungs to Mengele, Jung's wife, Margaret, recalled: "At the time that Dr. Mengele met my husband he was representing his Günzburg company and was an acquaintance of *Oberst* [Colonel] Rudel."

It was Rudel who persuaded Mengele that a lucrative market in farm machinery was waiting to be cornered in Paraguay, a country about the same size as California, especially in the well-watered luxuriant pastures of the southeast. Karl Sr. seems to have earmarked Josef to help the family firm's South American sales drive after successfully exporting a large con-

---

* Paraguay had the first Nazi party in Latin America, formed in 1932, and the last one to be dissolved, in mid-1946.

signment of farm machinery for wood cutting and milling in the early 1950s.[15] After Alois took over the business in 1954, when Karl Sr.'s health began to decline, Mengele products were sold through an Argentine company called Caffetti. Over the next few years Josef Mengele traveled to southeastern Paraguay and to farms deep in Chaco, the vast northwest region of the country, a flat wilderness of scrub thorn trees, dwarf shrubs, huge cacti, and scattered hardwoods.[16] Werner Jung said, "He really started to push the family business from 1954 on. I remember he was especially trying to sell a device to distribute farm manure, and carts to haul dirt and equipment."

It was during a trip to Paraguay in 1954 that Mengele met another key contact, Alejandro von Eckstein. He was then a captain in the Paraguayan Army, and together with Jung, he sponsored Mengele's bid for Paraguayan citizenship in 1959. Rudel was on a flying visit to Paraguay, having returned to Germany for an active role in neo-Nazi politics as a member of the *Deutsche Reichspartei*, when they had their first encounter, as von Eckstein described:

> Dr. Mengele was a friend of Rudel and Jung, and Rudel and Jung were friends of mine. And we just happened to be presented to one another. And it was from that time on that we would meet, on a sort of regular basis. He came here through Rudel. Rudel met him in Argentina and really was doing well in business here, so he told Mengele. That's why Mengele came here, to get in business.[17]

Alfredo Stroessner had just taken over Paraguay, ruling with the absolute power derived from Article 52 of the 1940 constitution.* Article 52 allowed him to declare a state of emergency and suspend habeas corpus. (This situation exists to the present day, Stroessner having declared himself President for Life.) Von Eckstein and the forty-four-year-old dictator were close friends, both being of German descent and having fought side by side in the 1930s in the Chaco war against the Bolivians. Both Stroessner and von Eckstein were decorated war heroes, as the president still likes to remind

---

* Now article 79 of the 1969 constitution.

visitors when he appears at ceremonial occasions resplendent in gold braid, half his chest covered in ribbons and medals.

According to von Eckstein, it was on one of Mengele's visits shortly after they met that Mengele was introduced to President Stroessner at a function with several others present. "The president didn't know who he was and all they did was shake hands," said von Eckstein. "But I remember Rudel telling Mengele that Paraguay under Stroessner was as fine a friend to expatriate Germans as Argentina under Perón."[18]

Jung and von Eckstein both found Mengele reluctant to talk about the war, even with his newfound Nazi friends. Jung said:

> We knew he was a doctor because he introduced himself as one. I didn't find it odd that he was a doctor who was involved in commercial business. We didn't talk about the war. Maybe if the Germans had won, there would have been a discussion as there always seems to be with the British and Americans, such as the inevitable question, "What did you do during the war?"
>
> But for Germans it is best left unsaid unless the other person brings it up. Mengele never brought it up. Everyone knew that those Germans who had come to South America had started a new life and there was nothing else that we needed to know. They were there because they didn't want to deal with the past.[19]

Mengele became a popular figure on his many visits to the Jungs. Their grand house on Calle General MacArthur in the Paraguayan capital of Asunción was a center for social activity. "We thought very highly of him," said Mrs. Jung. "Like *Oberst* Rudel he was a nondrinker for health reasons. He loved classical music, enjoyed reading good German poets, and praised our good and natural way of life. He was very good with the children and helped my second-eldest son to pass his biology exam."[20]

Back in Argentina by early 1953, Mengele had moved into a city center apartment on the second floor at 431 Tacuari Street, after leaving his lodging with the Malbrancs.* By this

---

* This several-month stay at Calle Tacuari was the only time Mengele resided within the city limits; all his other residences were in nearby predominantly German suburbs.

time, Mengele had invested some family funds in a small
carpentry business at the corner of Avenida Constituyente
and Avenida San Martín, in the Florida district of Buenos
Aires. Elsa Haverich, a secretary at the pharmaceutical company Fadro Farm, in which Mengele later became a principal
owner, recalls his carpentry workshop:

> Approximately in 1953 I met him as Doctor Gregor,
> that was in the Wander Laboratory [a pharmaceutical
> company in Buenos Aires]. He used to come every after-
> noon to visit Dr. Timmermann [a German medical
> friend who later became one of Mengele's two partners
> in the Fadro Farm business], and we talked, well, about
> nothing important, you know. And at that time he had a
> carpentry or a toy factory. I don't remember really if it
> was a furniture carpentry or a toy factory, but that is
> what he was doing at that moment. The factory had
> some winches and there some round things that could
> have been toys for children; they were made of wood
> and looked like little trains.[21]

Haverich remembers Dr. Gregor as "very kind, he was very
nice. He always used to come in very happy and he was always
making some jokes. He was calm, very calm."

Profits from Mengele's small workshop allowed him to buy a
Borgward car, "Isabella" model, in 1954. His application for a
license was granted after two friends, his former landlord,
Gerard Malbranc, and a recent acquaintance, José Stroher,
wrote that Mengele was a fine, upstanding member of the
community in response to a police question as to the "moral
condition of the applicant." Stroher wrote in similar glowing
terms a year later when Mengele needed a passport. Today
Stroher becomes excitable when asked about the basis for his
judgment on the Auschwitz doctor's morality. "It's all lies," he
shouts, "I don't know anything."[22]

Meanwhile, far away from Mengele's bachelor existence,
his estranged wife, Irene, was preparing to marry another
man, Alfons Hackenjos, who owned a shoe-store business in
Freiburg. She had met Hackenjos in 1948, shortly after he was
released by the Americans after being captured while serving
with Rommel in the Afrika Corps. At the time Mengele was
still hiding in Germany on the Fischer farm. Karl Sr. informed

his son, by letter, that Irene wanted a divorce, and Mengele did not stand in her way. He signed and notarized a power of attorney in Buenos Aires so that a local attorney in Günzburg could represent him and process the divorce by proxy. On March 25, 1954, their petition was approved by a court in Düsseldorf. Mengele was not especially heartbroken, nor was the Mengele family sorry to lose Irene. They had watched with disapproval as she had grown distant from Josef during the four years he was hiding on the farm in Mangolding. Irene's parting shot to the family was to tell them proudly that she did not want a penny from them.[23]

That winter, in 1954, Mengele moved again, this time to a medium-size Spanish-style house at 1875 Calle Sarmiento in the fashionable and predominantly German suburb of Olivos. There he rented half the house and was remembered by the owner's granddaughter as a model tenant. For a fugitive who had had such an impoverished start, life had by now become tolerably pleasant. Mengele had acquired a loyal clique of friends who shared his view of the world: embittered at losing the war, angered at Germany's capitulation to the Allies in agreeing to hold "war crimes" trials, fundamentally racist toward his indigenous South American hosts—"mentally low-level chattering," he once described their conversation. And there were regular visitors from home. His father once visited him, his old school friend Hans Sedlmeier, Alois's right-hand man, was often in town, and Alois himself made an occasional visit, once with his wife, Ruth. Mengele had also become an increasingly successful entrepreneur. His workshop now employed half a dozen employees, having expanded into machine parts for the textile business. While the workshop ran itself, Mengele made additional monies from commissions earned on sales of the Karl Mengele & Sons products from Günzburg.[24] As his fortunes increased he became a familiar figure at the leading German restaurants in the Argentine capital.

At about this time, Mengele struck up an extraordinary relationship with a German Jewish refugee, who has asked us not to mention his name, fearing the relationship would be misunderstood. The man is in his seventies now and ran a prosperous textile business in Buenos Aires. He arrived there before the war, escaping Hitler's persecution of the Jews. In the early 1950s he met a German girl who had been a wartime nurse. Like so many German youngsters, she had been a member of the Hitler Youth Movement. The businessman nonetheless was greatly attracted to the girl. She had settled in Buenos Aires with her parents, who happened to know Mengele.

On one of the businessman's visits to the girl's house, he found Mengele there, and the girl introduced them to each other. Mengele gave his name as "José Gregori." Neither the girl nor the businessman had any idea of his true identity. The two men soon found they were competing for the girl's charms, a contest that "Gregori" eventually won. However, the girl was not the only interest that "Gregori" shared with the Jewish businessman: "Gregori" wanted to go into partnership with him. They had several discussions about the possibility of a joint venture, but nothing came of it. During the course of this unlikely friendship, Mengele discovered that his prospective partner was Jewish, but he never once uttered an anti-Semitic remark. This is perhaps not as significant as it sounds. There is plenty of evidence from Auschwitz of Mengele's cynical exploitation of people whose skills he knew would further his career. And in the Jewish businessman he recognized someone with greater entrepreneurial skills than his own. "Gregori seemed to be quite a wealthy man," said the businessman, "and I remember wondering where he got his money. Later the girl told me that he had told her father he was getting help from his father."[25]

Karl Sr. had been helping in other ways as well. He wanted to see Josef married again. The girl he had in mind was Martha Mengele, widow of his youngest son, Karl, who had died when he was only thirty-seven years old, in December 1949. Martha was a handsome woman, "actually ravishingly beautiful," as Rolf described his aunt. She had fallen in love with Karl Jr. while still married to a businessman named William Ensmann. In 1944, a son was born, Karl Heinz, whose paternity was disputed in the local courts after Martha divorced Ensmann in 1948. After considering all the evidence in intimate detail, the regional court in Memmingen ruled that the boy was in fact Karl Jr.'s son.[26]

According to Rolf, Karl Sr. arranged a meeting between Martha and Josef in the Swiss Alps, having deliberately sabotaged an affair that she was having with another Günzburg man. Rolf, then age eleven, was to be brought along as well to meet his long-lost "Uncle Fritz," with whom he had walked through the Bavarian forests many years before. Behind Karl Sr.'s matchmaking lay a calculated plan to keep control of the Günzburg firm totally in the hands of the Mengele family. Karl feared that if Martha remarried someone outside the family, her voting rights, inherited from Karl Jr., could be influenced by that outsider. By marrying Josef, all key decisions would be made securely within the family. But there was another practical reason for the arranged marriage. Under German law, company assets in the amount of Josef's inheritance could be seized if an arrest warrant for Josef was issued. Karl Sr. therefore persuaded Josef to renounce his inheritance by secret legal agreement, thereby averting the possibility of the company being financially paralyzed. But it was just a cosmetic move. In practice, once Josef married Martha he would benefit from her share in the company, and although he had lost his voting power, she would be directly influenced by him.[27]

The travel plans for Mengele's reunion with Martha were laid months in advance. In April 1955, he applied to the Argentine federal police for a special passport for non-Argentine citizens. But first he had to satisfy the police that he had been a resident of "good conduct." Again his friend José Stroher obliged with a testimonial as to his integrity. On September 1, the police granted Mengele a "good conduct" pass, which allowed him to apply to the courts for the passport. Unfortunately for Mengele, his arrangements were interrupted by a successful coup against President Juan Perón.

Although there had been three previous attempts to oust Perón, he appeared to be solidly in power. But on September 16, 1955, Admiral Isaac Rojas led the entire Argentine Navy into rebellion. Rojas sailed the venerable U.S. cruiser *Phoenix*, later renamed the *General Belgrano*,* into Buenos Aires harbor and pointed its eight-inch guns in the direction of the presidential palace. Perón conceded: "Dammit, this fool Rojas is the sort of man who is likely to shoot." He sought refuge in

---

* The *Belgrano* was sunk by the British Royal Navy in the Falklands War in 1983, with the loss of more than 368 Argentine sailors.

the Paraguayan embassy and later boarded a Paraguayan gun-
boat which took him into exile. Walking up the gangplank,
Perón ingloriously slipped into the shallow water and almost
drowned before he was pulled out by Paraguayan sailors.

The coup brought the government to a standstill and frightened some Nazis who had relied on Perón for their continuing
safety. But they were soon assured that the new regime, composed of the military chiefs Rojas and Lonardi, intended to
maintain a business-as-usual attitude toward Nazis. When
Lonardi and Rojas were deposed in a second coup that November by another Prussian-style military reactionary, General Arambary, the Nazi community was even more pacified.

In the midst of all this governmental reshuffling, the Argentine Court of First Instance finally issued Mengele a 120-day
passport. In March 1956, Mengele flew to Switzerland with a
two-hour stopover in New York. There to meet him at the
Geneva airport was the ever-faithful Hans Sedlmeier, who
drove him to Engelberg, where he checked in to the Hotel
Engel, the best in town. At the hotel waiting to greet him
were Martha, her son, Karl Heinz, and Mengele's own son,
Rolf, then twelve years old.

Over the next ten days "Uncle Fritz," as he was introduced
to the two Mengele boys, regaled them with adventure stories
about South American gauchos and about his supposed experiences fighting partisans in the Second World War. Rolf was
impressed with his dashing uncle, who dressed formally for
dinner, had such exciting tales to tell, and gave him pocket
money, his first allowance ever. Rolf recalls:

Uncle Fritz was a very interesting man. He told us stories about the war and at that time no adults spoke about
the war. I liked him—as an uncle.[28]

Rolf also noticed how physically attentive "Uncle Fritz" was
to his Auntie Martha, although he thought at the time that it
was merely ordinary family affection. At the end of the holiday, Mengele traveled to Günzburg to tie up the legal arrangements that his father had prepared. Mengele visited his
family for nearly a week, his first open visit to Günzburg since
he had been on leave from Auschwitz in November 1944.
Following his stay there, he drove in a rental car to Munich to
visit his friends the pharmacist and his wife, who had assisted

Mengele after the war. Mengele had barely arrived in Munich when he was involved in a minor auto accident. Although he was not injured, the accident attracted the attention of the local police. They questioned him regarding his South American identification papers and told him not to leave Munich until he checked with them. Nervous about his real identity being discovered, Mengele telephoned his family in Günzburg and requested their assistance. Karl Sr. drove to Munich and settled the matter with the police. According to Rolf, "My grandfather paid the police some money to forget about the accident." Mengele left Europe the following day.[29]

Heartened by the prospect of more settled times with Martha, Mengele returned to Buenos Aires to unscramble the covert side of his fugitive life. In a moment of insecurity he had undergone one attempt at plastic surgery in Buenos Aires, haunted by a remark made by his first wife, Irene, predicting that his prominent forehead would give him away. Mengele himself stopped the surgery halfway through; he had had a local anesthetic and could see what was going on. "When he saw what the surgeon was doing, he realized he didn't know his subject," said Wolfram Bossert, who sheltered Mengele in Brazil during the last phase of his life. "He had scars at the top of his head that showed where the surgery was done. He permanently wore a hat because of what his wife had told him."[30]

But he need not have resorted to such drastic measures because by 1956 there was still no sign of a warrant being issued for his arrest. He felt confident enough to publicly relaunch himself as Josef Mengele. Besides, everyday life had become too complicated for a man living under a false name. Mengele had plans to take out a mortgage on a house so that he and Martha could enjoy a proper family life. He had his eye on a white stucco property at 970 Virrey Vertiz, a secluded cul-de-sac in the Olivos suburb that bordered on the back of what had been President Perón's palatial home. But the bank wanted proof of his identity. Also, his father had offered to set him up in partnership with a pharmaceutical company, for which, again, detailed evidence of his identity would be required.

Proving his real identity required a great deal of paperwork and the authority of the West German embassy, whom the

Argentine police required to certify that "Helmut Gregor"—
the name he was registered under—and Josef Mengele were
one and the same man. Mengele had to explain to the embassy, therefore, that he had lived under an alias for the past
seven years. He gave them his correct name, date of birth,
date of his divorce from Irene, and addresses in Buenos Aires
and Günzburg. On September 11, 1956, after checking with
Bonn, the embassy issued Mengele a certificate stating that his
real name was Josef Mengele and he was from Günzburg.[31]
"It doesn't seem to have occurred to anyone in the embassy to
say, 'Wait a minute, here we've got a man who clearly has a
past to hide, let's do some checking,' " said the Paris-based
Nazi-hunter Serge Klarsfeld. "No one in that embassy seems
to have checked with lists of war criminals. If they had, they
would have found Mengele's name on several of them."[32]

Armed with the embassy identity certificate and his birth
certificate, Mengele went before the national court in Buenos
Aires to swear that he and "Gregor" were the same person.
The court then issued a judicial certificate which he presented
to the Argentine federal police. They noted that all the information he had given on his arrival to Argentina in September
1949 was false, but any questions the police might have had
about this irregularity must have been perfunctory. In November they issued Mengele a new identity card, number
3.940.484. It listed his name as Josef Mengele, indicated that
he was divorced and a manufacturer by profession, and gave
his correct Buenos Aires address. Having got his new identity
card courtesy of the West German embassy, Mengele returned to ask them for a passport, a mere formality now that
the identity problem had been resolved. He even provided
his own picture, passport-size, in which he sported a moustache, and he filled in the following personal details himself:
"Height—1.74 meters; build—normal; form of face—oval;
color of eyes—greenish brown." The noninquisitive embassy
duly issued him a West German passport, number 3.415.574.

One explanation for the embassy's oversight might lie in the
fact that the West German ambassador at the time, Werner
Junkers, himself had been an active member of the Nazi party
and a senior aide to Hitler's foreign minister, Joachim von
Ribbentrop (who was hanged at Nuremberg in October 1946
for war crimes). From 1944 to 1945, Junkers was one of Rib-

bentrop's special envoys to Yugoslavia, where the Ustachi forces even outdid the SS in barbarity when dealing with Tito's partisans. Quizzed about the lapse at the embassy, Junkers said: "Ask the man who ran the consular section. I didn't know who Mengele was."[33]

The man in charge of the consular section in 1956 was Werner Schattman. As of July 1985, he was the newly appointed West German ambassador to Prague. Schattman insisted, "I didn't know anything about Mengele."[34]

In October 1956, Martha and her son moved to Argentina to join Mengele. For the next four years Mengele was effectively Karl Heinz's father, a tie which was to form the basis of a firmer relationship than he had with his own son, Rolf, whom he had seen only twice since he was a baby. Mengele was secure in his life with Martha. He took out a mortgage on his new house in Virrey Vertiz and registered the deed and the mortgage in the Günzburg company name, "Karl Mengele & Sons." Further evidence of just how secure he felt was shown by the fact that he allowed Martha to be listed in the telephone book under his name, Mengele.[35]

Meanwhile, using his brand-new passport, Mengele made a business trip to Santiago, Chile, in February 1957. According to Alejandro von Eckstein, Hans Rudel accompanied Mengele on the trip and they met Walter Rauff, the SS colonel who developed the mobile gas vans that killed 97,000 Jews, partisans, and Russians. (Rauff distinguished himself later in the war with the nickname "the Murderer of Milan," earned for his torture and execution of Italian partisans.) Rauff was living in Ecuador in 1957, but he was making one of his exploratory trips to Chile, which later became his permanent home until his death in May 1984. Rudel, Rauff, and Mengele spent a week in Chile reminiscing about times past. Like Mengele, Rauff was an uncompromising anti-Semite. Shortly before he died, he wrote to a friend renouncing his Catholic faith and saying, "Himmler was my God. The SS was my religion. Why can't people understand that all the big business in America is run by Jews."[36]

Soon after Mengele returned to Buenos Aires, he and Martha decided that the time had come to get married. In July 1958, they flew to Montevideo, Uruguay, for a civil ceremony followed by a three-week honeymoon. Again Mengele registered under his own name, giving his occupation as "businessman," the names of his parents, and his address in Germany. In mid-August, they returned to the house in Virrey Vertiz to resume a life that in all respects resembled that of a couple who felt they had nothing to hide.

Mengele's efforts to rehabilitate himself publicly took yet another crucial step. With his father's approval, he sold his workshop in Florida, and with the proceeds, bought a stake in a pharmaceutical company. Altogether, Mengele funded half of the 1 million Argentine pesos (approximately $200,000) venture capital needed to expand the fledgling company called Fadro Farm KGSA. Fadro Farm manufactured drugs and specialized medical products. "Dr. José Mengele" was registered as one of the founding directors along with two Argentineans, Heinz Truppel and Ernesto Timmermann. Truppel recalls:

> I saw Mengele for the first time in 1958, about the middle of July, because the Fadro Farm company had just been formed by two people, myself and Dr. Timmermann. This company started with the manufacture of products for the treatment of tuberculosis and we had our first factory, say office, at 1551 Acquenga Road in the federal capital [Buenos Aires].
>
> Dr. Timmermann presented Dr. Mengele, who also had another name which was Dr. Gregor. Effectively, Dr. Mengele contributed some capital to the company. Dr. Mengele was not in our company too much of the time. But his contribution of capital allowed us to expand our production department. . . .
>
> Dr. Mengele left the company within less than one year. When he worked here he used to do studies of new products for treatment of tuberculosis. He used to read many medical and scientific books. But I want everyone to know that he didn't carry out any experiments on human beings as some people may think.[37]

At first, Mengele introduced himself to his new business partners as "Dr. Gregor." Then he found that Elsa Haverich, the secretary who he had met three years before but had not seen since, was now working for Fadro Farm. She said:

He came into the office one afternoon. I called him "Dr. Gregor" at that moment because to me he was "Dr. Gregor." Then he corrected me and told me that, "No, it is Dr. Mengele." Joking a little bit, I asked him why he changed his name? He answered that it was for political reasons; when he got out of the war, he had to do it with another name.[38]

Mengele's life had now stabilized into the comfortable and secure routine of a family man in a nine-to-five job with good prospects. After thirteen years on the run, he felt the worst was over. The worst was still to come. Before long Mengele's luck began to change. Somehow he had attracted the attention of the Buenos Aires police on the suspicion that he might have been practicing as a doctor without a license. Exactly what triggered their interest is not known. A man who was a senior city detective at that time said Mengele was rounded up with several other doctors the police thought might have been involved in a back-street abortion clinic, where a young girl had died. The detective admitted to taking a $500 bribe for Mengele's release, which he split with another officer. Police files confirm that Mengele was held for questioning and freed after three days. At the same time, back in Germany a determined effort to bring Mengele to trial had just begun. As of August 1958, Josef Mengele's honeymoon had about a month to run.

C H A P T E R
6

———
———

Flight to Paraguay

———
———

There had always been an intention to pursue men like Josef
Mengele to the ends of the earth, as Prime Minister Winston
Churchill and President Franklin Roosevelt pledged as early
as October 1941:

> The atrocities committed in Poland, Yugoslavia, Nor-
> way, Holland, Belgium and in particular behind the
> German Front in Russia exceed anything that has been
> known since the darkest and most bestial ages in hu-
> manity. The punishment of these crimes should now be
> counted among the major goals of the war.[1]

But when the time came, this pledge did not extend much
beyond America and Great Britain's agreement with the Soviet Union in August 1945 to try twenty-two Nazi leaders
before an Allied military tribunal at Nuremberg, and a small
fraction of SS murderers at a limited number of other trials.
There was only one major Allied attempt to pursue the
Reich's murderous physicians in court. That took place in
December 1946, when twenty-three SS doctors and scientists

went before an American tribunal, also at Nuremberg, in the
so-called Doctors Trial. One man who felt that Dr. Josef Mengele should have been among the defendants was Hermann
Langbein, a left-wing political activist from Vienna who had
been arrested by the Gestapo and shipped to Auschwitz,
where he was put to work as a clerk in the chief physician's
office.

Although Langbein's opposition to Nazi tyranny was well
known, he survived Auschwitz and in the course of his imprisonment there became familiar with the gruesome activities of
the SS doctors, having seen some of the paperwork connected
with experiments. After the war he noticed that Mengele's
name cropped up at several trials of SS personnel.[2] He also
noticed, with dismay, how the determination of the Nuremberg trials lost some of its momentum after the Allies handed
over prosecutorial responsibility to the German authorities
and those in the countries where the atrocities had been committed. The record of the newly born Federal Republic of
Germany proved to be exceptionally poor. Although German
judicial authorities proudly point to 6215 convictions of Nazi
criminals, they disingenuously fail to note that more than 70
percent of those convictions were the result of indictments
brought under Allied jurisdiction. In all the cases brought by
German prosecutors, only 403 defendants were convicted of
premeditated murder. It became clear that the initiative for
bringing Mengele to trial was never going to come from
Bonn, and thus was the task left to the tireless industry of one
man.

Langbein began by compiling a dossier of evidence against
Mengele in the hope that the judicial authorities would take
an interest. On his own initiative—he cannot remember exactly how—he discovered that Mengele had been divorced
and that he had given power of attorney to a Buenos Aires
lawyer to handle the arrangements with a Frankfurt lawyer,
Fritz Steinacker, who later defended several prominent war
criminals. Langbein also tracked down many Auschwitz survivors and recorded their statements in order to build a case
against Mengele. In September 1958, only six weeks after
Josef and Martha Mengele had settled down as newlyweds,
Langbein took his file to the justice ministry in Bonn in an
attempt to persuade them to issue a warrant for Mengele's

arrest. But his visit to the capital was not very encouraging.
He encountered the first of many bureaucratic obstacles:

> I saw an official in the state prosecutor's office in Bonn.
> He told me that his office was not responsible for the
> question of Mengele. He said it was the responsibility of
> one of the eleven states of Germany—whichever one
> Mengele lived in. So he asked me, which state did Men-
> gele live in? I had to tell him that I didn't know. "In that
> case," said the official, "I can do nothing until you find
> out."[3]

Angered at the official's obstructive behavior, Langbein left
the file on the table, sternly telling him that he regarded
Mengele as the German government's responsibility. Coincidentally, in Buenos Aires that same September Mengele
signed over power of attorney to his new bride, signaling that
he intended to make himself scarce and needed someone to
make decisions that he could trust. There were two drafts of
this document, the first on September 13, 1958, the final one
signed and notarized in front of his Argentine lawyer, Dr.
Jorge H. Guerrico, on September 29. Three days later Mengele is reported to have entered Paraguay on a special ninety-
day visa.[4]

At first sight these two events suggest that Mengele had
somehow learned of Langbein's interest in his wartime activities, particularly since Langbein was simultaneously trying to
convince the state prosecutor's office in Kiel to include Mengele in an investigation concerning his Auschwitz colleague
Professor Carl Clauberg, who headed camp sterilization research. The likely explanation is far more prosaic, as are most
answers to the mystery of Mengele's amazing agility at evasion. The brush with the Argentine police regarding his alleged illegal practice of medicine certainly must have
alarmed Mengele, perhaps even made him consider whether
another haven might be more suitable. But the most compel-
ling reason for his departure for an extended stay in Paraguay
was probably nothing more dramatic than an attempt to sell a
new manure spreader that the Günzburg firm had just manufactured. It had broken all sales records in Europe. Mengele's
Nazi friend, Werner Jung, who lived in Asunción, recalled that
it was around this time that Hans Sedlmeier and Alois Men-

gele visited Paraguay, and that Mengele tried hard to sell the machine—without much success, however, according to Jung, who acted as agent for several major German companies:

> I never thought that he would make much money trying to sell that sort of machinery. I believe that Sedlmeier and Alois came at the same time and they were talking about expanding the business. Mengele himself constantly tried to interest me in becoming the official representing his company. He said I'd do it better than him and he would have given me a healthy percentage. But at that time I was already thinking about packing up and going back to Germany. I didn't want to take on new accounts.[5]

Jung's words are especially interesting in light of the statement made under oath by the Günzburg firm's purchasing director, Hans Sedlmeier, to the West German authorities in 1971 when they engaged in one of their periodic but half-hearted attempts to find Mengele. Sedlmeier told the investigating judge, Horst von Glasenapp:

> Our company has kept up business connections with South America. But since I have been with the company, for the last twenty-seven years, no business connections with Paraguay have existed. The accused in no way has been linked to the company affairs. Business deals are organized by our representative agents and for that reason there is no room to employ individuals on a private basis.[6]

According to the Jungs, when in Asunción Mengele stayed at a boardinghouse called the Astra, owned by a mutual friend, Peter Fast. Martha and Karl Heinz came to visit him there. "She was nice, everyone liked her," said Margaret Jung of Martha. She also remembered that Mengele had a preference for good German food, in sharp contrast to his later Brazilian tastes.[7]

Back in Germany, meanwhile, Hermann Langbein had made a breakthrough in his one-man effort to bring Mengele to trial. Although he had dumped his file of evidence with the obdurate bureaucrat in Bonn, Langbein had persevered in pinning down the state prosecutor's office within whose juris-

diction the Mengele case should properly fall, so that an arrest
warrant could be drawn up. From Mengele's war service record, Langbein discovered that his last recorded visit to Germany was in November 1944, in Freiburg, on leave from
Auschwitz, when he helped Irene move to Günzburg for the
remainder of the war. Langbein took the case to the Freiburg
prosecutor, Freiherr von Schowingen. "He was very helpful,"
said Langbein. "He couldn't have done more."[8]

Langbein also followed up on a tip that Mengele might have
studied medicine in Frankfurt. "By pure coincidence, the tip
proved to be right," said Langbein. "The university authorities would not let us see Mengele's file, but they did give his
date of birth, his date of graduation, and said that he was born
in Günzburg."[9]

On a visit to Günzburg, Langbein discovered the ubiquitous presence of "Karl Mengele & Sons." It was clear to him
that the Mengeles and Günzburg held many secrets about
their absent son but that he was not going to be privy to them.
All he could do was wait for von Schowingen to draw up the
arrest warrant and hand it over to the foreign ministry for
extradition proceedings. Although Langbein did not have
Mengele's exact address in Buenos Aires, he knew that he
lived there from the Buenos Aires notarization of Mengele's
divorce papers.

How much news, if any, of Langbein's efforts filtered
through to the Mengele family and was relayed to Josef is not
known. Langbein insisted that every move he made was conducted in the greatest secrecy. But the fact is that by March
1959, Mengele had decided that he would be safer living
permanently in Paraguay.

The strain of tearing up his Argentine roots just as he felt
they had taken hold soon showed itself to Mengele's friends.
On his return to Argentina from Paraguay early in 1959, the
staff at the Fadro Farm laboratory noticed he had become
edgy and that he often fell asleep in the afternoon. One of the
directors, Heinz Truppel, said:

> I suppose that he must have been thinking all the
> time that he would be found at any moment. That is
> why he used to sleep during the day and he looked very
> tired physically and mentally.

Yet a permanent move to Paraguay had its compensations. It meant Mengele could spend more time developing the family business there. He also had his sights set on buying land in the remoter areas of Paraguay, land that according to Jung, Mengele thought was a "valuable long-term investment." Perhaps, too, he feared that the climate toward men like him would change with the recent election in Argentina of President Arturo Frondizi. He was one of the most liberal leaders to come to power since the Second World War and was known to be sensitive to the first rumblings of international disquiet about Argentina becoming a Nazi sanctuary.

When Mengele returned to Buenos Aires from Paraguay to wind up his Argentine affairs, the $200,000 share that he and his father had invested in Fadro Farm was bought by an Argentinean named Ernesto Niebuhr.[10] Mengele's departure from the company was an abrupt affair and took everyone by surprise. "He just called me," said Heinz Truppel. "He told me he was leaving because of questions of different ideology. He said he was going to get out of the laboratory and out of the country." Elsa Haverich recalled the moment vividly. Mengele, she said, seemed to be a frightened man:

> I asked him "Why? What is going on?" I thought maybe it was his family, or an illness, or even an accident. Then he told me, very sadly, that no, it was because of political reasons. I didn't ask too many questions, because he looked a bit worried. The following day, the day he had to go, he arrived later at noon. He looked very quiet that day. He was very sad, very worried. It was about half past five. He took some books to return to the library—he was always reading science and medical books—and we got in the car. He gave me a lot of advice about the company and what we should do and I said, "I'll see you again?" Then he told me, "Elsa, we will never meet again."[11]

Although Martha and Karl Heinz stayed in Buenos Aires, they regularly visited Mengele in Paraguay, relieving the tedium of his life as a salesman traveling from farm to farm. As a sanctuary, however, Paraguay held many attractions. It had already become more popular among war criminals than Argentina, once described by Hitler's deputy, Martin Bormann, as *unser grosser Gönner,* "our great benefactor." Since the demise of Juan Perón in 1955, the Buenos Aires end of one of the more overt escape organizations had been raided by the Argentine police and a stash of false passports found.

Nazis had no such fear of robust police investigations in Paraguay. Far off the beaten track, impoverished and remote, Paraguay is still the most primitive country in South America. It is not the most captivating place for any fugitive to end his days. The World Health Organization lists tuberculosis, malaria, typhoid, dysentery, and hepatitis as endemic. Hookworm is the most common disease, and there is much venereal disease, goiter, and leprosy. It is a country where money buys everything. Its leading industry is smuggling. There is no proper tax system. American cigarettes, Japanese electronics, and whiskey of all nationalities provide substantial revenue, much of it finding its way into the pockets of Paraguayan government and military officials. Dozens of small seedy shops line the narrow streets, all selling contraband perfumes, cameras, transistor radios, and French nylons. Counterfeit Cartier and Rolex watches are sold on most street corners in the center of Asunción. Estimates of the illegal income produced by the contraband range up to $250 million a year. Middle-ranking officers claiming their fair share drive brandnew BMW and Mercedes automobiles and live on sprawling haciendas, even though their basic pay is only $500 a month.

For years senior military officers have been actively engaged in drug smuggling, according to an allegation by the U.S. state department in January 1985—an accusation that so stunned Paraguayan officials that for the first time in history the American ambassador was denied an audience with President Stroessner. Shortly after the state department's charge, Ambassador Arthur Davis's wife was killed in a mysterious Eastern Airlines crash on a flight from Asunción to La Paz, Bolivia. No evidence has been produced, but rumors abound that there was a link.

Presiding over this chaotic and corrupt state is the ironfisted rule of Alfredo Stroessner. Despite irrefutable evidence of systematic torture and imprisonment without trial, he brands all allegations of human rights violations as "Communist inspired." Those who share his philosophy have been welcomed with open arms—provided they keep their payments up. The deposed Nicaraguan dictator Anastasio Somoza reportedly did not, and was blown to pieces one day as he walked toward his car. Ellio Massagrande and Gaetano Orlando, the two Italian Fascists who blew up banks and trains in their native Italy for the fascistic organization *Ordine Nuovo*, have made a new life for themselves in Asunción. There has been a stream of others, all scoundrels, heading for the last refuge in the world. Sooner or later Josef Mengele was bound to join them.

By May 1959, Mengele was settled in Paraguay, still under his own name, ready to begin a new life. He moved to the southeast, in a region known as the *Alto Parana*, which borders Argentina. It may not have been Bavaria but it was the next best thing. Known locally as *Nueva Bavaria*, "New Bavaria," it is populated with settlers whose view of the world is still colored by the notions of one of the spokesmen of late nineteenth-century anti-Semitism, Dr. Bernard Förster, a schoolteacher from Berlin. In 1881 Förster organized a petition, which was signed by 267,000 Germans, urging the compulsory registration of all Jews and their exclusion from mainstream German life. Unfortunately for Dr. Förster, his views did not coincide with those of Bismarck's Second Reich, and he was so ostracized that he moved to Paraguay. There he established a colony of like-minded bigots. The result a century later is that 60,000 mainly fair-haired settlers live in squat Bavarian-style chalets set incongruously among dense palm trees. They have their own churches and cultural societies and schools, where portraits of the Führer and swastikas were prominently displayed during the war. Indeed, Nazi sentiment ran so deep in Paraguay that it did not declare war on Germany until February 1945, three months before the German surrender, and then only reluctantly as the foreign minister, Luis Maria Arganas, announced to a group of Paraguayan Germans:

> The Axis powers will know full well what Paraguay's real sentiments are and will take that into consideration when they finally triumph. But in the meantime it is imperative that Paraguay play along with the United States for urgent reasons of national self-interest.[12]

Mengele lodged at the home of one of the most diehard National Socialists in *Nueva Bavaria,* farmer Alban Krug, who was also head of the local farmers' cooperative. They were introduced by Hans Rudel. For the next fifteen months Krug's farmhouse in the hamlet of Hohenau, forty miles north of the border town of Encarnación, became Mengele's home. The grinding routine of sales rounds was broken by occasional visits from Martha and Karl Heinz and by weekends when Mengele either took a bus or drove a jeep to Asunción to relax by the pool at Werner Jung's palatial home.[13]

Everyday life in these new and austere surroundings was recorded in Mengele's diary which resumed at this point after the mysterious ten-year gap. In the diary, he referred affectionately to his host, farmer Krug, as "Major Domo." But he was not so charitable about the sophistication or intelligence of the Krug family:

> Sometimes these people get up in the middle of the night—at 5:00 a.m.—to celebrate that solemn ceremony . . . slurping their *mate* [herbal drink]. For their health and productivity it would naturally be a lot better if they would sleep one or two hours longer, rather than wasting their time with useless and mentally low-level chattering. It is interesting that these people, as early risers, consider themselves morally superior to late sleepers.[14]

Mengele traveled widely in search of business, to a Mennonite colony near Rosario north of Asunción, to Filadelfia in the heart of the Chaco, across to Pedro Juan Caballero on Paraguay's eastern border with Brazil, and to San Bernardino and Villarrica, southeast of the capital. "He was looking for business," said his friend Captain von Eckstein. "He would go where he could make a sale and stay two or three days at a time."[15] There were also sightseeing trips with von Eckstein to Indian settlements, although according to the Jungs, Mengele did not find President Stroessner's eccentric friend the most riveting of conversational partners. "Von Eckstein was a bit of a braggart," said Werner Jung. "He always liked to seem more important than he was. He used to claim that he had royal blood in him. A baron he's not."

A month after Mengele arrived in Paraguay, Hermann

Langbein's efforts in West Germany to call him to account
finally bore fruit. On June 5, 1959, a damning indictment of
his butchery was drawn up by Judge Robert Müller of Court
Number 22, Freiburg. The opening paragraph stated that
"Josef Mengele was to be taken into custody . . . on em-
phatic suspicion of murder and attempted murder." The arrest warrant set out seventeen counts of premeditated murder conducted by a man who had taken an oath to cure, not to
kill. The full range of Mengele's cruelty would not emerge for
more than twenty years. All the same, the results of the court's
preliminary investigation were gruesome enough:

> Killing numerous prisoners with phenol, benzene and/
> or air injections; killing numerous prisoners in the gas
> chambers; killing a fourteen-year-old girl by splitting
> her head with his dagger, the victim dying a slow, pain-
> ful death; injecting dye into the eyes of women and
> children, which killed them; killing several twins of
> Gypsy parents either with his own hands or by mixing
> lethal poison into their food, for the purpose of con-
> ducting specious medical studies on their bodies during
> autopsies; ordering a number of prisoners to be shot
> because they would not write to their families saying
> they were being well treated.[16]

The warrant was circulated to police stations and passed to
the Foreign Office in Bonn, in order to begin extradition proceedings from Argentina, where Langbein believed Mengele
was still living. Despite Langbein's request that the proceedings be conducted in the utmost secrecy, according to Rolf
Mengele, an informant in the Günzburg police tipped off the
Mengele family that the warrant had been issued. Yet by the
time the family was able to inform Mengele, by correspondence, of the gathering storm clouds back home, he had already made his initial application for Paraguayan citizenship.
He applied for this citizenship as "José Mengele." Had he
learned earlier of the developments in the Freiburg court, we
may assume that Mengele would have taken steps to change
his identity and adopt one of the variety of aliases he later
used when he fled to Brazil. As it was, Paraguayan citizenship
afforded him additional protection should the West Germans
seek his extradition. No formal extradition agreement existed

between the two countries, and President Stroessner, although he relied on the Germans for substantial investment, was less likely to make an exception if the request concerned one of his citizens. Next to his self-esteem, the president regarded Paraguayan citizenship as sacrosanct. Citizenship also helped facilitate land ownership, and Mengele had shown an interest. According to a CIA report, Mengele was "trying to acquire land [in] the zone of Alta Parana across from the Argentine province of Misiones."[17]

The lawyer chosen by von Eckstein to handle Mengele's citizenship application was Dr. Caesar Augusto Sanabria. According to Jung, Sanabria "was a prominent Asunción attorney with good government contacts," an important bonus since President Stroessner had a habit of taking a personal interest in new citizens of his country. Jung and von Eckstein both agreed to act as sponsors for Mengele. Dr. Sanabria clearly recalled them bringing him his new clients:

> I remember some German acquaintances in the capital brought in another German and said he wanted to become naturalized. I had never seen the man before but his friends vouched for him and told me he had been living near the capital for nearly six years. The man was quite distinguished, very well mannered, and appeared in every respect very correct. The request for completing naturalization papers was something I did as a lawyer so there was nothing unusual in the request. Also he was being sponsored by two prominent citizens [von Eckstein and Jung].[18]

Meanwhile, news that the West German foreign office had made preliminary inquiries about extraditing Mengele from Argentina had leaked to the press. By late 1959, the World Jewish Congress was appealing for Auschwitz survivors to come forward to supplement the evidence already gathered by Langbein and the Freiburg court.

It seems clear that by now Mengele was considering the possibility of life without Martha and Karl Heinz. As Dr. Sanabria said: "The man sought naturalization only for himself. He didn't have a wife or child with him and he didn't mention that he had either." As for Mengele's request, Dr. Sanabria may not have seen anything "unusual," but Jung and

von Eckstein should have known the application was illegal.
At that time, applicants for Paraguayan citizenship had to
prove they had lived at least five continuous years in the
country. Mengele had certainly made many visits but came
nowhere near to satisfying the residence requirement even
though von Eckstein and Jung swore in court that he did. Dr.
Sanabria, perhaps, also ought to have been alerted to the
deficiency, since Mengele gave his permanent address in Paraguay as that of Dr. Sanabria's office, thereby suggesting that
he did not actually have a home in the country. Airily dismissing any suggestion that he and Jung perjured themselves,
von Eckstein said: "He asked me for citizenship and he asked
Jung, and he asked me if we would be witnesses for him. I said
of course I would, and so I signed it and I became a witness
and he became a citizen."[19]

Jung claimed he did not know the law specified a five-year
permanent stay:

> That would be silly because how could anyone say
> with certainty that a man had lived continuously in Par-
> aguay for five years unless one had actually lived with
> him? But if the statement I signed is supposed to mean
> that I had known him for five years then it was true
> because I had. Mengele just asked me if I wanted to be a
> witness and I said yes. It was as simple as that. I thought
> it would be nice to have Mengele as a Paraguayan citi-
> zen.[20]

While Mengele's citizenship papers were being prepared,
he was involved in an incident which was used later by some
researchers and authors as an important piece of evidence to
show that Martin Bormann, Hitler's private secretary and
closest confidant in the latter half of the war, was alive and
associated with Mengele. A stream of Bormann sightings have
been reported since then, to the embarrassment of the newspaper whose suspects on closer examination have turned out
to be innocent South Americans with only a passing resemblance to Bormann. No proof has ever been provided to
counter the conclusion of West German prosecutors in 1973
that a skeleton unearthed half a mile from the site of Hitler's
bunker, between the Weidenhammer bridge and the Lehrter
Station in Berlin, was that of the former *Reichsleiter*. As of that

date, the West German courts ordered all outstanding warrants to be quashed and future sightings of Bormann to be ignored. But the incident featuring Mengele was first reported in 1966, by a Time-Life television production entitled, "The Search for Vengeance," and was later embroidered by Michael Bar-Zohar in his 1968 book, *The Avengers*. It was further embellished in 1973 by Ladislas Farago in *Aftermath: Bormann and the Fourth Reich*. All of this revived speculation that Bormann had after all eluded the Russian Army encircling Berlin in early May 1945.

The television documentary and both authors claimed that in the spring of 1959, an Asunción physician of Austrian nationality, Dr. Otto Biss, was escorted by a woman to the home of Werner Jung after Mengele had failed to diagnose the condition of a mystery guest who was seriously ill. Bar-Zohar reported Dr. Biss as saying:

> I examined the sick man and spoke to him in German, but the sick man wouldn't answer in that language or in any other of the European languages I know. He insisted on speaking in bad Spanish. So I found it rather difficult to get any help from him to establish the nature of his illness. The [other] doctor realized this, and he bent over the sick man and said, "You may speak German." And to my great surprise the men then spoke in fluent German.

Dr. Biss, who said his mystery patient "had a scar on his forehead," went on:

> A few days later a friend of mine came to see me in great excitement. He told me he had met the woman who had come to me and that the man I had seen professionally was Martin Bormann. I got hold of some photographs of Hitler's right-hand man at once. There was no possible doubt. The man I had seen was older than the man in the photos but it was the same man all right. He was certainly Martin Bormann.[21]

Ladislas Farago repeated Bar-Zohar's interview in his book, published six years later, as one of many incidents, some based on documents of dubious origin, cited to prove that Bormann was alive. The whole episode is worth dredging up only because it is one of many interesting examples of the sometimes wishful thinking engendered by Nazi-hunters, the kind that created such an elusive aura around Mengele. Interviewed ten years later, at the age of eighty-five, Dr. Biss was still convinced that his patient was Martin Bormann.[22] Had Jung been interviewed, a much more plausible interpretation would have emerged:

> I don't ever recall Mengele treating anyone in my house. But I myself was sick and I do remember being treated by Biss at my house for a stomach ailment. Mengele may have been there at the time, I don't remember.[23]

Unfortunately for Werner Jung, pictures of him taken around 1959 show a remarkable likeness to the wartime photographs of Bormann, and these pictures convinced Dr. Biss that he had just treated the world's most wanted war criminal.

The reality of fugitive life in Asunción at this time was much less Machiavellian. Bormann almost certainly was dead, and although Mengele was now wanted by the Germans, his application for citizenship, in his own name, was still proceeding smoothly. As a precaution, however, Hans Rudel asked the interior minister, Edgar Ynsfran, to expedite the case. Mengele knew he had succeeded when on October 24, 1959, he was issued an identity card as "José Mengele." Two weeks later the Asunción police gave him a certificate of "good conduct and residency."[24] His citizenship papers were vouched for by the obliging Dr. Sanabria; his application was brought before Judge Luis Martínez Miltos.* Court proceedings show that the police good conduct certificate was enough to satisfy Judge Miltos that there were no "outstanding legal or police records which could hinder his obtaining Paraguayan citizenship through naturalization." The judge was also satisfied that Mengele had "resided permanently in this country for more than five years" and that he had "shown repeatedly his intention to give up his former nationality as it is backed up by the statements of his witnesses Werner Jung and Alejandro von Eckstein." By law Mengele had to deposit the sum of 5,000 guaranis, in 1959 the equivalent of $41. All that was required

---

* Judge Miltos was later appointed Paraguayan envoy to the Vatican.

to complete the process was the rubber-stamp approval of the supreme court, where the papers were duly filed.

Almost at the time when the supreme court's approval was due, Mengele received word in Asunción that his father had died. Any thoughts Mengele might have entertained of going to Günzburg for the funeral were eliminated when he read the warning from his family. Local police informers had notified them that two undercover agents from the LKA (the German FBI) would attend the funeral in the hope of finding the fugitive doctor. Mengele instead arranged to have a wreath delivered to the grave, marked only with a wide sash inscribed "Greetings from Afar."*

Within days after Mengele learned of his father's death, the West German embassy in Asunción discovered that Josef Mengele was in fact living right under their noses in Paraguay. On November 13, four days before Mengele's father died, the West German consul, Winfried Engemann, asked the Paraguayan minister of the interior if he might make a brief inspection of Mengele's file. The request in turn alerted the head of police investigations in Asunción to make further inquiries of the Argentine federal police concerning "José Mengele's" background.[25] However, before the Paraguayans allowed Engemann to review the Mengele file, they removed any relevant information, and Engemann found the file useless.

At the same time that the West Germans were reviewing the file in Asunción, Interpol headquarters in Paris asked the naturalization section of the Paraguayan ministry of the interior to forward a copy of his file to their offices in Buenos Aires and Paris.[26] But Mengele had little to fear from this private organization, impressive though its membership list of more than one hundred countries seems to be. Interpol's contribution to the Mengele hunt was desultory. Files in the Brazilian

---

* A series of subsequent sensational newspaper reports said that Mengele did attend the funeral, using elaborate disguises including a nun's habit. Petra Kelly, the current Green Party member of the West German parliament, grew up in Günzburg. She said: "Everyone in town talks about how Mengele attended his father's funeral. It's a rather reactionary town. I was told by a nun that Mengele had in fact stayed in my old convent school, the English institute." One reported sighting came from Adolf Rogner, who had lived in Auschwitz and had been an engineer there for four years. "I know for a fact Mengele was here," he said.

Although the myth around Mengele's "visit" grew over the years, the overwhelming evidence, including his own diaries, is that he did not attend the funeral because of the timely police tip to his family.

and Paraguayan branches of Interpol contain mostly second-hand information. This continued to be the pattern in Interpol's approach.

Hunting war criminals has never been one of Interpol's priorities. It claims its broad charter prohibits this on the grounds that Nazi crimes were of a "political nature" as opposed to crimes of "common law." Its hierarchy also has an unhealthy history of close connections with National Socialism. In 1939 Reinhard Heydrich, chief of the Gestapo, was voted president of Interpol. In December 1941, Interpol moved its headquarters to the fashionable Berlin suburb of Wannsee, where it shared a villa with the Gestapo. Heydrich even made Interpol a division within the SD, the Security Police. When Heydrich was assassinated in June 1942, Himmler chose Heydrich's successor at the Gestapo, Ernst Kaltenbrunner, to replace him as Interpol's president. After Kaltenbrunner was hanged at Nuremberg in October 1946, a Belgian member of Interpol's executive committee, Florent E. Louwage, became president. He was succeeded in 1956 by Jean Nepote, who had collaborated with the wartime Vichy government in France. In 1968 Interpol elected Paul Dickopf president. He was found to have been an SS officer during the war, having worked in the very villa where Interpol was then headquartered. Nonetheless, he remained president until 1972.[27]

By mid-November 1959, both the Paraguayan interior ministry's naturalization section and the Paraguayan police knew that an extradition request was under way for Josef Mengele for war crimes. Alejandro von Eckstein, President Stroessner's friend, also admits to having known about this interest on the part of the West Germans and Interpol. But no one thought the circumstances warranted postponing Mengele's application for citizenship. Nor is there any evidence that these august Paraguayan governmental bodies brought this new information to the attention of the supreme court. If they did, the court ignored them. On November 27, "José Mengele" was issued his naturalization certificate, number 809.[28]

On the other side of the world, meanwhile, another government had been taking an interest in the case of Josef Mengele. Unlike the West Germans, the Israelis had little faith in the slow, ponderous, bureaucratic machinations of extradition requests to South America. Their skepticism was fully justified. On October 27, the Argentine foreign ministry told the West German embassy in Buenos Aires informally that they must expect their extradition request to be refused on the grounds that the allegations against Mengele were of a "political nature." For some time Israel's view had been that as long as Bonn stuck to the strict boundaries of international law, they were unlikely to succeed in bringing Nazi fugitives to trial in West Germany. The Israelis preferred to act within the broader concepts of international justice, as Mengele himself soon discovered.

C H A P T E R
7

Operation Mengele

The decision to deploy the limited resources of the Mossad to track down Nazi criminals marked a major departure from its role as Israel's foreign intelligence-gathering and special missions service. Until the late 1950s, events leading to the Suez crisis and, increasingly, the influence of the Soviet Union had been the Mossad's chief concern under its resourceful chief, Isser Harel. One of the more spectacular intelligence feats of Harel's fledgling service was his Moscow resident's success in "scooping" the Americans and the British by procuring the full text of Premier Nikita Khrushchev's explosive denunciation of Stalin in February 1956. In Harel's hands lay one of the West's most powerful propaganda weapons: Khrushchev, in a three-hour speech, had laid bare the totalitarian savagery of his predecessor at a secret session of the Soviet Communist Party Congress.

The stature of the diminutive Harel, just over five feet tall, was elevated overnight as he brought his prize to Washington to negotiate a deal. Publicly, the Central Intelligence Agency took the credit as news agencies broadcast the leaked text

around the world. Membership in the Western Communist
Parties was decimated almost overnight. Privately, Harel secured a new intelligence-sharing agreement with the Americans. With it, the Mossad's now legendary aura of intrigue was
born.

Late in 1957, Harel received a telephone call that was soon
to give the Mossad's reputation a public face. Walter Eytan,
director general of the ministry of foreign affairs, was on the
line from Jerusalem requesting an urgent meeting. It was not
a matter that could be discussed on the telephone. That evening the two men met at a café in Ramat Gan, where an
emotional Eytan told Harel that the foreign office had received word from West Germany that Adolf Eichmann was
alive and that his address in Argentina was known. Later, in
his own account of "Operation Eichmann," Harel wrote that
it may have been "instinct" that told him that this time the
information was accurate. For most of the 1950s, tips on Eichmann had proved to be wrong; the Israelis did not even have
certain proof that Eichmann was alive.

Back in Tel Aviv, Harel spent most of the night reading
Eichmann's file. It revealed how the SS bureaucrat had so
zealously administered the destruction of the European Jews.
By morning Harel had resolved that "come hell or high water" Eichmann would be caught:

> No agency in the entire world, no government, no
> police, were looking for him to answer for his crimes.
> People were tired of atrocity stories; their one desire
> was to dismiss those unspeakable happenings from their
> minds; they maintained that in any event there was no
> punishment on earth to fit the perpetrations of outrages
> of such magnitude, and that they were reconciled to the
> violation of law and perversion of justice.[1]

Harel had no difficulty persuading Prime Minister David
Ben-Gurion that capturing Eichmann was a proper function
for the Mossad. A deep and trusting relationship had devel-
oped between the two men in the first precarious months of
the new State of Israel, when it was under threat from the
Arabs outside and from Menachem Begin's right-wing Irgun
Zevai Leumi within. Then in charge of the Department of
Internal Affairs, the Israeli equivalent of the FBI, Harel had

neutralized the factions bent on civil war, both Begin's group and the remnants of the underground Stern terrorist gang that was opposed to the terms of the UN ceasefire in the first Arab-Israeli war following independence.* He accomplished this by flushing out the Irgun and Stern leaders and their arms dumps. Characteristically of Harel, the operation was carried out with zeal and determination, but not as revenge. The rebels were told, some personally by Harel himself, that the new State of Israel could not and would not tolerate private armies.

Pre-State Israel, then, and its early traumas were in Harel's bones. He was not a survivor of the Holocaust, but he was very much a State pioneer, a paternalistic keeper of its conscience. And so it followed that to Harel and the men under his command, capturing Eichmann was "a national and humane mission." Israel, he said, was the only country in the world "determined to leave no legal stone unturned" and by the rules of "law, logic and historical justice was the state most competent to pass judgment."[2]

But locating Eichmann precisely, proving his identity, kidnapping him, and spiriting him out of a country thousands of miles away posed enormous logistical problems for the Mossad. And although Harel had succeeded in persuading Ben-Gurion to allocate a generous budget for the Mossad, Operation Eichmann promised to devour a substantial part of it, as Harel himself explained in his autobiographical account of the affair.†

> In fact when Nahum Amir,‡ our "travel agent" in Europe, had told me that by his calculations it would cost a fortune to send a special plane to take Eichmann to Israel, I had said, "to make the investment worthwhile we'll try to bring Mengele with us as well."[3]

---

* Under Menachem Begin the Irgun plotted to keep a large arms consignment designated to be shared with the Israeli regular army. At the last minute Begin changed his mind about sharing the weapons because he regarded the truce terms being negotiated by Ben-Gurion's government as too favorable to the Arabs. Eventually Begin's soldiers pledged loyalty to the State but became a forceful political opposition, becoming the modern-day Likud.

The even more extreme Stern gang held out against any peace terms and assassinated a UN mediator on September 4, 1948, after he proposed that Arabs occupy the Negev desert. The assassination provoked Harel's big roundup.

† *The House on Garibaldi Street*, London: Andre Deutsch, 1975.

‡ As with all names of Mossad agents given by Harel on Operation Eichmann, "Nahum Amir" is a pseudonym.

Capturing Mengele was not quite the budgetary after-
thought that this quotation from Harel's account implies. As
he said later: "I thought it important for Israel to have a
Holocaust trial and I very much wanted Mengele there as
well. A trial would have allowed the world to explore a truly
evil mind."[4] Although the Mossad's intelligence on Mengele
was not as accurate as it was on Eichmann, it was clear from
the few scraps they had that the Auschwitz doctor was leading
a wholly different lifestyle than that of his murderous counter-
part. Mengele lived under his own name (Eichmann used a
pseudonym); Mengele's wife, Martha, was in the telephone
book (although at an old address); the Israelis even had some
details of Mengele's business activities. One complication,
however, threatened to torpedo both operations. Late in 1959
newspaper stories on Eichmann and Mengele began to appear. Ben-Gurion was asked in the Israeli parliament what
steps were being taken to bring Eichmann to trial. Fearing
that publicity might alert both men, who knew each other,
Harel encouraged false press speculation that Eichmann had
been seen in Kuwait.

One of the few men outside Israel who knew the truth was
Dr. Fritz Bauer, public prosecutor for the state of Hesse in
West Germany. In September 1957 he had sent word to the
Israelis that Eichmann had been traced.* The message to
Jerusalem was dispatched in the strictest secrecy. Only he and
the prime minister for Hesse, August Zinn, were privy to the
information. Harel agreed with Bauer that the Bonn government was most unlikely to deal with Eichmann. "Bauer told
me that no one else knew," said Harel. "He said that he didn't
trust the [German] foreign office and he didn't trust his embassy in Buenos Aires. He said we were the only people who
could be relied upon to do anything with the information."[5]

Aside from the fact that the West German ambassador in
Buenos Aires was Werner Junkers, a wartime foreign office
Nazi functionary, Bauer had one other reason for deeply mis-
trusting his own countrymen: he had been jailed twice by the
Nazis, both before and during the war, because he was a Jew.
Twice he managed to escape, the second time to Sweden, and

---

* Nazi-hunters Simon Wiesenthal and Tuvia Friedman have variously claimed credit for
pinpointing Eichmann, much to Harel's irritation.

on his return vowed he would do all he could to bring men like Mengele and Eichmann to trial.

The source of Bauer's information on Eichmann was a series of letters from a German Jew named Lothar Hermann, who lived in the remote Argentine town of Coronel Suárez. Harel sent agents out to meet Hermann, and at first he did not impress them as a credible witness. For one thing, he was blind, a condition that did not seem to lend itself to tracking Nazis. But after thorough questioning, the Israelis learned that Hermann's attractive eighteen-year-old daughter, by an extraordinary coincidence, was being pursued by a young German from Buenos Aires who called himself Nicholas Eichmann.*

As their relationship developed, the young Eichmann boasted to the girl that his father had held an important position during the war and regretted that the Nazis had not managed to wipe out all the Jews. Hermann correctly concluded that his daughter was dating the son of Adolf Eichmann, whose name had often been mentioned in the Argentine press. The Israelis employed Hermann to help them in the investigation, and within several months Hermann reported that he had found where Eichmann lived: 4261 Chacabuco Street, in the Olivos suburb of Buenos Aires. Hermann was convinced that the registered Austrian owner, Francisco Schmidt, was in fact Eichmann. In his first report to Tel Aviv, Hermann "presumed with certainty" that Schmidt and Eichmann were one and the same man. The Israelis took over the investigation, scoured Schmidt's background, and put him under surveillance. It took one Israeli agent little time to determine that Schmidt could not be Eichmann. Based on this discovery and Hermann's sometimes dubious claims for expenses, Harel began to lose faith in him. Harel was nothing if not consistent: correct to an almost puritanical degree in his private life, he expected the same high standards from his men, even if they were employed on a freelance basis. In any case, the hunt for Adolf Eichmann temporarily lost its momentum as Harel explained:

* His real name was Klaus, but he liked to call himself Nicholas. Eichmann's two other sons, Horst and Dieter, also used their correct last name. Only Adolf Eichmann used an alias, "Ricardo Klement."

These findings damaged Hermann's trustworthiness
irretrievably . . . in August 1958, instructions were
given to allow our contact with Hermann to lapse gradually.[6]

Yet Harel and his agent in the field had made a serious error
of judgment. Hermann had in fact been right all along in
pinpointing Eichmann's address; his mistake had been in as-
suming that the Austrian owner, Schmidt, was Eichmann.
From Harel's own account of Operation Eichmann, it appears
that not even the Israelis bothered at this stage to check on
the identities of all the occupants of the house. Had they done
so, they would have found that there were at least two tenants
under the same roof. Hermann had reported to Tel Aviv as
early as May 1958 that 4261 Chacabuco Street was split into
two units with two electricity meters registered in two names:
"Dagoto," and "Klement" or "Klements." Harel implicitly
blamed Hermann for the oversight because, he said, he had
"never even mentioned the possibility that it was one of the
tenants of the house—either Dagoto or Klement—who could
be Eichmann." In fact, a more thorough investigation by the
Israelis might have put Adolf Eichmann in their hands by late
1958. Then residing openly in Buenos Aires under his own
name, moreover, Josef Mengele might well have been part of
the roundup. As it was, the Israelis' failure to keep faith with
Hermann and exhaust all possibilities caused a delay of eighteen months; by which time Mengele was spending most of
his time in Paraguay.

According to one senior intelligence officer, the Eichmann
case was closed. "Harel basically didn't believe the information that Eichmann was using the name Klement," he said.
The case was reopened by the determined lobbying of Dr.
Fritz Bauer, who flew to Jerusalem in December 1959. Bauer
angrily complained to Israel's attorney general, Chaim Cohen, that Jerusalem had not acted on the information he confided to them late in 1957. Bauer said he had just received
independent confirmation, from an SS informant, that Eichmann was living under the name Ricardo Klement and that
he had fled Europe in 1950 using that alias.[7]

The attorney general asked Harel to reopen the Eichmann
case. Harel responded by "borrowing" Zvi Aharoni, then

chief interrogator of Shin Bet, the Israeli FBI. Harel dispatched him to Buenos Aires to check out the Chacabuco Street address for the third time. By a series of ingenious methods, including tailing one of Eichmann's sons on his motorbike and talking to neighbors without raising the slightest suspicion, Aharoni, with assistance from local Mossad agents, discovered that Eichmann had indeed lived at 4261 Chacabuco Street and had recently moved to a drab single-story stucco house in Garibaldi Street. At some risk, Aharoni's team snapped several photographs of Eichmann, with a hidden briefcase camera, while talking to him. There was another bonus too. Aharoni discovered that his quarry was a man with a regular job, and settled in his habits. His orderly routine, Aharoni reported back to Tel Aviv, boded well for a successful kidnapping.

Mengele, by contrast, was not a creature of habit. Unknown to the Israelis, sometime late in March or early April 1960, Mengele returned from Paraguay to Buenos Aires for one of his periodic reunions with his wife and stepson. Unnerved by news of the German arrest warrant for him, Martha and Karl Heinz had moved into a boardinghouse in the Vicente Lopez district of the city.

Coincidentally, shortly after Mengele's return to Buenos Aires, Harel decided to give the final go-ahead to Operation Eichmann, and Mengele was also chosen as a target for the Mossad. In April 1960, shortly before Harel's departure for Buenos Aires to take personal charge of the operation—an unprecedented move for an intelligence chief—he dug out Mengele's file and wrote down all the crucial information in a code known only to him. It was a wise precaution for Israel's intelligence chief to take in the event of discovery by the Argentine authorities. Although Harel had resolved to give himself up in such a crisis, he would have had his hands full trying to justify one infringement of Argentine sovereignty, let alone two.

Harel's plan was to go after Mengele once Eichmann was caught and held in one of the Israelis' seven safe houses in Buenos Aires, while they waited for the departure of a special El Al Britannia aircraft that would fly their prisoner home. The kidnapping was set for May 11. Harel had won the agreement of the national airline to divert one of its planes in order to bring a delegation of Israeli dignitaries, led by UN representative Abba Eban, to attend Argentina's celebration of 150 years' independence. But the aircraft could not arrive before May 19 because the Argentineans could not receive the Israeli delegation before 2 p.m. that day. Harel wanted to get Eichmann out of the country as soon as possible—within thirty-six hours at the outside. Yet that would be too soon for the Israeli delegation's planned departure. It was decided therefore that the delegation would have to return by scheduled airliner. But there was one complication. Eban had said he wished to travel back on the El Al plane. Since the Eichmann mission was so secret that none of the delegates, including Eban, knew the real reason for the plane's journey to Buenos Aires, Harel decided that Eban and his colleagues would have to remain in the dark. Eban was therefore told that the reason he and the other diplomats would have to return on another airline was that the airport fees for keeping the El Al plane in Buenos Aires for several days were too high. Since the El Al plane would depart from Buenos Aires on May 20, Harel would have just nine precious days in which to capture Mengele.

On May 11, 1960, Adolf Eichmann finished work at 7:10 p.m. at the Mercedes Benz plant, where he was an assembly-line foreman, and boarded the bus home to Garibaldi Street. He left the bus at his usual stop, paying no attention to a nearby car with its hood up. Two men were bent over the engine, apparently encountering mechanical problems. Nor was he unduly concerned by the presence of another car with three men inside, parked thirty yards from the bus stop. As Eichmann walked past the disabled car, the rear doors swung open and four men pounced on him and bundled him inside. The abduction took less than a minute. Eichmann did not offer much resistance. He spoke only six words before being bound and gagged. "I am resigned to my fate," he replied to Aharoni, who was driving the car and who had warned him not to resist. Eichmann's eyes were covered with a pair of opaque goggles, and he was shoved onto the car floor. An hour later the Israelis arrived at a safe house code-named "Tira" in the Florencio Varela district of Buenos Aires. With Eichmann safely in Israeli hands, Harel turned his attention to Mengele:

During that unenterprising—though by no means inactive—period preceding the arrival of the plane, with all the preparations for transporting Eichmann at an advanced stage, I decided to do something about Mengele. . . . Everything we knew about this man was written in my notebook, in a personal code which only I could decipher (and even I had some difficulty).[8]

The task of interrogating Eichmann was given to Aharoni. He spoke fluent German and had spent the last two years of the war interrogating captured German soldiers at the British Eighth Army headquarters in Egypt, Italy, and Austria. In 1949 he had joined Shin Bet and became its chief interrogator.

According to Harel, Mengele was the only subject Eichmann refused to talk about during his interrogation:

I asked Kenet [Harel's code name for Aharoni] to question Eichmann about Mengele. I told him not to ask if he knew Mengele or where he was hiding, but to tell him that we knew the man was in Buenos Aires and he must give us the exact address.

Eichmann's response wasn't very encouraging. He didn't disclaim acquaintance with Mengele, but he said he didn't know where he was and had never heard whether he was in Argentina or anywhere else in South America. Eichmann simply refused to say more, and to justify his refusal he told Kenet he didn't want to betray his friends. I regarded his reply as confirmation of two things: that Mengele was not far away and that he and Eichmann had been in contact.

When Kenet continued to press him, Eichmann brought up another argument in support of his refusal: he was afraid, he said, of what might happen to his wife and children. . . . I told Kenet to promise Eichmann that we would undertake his family's support if he would give us Mengele's address. But all our urgings and promises were of no avail.

My impression was that he went into a panic when we demanded Mengele's location, and I felt that his obduracy stemmed not from any sense of loyalty but from sheer fright.[9]

Eventually, Eichmann mentioned during the interrogation that Mengele might be found at a boardinghouse that had served as a refuge for several Nazis. It was run by a German woman named Jurmann. In fact Harel had known of this house, but he was excited to hear Eichmann corroborate it. "I was rather astonished that this information was well established," he said.[10] It was an isolated villa located on a narrow lane, surrounded by a white picket fence. To the consternation of Aharoni and several other senior members of the Eichmann task force, Harel decided to mount a surveillance on the house. Aharoni explained:

> I don't think I'd even heard of who Mengele was at that stage. His name hadn't surfaced in the newspapers and I must admit I was concerned only with getting Eichmann back to Israel. Harel had said nothing about this to us before. When he did, some of us felt that it was too ambitious and that it would risk the success of the Eichmann operation. As soon as Eichmann admitted his name, I personally wanted to get back home. I was very relieved the operation had succeeded so far and I didn't want anything to happen that might endanger the next stage of getting him out of Argentina. I thought we could always try Mengele another time.[11]

But Harel would not be dissuaded from making one attempt to capture Mengele. His problem was a shortage of agents. "Of the members of the task force only Menashe might be able to give me part of his time," he wrote, ". . . and when Shalom Dani heard about the new assignment he demanded that I allow him to take part in it. But these two were not enough—I had to have more, especially people who spoke Spanish."[12]

Harel requested the help of a third agent, Meir Lavi, who had acted as liaison man on the night of Eichmann's abduction. Lavi and his wife had emigrated to Argentina, and Harel considered having them rent a room at Mrs. Jurmann's boardinghouse. But he abandoned the plan after meeting Lavi because Lavi did not speak Spanish well enough to convince anybody that he was Argentinean. However, Lavi introduced Harel to another Israeli couple, Ada and Binyamin Efrat, who

lived in Buenos Aires and who had the qualifications. Harel
was impressed:

> The following morning, Binyamin Efrat was sitting
> opposite me in my "on duty" café. One look was enough
> to tell me that he was the man I wanted. He spoke
> Spanish fluently and looked exactly like an average Ar-
> gentinean. He had heard about Mengele but didn't
> know much about him. I told him we had information
> that this sadist was in Buenos Aires and we were trying
> to locate him. He said he was prepared—without any
> reservations—to undertake any assignment that he had
> to with Mengele.[13]

That evening the Efrats discovered from residents in neighboring villas that the tenants of the boardinghouse were
North Americans. The next morning Dani was assigned to
watch the house to see if any of the tenants looked German or
American. "To lend an air of plausibility," said Harel, he ordered Dani to go with a woman, so he chose Ada Efrat. They
saw no one who resembled Mengele. The next day Lavi and
Ada's husband, Binyamin, took over the surveillance. Lavi
had a briefcase camera, and Harel told him to photograph
everyone arriving at and leaving the house. But all they saw
were children. And although Lavi used the camera, the pictures did not come out clearly. It was therefore impossible to
know if Mengele's stepson, Karl Heinz, was among them. The
following morning Binyamin asked the mailman for the address of his "uncle," a "Dr. Menelle." He told the mailman he
knew "Dr. Menelle" lived in the area, but he did not have his
exact address. The mailman told Binyamin that a man by that
name had lived at the Jurmann boardinghouse, "until a few
weeks ago . . . maybe a month." But the mailman did not
have a forwarding address, nor did the nearby post office. The
letters that had come for Mengele had been addressed to him
in his real name, but the chief postal clerk told Efrat that he
did not have his new address and that all of his letters were
being marked "return to sender."[14]

Not wanting to admit defeat, Harel decided to pursue one
further lead. Word had reached the Israelis about Mengele's
small garage-workshop, where he had employed a handful of
people to make machine parts for the textile business as well

as furniture and children's toys. They knew that Mengele had at one time called himself "Gregor." "There was always the hope that Mengele had not severed his connections with the garage when he moved out of his house a month ago," said Harel. He briefed Binyamin to check out the garage with the cover story that he represented a big garage and needed a large quantity of left-hand screws, having failed to find any ready-made ones in the shops. At the garage, Binyamin told the secretary that "Mr. Gregor's" lathes had been recommended to him, and he asked to see him. Harel described the encounter:

> The secretary asked him to sit down and left the room. Binyamin heard her talking to somebody outside, though he couldn't catch the drift of their conversation. She came back, scrutinized him without saying a word, and went out again. Several minutes later, she appeared and told him that they had nobody there by the name of Gregor and they didn't do lathe work.[15]

Harel took the secretary's behavior to mean that she clearly did know a "Mr. Gregor," otherwise she would have told him immediately she did not know the name. Harel therefore reasoned that Mengele still had some connection with the workshop. Little did he know that Mengele had severed all links with it two years earlier, though the staff had doubtless been briefed not to answer any questions from strangers about "Dr. Gregor." In any event, Harel's ignorance was academic. He gave up trying to find Mengele through the workshop because, as he admitted, the only agents he could spare from Operation Eichmann lacked experience in undercover activities:

> . . . If we had a team of professionals like the task force at present occupied with Eichmann—who could invest the necessary time, patience and skill. But I had at my disposal—and for a few days only—a handful of people lacking experience in undercover activities. I had no choice but to give up trying to find Mengele that way.[16]

Instead, Harel drew up a final plan to capture Mengele before May 20, the deadline when the El Al Britannia aircraft had to leave Buenos Aires with Eichmann on board. He urgently cabled Tel Aviv and instructed them to send on the El Al Britannia a team of his own men trained as commandos. His plan was to storm the boardinghouse only hours before the Britannia was due to return to Israel with Eichmann on board:

> I was considering a commando operation on the house with the object of checking the identity of all the tenants of the house, and if Mengele was there, just to take him with force. What I had in mind was to bring Mengele to the plane just before takeoff, once Eichmann was safely on board, and to put him on at the last moment.[17]

Harel dispatched two men to make a final check on the boardinghouse in Vicente Lopez. Binyamin Efrat would pose as a repairman for the water heater, while Meir Lavi would pretend he was delivering a parcel. The "repairman" did manage to gain access and found, as the neighbors had said, that Americans were living at the house—and that there was no sign of Mengele. The "deliveryman" could not find a plausible pretext for going to the house. Instead, he merely telephoned the American manager and questioned her about previous tenants. Harel was furious at this breach of security. Failure to stick to instructions could have warned Mengele, had he been in the house. Efrat's and Lavi's results were, Harel said, a bitter disappointment:

> Though I knew the prospects of finding Mengele at his old address were pretty poor, I nevertheless hoped that luck might have been on our side. It was hard to reconcile myself to the fact that we missed the opportunity of capturing the murderous doctor by as little as a couple of weeks.[18]

Harel remains convinced to this day that Mengele had been at the boardinghouse only a matter of weeks before. In fact Mengele had spent most of his time since May 1959 in Paraguay, though he did make occasional visits to Buenos Aires in order to see Martha and Karl Heinz. It may well have been in the aftermath of one of these visits that Harel's agents picked up clues of his recent presence.

Either way, the Mossad team's main task had yet to be completed. At 9:30 p.m., the Israelis successfully transported a drugged Adolf Eichmann past the security guards at Ezeiza International Airport and placed him on board the chartered El Al plane.

A crude attempt has since been made to smear the prestige of this classic and daring operation with a set of documents prepared by SIDE, the intelligence organization which reports directly to the president of the Argentine Republic, then Arturo Frondizi. While the documents themselves appear to be genuine, what they report must be in doubt.* SIDE claims that each stage of the Eichmann kidnapping from beginning to end was followed by the Argentine intelligence services, who knew that Mossad agents were operating in Buenos Aires soon after they arrived. They even claim that one intelligence officer witnessed the entire abduction.

The SIDE reports are based partially on a report by the Alien Control office of Coordinacion Federal, the Argentine CIA, which claims to have "detected the presence of Israeli commandos in the Republic of Argentina as early as December 1959." It says Commander Jorge Messina, chief of the Argentine intelligence service, under direct instructions from President Frondizi ordered all Argentine security services to refrain from interfering with Israeli actions and merely to monitor their conduct. The report claims the greatest contribution to the success of the Eichmann abduction came at Ezeiza Airport when the Israelis attempted to pass the drugged Eichmann off as an ill member of the plane's crew. Inspector Hector Rodriguez Morgado of the Alien Police is said to have replaced the regular immigration personnel with his own agents and instructed them to let the Israelis pass without incident.

These extraordinary claims should be judged in the light of what must otherwise have been the acute embarrassment of the Argentine intelligence services when at 4 p.m. on May 23, Prime Minister David Ben-Gurion made one of the most im-

---

* Some of the documents were published in Ladislas Farago's book *Aftermath*, along with papers he claimed were written by SIDE relating to Bormann and Mengele. On publication of the book, the Argentine government said the Bormann and Mengele papers were fakes but made no reference to those claiming the Mossad team had been detected.

portant announcements in the short history of Israel's parliament, the Knesset:

> I have to announce . . . that a short time ago, one of the greatest Nazi war criminals was found by the Israeli security services: Adolf Eichmann, who was responsible, together with the Nazi leaders, for what they called the "Final Solution of the Jewish Problem"—that is, the extermination of six million Jews of Europe. Adolf Eichmann is already under arrest in Israel and he will shortly be brought to trial in Israel under the Nazis and Nazi Collaborators Law of 1950.[19]

If in fact President Frondizi did go to the extraordinary lengths of personally ordering his intelligence services to stand by while Argentine sovereignty was violated—even to assist at the airport—because he did not wish the Israelis to be hindered in their task, he certainly allowed an elaborate smoke screen to be laid at the United Nations. On June 5, Argentina requested and received an urgent meeting of the Security Council which unanimously voted to condemn Israel for "the violation of the sovereign rights of the Argentine Republic" resulting from the "illicit and clandestine transfer" of Eichmann to Israel. Even countries friendly to Israel were vehement in their criticism. The idea that any Argentine president had greater responsibility to the State of Israel than to the sovereignty of his own country is surely fanciful. The most plausible explanation is that the Argentine intelligence services were so badly caught out that they covered their dereliction by faking their reports after the kidnapping.

The kidnapping provoked a torrent of diplomatic rhetoric about the sanctity of sovereignty and the like. A breach of sovereignty it certainly had been. Yet the bedlam afflicting Argentina's bureaucracy when West Germany requested Mengele's extradition just a few weeks later showed that Israel's mistrust was justified all along. Fueled by Argentina's spasm of righteous indignation, the Eichmann kidnapping unleashed a wave of anti-Semitism that spread like a brushfire across South America. In the face of the UN furor, there was little Israel could do. Meanwhile, Jewish cemeteries were desecrated, Hebrew schools were set on fire, several Jewish restaurants were machine-gunned, and synagogues were bombed. In Colombia, Nazis held a memorial service for those war criminals executed at Nuremberg. Fascist youth groups held rallies in almost every South American capital. The home of the Israeli ambassador to Montevideo was bombed. A young Jewish woman, Graciella Sirota, believed to be the daughter of the owner of the safe house where Eichmann had been held by the Israelis, was kidnapped, sexually abused, and tortured, a swastika burned into her breast. Another young Jewish girl, Merta Penjerek, suspected of having brought food to the safe house during Eichmann's detention, was kidnapped and murdered. The noted Jewish scholar Maximo Handel was attacked by a group of Nazi thugs who beat him unconscious and cut swastikas into his body.[20] Despite these outbursts of anti-Semitism, Harel pressed on with his attempt to track down Josef Mengele. "Mengele," he said, "burned like a fire in my bones."

Back in Tel Aviv, Harel set up a special unit to track down major Nazi criminals, with Mengele heading the list. The headquarters for this operation was the Mossad's European station in Paris. The man in charge was Eichmann's formidable interrogator, Zvi Aharoni, who had run him to the ground in Buenos Aires before the kidnap team moved in. Harel had secured Aharoni's permanent transfer from Shin Bet to the Mossad.

From the spring of 1961 to the end of 1962, several agents from the Eichmann team were sent to Europe and South America. In Europe their assignment was to try to penetrate Mengele's family circle and shadow his mentor, the Luftwaffe ace Hans Rudel. In South America, the task was to infiltrate Mengele's Nazi friends. Harel claimed that the attempt to capture Mengele cost more money and manpower than Operation Eichmann. But Harel himself was to pay a heavy price. While he enjoyed the loyalty and respect of the majority of his team, there were those outside the Mossad who believed that its strained resources should have been more profitably used elsewhere. Although Harel did not know it then, his decision to concentrate on finding Nazis at the expense of other pressing tasks marked the beginning of the end of a distinguished career—and the end of the hunt for Mengele.

C H A P T E R
8

———
———

One Step Ahead

———
———

Memories of the homely embrace of Günzburg and the splendor of the rolling Bavarian pasture were now just nostalgic stabs of pain to Josef Mengele. South America was to be a life sentence after the Eichmann kidnapping, that much was clear. A period of gnawing anxiety followed while Mengele and other fugitives waited for news of Eichmann's ultimate fate after word spread that he was missing, presumed kidnapped and in Israeli hands. "One of father's friends, also an SS member, organized a network of checks at the harbors and airports," said Eichmann's eldest son, Nicholas. "There was no harbor, railway station, airport, or important intersection that did not have one of our men stationed there [in the hope of intercepting Eichmann when his abductors tried to move him out of the country]. This was how the 'small fry' came forward to help, while the 'big fish' simply ran away."[1]

Lying low in Alban Krug's farmhouse in southern Paraguay, one "big fish" was shaking like a jellyfish. The former Iron Cross hero was stricken with panic as his worst fears were confirmed by Ben-Gurion's announcement to the Israeli par-

liament. A few days later Mengele wrote that the "situation
[had] become unmanageable." His decision to make a permanent move to Paraguay a year earlier had clearly dismayed his
wife, Martha, who argued that he would still be safe in Buenos
Aires. But Mengele had no intention of returning there:

> It seems to me that things are coming to a head and
> might bring a drastic solution. Finally everyone will
> acknowledge how right an earlier conduct was, and that
> at the time, their advice was nonsense. That is now
> incontestable. But no one should blame the others. I
> alone knew and must know what I should and should
> not do. I hope my nearest will now respond cleverly and
> reasonably in order not to again endanger the new start.
> What is nevertheless depressing is how the entire situa-
> tion has become unmanageable. Despite this, I am
> somehow in a good frame of mind and optimistic.[2]

To Mengele the situation had become "unmanageable" because, contrary to popular mythology, he did not have a network of armed guards and the protection of President Stroessner. Indeed, the Paraguayan interior minister, Edgar Ynsfran,
was the only senior member of the government who had any
idea about Mengele's wartime background. It had been explained by Hans Rudel, confidentially, when he asked that
Mengele's citizenship application be expedited because of
"problems back home." The stark truth was that the only
protection Mengele could rely on was that of Alban Krug.
Krug may have been a muscular man, but his armory con-
sisted of precisely one pistol. What Krug lacked in firepower,
however, he made up for in loyalty to his fugitive guest. His
brother, Ewald, explained:

> How is it possible for one single man [Mengele] to
> have killed so many people? He actually saved several
> lives in Auschwitz. . . . Mengele did other things than
> what they say. He was there to select those who would
> live and those who would die. Don't you think in reality
> he did this to save lives? Why do you think Rudolph
> Hess is still in prison? He is a very old man. Look what
> the Jews did to Eichmann—it was terrible. These peo-
> ple only want to shame the Germans.

It's all the fault of the United States, which allows itself to be controlled by the Jews. The true war criminals, for having destroyed Germany, are in the United States. Germany was the last hope of the world to contain communism. But don't you believe that Germany is destroyed. The United States did not win the war and there are people ready to help us here in South America.[3]

While Mengele was living in fear for his life in Paraguay, in Buenos Aires the bureaucratic hunt involving West Germany's extradition request was progressing at a slow pace. Since Martha was still resident in Buenos Aires, the West Germans believed that Mengele would return there. But the arrest warrant took so long to process that by the time it had legal status in Argentina, Mengele was already hiding at Alban Krug's farmhouse in Paraguay.

The extradition process had begun with all due urgency and secrecy. On June 7, 1959, two days after the arrest warrant was issued, the foreign office in Bonn cabled the West German embassy in Buenos Aires to make inquiries about the prospects for extradition. But then the delays began. His Excellency, the Ambassador, the ex-Nazi Werner Junkers, was in charge. (He had been von Ribbentrop's special wartime plenipotentiary to the southeast region of Yugoslavia.) Junkers now claims not to remember anything connected with the Mengele case while his embassy was handling the extradition, although the case attracted enormous publicity in the European and South American newspapers at the time. It is worth recording in full a June 1985 German television interview with the former ambassador:

Interviewer: Were you confronted with the Mengele case in your time as ambassador?

Junkers: I can't remember.

Interviewer: In 1959, during your time, the first international arrest warrant was issued. Do you know about that?

Junkers: No, I don't know anything about that.

Interviewer: In 1959 or 1960, an extradition warrant went to the Argentine authorities. Do you know anything about that?

Junkers: No, I also don't know anything about that.

Interviewer: While you were ambassador, did you ever hear the name "Josef Mengele" mentioned?

Junkers: Not that I can remember.[4]

Junkers's amnesia aside, the first of many stages in a complex extradition request took an extraordinary length of time. For reasons never satisfactorily explained, the Argentine consul general in Munich, Alberto A. Maddonni, did not receive the warrant until March 11, 1960, a full nine months after it was issued. Another two months passed before Maddonni authenticated and signed the warrant on behalf of the West German court and sent it to his government in Buenos Aires.[5] Once in Buenos Aires, the document had to go through the West German embassy to the Argentine ministry of foreign and religious affairs, who then gave it to the president of the senate, José Maria Guido. Guido sent it to the procurator general, who in turn assigned it to Judge Raul Centeno of Federal Court Number One. Finally, on June 30, 1960, one year and twenty-three days after extradition proceedings were begun, the case was assigned to Judge Jorge Luque of District Court Number Three. Only then could the police begin their search for Mengele. But the question of extradition, if Mengele were caught, would be decided by the court.[6]

News of the West German extradition request broke in the last week of June, while Argentine president Arturo Frondizi was on a state visit to Bonn. Frondizi told a press conference that his country had "no intention of sheltering criminals from the justice they deserve." But, he said, the West Germans would have to provide proof of Mengele's crimes before he was sent back for trial. Smarting from the Eichmann kidnapping just two months before, the president said, "Some form of reparations would be sought from the Israeli government."[7] By contrast, a letter to the *Herald Tribune* in Paris that day expressed a view shared by many people around the world:

Rather than considering the question of "punish-
ment" of the Israeli "volunteers" for their abduction of
Eichmann, would it not be better to send them back
once more to gather up Mengele for us as well. . . .
Surely something has gone quite wrong, and we have
become somewhat distracted from the vital needs of
justice, when we begin bickering and feeling that "sovereign rights have been dangerously imperiled"?[8]

In Paraguay, meanwhile, Mengele's friends greeted with
disbelief the news that he was wanted for atrocities in Auschwitz. Captain Alejandro von Eckstein said:

When it did start to come out, he told us he was forced
to do some of those experiments and he really did not
carry out the experiments that so much has been written about. He made the remark that he had to do what
he was ordered to do because if he didn't carry out the
orders they would throw him in the same area as where
the others were. He also said he helped many people
who were very sick in the camp, but that none of his
good work was reported.[9]

Mengele's other citizenship sponsor, Werner Jung, said he
was "shocked, really shocked. I didn't get a chance to ask him
about it because I had already gone back to Germany when it
came out." But Jung's wife, Margaret, is still convinced that
the allegations were lies. She even claimed that Mengele's
Auschwitz pathologist, Miklos Nyiszli, who provided the most
detailed statement about his experiments, "is a pseudonym
and never existed."[10]

Werner Schubius, one of Jung's business colleagues, who
still lives in Asunción, also believed the allegations were invented:

When we met him we said, "He can't possibly have
done these things." I'm convinced of that. If he did
something it was only because he was acting under orders. I can imagine Mengele only as a human being and
as a human being he has my sympathy. He was modest
and well educated, much more educated than we are.[11]

But on the west coast of America, one former friend of Mengele's was stunned. Opening his morning newspaper, the Jewish textile executive from Buenos Aires saw a picture of the man with whom he had nearly gone into partnership several years before. "I simply did not believe it," he said. "I immediately telephoned the girl who had introduced us and I said to her, 'To think he'd been our friend.' She said they had just got the newspapers too and all they had done was look at the picture in disbelief."[12]

For Mengele, holed up on Alban Krug's farmhouse in southern Paraguay, matters went from bad to worse. Late in July, Mengele's great friend, Frederico Haase, the Argentinean architect who had introduced him to so many of his key Paraguayan contacts, fell off a ladder at a construction site in Asunción and died. It is clear from Mengele's gloomy diary entry for July 31 that the combined effects of the Eichmann kidnapping, the Argentine warrant for his arrest, and Haase's death had caused him to consider suicide:

> Like the rain that has covered the earth, sorrow has come over me. A good old unselfish friend has left me forever. The loss of him is irreplaceable for me anyway. For the moment I can only force myself to believe that I will never be able to see that friend again, who was always optimistic and prepared for a joke in any kind of situation. He still lives in me.
>
> The proof of his goodwill and helpfulness and comradeship are too much alive for me to imagine that only a couple of days ago we said good-bye forever. But thus it seems to be. The radio report has brought certainty. But his spirit and his love have left so much inextinguishable impact that this friend will always be present with us. It was he who told me to hold out and gave me new strength when I was doubting the future sense of life. "You must not give up now and lose your nerve! That's exactly what the others want with their hunt," he told me, and we said good-bye late in the night. Your words, my dear friend, will be your last legacy and my deepest duty.[13]

Mengele remained in this maudlin state for several days after Haase's death, and he was too frightened to attend the funeral. On August 5 he wrote:

Again and again my thoughts are with the tragic fate of my good friend. He must be resting under the earth by now. If only I could help take care of his wife. Is the son back from D [Deutschland] yet? He does lose something irreplaceable in his father. The death of his father has caused a break in the course of his development, both mental and professional.

Mengele soon had another source of anguish. By August, detailed stories about his crimes were appearing in the German press. A batch of magazine and newspaper reports were delivered to him by a friend he called "Don C," who landed at a private airstrip near the Krugs' farm. "All of a sudden I heard the sound of an engine . . . it was the arrival of 'Don C,' " Mengele wrote on August 15. "He had taken the chance to come by. We spent a nice Sunday afternoon and talked about the painful event and many personal questions."

That night Mengele read through the press reports, "which fascinated me until deep into the night." He went to bed deeply disturbed. Jews, he was sure, were behind the "lies" blackening his name:

It is unbelievable what is allowed to be slanderously written in German magazines. The magazines are the illustrated proof of the lack of character and lack of proper attitude of the current German government, that tolerates such self-defilement. The political lie triumphs and time and history have been warped and bowed. It drips of "humanitarianism and Christianity," and in this "God" is the most often quoted. Behind all this stands only one thing: that is all the Old Testament hate toward everything in the German consciousness, heroic and truly superior.

At about this time, a typist in the West German embassy in Asunción came face to face with Mengele while visiting the German colony of Colonia Independencia, where she dislocated her ankle. On her return to Asunción she told the embassy staff that a German doctor named Mengele had reset it.

She did not know that he was a wanted Nazi and asked why the embassy had no record of a German doctor by that name living in the area. The chargé d'affaires, Peter Bensch, went to southern Paraguay to investigate:

> I made some inquiries and it was clear to me that Mengele had been there under his own name. He was not practicing as a doctor full time but on an occasional basis, I thought, because he depended on the goodwill of the local people. There was no secret about his name. But I personally never found him. I met Alban Krug. He did not admit that he had helped Mengele although it was clear that he had helped several Nazis coming over the border from Argentina.[14]

The incident raises important questions about the degree of coordination and determination of the West German hunt. Despite Bensch's breakthrough in Paraguay, his colleagues in the Buenos Aires embassy a thousand miles away were pressing sedately on with their extradition request to the Argentineans. There appears to have been no attempt by the foreign office in Bonn to resolve these conflicting clues as to Mengele's exact location by putting their own agents on the ground. The West Germans were hunting Mengele with pieces of paper, from embassies, relying on hunches, but never in the field. What made Bonn's behavior even more questionable was their knowledge that the extradition request, despite President Frondizi's optimistic words, was unlikely to succeed.

First, there was no extradition treaty with Argentina. As a result, the case had to be submitted to the Argentine solicitor general for a recommendation in accordance with Article 652 of the Argentine criminal code. If a recommendation was forthcoming, the foreign office had to decide if the extradition was "in the best interests of Argentina," whatever that might have meant. If the foreign office decided it was in the best interest, the case would be left to the mercy of an Argentine court. But as Bonn had been informally warned, the Argentine attorney general was likely to object since the case was a "political matter, in which cases he generally refuses extradition."[15]

Nevertheless, the West Germans placed a 20,000 mark reward on Mengele's head in an attempt to excite some interest among Argentineans. It was the first time that Germany had offered cash for information leading to the capture of a Nazi sought for war crimes. The reward was widely publicized by the South American press in the hope of flushing out a reliable informant. None was forthcoming.

The search was left to the redoubtable Judge Jorge Luque, to whom the case had been entrusted by the Argentine foreign office. Although he set about his task with vigor, he did not know that Mengele had long since permanently fled Argentina. Luque was proud to take the case. He felt some old patriotic scores needed to be settled after the Eichmann affair:

> It was a high-profile case and it presented me with an opportunity to accomplish something for Argentina. I desperately wanted to catch Mengele to show the world, particularly the Israelis, that Argentina was a law-abiding member of the international legal community. I wanted to show the Israelis that the use of illegal methods to obtain Eichmann had been unnecessary.[16]

It was a noble but somewhat naive aspiration in view of the cumbersome legal process that the Argentineans were insisting upon—legalities especially inexplicable since Mengele was not an Argentine citizen and had violated their immigration laws by making false declarations when he arrived in 1949. Nor was Luque helped by the fact that the first set of extradition papers were drafted in German when the law required them to be in Spanish. But what really exposed the West Germans' feeble approach was the out-of-date information that the embassy had supplied on Mengele's various haunts. Some of the addresses were just street names without a listing for the suburb. Since the province of Buenos Aires is roughly the size of Italy, the task of pinpointing the streets was almost impossible. For example, one address the Germans gave was 1875 Calle Sarmiento. It meant the police had to check on five different locations many miles apart before they could be sure they had covered every possibility. The failure of the Germans to provide precise addresses created additional delays in a case which had already been delayed far too long.

Some of the German addresses were just plain wrong. The first address they suggested should be checked was 968 Calle Vertiz. It simply did not exist. After a futile two-day search the police zeroed in on Calle Virrey Vertiz, the small cul-de-sac adjoining the backyard of Juan Perón's former palace on Campo Grande Street in the Olivos suburb of Buenos Aires. Mengele's house turned out to be number 970. Although residents reported knowing him, they all said they had not seen him for several months. The police reported back to Luque that there was no trace. But Luque was suspicious:

> I was sure the police had obtained further informa-
> tion about Mengele's whereabouts but were holding
> back on me. I have never been able to prove this, but it
> could have been a bribe by Mengele's family.[17]

Another detachment of police traced Mengele to a boardinghouse at 1074 Calle 5 de Julio in Vicente Lopez. Unknown to them, it was the same premises that the Israelis had checked in May. Unlike the Mossad agents, the police found Bergilda Jurmann, the German proprietor who Eichmann had told his interrogators was sheltering Mengele. But there was no sign of the American couple the Israelis had found running the boardinghouse. Perhaps Frau Jurmann had coincidentally rented out the house while the Israelis were investigating it. Questioned by the police, she admitted she knew Mengele's wife, Martha, and stepson, Karl Heinz, whom she called "Carlos Enrique." But she claimed she had never met Mengele himself.[18]

The police, meanwhile, were becoming frustrated by running from one faulty address to another. Luis Acerbo, heading the hunt in Police District Number Three, asked Luque if he could be removed from the case. "While we have been motivated with diligence to find and detain Josef Mengele," he wrote, "none of the leads have proven positive, in part because the information provided on the locations of the houses in Olivos and Vicente Lopez has been incorrect."

Having drawn a blank in the province of Buenos Aires, Judge Luque asked the Argentine police to deploy their resources for a countrywide search. At first Luque was not successful. His request was turned down by the chief of the fed-

eral police, Admiral Ezequiel Niceto Vega.* "He told me that
he was not going to waste the time of the force looking for a
foreigner who hadn't committed any crimes in Argentina,"
said Luque. Two weeks later, Vega relented. On July 19 the
following message was telegraphed to all police stations.

> All stations are to seek the capture of José or Josef
> Mengele, Identity Card number 3,940,848, son of Karl
> and Walburger [sic] Hupfauer, born March 16, 1911, in
> Günzburg, province of Bavaria, West Germany; he is
> married to his second wife, Marta [sic] Maria Will; he has
> been frequently at 1074 Calle 5 de Julio in San Isidro,
> province of Buenos Aires, and has lived at Virrey Vertiz
> 790 [sic] in Vicente Lopez, province of Buenos Aires.
> Case number 575 from the Federal Republic of Ger-
> many has requested the extradition of Josef Mengele,
> assigned to offices 674 and 704 of the Federal Judge of
> San Martín, Province of Buenos Aires, Doctor Jorge
> Luque.[19]

The chaos surrounding the Argentine hunt was not of much
comfort to Mengele. News of the haphazard searches was
brought to him by Martha and Karl Heinz, who still managed
an occasional visit to his Paraguayan hideout on Krug's farm.
But it was not the Argentineans or the West Germans that
Mengele feared—it was the Israelis, as his diary shows. "I am
being taken care of in the best way by 'Major Dommo' and his
son," he wrote of Alban and Oscar Krug on August 24, 1960.
What he did not know then was that the Israelis had a task
force of agents, some permanently resident in South America,
now operational. It included surveillance of Martha's journeys
from Buenos Aires, as well as Alban Krug and his family. The
Mossad's strategy was long-term. They had no illusions about
the difficulty of finding and capturing the elusive Mengele.

By September 1960, Mengele decided that capture by the
Israelis was inevitable as long as he stayed at the Krug farm.
He resolved to get out of Paraguay and begin a new life
elsewhere. The choice was Brazil. "The strong change in my

---

* Vega was more interested in lining his pockets with bribes than in chasing Nazis. On
September 8, 1960, he and five other high-ranking federal police officers were arrested on a
variety of corruption and internal collusion charges. As he was taken to jail he shouted, "It is
better to have slightly corrupt policemen than no policemen at all!"

surroundings will definitely be mirrored in my writings," he wrote. For six weeks there were no diary entries. "So much happened in this time," Mengele later explained, "for a certain reason that I cannot explain, I cannot write about it."[20] By late October, Mengele had left Krug's farm and crossed the border into Brazil. There to bid him farewell were Alban Krug and Hans Rudel. Clasping his hands, Krug warned him: "For you the war is not over yet—be careful." By October 24, Mengele was at his new location. He noted that he had just met a "guest friend" who is knowledgeable about "astronomy and astrophysics. . . . I have always wanted to meet someone who knows more about these things than the usual compendium of knowledge. To my surprise that wish was fulfilled in my new surroundings."

These "new surroundings" were certainly a town, most likely São Paulo. His diary for October 27 spoke of a new life in a big city:

> The spiritual horizon of my new surroundings is as different as the real horizon. Up to now the flat wide landscape was the main characteristic of the country, but now it is the "hills." Ten meters from my window, the only shelter from the traffic is my hedge. The suburb traffic with cars, buses, and trucks is pulsing and especially in the early morning hours and evening when the city spits out its masses. With the passing of time one gets used to such noises of civilization, with which nowadays millions of people are able to live calmly.

The significance of Mengele's hurried departure from Paraguay, within months of the Eichmann kidnapping, is that he did not feel he could rely on the complete protection of the Paraguayan government. Images created by some Nazi-hunters and newspapers—of an elusive fugitive flanked by armed guards—all dissolve. According to one German intimately connected with the Paraguayan government, Mengele's name was not drawn to Stroessner's attention until late 1960, when a newspaper reported that he may have been hiding in Paraguay. Stroessner telephoned the interior minister, Edgar Ynsfran, and asked him who Mengele was. "Ynsfran told him to ask Rudel," said the German, "so he did. Rudel said he was just a lab expert who had worked in a chemical factory during the war and didn't do anything that the newspapers said. That was good enough for Stroessner."[21]

The man who gave Mengele his lifeline to Brazil was a thirty-six-year-old Nazi and former Hitler Youth chief in Austria, Wolfgang Gerhard. He had arrived in Brazil in 1948, leaving Europe because he could no longer tolerate "the oppressive Allied occupation," even though he disliked Brazil since it was filled with "half-monkeys, people of a sick and secondary race." He became the editor of an anti-Semitic fascist rag called *Der Reichsbrief,* the "Reichs Journal." Gerhard is described, even by his close friends, as a "fanatical and fervent Nazi." The link between Mengele and Gerhard was a fellow Nazi who knew both men—Hans Rudel. Rudel and Gerhard were friends, and both knew the family that Gerhard earmarked for Mengele in Brazil.

Mengele code-named the six-foot Gerhard "the Tall Man," or *Lange* in German. Gerhard helped Mengele wind up his financial affairs in Paraguay by selling land for a reported $20,000. By November 23, 1960, Mengele was confident that the arrangements Gerhard had made would ensure his survival. "I presume the best and consider the problem solved," he wrote. His son, Rolf, said he thought his father had amassed a small fortune, "by South American standards of living," from his Paraguayan land sales.

From this point on, Mengele's life fundamentally changed. Being a fugitive's wife was no life for Martha or her sixteen-year-old son. She and Mengele agreed to separate. Mengele had grown fond of Karl Heinz and treated him more as a son than his own boy, Rolf. Shortly before Martha and Karl Heinz flew home, Mengele wrote:

> I do not have to worry about my family, at least not financially. Karl Heinz has tried hard at school and has already made good grades. These things are not very important but I do want to jot them down because they bring me joy. How unlucky I am that I can't take care of the education of my own son. I especially would have liked to have started coaching Rolf, as far as that is possible through correspondence. As to Karl Heinz, I don't have any worries about his philosophy in life in spite of his having lived in such an alien environment.[22]

But Rolf, then age sixteen, was struggling hard to come to terms with who his real father was. His mother, Irene, had recently allowed his stepfather, Alfons Hackenjos, to tell him the identity of the man he had called "Uncle Fritz" on his skiing holiday in the Swiss Alps in 1956. Rolf remembers the event and how it affected him at the time:

> I was always told that my father had been missing in Russia. My father had always been Dr. Mengele who spoke Greek and Latin and who had been so brave.
>
> It was about 1960 when Hacki [Alfons Hackenjos] told me that Uncle Fritz was the same man as my father. It was very unpleasant and awkward for me. Now I understood why one time, a couple of years earlier, when I had shown a picture of my father in uniform to Hacki, he was disappointed and didn't like it.
>
> Now that I was told the truth, I would have preferred another father.

The newspapers were full of stories about his father's crimes. Young Rolf was confused. He was also rather jealous. When Karl Heinz and Martha returned to Günzburg, Rolf felt like an outsider. "Karl Heinz had lived with my father and I thought, 'That's not his father, it's my father,'" he said. At school his teachers complained that he was lazy. They put it down to a "father trauma"; it was only to be expected with a father like his, they said.[23]

Christmas 1960 was a bleak and wretched time for Mengele. His family had already left for Europe and Martha's present did not arrive. On December 28 he wrote:

> Again Christmas has passed. It was one of the most unenjoyable I have ever spent in my life. The details are so sad that I don't even want to talk about it. But I will remember it for the rest of my days.

Fifteen years after Auschwitz, and at the age of forty-nine, Josef Mengele had finally begun, in a small way, to suffer for his crimes.

Mengele's official SS photographs, stapled onto the front of his Nazi party file.

Mengele conducting a "racial purity" interview with an elderly Polish couple. This picture, taken in Posen in September 1940, is the only known photograph of Mengele performing one of his SS medical duties.

Mengele, now a member of the Waffen SS, just prior to his 1942 departure for the eastern front.

A rare picture of Mengele at Auschwitz. At the time this photo was taken, he had been at the concentration camp for four months.

This is one of the few SS photographs of the selection ramp at Auschwitz. The inmates have been separated into groups of men and women, and the SS doctors are waiting to select which will live and which will die. The officer with the soft cap at the far right has been identified by camp survivors as Mengele. He has a cigarette in his hand, not unusual for the chain-smoker.

A rare photograph from the period when Mengele was in hiding in Germany. This photo of her husband and their son, Rolf, was taken by Irene Mengele during one of their secret rendezvous near Rosenheim in 1947.

Hans Sedlmeier, Mengele's longtime protector and friend, in Günzburg with one of his children in the early 1950s.

The first known photograph of Mengele after his successful flight to South America, taken in December 1949, three months after his arrival in Buenos Aires.

The most widely circulated postwar photograph of a man believed to be Mengele. It helped to mislead Mengele's pursuers for nearly twenty years.

Mengele between his two Brazilian protectors, Wolfgang Gerhard, on Mengele's right, and Wolfram Bossert, on his left.

Hans Sedlmeier, Mengele's courier and German mail drop, in West Germany, near the end of the Mengele hunt.

Rolf and Josef Mengele in São Paulo during Rolf's 1977 visit to Brazil. It was the first time the two had met as adults.

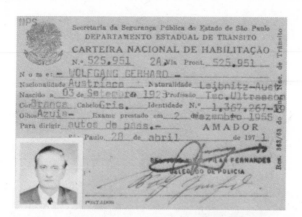

Wolfgang Gerhard's Brazilian identity card. Mengele covered Gerhard's photo with one of his own and then sealed the card in a plastic sleeve.

Wolfram Bossert, an amateur photographer, took this picture of Mengele for the identity card.

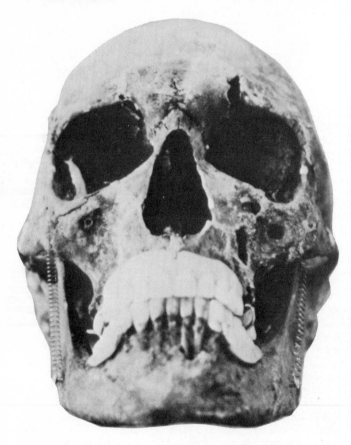

Mengele's skull, complete with reconstructed dental work, as assembled for the forensics examination in Brazil during the summer of 1985.

CHAPTER
9

———
———

The Man in the
Watchtower

———
———

Mengele's Brazilian savior, Wolfgang Gerhard, was as fanatical a Nazi as they come. Each Christmas he adorned his tree with a swastika. "You always have to take good care of swastikas," he used to say. He told friends he dreamed of "putting a steel cable to the leg of Simon Wiesenthal [the Vienna-based Nazi-hunter] and dragging him to death behind my car." His Brazilian-born wife, Ruth, was just as unhinged. She once gave her landlady two bars of soap, in their original 1943 wrappers, made from the corpses of Auschwitz inmates.[1]

After his wartime service as a Hitler Youth leader in Graz, Austria, Gerhard remained a Fascist for the rest of his life. He even christened his son "Adolf." "Wolfgang made no bones about being 150 percent Nazi," a former workmate recalled. In Brazil he was vague about what he did, having variously owned a small textile printing plant and worked in a publicity agency and as a welder. But what made Gerhard useful to Mengele was that he dabbled in real estate.

As a small-time property owner, Gerhard knew people with farms and estates that were far off the beaten track, ideal for a man like Mengele, now desperately seeking a Brazilian sanctuary. Gerhard had been introduced to Mengele in Paraguay, through Hans Rudel, the Luftwaffe ace. Rudel asked Gerhard to help his friend find a new refuge in Brazil and Gerhard jumped at the opportunity. Too young to have played an important role during the war, Gerhard relished the chance to protect one of the Third Reich's most notorious war criminals. Initially, Gerhard let Mengele stay on his farm at Itapecerica about forty-three miles from the center of São Paulo. After several months, Gerhard introduced Mengele to the family he had chosen to act as his next protectors. Their name was Stammer, a Hungarian couple who had moved to Brazil in 1948 to escape the Iron Curtain being drawn across Europe. Mengele was to spend the next thirteen years with them.

Gerhard had met Geza Stammer and his wife, Gitta, in 1959 at a special evening for Austrian-Hungarian expatriates. "You could say that we were firm anti-communists," said Gitta, "but we weren't Nazis." Even so, the Stammers shared with Gerhard some unpalatable revisionist views. "I think some things about the Holocaust may have been invented," Gitta said. "It's hard for people to believe all these things are really true."[2]

According to the Stammers, Gerhard introduced Mengele to them—as "Peter Hochbichler," a Swiss—as a suitable manager for a thirty-seven-acre farm in which they were planning to invest. It produced coffee, rice, fruit, and dairy cattle in a remote German community near Nova Europa, two hundred miles northwest of São Paulo. "Gerhard said he had a friend, an acquaintance, a lonely man who liked the country life far away from towns," said Gitta Stammer. "He said he could be of much help to us."* Gerhard told the Stammers that not only was "Hochbichler" an experienced cattle breeder but he had also recently inherited some money which he wanted to

---

* According to papers in the local property registration office, the Stammers never owned the farm at Nova Europa. It was purchased by an Austrian couple, Anton and Edeltraud Wladeger, on May 20, 1953. When it was "sold" by the Stammers to Jorge Miguel Marum in 1962, the deed was transferred directly from the Wladegers, and the Stammers appeared nowhere on the ownership records.

invest in Brazilian real estate. To the Stammers it was an attractive proposition, particularly since an extra pair of hands would fill the gap left by Geza Stammer when his job as a surveyor took him away for several weeks at a time.

One weekend, Gerhard brought Mengele to meet the Stammers, as Gitta Stammer explained:

> The first impression that I got from him was that he was a simple man, clean and tidy, but nothing exceptional. His hands showed that he was used to working hard because they were full of calluses.[3]

For Mengele, the arrangements to move took a nerve-wrackingly long time. But as would so often be the case in years to come, it was Gerhard who smoothed his path. From that period on, Wolfgang Gerhard was there, counseling, protecting, encouraging. Even though he could sometimes barely feed his own children, Gerhard somehow always found the time and money to help Mengele when it was necessary.

As Mengele waited anxiously for Gerhard's plan to materialize, he occupied himself with a temporary job in São Paulo. His diary suggests he was helping Gerhard with his textile business:

> I have had a very busy week behind me. The work isn't very enjoyable and comes right after sticking down paper bags. But it's important for my host because it earns him a fortune.[4]

The grinding routine of the job and anxiety about his uncertain future had begun to wear Mengele down:

> My life here is difficult, not only because of all the work (I have had to work a lot harder at times) but because of the entire situation: cramped conditions, monotony, primitiveness, noise and formlessness and which in the end, despite all this negativity, does not guarantee me any safety. I have only one aim and that is to change this, but unfortunately we haven't come up with a good idea. "One" also isn't in any great hurry because of all the other constantly unsolved problems. So I will persevere and continue to believe in my lucky star.[5]

Much to his irritation, Mengele also learned that further allegations—that he had dissected prisoners at the Auschwitz-Birkenau extermination camp—had appeared in the press:

> As you can see, my present mood is pretty bad, especially since I have had to deal these last weeks with this nonsense about attempting to strip bodies in B. . . . In this mood one finds no joy in a radiant sunny sky. One is reduced to being a miserable creature without love for life or substance.[6]

Eventually agreement with the Stammers was reached and "Peter" moved in with them to manage the farm at Nova Europa. But he declined any payment. According to Gitta Stammer, Mengele arrived at the farm looking thin and pale:

> . . . he seemed to be ill. . . . Gerhard said he suffered from a certain disease, and his stay with us would help him recover. He showed us a document, a simple paper with no photograph, that had allowed him to cross the border from Austria to Italy. This was the only identification document I saw with this name. But we were not suspicious about him. He seemed simple enough as he just wanted his food and laundry.[7]

In their attempt to convince skeptics that they were just innocent dupes, the Stammers insist that at first there was nothing suspicious about "Peter Hochbichler" or his refusal to take a salary. Nor did his parcels of letters and newspapers from Germany strike them as strange. But the farmhands who suddenly found themselves in Mengele's charge realized something was amiss. They noted that "Peter" read philosophy and history and loved classical music, especially Mozart. They also found that their new boss had a sharp temper which exploded as he struggled to make his orders understood in Portuguese, an alien language. "I didn't like him, but I couldn't do anything about it," said Francisco de Souza, who was working for the Stammers when Mengele arrived. "He loved giving orders and kept saying that we should work more and harder. The worst of it was that he didn't seem to understand much about farming or heavy work."[8]

Try as he would, Mengele failed to earn the respect of his

workers. They were amused when one of his experiments with farm gadgetry flopped badly:

> He was determined to build a machine to deal with the problem of hookworm and white ants that were spread all over the farm. He made me mount a hook on a cart. On the end of the hook he suspended a 175-pound weight, and with this crazy machine he accompanied me around the farm to destroy these enormous anthills, some of them three feet high. He just stared while I had to pull the weight up and release the rope. The weight smashed the mound, but within a few hours the ants were making a new home for themselves. We thought it was a crazy idea; it took hours and hours to prepare.[9]

Mengele did have one skill, however, that impressed the farmhands. He operated on a calf suffering from a hernia. "He reached for some instruments," said de Souza, who held the animal, "and cut its belly open quite expertly. He corrected the hernia and sewed up the cut. He said he could guarantee that the calf would get better, and it did. I noticed that he did everything with a high degree of dexterity."[10]

Although the farmhands did not care for "Peter," Gitta Stammer liked him. According to the farmhands in Nova Europa, from the moment "Peter" arrived, he and Gitta Stammer got on well together. They spoke in German, and she appreciated having a man on the premises since her husband was often away. But today Gitta Stammer tries to put a distance between herself and Mengele. She claims she mostly felt uneasy. "I don't even want to remember those thirteen years that he lived with us," she said. "He tried to order us— he was very authoritarian. Once he almost hit me."[11]

Unbeknownst to the Stammers and the farmhands, Mengele was difficult initially because he did not like the farm or his work. In this first phase of his Brazilian exile, Mengele found it hard to come to terms with his new lowly status. And despite his greater security at remote Nova Europa, his fear of capture by the Israelis plagued him. It revived his insecurity over his prominent forehead, which he nearly had had altered by plastic surgery in Argentina. As he went about his work on the farm, Mengele always wore a hat, even in the heat of

summer. "Whenever I got near him, he pulled the hat down
over his face and dug his hands into his pockets," said Enercio
de Oliveira, who harvested corn with Mengele. Zaire Chile, a
maid, said that Mengele usually wore a shirt buttoned at the
collar and a raincoat. "I never saw anyone on a farm dress like
that," she said.[12]

Mengele's fear of an Israeli strike was well founded. Since
the beginning of 1961, following the failed kidnap attempt in
Buenos Aires, a formidable task force of Mossad agents had
been assembled to track him down. Indeed, many members
of the new Mengele task force had also been on Operation
Eichmann.

The team was headed by Zvi Aharoni, the agent who had
provided the crucial confirmation that Eichmann was living
in Buenos Aires under the name Klement, pinpointed his
house, and interrogated him after his abduction. The headquarters of Aharoni's operation was Paris. One team concentrated on Mengele's friends and family in Europe, the other
turned to South America.

The Mossad's starting point was Paraguay, and their strategy was to try to establish links with those who knew Mengele
well, so that there was ready access to reliable information on
his location at any given time. Only when that was accomplished could the Israelis give serious thought to actually kidnapping Mengele. "It was not our intention at any stage to kill
him," said Isser Harel, head of the Mossad at the time. "That
would have defeated the whole purpose of the exercise. We
wanted him back in Israel for a public trial. That was more
important than anything."

According to Harel and another senior Mossad agent, Rafi
Eitan,* who was code-named "Gabi" in Operation Eichmann,
Mengele felt so at risk that he occasionally traveled to another
farm near São Paulo and went across the border to Paraguay.
Gitta Stammer said that when Mengele first came to live with
them, he "never ventured out." But Eitan insisted that Men-

---

* Rafi Eitan became the subject of headlines in the United States during November 1985,
but not for his work on Mengele. Instead, he was identified as the chief of the Israeli
intelligence unit that had spied on the United States government. The resulting investigation
ended in the arrest of U.S. military officer, Jonathan J. Pollard, and a public apology from
Israel.

gele hid at Alban Krug's farmhouse in Hohenau on several occasions in 1961 and 1962.

For the Paraguayan end of their operation, the Israelis resorted to a ruse to penetrate the Krug family and their circle of neo-Nazi friends. An Englishman working for the Mossad was asked to strike up a love affair with one of Krug's daughters. He was not very successful. But Eitan, who spoke no German or Spanish, claimed he once got close enough to Krug to catch sight of Mengele. "I saw him with my own eyes," he said. A Mossad colleague was more skeptical of Eitan's claim. "I'm surprised Rafi should say this," the Mossad man said. "How the hell he got that close I don't know. He couldn't even say *gracias* in Spanish."[13]

Zvi Aharoni, coordinating the Mengele hunt from Paris, said he was certain no Mossad agent ever saw Mengele in Paraguay. "I made several trips to Paraguay in 1961," he said. "I can tell you that we got nothing, not a thing from Paraguay." But it was not for want of trying. Aharoni's team adopted a variety of cover identities in the country. One agent was a financial consultant; another was a historian writing a book on the SS. He got as far as seeing the former *Gauleiter* of the Nazi party in Paraguay. "It was clear the man knew nothing about Mengele," said Aharoni.

Even to this day, Mossad agents disagree about exactly how close they got to Mengele in Paraguay, and about his degree of protection. Harel said his men became convinced in 1961 that Mengele was in Paraguay and was being sheltered by Alban Krug. "By the end of the year, we knew that he was moving between Paraguay and Brazil," said Harel. "He was completely panicked by the Eichmann abduction." Harel also claimed that Mengele was protected by armed guards and dogs on Krug's farm, though his agents in the field say they saw neither guns nor dogs. Harel did admit, however, that none of his agents actually saw or photographed Mengele in Paraguay.

The conflicting statements about Mengele's movements in the early 1960s reflects the soul-searching that surfaced within Israel's intelligence community after Mengele's death was disclosed. The discovery in June 1985 that Mengele had lived in Brazil for most of his fugitive life raised questions as to why the Israelis had never found him, much less apprehended him.

The difficulties confronting the Mossad were certainly daunting. By the end of 1961, Operation Mengele was a large and expensive venture, more costly than even the Eichmann capture. But according to Zvi Aharoni, despite the grand effort, his men had made little headway by the end of 1961. Attempts to follow Hans Rudel to South America to see if he was meeting Mengele had failed. Rudel wrote to his friend Wolfgang Gerhard in February 1961 that he had become aware that he was being watched.[14] It proved impossible to keep tabs on him once he arrived in Paraguay. Agents in Europe had fared no better in their efforts to intercept mail going to Mengele's estranged wife, Martha, who was living in Merano, in northern Italy. Another major problem for the Mossad was how to spirit Mengele out of a landlocked country like Paraguay or from the interior of Brazil. Harel explained:

> There were several major difficulties with Mengele which made the task of capturing him much harder than Eichmann. First, we had to be exactly sure where he was, and that information was proving hard to get. We thought we knew but since no one had actually seen him, we couldn't plan a commando operation. We had to be 100 percent sure before that stage could be seriously considered. Even if all that had been achieved, we still had to get him out of the country. There was no question of shooting him. The priority was always getting him back to Israel for a trial.[15]

Meanwhile, the more sedentary West German hunt was now progressing on three fronts. In February 1961, Bonn extended its extradition request from Argentina to Brazil. Word had reached Fritz Bauer, prosecutor for the state of Hesse, that Mengele might have fled to Brazil. But Bauer's information was more of a hunch than solidly based, perhaps nothing more tangible than what was available to the CIA station in Asunción at the time. The CIA reported that Mengele was "rumored to have gone to the Mato Grosso, Brazil."[16] In Asunción, Peter Bensch, the chargé d'affaires at the West German embassy, also continued to make inquiries. He had managed to procure a copy of Mengele's citizenship document. But the embassy's attempts to take evidence from Paraguayans who might have seen Mengele soon ran into trouble. "They told us that we had no right to mount what they said was a semi-judicial inquiry," said Dr. Bensch. Bensch's inquiries to the supreme court on the prospects of extradition were not very encouraging either:

> My own view was that Mengele was moving between Paraguay and Brazil at this time, but we had no precise information on him. The supreme court did tell me that if he was found in Paraguay it would not be possible to extradite a Paraguayan citizen. I personally did not talk to President Stroessner about the matter, but we did tell Bonn that as long as Mengele was a Paraguayan citizen, extradition from Paraguay would probably be impossible.[17]

In Argentina, meanwhile, a legend was being born. Mengele, it seemed, had almost superhuman powers of escape. He was wealthy; he had an army of agents; he was one step ahead of the Israeli secret service; and he was armed and extremely dangerous. The evidence lay at the foot of the Andes mountains near the Argentine resort town of Bariloche, where an Israeli woman had mysteriously fallen to her death. Argentine newspapers asked if she might not have been a Mossad agent sent to seduce Mengele and kill him, but instead Mengele had killed her.

The entire fiction was based on nothing more than a climbing accident that indeed had involved a woman tourist who had once lived in Palestine. She was Norit Eldad, an attractive, blonde, middle-aged woman, born in Frankfurt. She was reported missing in March 1960, only two months before the Eichmann kidnapping, after she went for a walk on the footpath of Cerro Catedral, the tallest mountain in the region. The leader of the search team, Professor Esquerra, president of the local ski club, was quoted as saying that when the body was finally found, he "immediately thought it was a strange place for a hiker to have a fatal accident. If it was a natural death, fate had done an excellent job in hiding the body from view." The body was deep in a crevasse, the result of an accidental fall from a precipice. Perhaps the "Angel of Death" had showed his hand? A simple spelling mistake in the hotel register had listed Norit Eldad as "Eldoc." Investigators mistook the error to be the pseudonym of an Israeli agent. The theory certainly appealed to local police inspector Victor Gatica, who said:

> The apparent motive now is that she was searching for Josef Mengele, the Nazi doctor. Now it is considered that Dr. Mengele may have been staying in Bariloche.[18]

No one proved that Mengele had stayed there. But neither could they prove that he had not. Thus Mengele was reported as having accompanied Norit Eldad on her fatal walk. They had become lovers, according to the story, she with the purpose of setting him up for an ambush by a team of Israeli hit men waiting in a nearby hotel. A false-bottomed suitcase had been found by Mengele's bodyguards while the couple were out: they had rushed out to tell Mengele; she was pushed over a precipice; Mengele had fled town. Now everything fit. The South American newspapers banner-headlined this news of Mengele's mountaintop encounter with an Israeli assassin.

On March 21, 1961, the Israeli embassy in Buenos Aires vainly tried to convince the newspapers that Norit Eldad was not a Mossad agent, saying she was known as a "timid and nervous person. Certainly it is not possible that she was an agent involved in a mission as difficult as finding Mengele." But after the cloak-and-dagger kidnapping of Eichmann, no one believed the Israelis. And when Simon Wiesenthal published his book, *The Murderers Among Us*, in 1967, claiming that Miss Eldad had been in a concentration camp, the story was accepted as fact. Wiesenthal even added one more touch of drama: Miss Eldad had been sterilized by Mengele, who recognized her while she was staying at the hotel. He had spotted her camp tattoo at a hotel dinner dance and had her killed because he feared she would betray him. Here was the genesis of *Marathon Man* and *The Boys from Brazil*.

The real hunt was a lot more hit-and-miss than that. Early in March 1961, the Argentine police followed up a tip from the West German embassy, a letter from a Señora Silvia Caballero de Costa. It claimed that Mengele was living under a false name and was engaged to a wealthy young woman in Santiago del Estero, the northern provincial capital of Argentina. Interviewed by the police, Señora de Costa proved to be illiterate; she could not possibly have been the author of the mysterious letter. The author was soon revealed to be a wealthy merchant whose only daughter was engaged to a man he was convinced was Mengele because he claimed to be a German doctor. The fiancé turned out to be a New York con man, Willy Delaney, twenty-five years older than Mengele, without the slightest resemblance to him, and with prior convictions for assault, bribery, and practicing medicine illegally.[19]

The Delaney case was followed by numerous press reports that the Mossad was back on Mengele's trail. The most spectacular, in the London *Sunday Dispatch*, quoted "reliable sources" who claimed that the Israelis had been given orders to "liquidate Mengele before the start of the Adolf Eichmann trial," scheduled to start on April 11. One of the five Mossad agents, code-named "David," had been relentlessly tracking Mengele for two years according to this story.

That same day another report came thundering over the wire services from Hamburg, where a German businessman, Peter Sosna, said he was sure he had met Mengele on a recent trip to Brazil. Sosna said that while he was in the Mato Grosso, in the town of Corumbá, a group of unidentified Germans introduced him to a doctor. Sosna reported that the doctor had Indian bodyguards and the meeting was held in great secrecy. On his return to Hamburg, Sosna went straight to the German prosecutor's office and after being shown photographs of Mengele, positively identified him as the man he had seen. Much credibility was given to the sighting. Sosna worked for a marine chandler supply company and seemed a reliable witness. The idea of Mengele living in a vast, virtually unexplored rain forest the size of Texas added a touch of drama to the reputation of the man fast becoming the world's most elusive fugitive.

In response to Sosna's report, the Brazilian police launched one of its biggest manhunts. Corumbá swarmed with policemen, who established blockades at all points crossing the Río Paraguay. On March 18, the police received a tip that Mengele was staying at a hotel in Corumbá and had registered in the name of "Juan Lechín"—yet another of the multitudinous aliases he was now said to be using. Brandishing guns, more than thirty officers stormed the hotel, where they found no one resembling Mengele but detained the hapless owner. "He seemed suspicious," said the police inspector who led the raid.

On March 23 farce turned to tragedy, however, with the story that Mengele had at last been captured. This time there was no doubt, said the reports. He had been hiding in the province of Buenos Aires all along. It was a fact.

The man the police arrested had lived in the town of Coronel Suárez for seven years, and three newspaper journalists claimed credit for his arrest. They were Alfred Senadom of *La Mañana* and Juan Vessey Camben and Geoffrey Thursby of the London *Daily Express*. The suspect's name was Lothar Hermann. By one of the strangest twists of fate, this was the same man who three years before had tipped off the Israelis that Eichmann was living in Buenos Aires. Hermann had suffered a complete nervous breakdown because he believed that the Israelis had ignored his contribution to that case. He had some cause for his grievance. Isser Harel wrote in his account of Operation Eichmann that he allowed the Mossad's contact with Hermann to lapse because of inconsistencies in Hermann's reports to Tel Aviv. In the end, of course, Hermann had been proved absolutely right.

At the La Plata police station, Hermann was almost incoherent. When asked if he was Mengele, he said he was. The poor man was in such a distraught state that he had no idea what he was saying. But it is difficult to understand how the police and the reporters seriously imagined they had got the right man since he was blind and bore no physical resemblance to Mengele.

Fortunately for Hermann, the police did take the trouble to check his fingerprints against a set of Mengele's, which they had taken when issuing Mengele an identity card in 1956. On March 25, a chastened provincial police chief announced that they had "determined that Josef Mengele is not the same person that we have detained." Hermann was released from custody and appeared quite mad when he gave a rambling interview to a group of reporters, threatening to sue the *Daily Express*, which he said had engaged in "yellow journalism."

The Hermann story did illustrate, however, the lack of urgency and the failure of coordination with which the West Germans were then conducting the hunt for Mengele. One year after the Argentine arrest warrant was issued, the West

Germans still did not have a copy of Mengele's fingerprints for distribution to other German embassies in South America. On July 24, 1961, the West German embassy wrote to the Argentine foreign office:

> According to statements in the press, the police have Mengele's fingerprints in their possession, since it was possible to prove that the fingerprints of Lothar Hermann were not identical to those of Josef Mengele. As there is a possibility that Mengele may be in another country, a record of his prints is of singular importance in helping to facilitate the competent German authorities in the continuing investigation.[20]

For four months the Argentine police simply ignored the request. On November 20, the West Germans sent a reminder to the foreign office, asking them to "please give attention to the request, which is urgent due to the character of the case." Finally, in December, the prints were sent.[21]

Little of the chaos and indifference surrounding the hunt filtered through to the public. They were treated instead to an almost weekly diet of new sightings and follow-up police operations. It was precisely because Mengele was portrayed as being able to elude such "dragnets" that his reputation flourished as a wily fugitive with superhuman powers of evasion.

On the farm at Nova Europa, meanwhile, Mengele remained unaware of many of the more imaginative press reports. According to Gitta Stammer, they rarely received newspapers. The irony was that although they did not know he was on their soil, the most active police hunts were conducted by the Brazilians.

On January 23, 1962, the Brazilian papers carried the headline that Mengele had been captured in the small border town of Pozos de Caldos. The prisoner was using the name "Solomon Schuller." He was German and he worked for Bayer, the German multinational conglomerate. He was said to be "definitely pro-Nazi, quiet and mysterious." The area Interpol director, Amoroso Neto, ordered Schuller's detention and was so confident he was Mengele that he released the story before fingerprint verification had been completed. Two days later the police withdrew the allegation. Fingerprints had arrived from the Germans and showed that Schuller was in fact Hans

Epfenger, a former member of the Waffen SS who was not wanted for war crimes but used an alias nevertheless.

The following month a hotel manager, Elias Cardoso, told the police that a suspicious foreign visitor had checked in to his hotel in the frontier town of Auto Posto. He was German. Once when he got drunk, Cardoso heard a friend call him "doctor." Later the mystery guest, in a drunken stupor, told Cardoso that he was a former member of the Gestapo and could not return home because the Germans "would slit my throat." Cardoso told the police he thought his guest looked like Mengele. The local police called in the Brazilian federal police.

At dawn on February 28, 1962, twenty-five armed militiamen stormed into the room where the Mengele suspect was staying. The room was empty. The guest had checked out during the night without paying his bill. It was the sixth Brazilian alert in less than a year. Surely, said the newspapers, this was Mengele's closest call?*

Midway through 1962, while several South American governments pursued a ghostlike fugitive, the real Mengele moved with the Stammers to a 111-acre coffee and cattle farm. Called "Santa Luzia," the farm was in Serra Negra, 93 miles north of São Paulo. The dry heat at Nova Europa, said Gitta Stammer, had become oppressive. "We wanted cooler weather," she recalls. Serra Negra is renowned for its rich soil, cool climate, and thermal springs amid gentle sloping mountains and woods. Once again Mengele provided capital, one half the purchase price of the farm.[22]

Although he had been against the move, once he arrived in Serra Negra Mengele began to relax for the first time in two years. He was involved in woodworking and construction on the farmhouse, work which he noted in his diary was "pleasing." In his first diary entries after arriving at Serra Negra, Mengele wrote enthusiastically about the "beautiful landscape," the "wondrous eucalyptus forests," and the "high plateau that fills my soul with awe." A month after his arrival, on

---

* The South American press was riddled with sensational but false Mengele stories for the remainder of 1962. The most imaginative claimed that Mengele had been kidnapped by Israeli agents and was on a banana boat steaming for Haifa. The boat docked in Israel in front of a full complement of the press corps. It was filled with exotic fruit but, alas, no Mengele.

August 19, 1962, Mengele summarized his feelings about his new hideout:

> Now I have been here for four weeks already and I am splendidly settled. As much as I was opposed to the move, I now feel comfortable in this spot. No wonder— it has all that is necessary to provide home and solace to a peaceless man.[23]

Mengele may have felt more settled in Serra Negra, but his hosts did not. The Stammers became increasingly uneasy about their new farm manager. Something, said Gitta Stammer, was not "quite right." He avoided meeting people; he was prone to quarreling with the farmhands, and would humiliate them. "His behavior," she said, "was very unpleasant. We were used to getting on well with the farmhands. I called his attention to the fact that we were living in Brazil and that we shouldn't be aggressive."

Most tiresome were Mengele's violent mood swings. One day he would be silent, brooding, a solitary man walking for hours. The next day, he was talkative, genial, captivating the Stammers with a sharp sense of humor. To them, it was clear that their guest was under great strain. They began to wonder who exactly was the man that Wolfgang Gerhard had brought into their lives. Their thoughts focused on the glaring inconsistencies in his background. Ultimately it was this that really aroused their suspicion. Whoever "Peter" was, his origins were not, as he had claimed, those of a man who had been farming all his life, as Gitta Stammer explained:

> He used to say that his family were farmers, but as time passed we began to realize that he was an intelligent man and educated as well. For example, we, the family, used to read a lot. . . . When we made certain comments about books or radio programs, he sometimes forgot and gave an opinion well above the level of a farmer. This was a sign that something was wrong, something wasn't true.
>
> Then we began to realize that he was afraid of everybody. When somebody came to the farm he would always disappear. Sometimes we had visitors from São Paulo, friends or acquaintances. When this happened he

looked very upset and started asking questions: "Who
are these people? Are they real friends?"

You know, all this was very strange and we began to
wonder why he behaved so strangely. We realized that
something was wrong.[24]

Gitta soon discovered what was wrong. She claims it was in
Serra Negra, on one of the rare occasions when there was a
newspaper in the house, that she learned the true identity of
"Peter Hochbichler":

A businessman buying our fruit came to the farm and
left a newspaper there. There was a piece of news about
the Nazi executioners, as they said. I saw this photo
there; he was a young man, about thirty or thirty-three
years old. Then I thought that this face was very familiar
to me, and his smile with gaps between his teeth. At that
time he had such teeth. I showed him the photograph
and told him that the man resembled him very much.

I told him, "You are so mysterious, you live here with
us, so please be honest and tell us whether it's you or
not." He was very upset after that, but he didn't say
anything and left. In the evening, after dinner, he sat
very quiet. Suddenly he said, "Well, you're right. I live
here with you and therefore you have the right to know
that unfortunately I am that person."[25]

Geza Stammer was at the farm the weekend when Mengele
admitted his true identity. He claims he was "very nervous,
very upset," that he wanted to immediately contact Wolfgang
Gerhard and arrange to move Mengele. But since there was
no telephone at Serra Negra, Geza had to wait for his next trip
to São Paulo, nearly a week later. Gitta recalls, "We didn't
want to take any risks; we weren't interested in politics; we
didn't want any confusions; we wanted to live our life without
problems."

In São Paulo Geza Stammer told Gerhard that he considered hiding Mengele "very dangerous." "My husband told
Gerhard that we were afraid, scared to keep a man hunted all
over the world," Gitta said. "Gerhard tried to calm us down
by saying that no one would find out. He said we ought to be
happy because before Mengele lived with us we were noth-

ing. 'Now there is something important in your life,' he told us."[26] Gerhard urged the Stammers to be patient. He promised to contact the Mengele family directly, arrange to move Mengele, and then come back to the Stammers when everything was resolved.

Mengele's younger brother, Alois, who was running the family firm in Günzburg, dispatched his old schoolfriend and most trusted confidant, Hans Sedlmeier, to Brazil to act as peacemaker. Gitta remembers what happened next: "One month later he [Gerhard] came over, by car, and brought an old man with him. This man was introduced to us as Mr. Hans, who came directly from Germany. Gerhard said the less we knew about him, the better."

Sedlmeier brought with him $2000, which Geza Stammer changed into Brazilian cruzeiros. He stayed with the Stammers in Serra Negra for two days. According to Gitta, although at first resistant, Hans eventually "promised to do everything to find another place for him [Mengele]."

Yet Sedlmeier did not keep his promise. Mengele stayed with the Stammers and "the problems got worse." Gitta recalls the deteriorating situation:

> During this period of time, Peter was very upset, very nervous. Actually, it was very difficult to deal with him. Whenever we asked something he gave us an aggressive answer. He used to say, "What do you think? This isn't a simple matter. There are many things at stake." He almost accused us of being the cause of his misfortune.[27]

Once more, the Stammers turned to Gerhard to find a way out, this time saying they were considering betraying him to the authorities. Gerhard's response was blunt, one that sounded to the Stammers like a threat. Gitta recalls:

> Gerhard said, "Do you really think it might be better that way? You should be very careful, because if you do anything against him, you'll have to take the consequences because he lives here with you. You should think about the future of your children. This is not so simple as you imagine. There are many obstacles, much difficulty."[28]

The sudden decline in their relationship caused by the revelation of his identity plunged Mengele into anxiety over his future:

> Again, outside flowers and trees give joy to that tired old heart. The cold wind whistles around the house and in my heart there is no sunshine either.[29]

For solace, Mengele immersed himself in studying flowers and trees and writing what he called his "childhood opus":

> That might be interesting later, looking back on them, on how everything came to be. I write them for my sons, R and K [Rolf and Karl Heinz], who will get to know much less about the past of the family than D [Dieter].[30]*

He became more and more self-obsessed, devoting no less than forty pages of this "childhood opus" to his own birth, including one and a half pages about the placenta, a phenomenon that caused Professor Norman Stone, the Oxford historian, to remark that Mengele's diaries were marked by "isolation, vanity, narcissism and nastiness."[31]

Yet despite the confrontation created by the revelation of Mengele's true identity, the Stammers remained loyal to him. Despite the risks they took in harboring Mengele and the abuse they endured from him, the Stammers stayed true to him for the rest of his life. They never breathed a word to the police, even after relations became so bad between them in 1975 that they went their separate ways. Nor did they consider going to the police after Wolfgang Gerhard had left Brazil in 1971 and was no longer a threat. Furthermore, the Stammers helped Mengele in his property deals right up to his death.†

The Stammer loyalty at first seems illogical. During the years they knew him, Mengele never threatened the Stammers. Nor were they paid direct protection money by the Mengele family in Günzburg. "If we had considered this ne-

---

* Dieter Mengele, the son of Mengele's younger brother, Alois, was at that time the only Mengele son living with his father.

† In 1985, when Gitta Stammer was asked if she would again provide shelter to Mengele, knowing what she does now, she said "I think . . . yes . . . politically speaking, in general, we help everybody."

cessity with G and G [Geza and Gitta Stammer] you might still have been together," Hans Sedlmeier wrote to Mengele years later, after he and the Stammers had split.[32] But the mystery of why the Stammers never gave Mengele up has several explanations. First, Mengele had become their business partner. He provided substantial capital that allowed the greedy Stammers to buy larger and better farms. They became financially dependent on him. Second, although a difficult person, Mengele's views were not so alien to their own. Gitta Stammer herself betrayed her own brutal historical perspective of the Holocaust when she tried to rationalize Nazi crimes. "The Germans thought that the Jews were working against Germany, so they had to get rid of them," she said. And she accepted Mengele's word that he had never conducted experiments.

Finally, and maybe most important, Gitta's unswerving loyalty to Mengele appears to be the result of a love affair between them. José Osmar Siloto, who helped harvest the coffee crop, said Mengele and she were "always together. They walked everywhere together and were always sitting and talking to each other." Ferdinando Beletatti, who worked on the farm, said:

> Mr. Stammer seldom came to the farm. Their children once told me that Peter and Gitta locked themselves in the bedroom to be by themselves, making it clear they had a romance.[33]

Wolfram Bossert, who sheltered Mengele later, says there was an "erotic relationship between Gitta and him [Mengele]." Evidence of the relationship is also scattered throughout Mengele's diaries. He wrote of the "beautiful" Gitta, and dedicated love poems to her:

Quiet Love

We only met so late,
When we both had experienced how bitter life could be.
Your love is never loud,
And quiet your words and gestures,
A fine smile, our secret knowledge.

Yet Gitta tearfully denies she ever had an affair with Mengele. She claims he "satisfied his sexual desires by having brief

affairs with almost every young female farmhand we hired."[34]
But Gitta's assertion that Mengele's only sexual outlet was
with local farm girls is contradicted by an episode recalled by
Wolfram Bossert:

> On one of my visits to the villa, I saw that a few girls
> had been invited to celebrate the coffee harvest, and
> one of them was a very pretty *morena*—that is to say, a
> dark girl. And Gerhard teased him [Mengele] later, say-
> ing that he had, surely, had a fling with her. Mengele got
> very cross and replied that he, as a race scientist, would
> never have an affair with a colored woman. You see,
> that's how persistent and stubborn he was in pursuing
> his course. Once he had made up his mind on some-
> thing, he would pursue the matter without compro-
> mise.[35]

Despite Gitta's denials, the evidence is that Mengele and
Gitta had an affair, which lasted until 1974, when she lost
interest, according to Bossert, during her menopause.

Satisfactory though the carnal side of life might have been,
Mengele's prospects for a more fulfilling lifestyle looked distinctly dim. On June 1, 1962, he learned that his colleague
Adolf Eichmann had been hanged at Israel's Ramale jail. Most
of Mengele's invective was directed at postwar Germany,
which he saw as the real villain in Eichmann's fate:

> The event which I learned of days later didn't sur-
> prise me, but I was deeply affected. One is tempted to
> draw comparisons, then one drops it again because one
> is startled by the reality of the path of history over the
> last 2000 years. His people have betrayed him miser-
> ably. As a human this has been the most difficult and
> upsetting part. Herein lies the core of the problem of
> the case! One day the German people will be very
> ashamed of themselves! Otherwise they will never feel
> shame.[36]

Determined that Eichmann's fate should not befall him,
Mengele became obsessed with his own security. Whenever
Mengele went for a walk he took a large number of dogs with
him. "He had about fifteen strays," Ferdinando Beletatti, the
ex-farmhand, said, "but he never went far from the farm."

Beletatti was also ordered to build an eighteen-foot wooden watchtower. When he asked Gitta Stammer why, she said that she and her husband wanted it for bird-watching, but he never saw them use it. The construction was fastidiously supervised by Mengele. "He was very abrupt," said Beletatti. "He spoke to me only when he was giving me orders on how to build it."

For hours on end Mengele scanned the countryside from the watchtower. Perched on top of a hill, the farm afforded him a perfect view of the surrounding fields and dirt tracks. He also had a clear sight of Lindonia, the nearest town, five miles away. There were no guns, no dogs or electrified fences, no praetorian guard—just a middle-aged man with a pair of binoculars anxiously surveying the scene. "A lot of people find it strange that Mengele managed to survive for so long without the aid of an organization or security," said Wolfram Bossert, who became one of Mengele's few friends. "I think he managed that exactly because he had no security apparatus."[37]

Mengele's obsession with security weighed on his mind and cast him into deep depressions. At such times, he believed his capture was inevitable, as his diary showed: "Out of the beautiful house of our ideal plans, one stone after the other breaks down, and the final collapse comes nearer and nearer." He even dreamed of death: "Occasionally, I dream of a double-headed guillotine."

Yet Mengele need not have worried. Certainly by the summer of 1962, he had fooled the West Germans, who thought he was probably still in Paraguay. On August 11 the ambassador in Asunción, Eckart Briest, formally requested Mengele's extradition. In November Judge Vincente Ricciardi of the Paraguayan Fourth Judicial Court issued a warrant for Mengele's arrest after the West German embassy said that their information placed "Josef Mengele as either visiting Asunción or in the Alto Parana region."[38] The Paraguayans knew, however, that the bird had already flown. Stroessner himself had actually responded quite helpfully to Briest. According to one reliable source in the interior ministry, Stroessner told the ambassador, "I don't know about extradition, but I can arrest him." Stroessner then telephoned the interior minister, Edgar Ynsfran, and ordered that Mengele be arrested. Ynsfran, recalling that he had expedited Mengele's citizenship at Rudel's request, telephoned the ex-Luftwaffe ace, who told him, "Forget it, he's gone to Brazil." As a precaution, the warrant was issued all the same.[39]

The warrant put an end to any idea Mengele may have had of using Paraguay as a sanctuary had his luck run out in Brazil. Even his friend Alban Krug was powerless to help. Although Krug was an influential man, he did not have an open door to Stroessner's palace; in fact he found the president quite intimidating. Once when Krug was summoned to the palace for a friendly chat, he mistakenly felt the atmosphere had relaxed enough for him to tell the president that many people in southern Paraguay felt the government was too remote. He also ventured to say that some of Stroessner's ministers were "assholes." When Krug realized he had gone too far, he began to feel uneasy and indicated that he would like to leave. But Stroessner kept him there for hours. Finally, when the president had finished, he walked Krug to the door, put his hand across Krug's broad back, and warned him, "If these intriguers ever make a revolt against me I will resist until not a stone is left in Asunción."

Since Stroessner seemed prepared, for the moment anyway, to have Mengele arrested, Krug could not risk giving him shelter, particularly since he was unaware that the president had ruled out extradition.

As for the Israelis, by the end of 1962, their hunt for Mengele had virtually ground to a halt, a casualty of competing priorities in a fast changing world. Once again the survival of Israel was threatened by President Gamal Nasser of Egypt. The cruel irony is that the hunt came to an end just as the Mossad made a spectacular breakthrough—one which in hindsight may well have ended in Mengele's capture.

C H A P T E R
10

———
———

"We Could Have
Had Him"

———
———

The Mossad's breakthrough in the spring of 1962 did not
come a moment too soon. For over a year their efforts to
penetrate Mengele's family's clannish circle in Europe had
come to nothing. But in South America many weeks of observ-
ing one of the first Nazis to befriend Mengele when he arrived
in 1949 had begun to pay off. In Willem Antonius Maria Sassen, a wartime SS officer and member of the *Abwehr,* the
Mossad detected an opportunity not to be missed.

Sassen was well known to the Israelis because just prior to
the kidnapping he had recorded a voluminous set of taped
interviews of Adolf Eichmann. Not privy to the closely
guarded secrets of the Final Solution, Sassen had always
doubted that millions died in the concentration camps. As a
neo-Nazi propagandist, he believed a firsthand account from
Eichmann would set the record straight. When Sassen finally
succeeded in persuading Eichmann to talk, he could not believe his ears. Once Eichmann started, he could not stop. Far

from dismissing the so-called Jewish Lie, he was supremely proud of what he had done. By the time he was captured by the Israelis, Eichmann had recorded sixty-seven tapes. Even Sassen flinched at some of Eichmann's shameless boasts. "I must say I regret nothing," he recorded on one tape. "It would be too early to pretend that I had turned suddenly from a Saul to a Paul. No, I must say, truthfully, that if we had killed all 10 million Jews that Himmler's statistician [Dr. Richard Korherr] had listed in 1933, I would say, 'Good, we have destroyed an enemy.' "[1]

For Israel's attorney general, Gideon Hausner, the tapes would have clinched the case against Eichmann, who was then awaiting trial in Jerusalem. However, although Sassen had sold the magazine rights for the tape material to Time-Life, he made that sale and the sale of other rights conditional on the original material not being given to the Israelis. Hausner was thus deprived of a vital weapon in his armory of evidence against Eichmann, which was what Sassen had intended.

Yet it was clear that a fundamental shift in Sassen's views had taken place. Caught off guard, he had been confronted by the awful truth about the Holocaust. Sassen had heard it from the "horse's mouth." The Mossad decided to turn this to their advantage in the Mengele case, gambling that Sassen was now vulnerable to another dose of the truth. It would be wrong to suggest that Sassen had undergone a complete change of heart. Although a complex man, he was still a Nazi ideologue in most respects and retained absolute faith in the integrity and honor of the SS. Since Sassen had faced one historical truth, the Mossad believed the time was right to give him a long hard look at another.

Mossad agents flew to Uruguay to meet Sassen. Patiently, they educated him about the unspeakable crimes in Mengele's past. After many hours, the approach seemed to be paying off. Zvi Aharoni flew from his Paris headquarters to meet Sassen and made one of the most bizarre recruiting pitches in the annals of espionage. Sassen emerged shaken, convinced that Mengele had sullied the honor of the SS, that band of noble fighting men. "We got him to a certain pitch," said one agent, "then Aharoni came in. He talked to him for eleven hours. He showed him some documents. After that

Sassen said he would try to help us." Although it was important, Aharoni's persuasive manner was not the only factor.
The Israelis also undertook to pay Sassen handsomely. His fee
was $5,000 a month.

Sassen, now cooperating with the Mossad, soon discovered
that Mengele had indeed fled Paraguay and was living near
São Paulo, although he did not know the address. Sassen also
learned the name of the man who was protecting Mengele in
Brazil. It was Wolfgang Gerhard. "Gerhard was supposed to
be Mengele's link to the outside world," said Aharoni. "What I
especially liked about this information was that it checked
with information we had had from two other sources."[2]

Aharoni kept watch on Gerhard and followed him wherever and whenever he moved. One day Gerhard drove out of
town. About twenty-five miles from São Paulo, Aharoni's
quarry turned right, off the road to Curitiba onto a dirt track.
Aharoni explained what followed:

> I couldn't possibly have followed him up so I had to
> drive on. We did all sorts of jobs to try and find out
> where the road led to. We also brought a guy over from a
> kibbutz, who looked like a local guy and spoke fluent
> Portuguese. He even went barefoot to look the part. It
> was an area that was partially wooded and we eventu-
> ally discovered it led to three or four farmhouses. You
> couldn't sit there all day long with binoculars so we had
> to think of something else, but our options were rather
> limited. One Sunday we decided to have a picnic there,
> me and two of our local guys. I was determined to do
> what I could. We had followed so many leads and they
> hadn't got anywhere. But at last it seemed as if we might
> be making progress.[3]

While Aharoni and his men were eating their sandwiches,
they saw three men approaching on foot, toward the direction
of the farmhouses. One was a European, and by his side were
two Brazilians. Before Aharoni had time to grab his camera
and sneak a snapshot, the trio was almost upon them. Aharoni
recalls:

> I thought the man may well be Mengele. In fact I was
> sure of it. Our information was so good. I said nothing

because I didn't want to talk, so the other two guys did the talking. They just chatted away. The man I thought was Mengele didn't talk, though he didn't seem at all worried about us. They stayed talking about five minutes, so I got a good look at his face. He had a moustache, he was the right height. There was a striking similarity with the photographs we had. The two boys with him weren't armed. They looked, well, tough. Local toughs.[4]

Aharoni watched the trio walk off and saw them enter the nearest farmhouse. The next stage was to get photo confirmation, and if that checked out, to draw up a kidnap plan. "I thought, 'Right, this is it, but I can't work alone,'" said Aharoni, "so I went back to Europe to make a start on the details of the operation."

Aharoni arrived at his Paris headquarters in June. "I was very excited and full of hope. Mengele was my one ambition then," he said. "I didn't know who Mengele was when we got Eichmann, but I had done a lot of reading since then." But Aharoni was in for a surprise. When he walked into the Mossad's Paris bureau, he found Harel there too—totally immersed in a manhunt of a completely different kind:

I went into Isser's office and tried to explain that I thought we had at last found Mengele. But before I could go any further he said, "Don't bother about Mengele now. I've got someone coming in from London tonight that I want you to interrogate." That was it. That was all Isser said. It was the end of the Mengele case. Having been a soldier I had learned to take orders, so I did what I was told. Isser was in no mind to argue. He was in a state of nervous tension.[5]

The case that was absorbing Harel's attention involved a religious kidnapping. For two years the issue had been moving Israel to the brink of a holy civil war.

In 1960 Yosselle Schumacher, an eight-year-old boy, had disappeared and was thought to have been smuggled out of Israel. One of the main suspects was Yosselle's own grandfather, who feared that the boy's parents, disillusioned with Israel, might take him back to their native Russia, where he would not be raised as an Orthodox Jew. The grandfather,

Nahman Shtarkes, held a deep loathing for the Soviet Union, having spent the war years in the Gulag, where he lost an eye and saw his youngest son murdered by a gang of Jew-baiting Russians. He was also a member of the ultra-orthodox sect known as the Hassidim of Breslau.

The whole family—Nahman, his daughter, Ida, her husband, Alter, and their two children, Zina and Yosselle—emigrated to Israel from Poland in 1957. But Ida and Alter soon found it hard to make ends meet, and Yosselle was sent to live with his grandfather while they sought to improve their fortunes. It was while the family was divided that Nahman learned his daughter was considering going back to Russia. Nahman believed it his sacred duty to save the boy's soul.

When Yosselle's parents realized their boy was missing, they called in the police, who arrested Nahman. The chief rabbi of Jerusalem urged full support for Nahman. The supreme court called him a criminal. It was Orthodox versus non-Orthodox. A decade into its fragile new life, the State of Israel was being torn apart.

Into this simmering feud stepped Isser Harel. He took the supreme court's view that a serious crime had been committed and that the parents' rights had been outrageously abused. The Mossad, he said, had a duty to find the boy, reunite him with his parents, and heal the country's wounds. Prime Minister Ben-Gurion agreed. It was not the first time Harel had acted as keeper of the state's conscience. But this time some people thought that he had gone too far.

Several of Harel's senior staff argued that finding the boy was a matter for the police. Harel did not agree. And to underline his point, he devoted much manpower and money to the hunt, code-named Operation Tiger. It was a challenging assignment to penetrate the Mafia-like secrecy of this most secret of Orthodox sects. As with the Eichmann search, Harel approached the task with crusading zeal; and as with Eichmann he succeeded, running the child to the ground in New York, displaying his masterly skills of instinctive intelligence and operational planning.[6]

According to Zvi Aharoni, however, Harel abandoned the hunt for Mengele after he became obsessed with Operation Tiger. Harel vehemently rejects the charge, claiming that in October 1962—three months after Yosselle Schumacher was

found—he sent agents back to Brazil to develop Aharoni's
lead that Mengele was hiding on the farm twenty-five miles
from São Paulo. Harel said:

> There were quite important signs that he had stayed
> or was staying there. But we did not succeed in confirm-
> ing that he was there. And we certainly had not suc-
> ceeded in identifying him. After weeks of many danger-
> ous attempts, we came to the conclusion that there was
> no point in going on.[7]

Harel said there was one overriding reason why the farmhouse outside São Paulo could not be investigated further: it
was guarded by armed men—just as he had claimed about the
Krug farmhouse in Paraguay.

> We couldn't take him by force any more than we
> could in Paraguay. There were armed guards at the
> Brazilian place and there were dogs, too, I think.[8]

Harel's suggestion of armed protection or guard dogs was
dismissed by Zvi Aharoni and other agents on the hunt:

> I certainly do not recall any reports at the time of
> guns or dogs guarding Krug's farm. When we were in
> Brazil we never saw armed guards or dogs either. All we
> ever saw there were the couple of young toughs who
> walked up to us with the man I believe was Mengele.[9]

The war of words between Harel and Aharoni, once the
best of friends, left them bitter enemies. Today they no longer
speak to each other.

Aharoni deeply regrets that he did not use his senior position to persuade Harel to devote more resources to his Brazilian lead:

> Looking back I have the feeling that if Israel is to
> blame for not doing more to bring Mengele to trial, I am
> as much to blame as anyone. As operational head of the
> case, I was in a position to demand that more should
> have been done and I did not. When Isser took me off
> the operation I did not question his decision at the time.
> I suppose I behaved too much like a soldier obeying
> orders.[10]

The main source of Aharoni's anger against his former close friend is Harel's historical analysis of the Mengele hunt:

> Isser says there were dogs and guns and that's why we couldn't get him. I say there were no dogs or guns and we could have got him. Where Isser gets dogs and guns from I have no idea. But if he's going to talk and write about historical events as important as this, he should stick to the facts. And the unpalatable fact is that Isser and I—both of us—could have pursued Mengele more forcefully. He was obsessed with Schumacher at the time. I should have pressed him to give Mengele as high a priority.[11]

Harel insists that his recollection of reports of guns and dogs is accurate and he roundly denies ever easing up on the hunt for Mengele. He also says that after the team he sent in October failed to confirm Mengele's presence at the farmhouse, he decided to go back to "the Nazi agent [Sassen] so that with our guidance and help he would supply us with more information from his sources."[12]

What is undeniable is that by late November 1962, Harel had ruled out a commando operation for the foreseeable future. It is also true that by that time Harel was fighting for his survival as chief of the Mossad.

Within days of the resolution of the Schumacher case, Harel was drawn into a second major operation, to counter what appeared to be the greatest threat to the security of Israel since its birth—ex-Nazi rocket scientists developing missiles for Israel's neighbor, Egypt. What made matters worse was that this new project brought with it a challenge to Harel's job from General Meir Amit, chief of military intelligence, a tough soldier with a distinguished career.

Only days after Yosselle Schumacher returned to Tel Aviv, Egypt's president, Gamal Abdel Nasser, successfully test-launched four rockets with ranges up to 350 miles. He boasted that they could destroy any target "south of Beirut." Matters came to a head after the rockets were paraded in the streets of Cairo, and Prime Minister Ben-Gurion was shocked to discover that the Mossad files were empty. Following this humiliating spectacle, Meir Amit fired a deadly broadside at Harel:

What are we spending our intelligence budget on if
we get our information from a public speech of Gamal
Nasser? All we need for that is a public radio.[13]

Harel was severely embarrassed. Never had there been
such a challenge to his competence. He immediately established a new department to gather intelligence on the state of
Nasser's rocket research. But Amit recommended that his
own military intelligence staff make a separate assessment.
He complained to Prime Minister Ben-Gurion that Harel had
neglected the rockets at the expense of less important but
more attention-getting projects, such as hunting for Adolf
Eichmann and Yosselle Schumacher. Amit believed that as
the head of the principal foreign-intelligence-gathering organization, and with limited resources, Harel had his priorities
dangerously wrong.

Harel now had two major projects underway. Both cases
involved Nazis, but one was an incontrovertible threat to the
very existence of the State. It was this dilemma, according to
those who support Zvi Aharoni's version of events, that prevented Harel from reviving a full-scale hunt for Mengele. The
crux of their argument is that Harel should never have allowed himself to be caught unaware by Nasser's rockets,
clearly of more immediate concern than Mengele. They con-
tend that all his energy was devoted to finding Yosselle Schumacher when he should have been keeping one eye on Nasser's German scientists and also sustaining the Mengele hunt.
Faced with the competing issues of Mengele and Schumacher, Harel had seemed unable to delegate authority. "Isser's problem was that he could only focus on one thing at a
time," said one senior Mossad agent who knew Harel well.
"He was very good on the ground and everybody had a lot of
respect for him. But he was a one-issue man. He had tunnel
vision." By the time the Schumacher case was over, Harel had
to pay dearly for his oversight concerning the rocket scientists. Perhaps if earlier and more reliable rocket intelligence
had been available, more money and manpower could have
been released for the Mengele hunt. The argument is a com-
pelling one. But explanations with the benefit of hindsight
almost always are.

Whatever administrative shortcomings Harel might have

had, it is only fair to note that no Mossad chief has been so publicly passionate about the justice, purpose, and duty of Israel to bring Nazi mass murderers to trial. Perhaps it is in that light that his denial of abandoning the Mengele hunt should be judged:

> After our disappointment [in Brazil] I came to the conclusion that we had to reach Mengele in other ways, more sophisticated ways. I started preparing plans for such ways and preparing the groundwork for a new strategy. But while doing so I resigned.[14]

Harel resigned in April 1963, because the trust between him and his prime minister, David Ben-Gurion, had broken down. This crisis followed Operation Damocles, a letter-bomb campaign against those rocket scientists who had not heeded Harel's anonymous letters warning them to return to Germany. Letter bombs were also sent to the Munich offices of the main Egyptian purchasing agency for the rocket program. Five people were killed, one seriously injured. There were also several failed assassination attempts.

Matters came to a head after a Mossad agent was arrested by Swiss police on suspicion of attempted murder. Furious that the Germans should seek his agent's extradition, Harel attempted to rally cabinet support to ask German chancellor Konrad Adenauer to withdraw the extradition request. But Ben-Gurion refused. Harel, he believed, was behaving irrationally. He thought that such a move would damage Israel's delicate new relationship with Bonn, and he knew the chancellor could not interfere with the due process of law.[15]

There was another factor. An updated assessment from military intelligence, under General Amit, suggested that Harel was now overreacting to the danger posed by the Nazi rockets. Amit's considered judgment was that Nasser had a long way to go before he could build an atomic bomb. And the rockets were much less sophisticated than claimed by Nasser's first bellicose announcement. Amit's agents discovered that research on a reliable rocket guidance system was still in its infancy.

The thrust of Amit's review, now playing down the rocket threat, maneuvered Harel onto the defensive. It was not an enjoyable position for a man who once counted on his prime minister's complete trust. So Harel went onto the offensive, accusing Amit of being complacent over Israel's security and implying that Ben-Gurion was being duped by the Germans in his quest for realpolitik. Had Bonn genuinely wanted to restore meaningful diplomatic relations, he argued, more pressure would have been put on the rocket scientists to disengage from their murderous work with Nasser. "If that is what you believe," Ben-Gurion told Harel, "then I just tell you that I have no faith in the source of your information or the information itself." Such a lack of confidence meant that Harel had no choice but to resign.[16]

Whatever plans Harel might have had for reviving Operation Mengele died with his resignation. "I have often been asked," he said, "what I most regretted about going, and I have always replied that more than anything, I regret not getting that abominable man."[17]

Harel's successor was General Meir Amit. His policy was very clear: the Mossad should devote virtually its entire effort to guaranteeing Israel's future. Faced with the assembled might of the Arab states, the Mossad did not have the resources to resurrect the past. Nazi criminals would be pursued only if solid evidence was presented to the Mossad. Although under General Amit a watching brief was kept on Mengele until the late 1960s, he was no longer a high-priority target. Given future events, it was not a policy that could be seriously challenged. Amit did not know it then, but he was preparing for the 1967 Six Day War. Certainly he has never doubted the wisdom of that fundamental policy change:

> I was not happy with the flow of information on matters that we needed to know about. I came to the conclusion that the information did not flow because the organization was engaging in other things. I think I was right then and I think that I am still right today.[18]

The question that will never be satisfactorily resolved is: just how near did the Israelis come to kidnapping Mengele on the farm twenty-five miles from São Paulo? Were they, as Harel said, not that close? Or was Mengele, as Zvi Aharoni claimed, within their grasp?

Aharoni admitted he did not have conclusive proof that the man he saw on the dirt track near São Paulo in 1962 was Josef

Mengele. But three vital facts now suggest that Aharoni may well have been right. Early in 1962, Mengele was staying with Wolfgang Gerhard while he made the final arrangements for Mengele's move to join the Stammers in Nova Europa. The Mossad's informant, SS man Willem Sassen, was also correct in naming Wolfgang Gerhard as Mengele's protector. Finally, the photographs of Mengele taken during the 1960s—released in 1985—have reinforced Aharoni's belief that the man he saw was indeed his quarry.

One senior Mossad agent on the Mengele hunt recalled that it was Aharoni who finally obtained conclusive evidence of Adolf Eichmann's hideout in Buenos Aires. "Zvi would eventually have found Mengele," the agent said. "It was just a question of time. If we had one more year, we'd have got him. Just one more year, and we'd have had him in Israel, and he would have hanged."[19]

CHAPTER
11

Chasing Shadows

Braving the intimidating stares of President Stroessner's secret police, Nazi-hunter Beate Klarsfeld was testing the limits of Paraguayan free speech. "President Stroessner, you lie when you say you don't know where SS Mengele is," her banner proclaimed in May 1985. It was unfurled on the steps of the supreme court that had granted Mengele Paraguayan citizenship a quarter of a century before. An hour later, the patience of the police ran out. Mrs. Klarsfeld had attracted a small but resolute band of young opponents of Stroessner's unsavory regime, and she was told to move on. Back at the Guarani Hotel in Asunción, the management asked Beate Klarsfeld to pack her bags. Disrespect to the aging dictator is not tolerated by the fawning acolytes of his ruling Colorado party.

Throughout her visit, Beate Klarsfeld had been challenged by an indignant presidential spokesman, Anibal Fernandez, and the owner of a pro-government TV station, Simon Bo, to back her allegations about Mengele with proof. Bo accused her of "making a business of hunting Dr. Mengele." Fernan-

dez said, "She says he is here, but tell us where he is." Beate
Klarsfeld could only respond, "If you think logically, there is
nowhere else he could be."[1]

Two weeks later, on a brilliant autumn afternoon, Josef
Mengele's bones were exhumed from a weed-covered tomb,
his skull held triumphantly aloft for all the world to see. The
place was Embu, Brazil, twenty-five miles from São Paulo,
seven hundred miles east of Asunción.

But the Klarsfelds were not the only casualties of the discovery of the grave at Embu. Simon Wiesenthal, who often
claimed to have been a breathless few paces behind Mengele,
had also been "one hundred percent sure" he was hiding in
Paraguay. For those who have wondered at Wiesenthal's ele-
vation to a kind of international Sherlock Holmes, his charge
was typically absolute. For the Klarsfelds, whose real successes
as self-appointed Nazi-hunters are no idle boast, their certi-
tude in this case was an untimely lapse. How, then, did Paraguay endure as part of the Mengele myth? The Klarsfelds and
Wiesenthal alone cannot be blamed. They were just part of a
stream of bounty hunters and journalists, the authors included, who were certain that somewhere in the darker re-
cesses of the Paraguayan jungle lurked the "Angel of Death."

President Stroessner himself carries a share of the guilt for a
wound to his country's reputation that was largely self-inflicted. As Beate Klarsfeld pointed out, "If Mengele left, the
police must know it; it must be in their files." Stroessner tried
to persuade the world that Mengele had left in 1961 or 1962.
Not once did he or his police attempt to find out exactly where
Mengele had gone. That his government could have done so
through Hans Rudel or Alban Krug is not in doubt. The real
question is why no one believed Paraguay's claim that their
most infamous citizen had flown.

The myth was based on fact. Josef Mengele *had* been in
Paraguay, and as the West German chargé d'affaires, Peter
Bensch, discovered in 1961, he had become a citizen. Thereafter, the onus was on the government of Paraguay to prove
that he was no longer there. It was largely the diplomatic
skirmishes between the West Germans and the Paraguayans,
and their failure to resolve the mystery of Mengele's whereabouts, that allowed fiction to develop out of fact.

Certainly for most of the 1960s and much of the 1970s, the

West German government led everyone to believe that Mengele was likely to be in Paraguay.* As early as 1963, West German chancellor Konrad Adenauer, in one of his last major decisions in office, offered President Stroessner 10 million deutschemarks, about $2.5 million, to extradite Mengele. Eckart Briest, the West German ambassador in Asunción, was told that Adenauer's offer would not be accepted. The suspicion lingered, therefore, not just that Mengele was in the country but that he was being actively protected by the top echelons of the government.[2]

On February 7, 1964, several months after the Adenauer offer had been rebuffed, the foreign ministry in Bonn issued the following statement:

> We can confirm that Mengele is in fact a citizen of Paraguay. He has obtained an identification card and citizenship in Paraguay. The Paraguayan Division of Investigations issued Mengele's file 425.0066 in 1959. That file says that Mengele first visited Paraguay in 1959. The identification document given him in 1959 was 293.348 and on November 27, 1959, citizenship number 809 was issued by the supreme court and signed by Werner Jung and Alejandro von Eckstein.
>
> In the early part of the 1960s, he was often in the south of the country in the frontier of Argentina and Brazil. He later came to Asunción and stayed at the "Astra" boarding house under the name "Peter Fast."
>
> At this time he is in the triangle of three countries and may even be in Brazil.[3]

The statement drew an immediate rebuttal from Paraguayan interior minister Edgar Ynsfran. Smoothly fielding questions at a press conference, the British-trained lawyer noncommittally offered only that Mengele was "not in Paraguay at this time."

For all the ambiguity in the German statement, they clearly

---

* Indisputably, most amateur hunters looked in Paraguay most of the time. But there was police activity in neighboring countries too. In 1964 the Argentine federal police burst into a jungle compound in the north of the country and arrested an eccentric seventy-one-year-old Hungarian doctor on suspicion that he was Mengele. In Brazil, press reports circulated that an Israeli agent close on Mengele's heels had been killed. And in Rio de Janeiro, a former Auschwitz inmate fainted when she saw a man she thought was Mengele. Nonetheless, Paraguay continued to be the focus of the hunt.

believed Mengele was in Paraguay. The following day, Ambassador Briest met with President Stroessner in order to make one final attempt to secure some Paraguayan assistance in the Mengele hunt. In Bonn's statement, the Germans had quoted the Paraguayan government's own police file on Mengele as saying he had entered the country in 1959. That was wrong, of course, since Mengele's first visit was in 1951. But Briest now sought to use this factual error as a reason for Stroessner withdrawing Mengele's citizenship. Briest based his argument on the Paraguayan requirement that an applicant for citizenship reside in the country for five consecutive years prior to filing the application. Briest told Stroessner that since the Paraguayan police file listed Mengele's entry as 1959, it was impossible that he had satisfied the five-year residency requirement for the citizenship granted in November 1959. His citizenship could be revoked, therefore, because it was granted on the basis of a false declaration. Once the citizenship hurdle was out of the way, Briest argued, Mengele could be extradited.

This time the president did not equivocate. Clearly Bonn had not believed his government's numerous denials that Mengele was still on Paraguayan soil. Stroessner took this persistent skepticism as an attack on his personal integrity. He began to bang the table and raise his voice. "Once a Paraguayan, always a Paraguayan," he thundered at Briest, who was warned that if he pursued the matter he would be declared persona non grata.[4]

The president's tantrum had only one effect; it heightened the suspicion that Mengele was indeed in Paraguay, with Stroessner's tacit approval. The absurdity was that for Stroessner the issue had little to do with the question of whether he was conniving with one of the twentieth century's most evil men. It had everything to do with the sanctity of Paraguayan citizenship, which a close ally had dared to question. By such strange axioms did the president rule.

Following Ambassador Briest's humiliating slap-down, the West German judicial authorities toughened their approach. In July 1964, Fritz Bauer, the indefatigable chief prosecutor for the state of Hesse, who was responsible for the Mengele case, raised the reward for his capture from 20,000 to 50,000 deutschemarks, the equivalent of $12,500.[5] Much to the consternation of the West German foreign office, Bauer fired the opening shots in what became a war of words with Paraguay. Bauer's secret dealing with the Israelis during the Eichmann case had shown that he was not a man to sit on the fence. This time, he went public.

Bauer charged that Mengele spent much of his time in Paraguay under his own name, visited Asunción, had a great deal of money and important friends, and freely visited southern Paraguay and a Paraguayan Indian reservation as well as Brazil. But Bauer had scrapped together just fragments of the truth. His information was long out of date. Yet in a truth contest between a senior and respected judicial figure like Fritz Bauer and the interior minister of a government that resembled a bargain-basement version of Benito Mussolini's regime, Bauer was always going to win. Edgar Ynsfran's response two days later—that Mengele was "definitely not in Paraguay but either in Brazil or Peru"—was greeted with contempt.

The storm that Ynsfran provoked broke in the midst of the long-running trial in Frankfurt of SS personnel from Auschwitz. Twenty-one officers, doctors, and guards had been in the dock since December 1963. Gruesome details had emerged about how clerks worked night and day, in shifts at seven typewriters, to make out death reports of prisoners selected by doctors to die in the gas chambers. One name that kept cropping up, and was made most notable by his absence, was that of Josef Mengele. Back came the chilling reminders of his satanic gaze at the railhead ramp. "His thumbs were in his pistol belt," said one witness, Dr. Ella Lingens. "I also remember Dr. König, and to his credit I must say he always got drunk beforehand, as did Dr. Rhode. Mengele didn't; he didn't have to, he did it sober."[6]

The trial itself was covered extensively by the press. Hundreds of witnesses were called, and twenty prosecutors and forty-five defense lawyers were involved. Now Bauer instructed his chief prosecutor, Hans Kuegler, to go on the offensive against the Paraguayan government. Bauer's anger had been provoked by the Paraguayan claim that Mengele was in Peru. Bauer regarded this as a deliberate lie, based on a public-relations fiasco committed by the Lima government just the previous month. The Peruvian minister of government and police, Dr. Juan Languasco Dehabich, had said at a press conference that Mengele had been captured in a straw hut in the Peruvian jungles. His remark had sent newspaper reporters scurrying to Lima from all over the world. On the basis of this report, Bauer himself had asked Bonn to immediately process an extradition request to the Peruvians. The day following the announcement of the Mengele "arrest," the Peruvian government said the minister had been wrong. An official statement claimed that he had thought a reporter was asking about the arrest of a communist agitator named David Livingstone Penn, not Mengele, and it had all been a "momentous misunderstanding."

What had so angered Bauer was his belief that the Paraguayans had prompted the confusion in Peru. Bauer was convinced that the Paraguayans knew Mengele was not in Peru, and that Paraguayan interior minister Ynsfran had issued a public statement placing him in that country in the hope of taking the spotlight off Paraguay. Coupled with the genuine blunder of the Peruvian government regarding the Mengele "arrest," it had been a cheap but effective ploy by the Paraguayans. Bauer did not want them to get off the hook so easily. The Frankfurt trial prosecutor, Hans Kuegler, did not mince words:

> Paraguay is protecting Mengele. We are convinced the protection comes from the highest spheres of the Paraguayan government.[7]

The gloves were off. No statement could have been more precise, more deliberate, more provocative. Three days later, Bauer pursued the matter by calling a press conference to provide evidence for Kuegler's claim.* He announced that he was in possession of "absolutely reliable" information that a Paraguayan of German descent, Werner Jung, had co-sponsored Mengele's citizenship in 1959. He also claimed that the Paraguayans had adopted a new tactic:

> Paraguay is now saying that the Paraguayan citizen José Mengele is not Josef Mengele, the wanted fugitive.

---

* In the midst of this diplomatic flap between Paraguay and West Germany a reporter for the magazine *Bild Zeitung* visited Günzburg to write about Mengele's hometown. On July 8 he was beaten unconscious by a group of youths. No arrests were made.

But it does not sound as though Paraguay is serious in any effort to find Mengele. Interested parties are protecting him.[8]

This time the Paraguayan government did not respond. It was left to Ezequiel Gonzalez Alsina, editor-in-chief of Stroessner's Colorado party newspaper, *Patria*, to tell a group of foreign correspondents that Bauer was "talking garbage."[9] Bauer had certainly got it wrong, well-intentioned though he was. But Ynsfran's head-in-the-sand attitude, offering no proof, responding to the attacks with diplomatic grunts, and smearing Peru, led to Paraguay's defeat in the public-relations battle. Most newspapers now firmly believed that Mengele was being hidden in Paraguay because that was what the West German chief prosecutor believed. What the German foreign office believed is not clear, although it was uniquely placed to find out from its embassy in Asunción. Their staff occasionally met Asunción's seedy clutch of neo-Nazis, who had fastened on to the cocktail party circuit. It would not have been difficult to have gleaned some information from them.

Chastened by Stroessner's attack on Ambassador Briest, the embassy was in fact adopting a very rigid stance. A speculative article in the German magazine *Der Spiegel*, in August 1964, claimed that Mengele had been seen recently in Paraguay. The article prompted the German embassy to ask the Paraguayans if this was so. On September 23, the Paraguayan government issued a statement saying that not only was Mengele not in Paraguay but that "he departed four years ago." Although the statement was true, repeated angry and defensive rebuttals, with no evidence that they were prepared to help in the search for Mengele, had almost exhausted Paraguay's credibility. President Stroessner had become his own worst enemy.[10]

The *Spiegel* article also drew an angry letter from Hans Rudel, who was described in it as one of Mengele's closest friends. The article claimed the two men had recently been on a drinking spree and that Rudel also knew Alban Krug. Mengele, Rudel, and Krug were indeed friends, but the drinking spree was an unlikely event since Rudel was a teetotaler. Of course Rudel denied any knowledge of Krug, to whom he had introduced Mengele. Of more interest was the way he publicly disowned his friend, saying that the suggestion of the relationship was "libelous":*

> Both Mengele and myself lived in former years in South America and that is where I know him from. We were part of the German colonial community and participated in their events. Since then I have had no contacts with Mengele. I was not a friend of his, nor have I ever gone on a drinking spree with him, especially not two or three months ago. My last business trip to South America was in April of this year. I neither saw Mengele nor did I speak to him. I don't know any farmer by the name of Krug and I never spent any time with him in his hunting lodge. I am asking you to print this correction and I would appreciate if you would let me know your sources for those libelous stories about me.[11]

Six days after the Paraguayan announcement that Mengele had not lived in the country since 1960, the West German justice minister, Ewald Bucher, wondered aloud if the solution to Stroessner's intransigence might not be another Eichmann-style kidnapping. There could be no clearer message that Bonn believed Mengele to be hiding with presidential blessing. Bucher told the Haifa Nazi Crimes Documentation Center that his government could never contemplate such action, but perhaps the Israelis should. Behind Bucher's remark lay an undeniable truth. Again and again, the record showed that information trickling through to Bonn was out of date and poorly researched. It was a deficiency that could be remedied by a full-time team of agents, such as the Israelis had deployed in the early 1960s and then abandoned.

But the Germans did not seriously consider extralegal methods of bringing Mengele to justice. Instead they pursued the case within the confines of their legal system. In an effort to make a breakthrough, the West German prosecutors applied to the courts for a search warrant to inspect the house of Hans Sedlmeier, Mengele's longtime friend and family company executive. Fritz Bauer was convinced that if anyone in Germany maintained contact with the fugitive doctor, it was

---

* Mengele's private correspondence, in fact, showed that he and Rudel maintained contact for the rest of their lives. Rudel even intended to visit Mengele in 1978, but had to postpone the trip due to medical treatment at the Mayo Clinic in the United States.

Sedlmeier. Simon Wiesenthal was also convinced that Sedlmeier was a key figure in the Mengele case, and he informed the German prosecutors of his suspicion in a 1964 letter. Their hunches were right. Not only was Sedlmeier the family courier for South American visits to Mengele, but he was also the "post office" for receipt of dozens of Mengele letters. However, when West German police agents burst into Sedlmeier's home in mid-1964, they did not find one scrap of incriminating evidence.* According to Rolf Mengele, unknown to Fritz Bauer and the federal police, Sedlmeier had a high-ranking contact in the local police who warned him of the impending raid. Sedlmeier received a telephone call from his police friend and was told: "We are coming to search your house, make sure we do not find anything." Sedlmeier had plenty of time to ensure that all relevant documents were removed. If there had not been police collusion with Sedlmeier, the Mengele case might very well have been over in 1964, and Mengele would have joined the ranks of defendants at the Frankfurt trial.

The abortive raid on Sedlmeier's house was not publicly disclosed. Yet the Mengele case continued to maintain a high profile in West Germany, based in part on the deep mistrust of Paraguay's public responses and in part on the publicity surrounding the Auschwitz trial. It was not a climate much given to sympathy for Mengele's estranged wife, Martha, when she appealed against the decision by the universities of Frankfurt and Munich to strip Mengele of his medicine and anthropology degrees. In early 1964, Frankfurt University had publicly invited Mengele to come and defend himself against charges that he had violated the principles of the Hippocratic oath, an invitation he declined. Instead, Martha employed Dr. Hans Laternser, one of the defense lawyers at the Auschwitz trial, to act on Mengele's behalf. Laternser claimed that the 1959 indictment against Mengele contained untried allegations, and that some other wartime doctors convicted of experimentation crimes had not forfeited their degrees. But the rectors

---

* On May 31, 1985, West German federal police raided Sedlmeier's house and discovered letters from Mengele, which led directly to the South American protectors and the grave in Brazil. According to Rolf, the 1985 raid was successful because not only had Sedlmeier's local police contact retired but the Mengele case had gone so high in the federal government hierarchy that the local police could no longer interfere.

of Frankfurt and Munich were not impressed. They rescinded his degrees "because of the crimes he committed as a doctor in the concentration camp at Auschwitz."

As a foretaste of what might happen were Mengele ever brought to trial, the rectors' judgment did not bode well. Having read the seventy-five pages of witnesses' statements, they found the testimony credible enough to pronounce Mengele guilty.[12] But most wounding to him must have been the unspoken judgment that academically his work had been devoid of any real scientific merit. Achieving academic status had always been Mengele's driving ambition. The title "doctor" was important to him, as he showed later when he wrote to Rolf urging him to reconsider his decision not to take his doctorate in law:

> From all the arguments you had concerning your intention not to get that doctorate level, I accept the one that says that you lack interest and diligence and hard work. I can't find the right word to express myself . . . anyway, it has affected me badly. Getting the doctorate was actually the only desire which I asked of you in your whole life.[13]

Back in Asunción, meanwhile, Paraguayan credibility was dealt a mortal blow with the arrest of Detlev Sonnenberg, a former SS officer living in Zarzedo, Brazil. He told the police he had seen Mengele several times, the latest being in Paraguay in late 1965. Sonnenberg claimed that Mengele was then practicing medicine. While there was no doubt that Sonnenberg's credibility was suspect—he was given to boasting of his contacts with wanted Nazis—the response by Paraguay's interior minister, Edgar Ynsfran, was breathtaking. Having denied that Mengele was in Paraguay, Ynsfran then asserted that he did not even have Paraguayan citizenship.[14]

One of the few triumphs the West Germans could boast in their hunt for Mengele was a copy of his Paraguayan citizenship paper. Ynsfran's remark was a blatant lie. It gave the West Germans and the press a wholly distorted view of the Paraguayan connection with Mengele, but one which the Paraguayans' dissembling entitled them to hold.

When Hubert Krier succeeded Eckart Briest as ambassador

in 1965, Bonn had given up trying to exert any more pressure on Paraguay. Krier said:

> Before my departure I was given instructions not to do anything concerning the Mengele affair. I was given no explanation for this. An explanation for these instructions was later given to me in Paraguay by the secretary of state. On a visit, he told me that they had come to the conclusion that to demand the extradition of a Paraguayan citizen would be grotesque and senseless. It made sense. Mengele was a Paraguayan citizen and in the government's opinion and my opinion it broke an unwritten international law, namely that a strong state should not demand of a weaker state that it extradite one of its own citizens.[15]

Krier certainly seems to have held to that advice. He adopted a most gentlemanly attitude when he made one inquiry about Mengele at a reception. As Alejandro von Eckstein, who co-sponsored Mengele's Paraguayan citizenship, recalled:

> The ambassador approached me and asked me if I could come by and have a word with him. I said, "Of course, I would be delighted." I was a captain in the reserves then. And I went by and he wanted to talk to me about Dr. Mengele, and I told him that Dr. Mengele had left and I had not heard any more from him since he left. He said, "Excuse me, I'm just carrying out orders from Bonn. Excuse me." We shook hands and that was it.[16]

West Germany's decaying image as a country making amends for its Nazi past suffered another setback on June 30, 1968, with the untimely death of Fritz Bauer, the only man in the country's judiciary who had consistently pursued Mengele. Bauer's tendency to overreact in his public pronouncements had significantly influenced the Paraguayans to excessively defend the integrity of their president. The truth was a casualty lying somewhere in between. Nonetheless, as the *New York Times* recorded in Bauer's obituary, he was a man who had "achieved international recognition for his work to bring Nazi war criminals to justice."[17]

Amidst the confusion as to exactly where Mengele was, only one country knew for certain, and that was Israel. According to a senior Mossad man, they had received reports that Mengele was in Brazil. But the Mossad kept this information to itself. The Six Day War in 1967 had confirmed the view of General Meir Amit, chief of the Mossad, that resources had to be concentrated on the Arab threat. There appeared to be no justification for funding a special task force to review the leads developed by Harel's agents in the early 1960s. In the wake of the war, Israel also underwent a major shift in foreign policy. Jerusalem decided to open an embassy in Asunción. It would have been an ideal base from which to pursue the Mengele hunt clandestinely. But Benjamin Weiser Varon, ambassador from 1968 to 1972, had a much more straightforward mission: "I was sent there to create friends and influence people," he said.

The decision to open an embassy in Asunción was taken soon after January 1, 1968, when tiny Paraguay assumed disproportionate power on the world diplomatic stage by becoming one of two Latin American countries in the UN Security Council. In Varon's view the Council had been a "kangaroo court against Israel for far too long." His special task was to persuade Paraguay to "join a small minority that occasionally still cast a vote for Israel." Hardly a week passed without Varon asking the Paraguayan foreign minister, Dr. Raul Sapena Pastor, for a vote in Israel's favor at the UN. Raising the subject of Mengele was not likely to assist that goal. Thus, on his appointment Varon was "not given any instructions by the foreign office on Mengele of any kind. It wasn't even mentioned."[18]

Nor was Varon told that the Mossad had had teams in Paraguay and Brazil from 1960 to 1962, or that Harel had considered a commando raid on a Paraguayan farmhouse. Indeed, Varon heard of this only after he left office, when Granada Television screened a special *World in Action* program on Mengele, researched by John Ware, in November 1978:

> It was strange that I had to learn all this from the script of the program which Granada sent me after the docu-drama [sic] was shown in England. It proved that it had not been deemed wise to burden me with that

knowledge when I set out on my mission in Paraguay. It also proved that Israel's secret service acts in complete independence of the foreign ministry. On the other hand, Harel's revelations coincided with conclusions that I had reached on my own.[19]

The autocracy of the Mossad aside, Jerusalem had one other good reason for not mentioning the issue to Varon: they knew that Mengele was living in Brazil. But the effect of the diplomatic furor between Asunción and Bonn—in which presidential protection of Mengele had become part of the mythology —soon made its presence felt, according to Varon:

> I was standing with my family at the Buenos Aires airport en route to Paraguay. We met a young Jewish woman and her husband. She introduced us to his father, who was puzzled that Paraguay with its tiny Jewish community rated an Israeli ambassador. Suddenly he had an illumination: "I know why you're going there," he said with a wink, and as I stared at him incomprehensively he whispered into my ear, "Dr. M." Strangely enough, I understood at once.[20]

Varon himself became a victim of the mythology. "Was Mengele really in Paraguay while I was serving there?" he later wrote. "I couldn't have the slightest doubt about it."[21] What really persuaded Varon of this, he said, was the reaction of the government to the plethora of newspaper allegations that Mengele was there. The subject was raised with Varon on several occasions by the foreign minister, Dr. Sapena Pastor, at the request of President Stroessner. But Pastor always stopped short of denying that Mengele was in the country, a sign that Varon, with the notion of Mengele's presence now deeply embedded in his subconscious, took to mean that "he really had at that time one of his homes in Paraguay."[22]

The Paraguayan foreign minister once asked Varon about the source of the Mengele stories and what he could do about them. Many of these stories emanated from Tuvia Friedman, who ran a Nazi crimes documentation center in Haifa, Israel. As Varon explained, the minister was theoretically entitled to his "quid pro quo because of Paraguay's support in the UN."

Varon's task was to persuade him there was genuinely nothing he could do:

> I said, "I hope you will understand the handicaps of a democratic regime. It is utterly beside the point that from government to government the relations between our two countries could be no better. You can believe me that Paraguay's gallant stand at the United Nations is fully appreciated. But we have a free press; it may say whatever it likes. If tomorrow one of our papers were to say that Mr. Eshkol [then Israel's Prime Minister] is a scoundrel and that Mrs. [Golda] Meir is a fool, nothing could be done about it. Now in Israel there are half a million survivors of the Holocaust. For you, *Señor Canciller*, the existence of Dr. Mengele may be a nuisance. For these half million survivors it's an outrage, a provocation, an abomination. There is absolutely no way to silence Mr. Friedman."[23]

Varon's belief that Mengele was in Paraguay was further confirmed when Dr. Pastor seemed to hint that he could not solve the Mengele question alone and that perhaps it would best be dealt with by Israeli commandos. Varon interpreted that to mean that Mengele was hiding within the country's borders, but that the matter was out of Pastor's personal control:

> Possibly it was an intimation of Sapena Pastor's feelings—"Take him away, take him away out of our hands." But he did not speak for the president. And in Paraguay, President Stroessner has the first and the last word.[24]

Although Varon was not privy to the policy of General Amit's Mossad, he did experience firsthand one of the reasons the Mossad had placed other priorities over hunting Nazis. On May 2, 1970, two PLO gunmen charged into his embassy and began shooting wildly. Four Israeli officials were wounded and one was killed. When the terrorists finally reached the ambassador's office, they kicked open the door and aimed at Varon's head. Mercifully for him, all he heard was the click of the gun. Both gunmen had exhausted their bullets. Before they could reload, the Paraguayan police arrived and arrested them. Embarrassed that a diplomatic mission, especially one so newly established, should have been violated on its own soil, Paraguay sentenced the PLO men to fifteen years at hard labor.

In the absence of a "Mengele policy," Varon developed a standard answer to the tips that came in to the embassy about his latest hideout: the Israeli government was not searching for Mengele; the Federal Republic of Germany was. Thus did Varon tell each informant that the appropriate recipient of their information was the West German embassy. "I must confess, I was not so eager to find Mengele," Varon said. "He presented a dilemma. Israel had less of a claim for his extradition than Germany. He was after all a German citizen who had committed his crimes in the name of the Third Reich. None of his victims was Israeli—Israel came into existence only several years later."[25]

Varon's rationale seems heretical in view of the serious, frenzied search for Mengele that began fifteen years later, in 1985, as a last and desperate attempt by West Germany and Israel, at the behest of the United States, to salvage their collective consciences. As the world now knows, they were six years too late.

But into this fifteen-year vacuum, created by Israel's abandonment of the hunt and West Germany's conclusion that it could not locate nor extradite Mengele, jumped the self-appointed Nazi-hunters. The tragedy was that, laudable though their intentions were, their judgment became clouded by their need for publicity. By working to sustain the interest in their search, they inadvertently kept the spotlight on the wrong country—Paraguay.

CHAPTER
12

———
———

"I've Seen Mengele"

———
———

Josef Mengele was a regular visitor to the best restaurants in Asunción, the Paraguayan capital. Naturally, he also visited the German Club—his black Mercedes 280SL regally sweeping up and armed guards jumping out, anxiously surveying the scene. One evening he made a spectacle of himself by slamming his pistol on the bar.[1]

To most people the source for this colorful story was a credible one. It was Simon Wiesenthal, the Nazi-hunter from Vienna, a familiar figure on TV screens. The evidence had come from his network of informants who were said to be scattered around the globe.

Wiesenthal would often claim that his informants had "seen" Mengele. Sometimes they had "just missed" Mengele. One of the closest shaves, according to Wiesenthal, had occurred in the summer of 1960, when Mengele was seeking refuge in Egypt. Concerned for his international image, President Nasser barred Mengele's entry, and the doctor was taken by a former SS *Obersturmführer* Schrawz on a chartered yacht, together with his wife, Martha, to the tiny Greek island of Kythnos. "I was about to leave for Jerusalem to attend the Eichmann trial," Wiesenthal wrote in his book about his sleuthing exploits:*

> If I notified the Greek authorities through international channels, several weeks would be lost. This time, as I often had in the past, I chose a non-routine approach. I called up the editor of a large illustrated magazine in Germany with whom I had cooperated before. The magazine wanted the story. I wanted the man.[2]

Two days later, said Wiesenthal, a reporter from the magazine arrived by boat and was told by the owner of the island's only inn that a "German and his wife left yesterday. A white yacht came into the harbor. The German and his wife went aboard and the yacht left again, heading west."[3] The reporter showed the owner a batch of photographs. "Without hesitation, the innkeeper picked a picture of Mengele. Two monks who happened to come in also agreed that this man had been there only yesterday.

"We had lost another round."

Wiesenthal did hire a magazine reporter. His name was Ottmar Katz. But according to Katz, the rest of Wiesenthal's story was fiction from beginning to end:

> I got the OK from my editor after Wiesenthal asked us by letter to check. Not a single detail in the letter was correct. I spent four or five days on Kythnos. Mengele was certainly not there. There was no monastery. I spent two days with the local justice of the peace, who was strongly anti-Nazi, and we inspected the register of the only hotel, and the only name we thought that was worth checking we discovered belonged to a Munich schoolteacher. I did explain to Wiesenthal that it was all wrong and then seven years later I read his book and he said we'd missed Mengele by a few hours.[4]

In 1967 Wiesenthal claimed to have traced Mengele's movements "quite exactly." At various times he boasted of tracking him to Peru, to Chile, to Brazil, to military installations in Paraguay, always a few paces behind. Mengele was a

---

* *The Murderers Among Us* (London: Heinemann, 1967).

"millionaire," a "doctor"; he was "surrounded by comforts
. . . moreover he lives very close to where Martin Bormann
lives." In 1978 a typical Wiesenthal bulletin on his hunt for
Mengele read:

> Mengele is living in Paraguay, where he is protected
> by the local junta, which is dominated by ethnic Ger-
> mans. Mengele is Number One on our wanted list. Al-
> though his observation in Paraguay and the monitoring
> of his occasional trips abroad has cost us a lot of money,
> we have continued our activities against this arch crimi-
> nal through 1977 and will continue to do so in the fu-
> ture.[5]

The extraordinary thing is that the myth of Wiesenthal's
hunt remained intact even after Mengele's body was discovered. He told reporters that it was he who had tipped off the
West Germans and persuaded them to raid the Günzburg
home of Hans Sedlmeier, where coded letters giving
Mengele's Brazilian address were found. In fact, the breakthrough came from a university professor in whom Sedlmeier
had confided his relationship with Mengele. The few—like
Benjamin Varon, former Israeli ambassador to Paraguay—
who dared to challenge Wiesenthal's role as the world's pre-
eminent Nazi-hunter have been savaged by his supporters at
the influential Simon Wiesenthal Center in Los Angeles. Gerald Margolis and Martin Mendelsohn, counsel to the
Wiesenthal Center, complained about this statement by
Varon:

> He [Mengele] would be a prize catch for any Nazi-
> hunter. But no one has specialized in him. Simon
> Wiesenthal makes periodic statements that he is about
> to catch him, perhaps since Wiesenthal must raise funds
> for his activities and the name Mengele is always good
> for a plug.[6]

Varon's observations drew an intemperate blast from
Messrs. Margolis and Mendelsohn:

> To denigrate Wiesenthal's efforts, as Varon does, is to
> defame a man who has successfully brought to justice
> 1,100 Nazi war criminals; a man who embarked on his

sacred mission in 1945, unlike some recent arrivals who
have embarked with much passion and fury and scant
results in the 1980s.[7]

Varon's response to them went to the very heart of the
matter: money.

> Sometimes in the seventies Wiesenthal confided to
> me in Boston that it was not at all easy to keep his outfit
> in Vienna going. [There was as yet none in Los Angeles.]
> He said that his lecture fees and the contributions of
> some 17,000 Dutch Gentiles went into it. I recounted in
> my article that Wiesenthal maintained for several years
> a steady flow of statements about Mengele sightings in
> different countries. He said in 1980: "Now I cannot say
> where he is, but . . . I am much closer to catching him
> than I was a year ago." In 1982 he offered a $100,000
> reward for information leading to Mengele's arrest and
> claimed that because of the reward "even his body-
> guards would sell him out." It is 1984, and none of these
> predictions have come true. Wiesenthal must be fully
> aware that just finding Mengele does not equal "catch-
> ing" him. And how opportune is it to warn him every
> few months that he is about to be "caught"? On the
> other hand an award of $100,000, which is in no danger
> of ever having to be paid out, is subtle inducement for
> contributing to the Simon Wiesenthal Center: who
> wouldn't gladly part with some money for the prospect
> of catching a genocidal monster?[8]

Margolis and Mendelsohn accused Varon of "profaning
what is profound and trivializing the Holocaust"; Varon replied that the Holocaust was "no one's private property and
should not be invoked in vain." It was an unseemly row,
provoked by a man who avoided pursuing Mengele leads in
South America while he was uniquely placed to do so as the
Israeli ambassador. But Varon had raised an essential truth. As
a survivor of several concentration camps, Wiesenthal's
sincerity was never in doubt. It was financial constraints and a
knack of playing to the gallery that ultimately compromised
his credibility. The truth is that for many years Wiesenthal's
Mengele file at his Vienna office had been a potpourri of

information, which as the London *Times* said, "only sustained his self-confirmatory myths and gave scant satisfaction to those who apparently needed a definite answer to Mengele's fate."[9]

What no one can take from Wiesenthal is his missionary zeal, his success in ensuring that many people and some reluctant governments pursued Nazis when they would have preferred to forget. One must ask: if not Wiesenthal, who else would have performed that role? He really was the public conscience of the Holocaust when few others seemed to care. It was largely on Wiesenthal's self-image of a tireless, dogged sleuth, pitted against the omnipotent and sinister might of Mengele and a vast Nazi network, that two full-length Hollywood films were made. Both *Marathon Man* and *The Boys from Brazil* were box-office hits. They played an important part in keeping Mengele at the forefront of the public's mind, an easily identifiable symbol of the Allies' betrayed pledge to pursue Nazis wherever they fled. But these movies also created a mood of despair: Mengele was simply too powerful, he was too clever, he was "bionic," he would never be caught. And yet . . . he was here, he was there, he was everywhere, said Wiesenthal. He had been seen: he really could be found.

Wiesenthal's information was right on target sometimes, as when he pinpointed Hans Sedlmeier as a key figure in the Mengele conspiracy, as early as 1964. But often Wiesenthal's pronouncements raised the public's expectations, only to dash their hopes each time. But he was not alone. Beate and Serge Klarsfeld, in Paris, once claimed that Mengele was within their grasp. Tuvia Friedman, in Haifa, said his network of informants "provided definite and precise information by which to identify him [Mengele]."[10]*

And there were many others, quite independent of the full-time Nazi-hunters, who claimed to have seen Mengele. They seem to fall into three categories. The first consists of those people who were thirsting for what American artist Andy Warhol once called "the fifteen minutes of fame to which everyone is entitled in their lives." The second category was

---

* Both Wiesenthal and Friedman claim to have found Adolf Eichmann. Wiesenthal says he proved that Eichmann was still alive; Friedman says that Eichmann's first words to his Israeli kidnappers were: "Which of you is Friedman?" Isser Harel, chief of the Mossad team that captured Eichmann, denies that either Nazi-hunter played any role in finding Eichmann.

made up of Fascists who got a sick satisfaction from disseminating false information to throw legitimate hunters off the track. This role was best exemplified by Wolfram Bossert, Mengele's protector in Brazil for the last four years of his life. When Bossert wrote to the Günzburg clan informing them of Mengele's death in 1979, he suggested that it should not be announced so that "the opposing side waste time and money." The third category of Mengele "witnesses" were those who reported in all good faith that they had caught a glimpse of the world's most elusive Nazi criminal.

Sonia Tauber, a survivor from Auschwitz-Birkenau, was a witness whose sincerity was not in doubt. She claimed she saw Mengele in April 1965, when he walked into her jewelry shop in the Casa Inolvidable in Asunción. She said she was paralyzed when she realized that the customer browsing through her showcase diamonds was the man who had spared her life with one flick of his thumb. Her husband said she ran to the back of the shop, ashen, and stammered: "Mengele, that was Mengele."[11]

Even before the Israeli embassy had opened in Asunción, Ambassador Varon was swamped with Mengele sightings:

> I was not yet installed in Asunción when a Paraguayan asked to be received. I let him come up to our hotel suite. He acted mysterious, lowered his voice, and said, "I know where you can find Dr. Mengele." I did not know how to react. I suspected the man had mercenary motives and did not encourage him to go on. He assured me he was not out for the money, he just wanted to see justice done. He described a setting near the Brazilian border, where behind a wire fence surrounding his hideout, I would be able to see the doctor take his daily walk. I thanked my informer and took his name.
>
> Any temptation to take the tips I received seriously was dispelled as soon as the embassy offices were inaugurated. Hardly a week passed without somebody dropping by to offer me news of Mengele's whereabouts. The visitors were old and young, simple and educated, idealists and bounty hunters. But strangely enough, and no matter how sincere many of these informants were, no two tips I received during all these years coincided.

Mengele seemed ubiquitous. He was in the north, east, and west. He was an army doctor, a farmer, a cobbler, an idler.[12]

Another witness whose sincerity was not in doubt was William Orbello, a U.S. Army lieutenant colonel assigned to the American embassy in Asunción. Orbello said that on a visit to the Guarani Hotel in 1969, the Paraguayan army officer accompanying him pointed out Mengele:

> My Paraguayan colleague pointed to this man of dapper appearance wearing a dark gray suit and with close-cropped hair. He told me that it was Mengele. I had no personal knowledge that it was Mengele, but I had no reason to doubt my colleague's word.[13]

Sightings like those reported by Tauber and Orbello came from witnesses who genuinely thought they had seen Mengele. Almost certainly they had not. Mengele's diaries, autobiography, and letters to his family describe his short excursions during the 1960s and 1970s. The overwhelming evidence is that Mengele never risked a venture into Paraguay after late 1960. None of the Mengele sightings reported over the years coincides with a place and time where Mengele is now known to have been. Such sightings, although well-intentioned, mainly served to pinpoint Paraguay, the wrong country, as Mengele's refuge.

Unlike those witnesses who genuinely thought they had seen Mengele, there were many others whose reports served to perpetuate the Wiesenthal fantasy of a fugitive who was armed, dangerous, and wielded presidential power. One imaginative example followed the violent death, in February 1965, of another Nazi on the run in South America, Herbert Cukurs. Cukurs had been a notoriously cruel SS officer, who supervised massacres at the Riga concentration camp from horseback. His battered body was found in a derelict house in Montevideo, Uruguay. He had been savagely bludgeoned to death by a group claiming to be Jewish avengers, as a cable from Bonn to a Montevideo newspaper announced:

> Herbert Cukurs, the executioner of thousands of Jews in Riga, was murdered two days ago in Uruguay by THOSE WHO CANNOT FORGET. His body lies in a

trunk in an abandoned house in Colombia Street near Carrasco.[14]

The Brazilian police became involved in the investigation because Cukurs had traveled to Montevideo from his home in São Paulo shortly before his death. At first they speculated that Cukurs may have been murdered by a group of fellow Nazi fugitives, whom Cukurs, having financial troubles, was preparing to sell out for a reward. But the police soon ruled this out when evidence of Jewish involvement came to light. However, years later, nationally syndicated Washington columnist Jack Anderson resurrected the Nazi reward story. Anderson claimed the fugitive Cukurs was about to betray Mengele himself:

> Cukurs tried to make a deal with the Jewish underground after I published his whereabouts. In return for his own safety, plus $100,000 in cash, he offered to lead them to Mengele. . . . Mengele clearly was the bigger catch.
>
> Cukurs informed the Jewish agents that Mengele was hiding out in Paraguay across the Parana River from the small Argentine town of Eldorado. . . . He warned that it would be impossible to approach the Mengele hideout without being spotted.
>
> Cukurs offered, upon payment of $100,000, to fly the Jewish commandos into the area by seaplane. They could land secretly and approach the unsuspecting Mengele by water.
>
> My sources say that Mengele got wind of Cukurs' doublecross. Not long afterwards, two men showed up in Uruguay on a Lufthansa airliner from Düsseldorf, Germany.
>
> My sources believe he [Cukurs] was slain by the Nazi underground although he had been one of its heroes.
>
> Did Mengele, on hearing of Cukurs' offer to sell him out, order his assassination? My sources believe so.[15]

In fact, Cukurs was killed by a team from the Israeli Mossad.[16] The Anderson story was a well-written piece of fiction, which enhanced the growing legend of Mengele. The image of the well-armed avenging demon was complemented by another from Simon Wiesenthal, portraying Mengele as a man with Houdini-like powers of escape. Wiesenthal claimed that a dozen Auschwitz survivors calling themselves "The Committee of Twelve" missed Mengele by minutes when they tried to kidnap him at the Paraguayan jungle hotel Tirol, near the Argentine border in March 1964. He wrote:

> It was a hot dark night. . . . A few minutes before 1:00 a.m. the men entered the lobby of the Hotel Tyrol [sic], ran up the stairway, and broke open the door of bedroom No. 26. It was empty. The hotel owner informed them that "Herr Dr. Fischer" had left in a hurry ten minutes earlier after getting a telephone call. He had been in such a hurry that he hadn't even bothered to take off his pyjamas.[17]

The story was embellished by Michael Bar-Zohar in his book *The Avengers*, in which he said one of the avenging group was found dead a few days later, shot in the head. According to Bar-Zohar, Wiesenthal claimed the gang first came to see him in Vienna:

> I know about these men. . . . They came to see me, here in my office. They were after Mengele and they asked me for information as to where he was hiding. This "Committee of Twelve" had plenty of money and planned to kidnap Mengele to take him to a yacht and judge him when out at sea.[18]

The difficulty with this story is that the Hotel Tirol had no Room 26, or even a second floor. There was no telephone by which Mengele could have been warned. Finally, Paraguay is landlocked, making the possibility of an escape by yacht to the open sea somewhat ambitious. Nevertheless, the story flourished and was expanded in subsequent retellings.

Even sober people were infected by the fever of the mythical hunt. Alejandro von Eckstein, the Paraguayan army captain who co-sponsored Mengele's Paraguayan citizenship, recalled that during 1965 he was told by the chief of Paraguayan security that Mossad agents were scouring Asunción, looking for Mengele. In fact, Israeli agents had not been in the country for several years. But von Eckstein did not know that:

I was told there were five Israelis that had come to
Paraguay to search for Mengele. I was told to be very
careful.

So I sent my wife to her sister's house. I stuffed my bed
with pillows under the sheets so it appeared that a man
was sleeping there. Then I slept next to the front door,
on the floor, with a pistol next to me. I was ready for
them if they came to my house.[19]

The myth of the "bionic" Mengele was growing. The mere
mention of Mengele's name seemed to provoke a sense of awe
and fear, as if anyone who followed his trail was sure to die.
Rational people did not act in rational ways. The old pistol
that von Eckstein kept by his side in readiness for a shootout
with the Mossad was rusty and had not been fired for twenty
years. Right up to the moment Mengele's death was revealed,
reporters were scouring the Hotel Tirol looking for souvenirs
left by the fictional "Committee of Twelve."

One other sensation-seeker on the Mengele trail also succeeded in fooling everyone right up to the day Mengele's
bones were found. Adolfo Cicero, a Brazilian TV reporter,
claimed to have shot a three-second film clip of Mengele in
1966. This now famous film shows a slightly built man dressed
in a light sport shirt, with dark receding hair and a moustache,
half turning toward the camera. A blowup photograph from
the film was used to illustrate every major Mengele story in
newspapers, magazines, and TV stations around the world.
For a time even camp survivors, the West German prosecutors, and the Nazi Crimes section of Israel's police believed
the picture was Mengele. It was also printed on Interpol
memoranda. The skull shape, jawline, ears, and hairline of the
man in the photograph did show a remarkable degree of
consistency with known pre- and postwar photographs of
Mengele. On this basis, Dr. Fritz Bauer, in charge of the West
German judicial investigation, said he believed the picture
was genuine.

The film was shot by Cicero for a documentary on Mengele
by Czechoslovakian TV. Cicero claimed that he had paid for
information from an Argentine intelligence agent, and that
Mengele was traveling under the name "Dr. Engwald" from a
jungle hideout in Paraguay to Eldorado, Argentina. He would

be sailing up the River Parana on a boat called the *Viking*, named in honor of his Waffen SS division.

Cicero claimed that he waited for several days with ten-year-old photographs as his only reliable guide for identifying his quarry. Just as he was losing hope, Cicero spotted a man he thought was the fugitive doctor. Using an 8 mm camera, he immortalized him for precisely three and a half seconds:

> Suddenly I saw him walking in front of me. It was so simple. Then when he realized he was being filmed, he ran off immediately.

Perhaps the next part of the Cicero adventure should have been more closely scrutinized by those who believed he had got his man:

> I was told that night by a local policeman that I was running a high risk and playing with my life. He told me that within the past several weeks two bodies of Jewish avengers were found in the Parana, one mutilated but disguised as a priest.[20]

As a result of the Cicero story, everyone was looking for the wrong man. Notwithstanding worldwide media attention and distribution of wanted posters (with the wrong face), neither the man in the photo much less the real Auschwitz doctor was ever found. But Cicero's initial credibility added to the feeling that Mengele was ubiquitous, with a finely honed sixth sense for danger. The sighting sickness spread.

"Gustav M.," a German immigrant in Altos, on Paraguay's border with Argentina and Brazil, told an Argentine journalist that Mengele lived on a large farm in Altos with "a beautiful woman. He certainly liked women. He looked great for his age; he looked fit and his skin was tight. And he liked to dance and socialize."[21]

Detlev Sonnenberg, the former SS man who the Brazilian police were convinced was intimately linked with high-ranking fugitive Nazis, claimed in 1967 to have known "both Josef Mengele and Martin Bormann very well. I've recently seen Josef Mengele twice." He said that Mengele was living in Paraguay and, like Bormann, had had plastic surgery. "I can even give you the hours they go out and the places they frequent in La Paz and Asunción," Sonnenberg boasted.[22]

Joao Alves, a light-aircraft pilot, claimed that several times he had ferried Mengele under the alias "Dr. Fritz Fischer" between southern Brazil and a small hotel in southern Paraguay. "He was a peaceful man who liked to play with German watchdogs," Alves said. "Another doctor accompanied him but I don't remember his name. One day, a year ago, these two stopped coming here. It's no fun to be around a Nazi, you know. These people are half crazy."[23]

At the same time, a boatman named Osnelho Canilha claimed to have taken Mengele many times across the River Parana, which separates Paraguay from Brazil and Argentina:

> I took this bearded man to Puerto Lopez. He remained silent but I recognized him even with his beard. He had a sport shirt on and did not carry any luggage. He was in a terrible hurry to get to Paraguay. We traveled alone and we did not say a word to each other. When we arrived he did not even thank me.[24]

However fanciful these sightings were, they made the South American authorities look inept and indifferent, and put them on the defensive. The Brazilian police, with commendable vigor, went on the offensive. But the result was a fiasco. In May 1966, they announced they had arrested Mengele at the frontier outpost of Cascavel, near the Paraguayan border. It was their sixth false alarm in five years. This "Mengele" turned out to be a young German wanderer whose requests, in German, for immediate release were misinterpreted by his Portuguese captors as a confession that he was the Nazi doctor.[25] Before the mistake was discovered, prominent South American newspapers and foreign wire services had extensively covered the "arrest."

This was soon followed by one of the most extravagant claims. The London *Sunday Times*, a paper not usually given to flights of fancy, reported the assertions of a former Nazi corporal, Erich Karl Wiedwald, that Mengele had joined the Paraguayan army as a doctor, with the rank of major, and was posted in a military zone in northeastern Paraguay. Wiedwald boasted that his inside knowledge stemmed from his days as "bodyguard to Martin Bormann," who, he said, had undergone plastic surgery and was dying of stomach cancer. The giveaway was Wiedwald's claim that SS *Gruppenführer* Richard Glucks, the second inspector of concentration camps, was alive in Chile. Actually Glucks had committed suicide in British custody at Flensburg prison on May 10, 1945. Yet the Mengele part of Wiedwald's claims somehow stuck.[26]

There was one witness, however, whose sense of adventure on the Mengele hunt outmatched everyone else's. Erich Erdstein, a former Brazilian policeman, actually claimed to have shot the man dead. Erdstein was born in Vienna but moved to South America, where he served in Brazil's criminal investigation division in the state of Parana. As an ex-cop, Erdstein managed to convince some newspapers that he was about to kidnap Mengele, and he sold the European rights to his story in advance to a German correspondent representing a leading daily. He also sold the South American rights to the editor of Parana's largest-circulation paper. The sight of Erdstein ludicrously decked out in wraparound dark glasses at all hours of the day and night, permanently carrying his "best friend," a Taurus .38-caliber revolver, seems not to have alerted those newspapers to the possibility that they were dealing with a spinner of tales.

Erdstein claimed to have the approval of the Brazilian police for his kidnap plan. He said he would seize Mengele on one of his frequent trips from Argentina to Paraguay. Then he would hand him over to the Argentine frontier police. They in turn would dispatch Mengele to Judge Jorge Luque in Buenos Aires, who would activate West Germany's long-standing extradition request.

Erdstein claimed to have four armed agents scouring southern Brazil for Mengele. He said they had succeeded in capturing Mengele, only to have him freed by corrupt police in the Parana state capital, Curitiba. But word soon reached Erdstein that Mengele planned to cross the River Parana from Pôrto Mendes, as he explained:

> I took two of my best agents and my son to Pôrto Mendes and laid a trap for Mengele. He arrived with Walter Bernhardt, a former sailor from the battleship *Graf Spee*, who was to navigate him across to Paraguay.

This fiction appeared prominently as a blow-by-blow account in many reputable European newspapers and magazines, and later in Erdstein's book, *Inside the Fourth Reich*. It went on to describe how Mengele was bundled onto a boat that was intercepted as they sped to rendezvous with an Argentine patrol boat:

> Then an antiquated Paraguayan gunboat came out of the darkness and started shooting. Before we knew it, six men with submachine guns clambered aboard our boat and tried to take Mengele away. I drew my pistol and my son took out his gun. We opened up at the same time. I hit Mengele twice in the chest and neck and then I saw him slump over the side with his head and torso under the water and his feet caught in some ropes.
>
> I was sure Mengele was dead. If the bullets didn't kill him, he would have drowned because his head was under water for several minutes.[27]

The date Erdstein gave for succeeding where the Mossad and everyone else had failed was September 1968. In October, Erdstein fled South America. "After I killed Mengele, there was no way for me to stay," he said. "I wouldn't have lived long."[28] The real reason for Erdstein's hurried departure was that he was wanted by the Brazilian police for passing bad checks. Today, at seventy-seven, he still sticks to his story. Confronted by the evidence that Mengele died of a stroke while swimming, the feisty Erdstein said, "Well, I must have shot a double then."[29]

The only consolation to the authors of all these inventive accounts was that the world's most touted gatherer of information, the Central Intelligence Agency, did not fare much better. On November 19, 1970, the CIA considered the following report from one informant worth recording:

> He had heard from an unnamed friend that Dr. José [sic] Mengele was residing [at] Villa Curuguaty as recently as 25 October (Curuguaty located N.E. of Asunción approx 24 Kms from Brazilian border in department of Caaguaz). Mengele was working as an auto mechanic.[30]

The next day, however, unnamed informants told the CIA station in Asunción that, although others were skeptical, they "agree with the pronouncements of the GOP [Government of

Paraguay] to [the] effect [that] no information has come to light in recent years to indicate Mengele in Paraguay."[31]

It took ten years of wild rumors before this first sane glimmer of analysis appeared. Mengele may not have been a mechanic, but he was leading a mundane lifestyle. And as the report said, he was not in Paraguay.

Little of all this drama filtered through the Brazilian bush to "Pedro" on his farm in Serra Negra, cut off as he was from the daily news. Jungle hideouts with armed guards and killer dogs, face-to-face confrontations with Israeli secret agents, last-second reprieves from Wiesenthal's worldwide network of sleuths, Eric Erdstein's bullet through the head—no one would have marveled at his immortality more than the authoritarian farmhand at Serra Negra.

C H A P T E R
13

"He Was an Impossible Man"

A tense psychodrama—with the two warring factions under one roof—had developed on the farm at Serra Negra. Mengele and the Stammers were now inexorably joined within the same four walls, each dependent on the other, and there was no retreat from the developing friction between them.

Mengele had never lived alone in South America, and he felt that he needed the protection of the Stammers. He was prepared to pay any price—and that was why the Stammers needed him. Mengele bought a one-half interest in the spartan Serra Negra farm with the money he made from his business ventures in Argentina and land sales in Paraguay. Although they had no electricity or telephone, their standard of living had noticeably improved thanks to Mengele. They had bought new farm machinery, and the Mengele family in Günzburg had financed a new car.*

---

* In his letters, Mengele often complained that his family was not providing him with enough money. Both Mengele and Geza Stammer thought the car was too small and cheap.

But sharing their lives so intimately with this authoritarian intruder was exacting a terrible strain on the Stammers. During the thirteen years Mengele stayed with them, he tried increasingly to dominate the household. He interfered in almost every part of their daily lives. He told them how to spend their money, and he criticized them for failing to provide their children a "classical" education. He interfered in their married life, often counseling Gitta on what he considered the "character flaws" in her husband. Mengele even forbade the Stammers to speak their native Hungarian in the house or at the dinner table. He became so paranoid that he thought they were plotting against him whenever they spoke in Hungarian. Gitta recalls, "He said, 'I forbid it. In my presence you have to speak German.' "

To make matters worse, Geza Stammer enjoyed provoking Mengele. A carefree Hungarian who liked to drink and sing and enjoy the good life, Geza resented the authoritarian and grumpy Mengele. He might also have suspected that his wife and Mengele had more than a platonic relationship. Geza thought it was good sport to taunt Mengele by ridiculing his race theories: "We are a different race. We are Hungarians. But we are certainly every bit as good as you Aryans." Mengele would get furious. There were shouting matches, sometimes lasting day and night. "They were always fighting; they were never close," says Gitta. Wolfram Bossert, Mengele's last protector, once told Mengele that he should respect the opinions of the Stammers since he was merely a guest in their house. Mengele shouted, "I own half of all of this and I will do as I please."

Since Geza Stammer refused to be intimidated by Mengele, and the Stammer children, Miki and Roberto, tried to ignore him, only Gitta was left for Mengele's abuse. Through the years, Gitta became an intellectual punching bag for Mengele. Usually she was the only audience for his interminable lectures on evolution, philosophy, morality, and housekeeping budgets. The decadence and decline of West Germany was a favorite theme: "The new stratum of leaders in Germany is made up for the most part of traitors, separatists,

Stammer eventually gathered the extra money and purchased a larger car. Mengele wrote a bitter letter to Günzburg telling them of the "luxurious" new car, bought without their assistance.

deserters, rats and clerical shady characters," Mengele wrote
in his diary.[1]

But it was his sermons on parental discipline—advising the
Stammers on their two children's education, urging them to
be stricter—that they found hardest to take. The Stammers'
eldest boy, Roberto, grew to resent Mengele, because he attempted to behave like a father when Geza was away. "My
son detested him," said Gitta. "Peter was always ordering him
to do this, do that. My son would say, 'Well, why should I?
You're not my father.' "

To the Stammers, Mengele was becoming an impossible
man, now cold, distant, as well as authoritarian. "As time
passed he even began to behave as if he was a superior human
being," said Gitta Stammer. What's more, there seemed to be
no escape. "We were far away, isolated, alone," she said, "far
away from everything and everybody. We waited and things
became more complicated because everybody was nervous
and tense."[2]

As Rolf Mengele later learned, the tension became unbear-
able:

> The relationship was terrible for both my father and
> the Stammers. He was very organized and precise and
> they were much more like the local Brazilians. It used to
> drive him crazy, even little things. For instance, he
> would put pencils and pens in one place. They would
> use them and leave them scattered everywhere. It used
> to make him furious. They were very different people.[3]

At times of crisis, Wolfgang Gerhard appeared and tried to
calm things. During one explosive period in 1969, Hans Rudel
suggested to Gerhard that Klaus Barbie, the "Butcher of Lyons," who was hiding in Bolivia, was willing to provide refuge
for Mengele. But Mengele balked at the idea. He did not want
to move again. He had become used to his solitary life, sinking
deeper into a state of isolated introversion, seeking refuge in a
newfound passion for flowers, Mozart, Haydn, existentialism,
and German philosophers. "Time and again," Mengele wrote,
"I find consolation with Goethe, Weinheber, Mörike, Rilke,
Novalis and all the others. Because of them it's worth being
German."[4]

To the farmhands, their boss, "Pedro," remained a complete enigma—silent, morose, patrolling the coffee plantation and cattle fields with an entourage of fifteen or more yapping mongrel dogs. As one farmhand described them, they were "thin, skeletal-like, standing next to him like toothpicks." And always there was the bush hat, pulled down over the prominent forehead that he feared was his Achilles' heel. To "Pedro" all visitors were still deeply suspect. Mengele would ask, "Who are these people? What side are they on? What are their politics?"

As at Auschwitz, orders were signaled, not spoken—a finger waved in disapproval, with a frown. Monotonously, he complained to the Stammers that the Brazilians were work-shy. "He was hard to work for," said farmhand Ferdinando Beletatti. "I never saw him smile."[5] "Pedro" did not tolerate mistakes. Gitta recalls one incident in which a farmhand finished a small construction job poorly: "Peter started a fight with the worker. He even wanted to stab the old man. We tried to calm him down because we were afraid of the police. We gave the old man money [$250] and sent him away."

Mengele's hero, according to another farmhand, was Hitler. "He told me he was a German who came to Brazil after the Second World War," said José Siloto. "I asked him what he thought about Hitler. He said Hitler was a great and very intelligent man."* At the mention of Jews he just went "totally cold," according to Gitta Stammer. "He didn't talk much about Jews but when he did he did not fly into a rage. He said they were a people who had no reason to be in Germany."[6]

To avoid the increasing conflicts Mengele spent more time in solitary pursuits. Carpentry became a favorite pastime. After five years of manual labor, he had begun to show real skill as a craftsman. He completely remodeled and rebuilt the farmhouse. He relaid the floorboards and rebuilt the windows, doors, and ceilings too. Mengele displayed a curious fascination for arches. He used them everywhere in his building work, on bookshelves, tables, even the windows in his watchtower.

---

* Mengele's writings offer conflicting opinions regarding Hitler. In a letter to Rolf dated August 17, 1975, Mengele referred to Hitler as the "Man of the Century," and compared his regime to "those of Alexander the Great, Charles XII of Sweden, Frederick the Great (of Prussia) or Napoleon." However, in a July 27, 1962 diary entry, Mengele had not been so complimentary. He wrote that Hitler "was a mixture of brilliant intelligence with a smattering of superficial education, that necessarily led to oblique and wrong ideas."

Early in 1969, the Stammers moved to within twenty-five
miles of São Paulo because their two sons had finished school
and Geza wanted to be nearer the city for his job. They
bought a comfortable four-bedroom house set on two acres on
a hilltop at Caieiras, in Jardin Luciana, in the state of São
Paulo. Mengele financed half the purchase of the new house
with the proceeds of the Serra Negra sale, which he had
helped buy in 1962.[7] This time Mengele stayed behind for
several months and joined the Stammers only when all the
arrangements were completed.

At Caieiras Mengele tried to spend more time working on
the grounds and less time arguing with the Stammers. He
built a stout log fence around the farmhouse, with a white
wooden gate and a secure lock. He devoted much care to
planting lemon trees and lovingly tended young shrubs. He
also developed a fondness for an elderly horse and felt safe
enough to be photographed feeding it, the first photographs
he allowed the Stammers to take. He was an eccentric figure,
fifty-eight years old now, white-haired, still wearing the hat,
puttering around the grounds, sometimes unshaven, wearing
knee-high boots. "He was clearly an educated man," said Luiz
Carlos Luz, who was friendly with the Stammer children.
"But he didn't speak Portuguese very well, and sometimes I
had difficulty understanding him."[8] Laerte de Freitas, who
later bought the Stammers' house, thought he had an "intelligent and contented face. When I went to the house Pedro
would meet me at the gate, make conversation and get me
something to drink. When he talked about a plant or a tree he
showed that he really enjoyed it."[9]

But the change in scenery did nothing to relieve the tension
between the Stammers and Mengele. "The same old story
happened again," said Gitta. "He had just become an impossible man." Wolfgang Gerhard, realizing the relations between
the two sides were approaching the breaking point, played
one last card. He decided there was no choice but to integrate
Mengele into another set of friends in the hope that they
would eventually take him off the Stammers' hands.

The couple he chose, Wolfram and Liselotte Bossert, were
Austrians like himself. Politically, the Bosserts were, as Gerhard later said, "reliable." Wolfram was a former German
army corporal and spoke passionately of the injustice Ger-

many had suffered in being "dragged before the victors." In Bossert Gerhard discerned a quality that was missing in the Stammers. Wolfram was something of a philosopher, known to his neo-Nazi circle of friends as "Musikus." He and Gerhard had often discussed German literature, politics, and philosophy, though Gerhard confessed to being rather out of his depth. Mengele would be a more suitable conversational partner in every way. Bossert wanted to broaden his horizons. Gerhard calculated that he would be an ideal student and recipient of Mengele's monologues.

One day soon after Mengele and the Stammers had moved to Caieiras, Gerhard appeared with the Bosserts. Wolfram Bossert remembers his introduction to Mengele:

> It was only when I moved to the vicinity of São Paulo, to Caieiras, where I worked as a maintenance manager with a paper manufacturing company . . . [that] Gerhard took the opportunity to find another discussion partner for Mengele, who was leading a very isolated life.
>
> I was introduced to Mengele—he introduced himself as Peter Hochbichler. The Stammer family knew him only as Peter, while the other people called him Señor Pedro. After that, some form of mutual relationship developed.[10]

Even though the Bosserts did not know that "Peter" was a Nazi fugitive, it is doubtful that would have made any difference. "When I discovered who he was I felt sorry for him," said Wolfram. "He was the most hunted, persecuted man in the world." Liselotte Bossert shared her husband's sympathy when she discovered he was the Auschwitz doctor:

> I found out a bit later than Wolfram. I know that I was shocked and that I felt it unfair he had involved a family with small children. But, somehow, we had already developed friendly relations, and for humanitarian reasons, and out of Christian love for one's neighbor, we simply went along with it. Although the man was being sought, we only knew him as a highly cultivated gentleman. And we carried on as though we didn't know anything.

There was some sort of suppression psychosis in that we simply pushed it out of the way. Because it was simply too dangerous to think about it, to realize that this was the man. And that's how we left it. And because our children were still very young, he was simply the Uncle for us and for our children.[11]

As Gerhard predicted, a solid relationship was established, and soon Mengele became a regular guest at the Bosserts' home. Every Wednesday, Wolfram collected him from the Stammer farm, and drove Mengele to his comfortable home a little over a mile away. There Mengele had supper, played with the Bosserts' two children, talked, and listened to music. Shortly before midnight, Bossert drove Mengele back to the Stammers'.

At the weekly meetings, Bossert and Mengele talked long-ingly of the "eternal values" of prewar German life. Personality differences surfaced but politically, ideologically, philosophically, they thought as one. Mengele developed a powerful hold over Bossert, who came from humbler origins, having finished the war as an army corporal. In Mengele, Bossert found a spiritual home for his obsession about restoring "the virtues of race, creed, class, and kind." He admired Mengele. Bossert fondly recalls their discussions:

Since he lived in a permanent state of fear, fear that someone, somewhere, might find him, he was filled with an anxiety and a tension. This tension was released in his chats with me. He sometimes became very agitated in discussions, very authoritarian, very domineering.

The talks between Mengele and myself were very interesting at all times. . . . We hardly ever talked about political matters. It was generally about our views of the world, the future of mankind, the evolution of man, archeology, and the ecological problems, i.e., the destruction of nature and about the evil of materialism.

These were perhaps the main topics of our discussions. And these always took place at a certain intellectual level, because Mengele was a doctor of philosophy [sic—Mengele's PhD was in anthropology] as well as medicine. I tried to follow his thoughts and contributed as an interested layman, so to speak. I could imagine that, in earlier days, he would have been the life and soul of café society—a person who liked to look elegant and to be surrounded by beautiful women, a witty talker, always at the center of things, organizing parties.[12]

Not only did Bossert fawn over Mengele but they also shared the same views on important ideological issues. They both held the elitist racial view that "it is a fact that the poorer strata of society, the more primitive people, the intellectually less endowed, have large numbers of children, while those who are more intelligent and who have got somewhere in academic or material terms hardly have any children." They favored forced sterilization, "although we realized that this would be difficult," in order to reduce the number of "primitive births." Mengele and Bossert also shared the same anti-Semitic bias. Bossert recalls that he and Mengele agreed that Jews had created their own problems during the war by dominating most of the professions, and "dishonorable money businesses, like money-lending and money-changing," before the war.

In Bossert, Mengele had found a true ideologue and soulmate. Even today, six years after Mengele's death and confronted by the mass of evidence of Mengele's wartime crimes, Bossert defends his former friend: "He was not an evil person. He always had the greatest respect for human life. I believe only a fraction of all the things he is accused of." Not once did Bossert think of handing Mengele over to the police:

Once you know someone well and become friends, someone who likes nature, children, animals, and is interested in literature and philosophy, it becomes very difficult to believe that this person could have committed such cruel crimes. It's easy to say that knowing a criminal, every citizen has an obligation to denounce him. But if you know someone intimately, even if he's a wanted man—I just couldn't do it.[13]

Soon after Mengele formed his friendship with the Bosserts, Hans Sedlmeier flew in from Germany, on behalf of the Günzburg clan, to test the rising temperature in the Mengele-Stammer feud. He tried to pacify the Stammers, promising that alternative arrangements would be made but apparently not offering any more money.[14] Sedlmeier asked Bossert to report on the state of both parties. Bossert, despite his admiration of Mengele, later confided one criticism: "He thinks everybody else ought to devote themselves to him in a selfless fashion, while he himself must only use them according to his own aims." In another dispatch to Sedlmeier, Bossert described the tensions produced by the complex interdependence between the Stammers and Mengele:

> From one side—cleverly—an ensnaring net of human and financial threads is being woven, from which the other side is struggling to escape in order to get away from this attrition of nerves.[15]

The Bosserts certainly did what they could to defuse the situation, offering to take Mengele on a jungle exploration holiday with them in the autumn of 1969. Mengele was delighted. For the first time, his diary betrays just how unhappy he had become with his fugitive life. After years of isolation and feuding with the Stammers this simple holiday, Mengele's first in a decade, was an adventure of a lifetime:

> The sun had come up and "sang as of old," white flags hung in the sky which started to pile up in large shapes in a southerly direction. A wind, full of morning freshness, from the northeast, kept these cloud ships moving softly and rustled through the leaves of the neighboring eucalyptus trees. The beautiful day had been well chosen for the start of the holiday and promised to give our journey a good start. All I needed was my traveling companion and the Volkswagen that went with him.
>
> I had just carried my luggage into the covered porch of the house when the pack of dogs, with their excited barking, announced the arrival of a vehicle on the approach road, which was hidden by woods. One can always rely on their announcement because our house mongrels can distinguish between an arriving car and one that is rushing past on the tarmac road.
>
> Shortly afterward Mu* stopped in front of the house

---

* Mengele's code name for Wolfram Bossert.

with prearranged holiday punctuality. As always, his even-tempered good-morning smile pleased me . . .

We were nevertheless still more than 400 kilometers away, and from base camp "O" of our expedition onward, we would have to carry these many kilos on our male shoulders. But even this proposition could not reduce our pleasure at the beautiful autumn day that we drove into. . . . Our guides took us through various little towns and industrial suburbs of the capital. Its dusty, smokey, and smelly ugliness we only perceived from the perimeter, because our senses were so preoccupied by the expectations and promises of the jungle days.

On the three-lane "highway" which had been built according to the most modern road construction techniques, zooming along at top speed one really had more of a sensation of flying than driving. . . . Pretty whitewashed farm and tourist houses greet us, light green patches of canna plants interrupt the monotonous tired green of the grazing land. . . . If a little village has been formed, then usually a pointed church spire sticks out, and unfortunately, yes, unfortunately, also the ugly TV antennas.

Beautiful white clouds on a radiant blue sky remained our faithful companions throughout the rapid journey. . . . A mountain chain, which had appeared on the horizon, informed us that the end of our winged motorway journey was near.[16]

This holiday at the turn of the decade was a watershed for Mengele. It marked the point at which he finally felt able to venture out, sensing perhaps that the hunt for him had long since run out of steam. For nearly ten years Mengele had bided his time in rural isolation. The move within reach of the São Paulo suburbs changed all that. "Until he knew the language, until he got inside Brazilian life, he was afraid," said Gitta Stammer. "But when we lived in Caieiras he felt more secure. He would go on a bus, go to the city, do some shopping, get the train."[17]

The Bosserts were the motivating factors in Mengele's change from strict isolation to a more open lifestyle. Liselotte Bossert recalls the gradual change:

Shortly before he came to São Paulo, he was incredibly shy, trying not to look if someone went by. But because we behaved normally, we helped him regain his normal social behavior, to become a social animal again. He realized that not everybody was seeking to find something else in him than the person he appeared to be.

I remember it well; in Caieiras, he was always frightened and wanted to escape if we met someone on our walks. So that we said to ourselves that this could not continue because otherwise the whole thing would become known and people would soon find out that he was somebody else.[18]

The Bosserts resolved to help bring Mengele out of his frightened shell. Wolfram began by persuading Mengele to stop wearing his hat in the middle of the sweltering Brazilian summer. He convinced him that by placing his hands in front of his face when people passed near him, he attracted attention as a suspicious person. Bossert had his children take Mengele on the subway so that he could learn how to use it and how to get around the city. He took many pictures of Mengele so that he could "become familiar and comfortable with his own appearance." He even took Mengele into crowded public areas, so that he would realize that people did not recognize him as the Auschwitz doctor. Bossert recalls, "Once I took him to the supermarket. The tension and stress he was under in that place made him sweat. He thought all the people in there were looking at him and nothing else. But eventually, he managed to go into town by himself. He went to the doctor, the dentist, and even for walks on his own." He had begun to lose his sense of fear.

C H A P T E R
14

———
———

Greetings from Afar

———
———

The "new," confident Mengele had also become a man of
property, as owner of a $7000 apartment in a high-rise build-
ing in the center of São Paulo. He acquired it as partial settlement for his share of the farm sale at Serra Negra. For security, the deed was registered in the name of the Stammers'
son, Miki. But the rent went to Mengele.

Although he led a frugal life at the Stammers' farmhouse in
Caieiras, Mengele never had a surplus of cash. His personal
writings often reflect his money concerns. Occasionally he
borrowed money from either the Stammers or the Bosserts to
tide him through difficult periods. "I'm running out of money,
but Mu [Bossert] loaned me 400 [currency not mentioned] on
our last Wednesday meeting" is typical of many diary entries.
On other occasions when his cash completely dried up, Hans
Sedlmeier flew in from Günzburg with bundles of dollars. His
air fares were paid by the family firm, the cost disguised in the
form of miscellaneous expenses. The cash payments, however, came straight from the pocket of Mengele's nephew,
Karl Heinz. But Mengele was hopeful that his new apartment

investment would provide him with a steady and plentiful income. When he later rented it for $225 a month, he noted, "With that amount I shall try to make my living, and believe me, it's not so easy."

As he tried to develop some financial independence, a further boost to Mengele's confidence came in 1971 when he inherited a priceless Brazilian identity card. It belonged to Wolfgang Gerhard, the man who had helped him through every major crisis, from his darkest days after the Eichmann kidnapping to his explosive rows with Gitta and Geza Stammer. The opportunity to assume Gerhard's identity arose when he decided to return to Austria to find his "fortune" there.

With the help of Wolfram Bossert, a competent amateur photographer, Mengele accomplished a tolerable forgery. Bossert took dozens of passport-size photos of Mengele and then selected the one that best fit Gerhard's description. The laminated identity card was spliced open, pictures of the moustachioed Mengele, his hair neatly combed, were stuck over the photograph of his Nazi friend, and the card was relaminated. All the other details remained Gerhard's, including his thumb print and his date of birth, which transformed Mengele, then sixty, into a very old-looking forty-six-year-old, the age listed on the card. Although Mengele was terrified of having to produce the card, it reassured him that in a tight spot he at least had a first line of defense.

Mengele soon found that Gerhard's parting gift would cost him dearly. After he went back to Austria, Gerhard's wife, Ruth, developed terminal cancer. And then his son, Adolf, was also found to be suffering from cancer. With his wife dying and his son fighting for his life, it was now Gerhard who needed help—to pay the enormous medical bills. Mengele could hardly refuse. He owed Gerhard his liberty, and probably his life.

In July 1972, Mengele himself fell ill. Over the years he had lived in such a state of tension and anxiety that he had developed a nervous habit of biting the end of his walrus moustache. Eventually he swallowed so much hair that it developed into a ball that blocked his intestines. His condition became so painful and dangerous that he took the risk of admitting himself to a hospital in São Paulo. For the first time his new identity card was put to the test, and it nearly failed. A puzzled doctor treating Mengele told Bossert that his patient seemed physically very old for a forty-seven-year-old man. Bossert told the doctor that the date of birth was incorrectly entered on the identity card, and that the Brazilian government had promised to correct it with a new card. The doctor accepted the barely credible explanation. If the doctor had taken a slightly greater interest in the physical discrepancy he noticed, the Mengele case might have ended seven years before his death. Instead, Mengele was treated, paid the bill in cash, and was released, under the name of Wolfgang Gerhard. Mengele later wrote that his biggest problem was that he had constantly to fight the temptation to discuss his ailment with "my fellow peers," lest this betray his extensive medical knowledge and arouse the suspicion that the patient was himself a doctor.

This early period of the 1970s, when Mengele integrated himself into modern-day life, also marked the start of a period of prolific correspondence with his family, particularly his son, Rolf, and his childhood friend Hans Sedlmeier. Usually several pages long, these letters laid bare Mengele's emotions. As private correspondence they were stripped of the literary excesses that often marked his personal diary and autobiography, for Mengele never intended his letters, unlike his other writings, to be read by outsiders.* That is why they are probably a more accurate guide to his real nature. They portray an embittered Nazi of failing health, dissatisfied with almost everything, an unrepentant, tiresome, and inhumane old man, yet one who is tortured by the human anguish of being separated from his family.

All the individuals mentioned in Mengele's letters were given coded names, though a child could have broken the code. "Ro" was Rolf; "Kh," his devoted nephew, Karl Heinz; "Ma," Martha, his loyal second wife, and so on. The letters were sent primarily to Sedlmeier by way of a post office box in

---

* Although Mengele's letters to his family began in the early 1950s, the family has saved only those letters from 1973 on. The earlier letters were handwritten, and the family feared that if they were discovered by the authorities, the writing could be identified as Mengele's. The letters from 1973 on are typed. (The typewriter found in Mengele's home by Brazilian police in 1985 matched the script in the letters sent to the family during the 1970s.) Mengele signed the letters with the code-name "Dein." According to Rolf, once Mengele began typing his letters to the family, he sent many more than he had in the previous fifteen years.

Switzerland and Sedlmeier distributed them to the family.
Sometimes letters were sent to a trusted family acquaintance
and Mengele's friend from childhood, Dr. Hermann
Schweigert, in Augsburg, Germany. Schweigert played only a
passive role, merely passing the letters on to Sedlmeier. For
West Germany and its judiciary, the regular and unscru-
tinized transmission of these letters has redounded to its
shame. Over the course of two decades more than two hundred letters were exchanged. The authorities have pleaded
that mail intercepts were not possible because of the Federal
Republic's strict criteria for securing a warrant.

Letters sent from the family to Mengele were again chan-
neled through Sedlmeier, who mailed them to a post office
box in the Bosserts' name. Each letter meticulously confirmed
the receipt of the last; Wolfram Bossert passed the original on
to Mengele and kept a copy for himself. A typical dispatch
from Sedlmeier in his role as courier read:

> Your letter dated 8.7.77 [July 8, 1977] I received only
> two days ago—the recipient was probably away. [My
> short letter of 18.7 which I had sent, included the enclo-
> sure from Ro, which you had long been expecting.] The
> two letters to Ma and Kh were passed on, including a
> copy of the letter mentioned at the beginning for Kh.[1]

The slightest hitch or mistake provoked anger and anxiety,
as revealed by this letter from Mengele to Sedlmeier asking
him to reprimand Rolf and his second wife, Almuth:

> Mail from Ma and Kh arrived on 14.12.77 [December
> 14, 1977] but a parcel containing letters from Ro and
> Alm was only received on 28.12. They mixed up the
> house numbers and wrote 10 instead of 7! [7 Missouri
> Street was the Bosserts' home.] This could be danger-
> ous! Please tell them to adhere to the exact postal de-
> tails.[2]

According to another letter to Sedlmeier, Mengele's worst
fears were realized when a letter was actually lost in the mail:

> I'm amazed that you didn't think one of my letters
> could have "gone astray" in some way. One can easily
> conjure up a whole series of possible ways my letter of

23.6 could have become lost. It was a bulky letter with enclosures to Ma, Kh, and Ro apart from the letter to you. I personally handed over the 15 typewritten pages and watched how the girl at the post office ran it through the franking machine. That doesn't exclude the fact that she could have set the machine at O, stolen the money (17 dollars after all), and destroyed the letter. This or the action of an empty-headed letter robber would be the most harmless explanation of the loss of the letter. It's neither here nor there.

What would be more upsetting is if the contents of the enclosures to Kh and Ro fell into the wrong hands. It mustn't be ruled out that the censor has been at work here. This would mean delay and ensuing consequences. Mu [Bossert] had already made Xeroxes of my copies so I can send these if you really don't receive my letter of 23.6 and you can tell me direct that there are no suspicious circumstances. We would have to draw the logical conclusion if the latter happened, and find other ways.[3]

Mengele's private correspondence highlighted how much closer he was to Karl Heinz than to his own son, Rolf; he had corresponded regularly with Karl Heinz and Martha since they left South America in 1961. He tried to compensate for this by making overtures to Rolf, with whom he had no relationship worth speaking of. Rolf was brought up by his mother, Irene, and stepfather, Alfons Hackenjos, of whom he was very fond. Since 1960, when at the age of sixteen, he was told his real father's identity, Rolf's confusion of loyalties and doubts had become a heavy burden to bear. He recalls:

My father had always been Josef Mengele, the war hero who died on the eastern front. He was the educated man, versed in Greek and Latin. Now he was the doctor of Auschwitz. It had a very strong impact on me. It was not so good to be the son of Josef Mengele.[4]

Always there was the question from strangers: "Rolf Mengele? Not the son of the Josef Mengele?" Awkwardly, Rolf would make light of his inheritance by saying, "Oh, yes, and I'm also Adolf Eichmann's nephew."

Mengele attempted to draw closer to Rolf by regularly writing letters to him. But Rolf was unmoved, knowing that his father held him in lower esteem than his cousin, Karl Heinz. As early as Christmas 1960, Mengele had written in his diary that a letter he received from Karl Heinz was "good, but the one from Rolf was too factual." The knowledge that his own father preferred Karl Heinz, who had shared four years of his father's life, created a tension and rivalry between the cousins. For Rolf it seemed that his father wanted him to model himself on Karl Heinz. Rolf rebelled by opposing his father and family on almost every issue. He went out of his way to prove to others that he did not share his father's views:

> I had nothing in common with my father's views at all. On the contrary, my opinions were diametrically opposed. I didn't even bother to listen to him or think of his ideas. I simply rejected everything that he presented. My personal attitude to national and international politics was never in doubt. My liberal political views, partly even "to the left," were known. As a result of my many critical remarks, sometimes I was even suspected of being a communist.

When Mengele tried to open a dialogue with his grown-up son in the early 1970s, his barely repressed criticism of Rolf soon came to the surface. In almost every letter Mengele extended fatherly affection to his son in one sentence, only to take it back with hurtful chiding in the next. He treated Rolf in a cold and distant manner, much as his own father had treated him. A letter congratulating Rolf on his first marriage is a good example:

> From the photographs one can deduce that you are happy. And why shouldn't such a good-looking young man and his pretty and lovable wife not be that. I think I have already shown too much fatherly pride in my newly acquired daughter. Unfortunately I hardly know her, or rather I only know her as much as the few photographs reveal. But do I know the son better? . . . The description accompanying the photos—you really could have tried a little harder. I myself would have realized

that these were your friends and not your enemies that accompany you to the registry office![5]

Mengele's concern for his son's happiness always took second place to detailed accounts of his own dire predicament. He cynically manipulated Rolf's feelings of guilt about having ignored him for so many years in order to make him feel sorry for his plight:

> I suppose you know each other and your decision was a good and mature one. Now this is your responsibility: to have a proper marriage even if it was without a veil, top hat and organ music. One can't recommend more, especially seeing that I am as unsuited to being a marriage counselor as a bald hairdresser is to selling hair health products. One more little contribution I do nevertheless want to make to your new start: I will forget the pain and bitterness and not being informed of anything for years.[6]

In the same letter, Mengele said that he was hurt to have discovered from Sedlmeier that his son was getting married, rather than hearing it directly from Rolf. But, he said, he was relieved to hear that Rolf had "initiated Irmi into our circumstances. I am not only pleased about the fact, I see it as your duty. As your wife she has a right to be fully informed about the family circumstances." Mengele could not, however, resist an anthropological inquisition about his future daughter-in-law, even on the basis of one photograph:

> From the little photograph I could deduce some "anthropological" facts and make some psychological deductions. She can be classified as one of those pretty, dark, gentle, lovable, and surely good-tempered and hardworking young ladies from your hometown.[7]

As a wedding present, Mengele pledged his center-city apartment. He said it had a cash value of about $7000, though it was not a gift he could part with at the time, since "I require the rental income for my sustenance." Rolf and his wife would own it, he quipped, "only after my situation has fundamentally changed."

Mengele then broached a subject on which he berated Rolf

time and again. He was obsessed with the idea that his son should achieve a doctorate in law. But Mengele was worried that he might not be capable of this:

> In September and December you passed your attorney's exams and you received the mark "satisfactory." I am very pleased with that, and I am very proud of you, as a father who in his lifetime has sat for several exams. The title means nothing much to me because I am not familiar with this system of school marks and I don't have anything to compare it with. Nevertheless, permit me to make a comparison with Ha, jr. [Sedlmeier's son], who was in the top quarter and still did not do well enough by 10 percent to obtain his doctorate [in Munich]. Your exam results, upon examination, obviously won't stand in the way of completing your doctorate. Is there a regional difference? Now all that is missing is that last academic hurdle, and I hope that in a short while I will hear from you that it has been mastered.

Another theme that Mengele raised in this letter and in many of his later dispatches was the state of his health. In 1972 he disclosed that he was suffering from spondylarthrocace, a painful condition in which the discs in the lower spine degenerate, as well as an enlarged prostate gland. (The intestinal blockage mentioned earlier was removed in the same year.)

To the irritation of everyone, including his new friends the Bosserts, Mengele never stopped complaining about his ailments. Wolfram Bossert told Sedlmeier:

> He can really make one furious. . . . For weeks on end, all he talks about is his illness, one hundred times in all its detail. And he's always accusing everyone: "Nobody cares about me. Now it's too late. My health never was what it seemed."

Wallowing in self-pity and dramatic threats, Mengele complained that he was too poor to pay for a doctor: "If money is a problem, and my family won't pay the doctor, then I have no option but to finish myself off."[8] Bossert said that when Mengele finally got to see a doctor, he always ended up questioning his competence. But all of Mengele's health concerns paled into insignificance when Rolf first tentatively suggested that he might travel secretly to Brazil to see his father.

For some time, Rolf had been openly skeptical of his father's protestations that he was innocent of any crimes at Auschwitz. There was a clear conflict between what was alleged in the press and the scorn with which those charges were greeted by the rest of the Mengele clan in Günzburg. As the son of the criminal portrayed in the newspapers, it was a conflict that Rolf knew he would have to resolve for himself. He decided to confront his biological father in the flesh. From the outset, Mengele reacted eagerly to the idea of a visit. But he soon sensed that its real purpose was more than just a father-and-son reunion:

> You wish to have a dialogue with me—the game: question and answer. . . . Of course a discussion is always the best way of exchanging ideas, even though during discussions one tends to defend certain positions for reasons of prestige, because during such exchanges one gets bogged down in one theme. When one has a discussion by letter, this doesn't tend to happen, which is an advantage. I'm sure I don't have to stress how much a meeting between us would mean to me. For want of a better way, I have always tried to be in close contact with you by writing to you. If this would now be possible, nobody would be happier than me. It is quite natural and understandable that you want to get to know me through personal contact and that you want to find out for yourself, independently from all that you have heard and read, what I am like. I after all feel the same about you.

Mengele invited Rolf to come with an open mind, "free of prejudices, biased wishful thinking, uncritical simplification, cheap resentment and patronizing arrogance." Yet he made it clear that his own mind was closed on the subject:

> Without sufficient "maturity," greatness, and a sense of "proportion," one should leave certain historical events as they are. . . . Your fears show me how misinformed you are about me, and that is why I am almost not upset about the way you formulate things![9]

It soon emerged that Karl Heinz and Sedlmeier were the
moving forces behind the idea of a meeting. According to
Mengele, Karl Heinz believed that Rolf had "not shown
enough interest in my problems." Mengele hoped that the
lifelong rift between the cousins—both of whom he regarded
as sons—would heal as a result of their discussions about a tête
à tête:

> Nothing would please me more than to hope that my
> "sons"* would find brotherly common interest. Obvi-
> ously in your natural state you are as different from each
> other as I was from my brother [Karl Jr.], but surely
> there is enough mutuality, which only needs to be un-
> earthed. The closed nature of Kh might mean this lies a
> little deeper. His willingness to cultivate closer relations
> with you can surely be taken for granted. Maybe as you
> both become more mature, the concern about me will
> bring you closer together, unlike the years when you
> were growing up.[10]

For all the issues dividing father and son, when Mengele
signed off he was pathetically grateful that Rolf had even
bothered to write. "Your heartfelt words at the end of your
extraordinary long letter have done my lonely heart a lot of
good," he wrote. "I would like to thank you for your nice
letter and hope to get one soon again, which I will read, even
if it has to be read by the light of a paraffin lamp. Till then, I
and my friends greet you and I give you a fatherly hug and
kisses."

Several subsequent letters were taken up with Mengele's
views on the evils of communism, the virtues of the free
market economy—"the free play of forces has the same function as it has in all manifestations of life on our planet"—and
snipes at the Stammers, with whom relations continued to
deteriorate because of Mengele's interference in their affairs.
Even Mengele's younger brother Alois had a taste of just how
intrusive he could be, receiving lengthy instructions on running the Günzburg firm. Mengele advised Alois on how to
rear his own children, and he presented Alois with a list of

---

* Mengele often referred to Karl Heinz as a son because he was his stepfather in Argentina,
and, in theory at least, continued to be since he and Karl Heinz's mother, Martha, were never
divorced.

Günzburg families that were "so disreputable" that Alois should not allow his children to marry into them. Alois became so irritated that he did not send greetings to Mengele on his sixtieth birthday. Mengele complained to Sedlmeier that it was "one of the saddest days of my life that I have to occupy myself at all with my brother's hostilities."[11]

In February 1974, Alois died. Despite their rift, Mengele paid tribute to Alois's assistance over the years: "We owe him honest thanks for 'quite some things,' " he wrote. In the same letter Mengele scathingly took Rolf to task for his youthful idealism of the simple life: "You say you have an appreciation for the simple life, which I do know, and you condemn all those Mercedes Benz drivers and swimming-pool owners. You only talk the simple life, but I live it. I hope you are prepared for the consequences of such recommendations. If not, it is only pure jealousy, which I consider human and understandable but unproductive and the product of a second-rate mind."[12]

It was Mengele's second "son," Karl Heinz, who continued to be the apple of his eye. It was rare that a letter to Rolf did not mention his cousin's name and always in the most praiseworthy terms. Directly after Alois's death, Karl Heinz took over the family firm, a job which had "rapidly matured him," wrote Mengele. Again, he urged Rolf to draw closer to his cousin. "In your letter I was looking in vain for a few personal words about him and his visit on your birthday."[13]

Mengele constantly harangued Rolf by comparing his failures with Karl Heinz's successes and by taunting him for his lack of academic ambition. Mengele somehow always managed to make Rolf feel he was second best. When Mengele received news that his son's first marriage had broken up after only a year, it was Rolf's decision not to pursue a doctorate that preoccupied Mengele. He was convinced Rolf's laziness was the root of the problem, and he castigated Rolf for letting him down on the only thing "I asked of you in my whole life." He further chided Rolf:

> I doubt that being an attorney would satisfy me. If I compare it to being a medical doctor or any kind of PhD, then I must draw a negative conclusion.[14]

In this same letter Mengele had only harsh words for Rolf on
the failure of his marriage:

> When it finally finished it did not of course surprise
> me. The speed with which you ruined your marriage
> can only be considered in a favorable light in that the
> liquidation of a marriage without children is much less
> complicated than one with children. But at the same
> time one gets the impression of a vicious circle because
> one could imagine, at least, that the split was encour-
> aged by the fact that you have no children. . . . (The
> fact that it took longer for me to find out my daughter-
> in-law's name than the marriage lasted is a long-stand-
> ing joke in our family.). . . . I do personally lose a mail
> partner with Irmi, who connected me indirectly with
> you. It wasn't so much, but one who has so little suffers
> any loss.[15]

Their relationship worsened when Rolf responded by telling his father that he would be unable to support him financially. Mengele retorted: "I can relieve you of your worries
about myself. Let us keep things as they are. In any case I
haven't been a financial burden to you up to now. I am sure
however you will manage one or two letters a year."[16] Although Rolf had by now qualified as a lawyer, Mengele continued to remind his son that his greatest wish was for him to
become a doctor of law. Rolf had just lost his job as a lawyer
with a construction company, which had gone bankrupt.
Mengele advised:

> I would like to express—apart from any regret—the
> suggestion that, when looking for a new engagement,
> you should look for one with a more pronounced use as a
> lawyer—considering that you have already thrown
> yourself into the arms of jurisprudentia. I suppose this
> would be very appropriate with regard to becoming
> more proficient on the subject, whereby I am also think-
> ing about doing your doctorate! Between you and me,
> this [doctorate] is also part of the family prestige.

Meanwhile, Rolf concentrated on setting the agenda for
their meeting. He criticized his father for his racist views. At
first Mengele said he felt compelled to respond to what he

called Rolf's "didactic explanations about the lack of racial differences among the human species. I had worked out a long exposé on the subject for you." But Mengele changed his mind because, he said, "It seems to me rather silly that I of all people should have to enlighten my son about something the Jews have known for 4000 years."

But in early 1974 the plans for the visit were interrupted by a more pressing problem. Relations between Mengele and the Stammers had finally and irretrievably broken down. What flicker of attraction was left between Mengele and Gitta Stammer had finally died. Mengele had so intruded into their lives that Gitta and her husband Geza were spending more and more time apart. Geza was camping in the Rosario hotel in São Paulo's red-light district, vowing not to return until Mengele had gone. "The situation," Bossert warned Hans Sedlmeier, "is explosive." Gitta said, "We decided we couldn't stand the situation any longer. I told Peter 'It's all over, it's all over.' "[17] An eleventh-hour peacemaking attempt by Sedlmeier, who hurriedly flew in from Günzburg, failed completely. He arrived with $5,000 for Mengele that was also enticingly waved before the Stammers. But three days of efforts by Sedlmeier were all to no avail. With Wolfgang Gerhard back in Europe, all avenues had been exhausted.

When Bossert realized that the Stammers and Mengele were about to split up, he attempted to place Mengele in a new home with a new protector. His choice was Erich Lissmann, the owner of the textile factory where Wolfgang Gerhard had worked when he lived in Brazil. Lissmann had emigrated from Germany after the war, had been a good friend of Gerhard's, but knew Mengele only as "Peter." Bossert went to Lissmann and told him of "Peter's" true identity. For the next two weeks, Lissmann literally trembled with fear. He became acutely paranoid, thinking that cars and people were following him around São Paulo. One dawn at 4:00 a.m. he knocked on the door of the Bossert home and pleaded to be allowed to sleep in the closet of their bedroom, as he was sure he was being followed. Bossert discarded the possibility of placing Mengele with Lissmann, and Lissmann, out of sheer fright, never told anyone of "Peter's" true identity. Even today he denies he knew "Peter" was Mengele.

As the Stammer/Mengele relationship fell apart, Rolf offered to intervene. But his father told him not to bother:

> I acknowledge your good intentions of wanting to help me in this way but you must realize that it is not possible like that. The information you receive about my situation is not accurate enough for you to make a proper judgment. The facts are these: my alleged attempts to influence are strictly within the limits of what is "suitable to my station" and necessary for life; my behavior has remained unchanged for all these many years; and I also have identified with the family's lot in every respect. For logical reasons alone one can be convinced of my tireless efforts to keep the domestic atmosphere as pleasant as possible. It is not always possible. The fault is not just mine![18]

The Stammers decided to make the final break with Mengele by selling their Caieiras farm and moving to São Paulo—they did not take Mengele with them. In November 1974, the Stammers sold their house at Caieiras to Laerte de Freitas, a Brazilian millionaire, and bought a large 10,000-square-foot villa on the outskirts of São Paulo. They moved to their new home in December, and Mengele stayed at Caieiras until February 1975. He felt the Stammers had deserted him, and he bitterly complained and moped in self-pity. Despite the extent of the problems between them, Mengele, until the final breakup, thought that he and the Stammers had decided to buy one large house and live together once again. "But they tailed off on their own. That is their malicious cunning," he wrote in his diary. "Again it is not so much to be alone but to be left in the lurch that hurts so much."

Mengele grew anxious about where he would live. "Now it is naturally much more difficult for me to find suitable housing," he wrote in his diary. He did not want to move into his center-city apartment because he needed the monthly income from its tenant. He did not ask the Bosserts if he could move in with them because they and their two children lived in a small two-bedroom house that had no room for another boarder. Moreover, it is doubtful the Bosserts would have agreed to let Mengele move in. They had witnessed firsthand the destruction of the Stammer household by the authoritarian and domineering Mengele. They realized that he would use them. Wolfram Bossert said, "We weren't his only true and bosom friends. We knew that he had a selfish personality and he used us as an essential tool. Although there was a certain human bond on his part, there was not real fondness." The Bosserts differed from the fanatically dedicated Gerhard. Wolfram Bossert recalls:

> We didn't indulge him [Mengele] in all his wishes and moods, because we had our own life. That was the difference between us and Gerhard. Gerhard placed Mengele's fate above that of his family. He would leave his family, even if they didn't have anything to eat, he didn't care. He would go away for days to do something for Mengele if he thought that was necessary. We always said, "Our family comes first, and then comes Mengele." That was the difference, you see.[19]

Yet before the end of January 1975, Mengele's housing worries were solved. The Stammers, who had given a Christmas promise to help him, used his $25,000 share of the Caieiras sale proceeds to buy a small bungalow, which they then decided to rent back to him. It was little more than a shack, a yellow stucco bungalow with one gloomy bedroom, an antiquated bathroom, and a tiny kitchen. It was in one of the poorer parts of town, at 5555 Alvarenga Road in the Eldorado suburb of São Paulo, but it was only a few miles from the Bosserts, the only people he could depend upon for regular visits and support.

The deed of the house was registered in the name of one of the Stammers' sons, Miki. To the electric company, the new elderly and solitary inhabitant was "Peter Stammer"; to the legal authorities he was "Wolfgang Gerhard"; and to his neighbors and house employees, he became known as "Mr. Pedro."

For the first time since becoming a fugitive, Josef Mengele was living completely alone. He was now deeply unhappy. His diary entry for April 7, 1975, shows the depth of his depression: "It has a wearing effect on me, to be left so very much isolated and excluded and all alone."

C H A P T E R
15

————
————

"We Don't Know Where
Mengele Is"

————
————

On November 9, 1970, the president of West Germany, Gustav Heinemann, made an important announcement about the hunt for Josef Mengele. It implied defeat for the first time. Dr. Heinemann personally asked President Stroessner of Paraguay for assistance in finding Mengele. When none was forthcoming, his office issued the following statement:

> We do not know where Mengele is in Paraguay. Before he lived in the frontier triangle formed by three countries, near the waterfall of Iguazu, and depending on the political situation he moved between Paraguay, Brazil and Argentina. He has access to houses of friends in the region, filled with many Germans, and he travels easily along the river [Parana]. The region is almost impossible to cross.
> Paraguay has rejected a previous request for extradition saying that Mengele had already obtained Paraguayan citizenship. Even assuming Mengele is in Para-

guay, it is impossible to attempt any further official measures.[1]

To placate the West Germans, Judge Antonio Perez Dominguez, of the First Section of the criminal court in Asunción, reminded the police that the warrant issued in 1962 for Mengele's arrest was still in force. News of the directive soon leaked out. But as had happened so many times before, the result was a public relations fiasco. The judge's action was interpreted by the press as an admission by Paraguay that Mengele was within her borders. In reality, it was a cynical exercise in public relations because the Paraguayans knew that Mengele had long since departed. But Paraguay's ambassador to Bonn, Venceslao Benitez, was apparently caught off guard. Questioned by reporters, he was refreshingly candid:

> I don't believe these reports, but it is only my opinion and I have not received any communication from my government. This is a political conversation that is really only intended to take place between the Paraguayan embassy in Bonn and the German embassy in Asunción.

Benitez then made a most revealing statement. Pressed further, he said in exasperation: "Let's talk about Brazil." In hindsight, one wonders if Benitez was trying to signal that his government knew Mengele was in Brazil. But at the time the ambassador would not elaborate, saying that he knew nothing about Mengele, and: "I think it much better for my country to know nothing about him."[2]

Into this murky sea of hints, half truths, and speculation jumped the irrepressible Tuvia Friedman, the Nazi-hunter from Haifa. His Nazi Crimes Documentation Center offered a $50,000 reward for Mengele's capture, and Friedman urged the West Germans to match it with a $10 million reward.* "That would be a dollar for every one of the ten million killed," said Friedman, adding confidently: "It will help find

---

* Had West Germany offered that sum to the public, rather than in the form of extra aid to the Paraguayan government as had former chancellor Konrad Adenauer, it might well have succeeded in bringing Mengele to justice. While the Bosserts and Stammers were unlikely to have been bought, there were two other people who learned of Mengele's true identity in São Paulo before he died, and both said they would have been sorely tempted by a large sum. By the time the government and private rewards totaled $3.5 million in 1985, Mengele had been dead six years.

him. We are not interested in killing him. That would be too good for him."[3]

A few days after Friedman's offer, he claimed he had found Mengele. Brandishing a postcard from South America, he claimed it "told me where Mengele has been for the past two months and it provides definite and precise information by which to identify him."

Friedman's reward offer was the first involving private funds, and it drew extensive coverage in the South American press. Simon Wiesenthal, not to be outdone, then dropped a bombshell. In a television interview with Israel's former prime minister David Ben-Gurion, Wiesenthal claimed he had "new information that Dr. Mengele is in Puerto San Vincente in Paraguay. I hope the authorities in Bonn will act immediately." He said the area was a military zone located in the Alta Parana region which civilian police could not enter. The Paraguayans responded that no such place as Puerto San Vincente even existed in the Alta Parana, and they were right. The Mengele affair had begun to look like a circus.

This was Wiesenthal's first major statement on Mengele since November 1968, when he had claimed that his "agents" had snapped pictures of Mengele on the streets of Asunción. That too had been a mistake, and to his credit, Wiesenthal admitted as much twenty-four hours later.

The Israelis did nothing to relieve Wiesenthal's discomfort about this new claim. A government spokesman said that Jerusalem "did not have conclusive evidence that Mengele is in Paraguay." In fact, by then the Israelis had no up-to-date information on Mengele at all. The Mossad was no longer watching Mengele, since his capture had long since ceased to be a priority target under General Meir Amit's administration. That policy was continued by Amit's successor, Zvi Zamir, who ran the Mossad from 1969 to 1976. "I don't think I spent more than about ten minutes on Mengele during my term of office," said Zamir. "It was something to do with fingerprints, or something like that. Whatever it was, it didn't come to anything."[4]

One of the few people who did know Mengele's precise location was tracked down by an Argentine reporter and his Italian colleague in February 1971. They persuaded Mengele's estranged wife, Martha, to briefly answer questions from the balcony of her apartment in Merano, in northern Italy. Martha had maintained regular contact with Mengele ever since he went to live with the Stammers in 1961. She had also received letters from him. But, with a convincing act of complete ignorance, Martha breezily lied:

> It's been years since I heard anything. I've heard nothing from Herr Doctor. But the stories they print about him—they're just stories. Lies. No, no, they're just not true. He's a very educated, very gentle, very affectionate man, a wonderful husband, a wonderful father.[5]

The following month, Wiesenthal claimed he had just missed catching Mengele on a lightning visit to Spain. Mengele, he said, had been seen driving a car. But by the time Wiesenthal had learned of the trip, it had been too late. Near misses became a familiar cry from Wiesenthal, but the world did not know there was no foundation to his claims. To Wiesenthal, the overriding purpose of his announcements was to keep Mengele in the public eye, something he achieved with great success.

By the end of 1971, Mengele's name had attracted such notoriety that it was used by a fellow Nazi, Frederick Schwend, as a bargaining chip when he was arrested in Peru, suspected of murder. Schwend was the Third Reich's master con man, a former SS major who tried to persuade Hitler to sink the British economy by dropping counterfeit pound notes all over the world. He fled Europe after helping to run an escape organization working for the American counter-intelligence corps, and ended up in Peru.

On December 31, 1971, one of Peru's wealthiest men, Luis Branchero Rossi, was found shot dead at his palatial home outside Lima. Herbert John, a West German journalist, had once worked for Rossi and was still intrigued by the shadowy world of Nazis in South America. John told the investigating judge, Santos Chichizola, that he suspected Rossi had been murdered by a neo-Nazi group, of which Schwend was the mastermind. In mid-February the police arrested Schwend, who offered details about Mengele's "involvement" in the case in return for immunity. The Peruvians jumped at the opportunity.

Schwend's lively imagination did not desert him in his hour

of need. He spun a whole series of stories about Mengele's business interests in Rossi's empire and even about Mengele's plot to take it over. At first the Peruvians fell for the ruse. On March 5, 1972, Judge Chichizola announced that Mengele was a suspect in the case. Rossi's glamorous secretary, Eugenia Sessareyo de Smith, and Juan Vilka Carranza, the nineteen-year-old son of a neighbor's gardener, were already being held as suspects. The press speculated that Mengele had been the mastermind behind the killing, which took place when Rossi and Eugenia Sessareyo had gone to his home for an afternoon's lovemaking.

On March 6 the Peruvian police announced that they had incontrovertible evidence that Mengele had visited Peru during 1971. Their inquiries suggested he had been in the country when Rossi was killed, then left shortly afterward. That same day Judge Chichizola said that Schwend was cooperating with their investigation into Mengele's alleged involvement. This time Simon Wiesenthal showed an uncharacteristic degree of caution. He warned that Schwend was pulling the wool over the Peruvian police's eyes, saying that Mengele was "not an appropriate suspect in the Rossi murder in Lima. It is a diversionary tactic." Not long afterward, Judge Chichizola agreed and said so publicly. Schwend was released, and the gardener's son was convicted of Rossi's murder, though neither a motive nor Schwend's involvement was ever properly established.

Another Nazi-hunter in Peru was not so restrained. Flushed with her success at identifying Klaus Altmann as Klaus Barbie, the "Butcher of Lyons," Beate Klarsfeld announced that Mengele was living in a jungle zone 250 miles from Lima. She said that Martin Bormann might be there too. Soon afterward, Mrs. Klarsfeld issued a second bulletin on Mengele. She said that a knowledgeable German had told her that Bormann, Mengele, and sixteen other prominent Nazis lived in South America and had business ties in an organization called "Telerana." She added that Bormann himself often lived in Bolivia disguised as a priest, and that she knew of a photograph of Bormann hiding in a fortress with Freddy Schwend. No trace of an organization dubbed "Telerana" was ever found, and Bormann's survival of the war remained much in doubt. But Beate Klarsfeld was new to the Nazi-hunting business, and this was a salutory lesson in the hazards of relying on the tales spun by informants in the shadowy business of tracking Nazi fugitives.

Back in Bonn, the government's hunt had halted. Following President Heinemann's handwringing admission that no further progress could be made, a *Catch-22* deadlock had taken hold. As far as Bonn was concerned, the hunt began and ended with Paraguay, which the government continued to believe was Mengele's likeliest hideout. Since the Paraguayans had made it clear that as a citizen Mengele could not be extradited should he be found, Bonn was convinced Mengele was there and he was protected. Therefore the West Germans made no serious effort to search elsewhere. Although President Stroessner was in a position to provide the information that would have led the West Germans to Brazil, Bonn never played its ultimate card—threatening to withdraw foreign aid. West German conglomerates had too much to lose. Instead, the judiciary became bogged down in an exercise of secondary importance to the hunt.

Judge Schneider of the land court in Frankfurt, to whom the case had been transferred from Freiburg, ordered a review of the entire prosecution case. An exhausting program was begun, taking depositions before a judge from all the witnesses who provided evidence for the original arrest warrant in 1959. This was important in that it guaranteed that evidence from witnesses who might die before Mengele's capture could still be brought before the court. But since the hunt had been effectively abandoned, the procedure was almost academic. Called *Vorferschelung,* it was the equivalent of a preliminary investigation, aimed not at finding Mengele and arresting him but at adding evidence to a record which was already abundantly clear.

The task of rehashing the old arrest warrant went to Horst von Glasenapp, an investigating judge who had ended the war as a master sergeant in an antiaircraft battalion in Berlin. Captured by the Russians, von Glasenapp spent May to October 1945 in a Soviet prisoner-of-war camp in Siberia. Unlike several other members of the German judiciary, von Glasenapp's wartime background did not link him with Nazi atrocities.

Von Glasenapp went about his evidence-collecting task

with some enthusiasm, not just because he wanted to unravel the horror of Mengele's crimes but also because he liked to travel. From 1969 to 1975 he became a seasoned globe-trotter, interviewing three hundred witnesses and making several visits to Israel, Canada, the United States, the Soviet Union, Poland, France, Italy, and Austria. He assembled a formidable document, listing seventy-five witnesses who testified to the monumental scale of Mengele's savagery.

Von Glasenapp had no authority to engage in a hunt for Mengele, but on December 9, 1971, he interviewed Hans Sedlmeier, who gave sworn evidence before him in a court in Ulm. Under paragraph 57 of the criminal code, Sedlmeier was warned that he could be prosecuted if he gave false evidence. But loyalty to Mengele and the Günzburg family caused Sedlmeier to do just that. He told von Glasenapp:

> I also do not know what connections there are between the accused and his living brother [Alois] in Günzburg. I can even state with a certain amount of conviction that Alois Mengele does not know where the accused is residing. The son [Rolf] of the accused is now a lawyer in Freiburg, and I have known him since his childhood. I know he is very close to his family and frequently comes to Günzburg. My personal relationship with his son is such that I can categorically state that he would have told me had he any connection with his father, the accused.[6]

Sedlmeier was acting as the clearing center for letters from Mengele to Alois, Rolf, and other members of his family, and he posted back their replies, so the statement was clearly a lie. But Sedlmeier was confident that his dissembling could never be proved. Out came a further stream of lies:

> I would like to say the following. The accused was once, in the 1950s, in Günzburg, after his divorce. I had the opportunity to speak to him then. Since then he has not been here and, I can safely assume, nowhere in the Federal Republic. Should he have been here, I would definitely have heard about it. He would have spoken to me. I would also like to say that I visited the accused when he was still a resident in Buenos Aires. These were

business trips and I would like to emphasize that my trips were for business reasons. I visited the accused solely for business reasons. If my memory serves me right, the last time I saw the accused was about ten years ago. I seem to remember it was at the airport in Buenos Aires. I also heard that at about the time that Eichmann was captured, the accused went to live in Paraguay. Since then, all connections between Günzburg and the accused have been severed, and no more correspondence passed. I personally am not in a position to state where the accused is residing nowadays. . . . The accused has in no way been linked to company affairs.[7]

Virtually this entire statement was false. Sedlmeier had seen Mengele in Brazil—after the Eichmann kidnapping— when he visited the farm at Serra Negra. Mengele and Günzburg were in regular touch, and as their link man, Sedlmeier knew exactly where Mengele was. Von Glasenapp said he knew that Sedlmeier was lying but claimed he was powerless to act because he could not prove it:

We had stretched the system to its limits. There was nothing more to go on with Sedlmeier. Since we could not prove he was lying, we could not raid his house or get warrants to intercept his mail or his telephone. We did as much as we were legally entitled to do. In order to grant a warrant, there has to be reasonable grounds for suspicion. I was suspicious, but I had no grounds.[8]

Von Glasenapp had already been told by Fritz Steinacker, Mengele's lawyer in Frankfurt, that he would be wasting his time talking to Sedlmeier and the Mengele family. Steinacker had represented Mengele in his divorce, and he assisted Dr. Hans Laternser in their unsuccessful appeal against the decision by Frankfurt and Munich universities to strip Mengele of all his professional degrees. "I knew Steinacker quite well," said von Glasenapp, "but there was not much point in pressing him for information because of his confidentiality to his client. He did tell me, however, that he had received his instructions through a Swiss intermediary when he acted for Mengele in relation to his divorce and degrees. I don't imagine he knew where Mengele was for that reason."

Von Glasenapp decided not to travel to Günzburg, taking Steinacker's advice that he would find the family and their close friends "had lost their memory." He turned to Simon Wiesenthal, whose many claims to have known Mengele's movements von Glasenapp had read:

> I met Wiesenthal several times but I never got much out of him. I naturally wanted to know if he really did have anything of value. It was difficult to make that judgment from the various newspaper articles I had read.[9]

On one occasion von Glasenapp arranged to take evidence from Wiesenthal before a judge in Vienna:

> I put my questions to the judge and he in turn put them to Wiesenthal. The hearing had been specially convened for Wiesenthal himself. I had told the judge that I was eager to learn the names and addresses of persons who might have accurate information as to Mengele's whereabouts. Wiesenthal was quite angry that I had asked him these questions and he refused to answer them. He said he was bound by confidentiality to his informants, which I understood.
>
> I left feeling he was eager to convey that he was leading the field on this question, that he was the man out in the front. Perhaps behind his refusal to answer the questions was a feeling that the people he had in mind were not so reliable after all. I myself remained a little skeptical and did not raise the subject with him again.[10]

For a man with a healthy degree of skepticism about Wiesenthal's evidence, von Glasenapp's relationship with another Nazi-hunter, who made even more extravagant claims, was strange. It raised serious questions about his integrity as a senior member of the West German judiciary.

At the end of 1972, Ladislas Farago, a best-selling American author and wartime naval intelligence officer, claimed to have pinpointed Mengele's hideout. Farago was wrong, and his bogus information may have cost the life of an innocent man.

The origins of Farago's relationship with von Glasenapp can be traced to the grueling circulation war in which Britain's popular newspapers engage periodically. Late on the afternoon of November 26, 1972, word spread that the *Daily Express* was taking delivery of a very large order of newsprint for that night's print run. The *Express*, which enjoyed an enviable reputation for exclusives, believed it had a major story. It was confident its circulation would rise dramatically.

Shortly before midnight, the paper's first edition came out with the claim that reporters had tracked down Hitler's elusive deputy, Martin Bormann, and the news was flashed around the world. The source of the *Express*'s "scoop" was Ladislas Farago, who said he had run Bormann to ground in Buenos Aires. Farago's evidence was a balding man with a passing resemblance to Bormann. He turned out to be a respectable Argentine schoolteacher named Nicholas Siri.

In his Bormann article, Farago also claimed to have spoken to Josef Mengele, who he said was living under the alias "Dr. Nadich." Farago said he had tracked Mengele to the Paraguayan border town of Pedro Juan Caballero. The Paraguayans scornfully invited reporters to the town to see if they could find him.

The discovery that the Bormann information was a fabrication provoked a bitter row between Farago and the *Daily Express*. The editor, Ian McColl, demanded that Farago repay a $5000 advance:

> As far as producing Martin Bormann is concerned you have gone on record, on television and in print, saying that you know where he is, how he is living, and promising to produce him. . . . Perhaps you might consider that the honorable course at this stage would be to repay the advance, as you pledged.[11]

In the same letter, McColl said that he had learned from his reporters that documents Farago had supplied to support his Mengele claims were also fakes:

> If, as you admit, you have been duped over one set of documents which have turned out to be Spanish translations of old articles extracted from *Der Spiegel*, it begs a number of supplementary questions. Are the other documents fakes as well? Have we been chasing the body that does not exist?[12]

Farago was mortified. He said his South American documents on Mengele and Bormann were genuine but that he had never claimed the Bormann picture was. He accused the *Daily Express* of jumping the gun:

> I would like to remind you that I undertook the writing of the series under duress in a climate of phony competition conjured up by you. I had no choice but to go along with your demand that the series be written then and there, when you wanted and needed it, especially when I found out that you had already prepared a series of your own, to be by-lined by Mr. Steven [a *Daily Express* staff writer] alone, although based on my material. I have copies of this article in my possession, and it is a sad and sorry reminder of the lengths to which the *Daily Express* was willing to go to score this confounded scoop.[13]

Despite Farago's denial that the onus was on him to "deliver Bormann . . . on a silver platter," he went on to make some astonishing claims about having met Bormann in a convent high in the windswept Andes. This claim appeared in 1974, amid another spate of publicity for his book *Aftermath: Martin Bormann and the Fourth Reich.*

> When I was in contact with him in February 1973, he had just moved from Chile to southern Bolivia. A very sick man, he was cared for by four German nursing sisters of the Redemptionist Order in their convent near Tupiza, a remote region of Potosi Province in the Andes.[14]

Notwithstanding Farago's extraordinary fabrications about Bormann and Mengele, it is clear from his voluminous files that some of his information was tantalizingly good. Farago certainly impressed respected historians like Lord Dacre, then Hugh Trevor-Roper, Regius Professor of Modern History at Oxford University, even after the *Daily Express* published the phony Bormann story. When Trevor-Roper was asked by the *New York Times* to vouch for Farago in their attempt to unravel the mystery of whether Bormann was dead or alive, the British historian was quite flattering, as he later told Farago himself:

I told them that you should be taken seriously and that although I had certain reservations about certain parts of your story (reservations which might well be dispelled when your evidence was produced in full), I considered your researches were valuable and that you had made an important contribution to the solution of the problem.[15]

But after Farago's book was published, Trevor-Roper was not so sure:

My recollection is that when we met in London you told me that the [Bormann] photograph was not genuine and that this was before its falsity was publicly declared. I therefore deduced that the responsibility for printing that photograph rested not with you but with the *Daily Express* and that you had disapproved of its publication. Since you were heavily committed to the *Express* I can see that it would have been difficult for you, at that time, publicly to disown the photograph which they had printed. However the problem remains, how did the *Express* obtain the photograph and accept it as genuine? You do not in the text, that has been sent to me, refer to the matter; but it is a question which the critical reader is bound to ask and I would be very interested to know your answer to it.[16]

Farago never did provide a satisfactory answer.

Overeager though the *Express* may have been to publish a Bormann story, Farago bore a heavy share of responsibility for its publication. Farago made substantial payments to all his important sources, and in doing so attracted many unscrupulous informants who presented false documents to support their phony claims. Probably he had become so financially committed to his book publishers, Simon and Schuster, that he had to press on. But in casting his net so wide, Farago also attracted several civil servants from South America and West Germany who were officially working on the Bormann and Mengele cases.

One of Farago's key informants was Judge Horst von Glasenapp, who was investigating both the Mengele and the Bormann allegations. They became well acquainted on von

Glasenapp's visits to the United States and on Farago's research trips to West Germany. In January 1973, Farago paid von Glasenapp $500 in cash and a further $1000 by check in exchange for information.[17] Von Glasenapp admitted he received the payments, but claimed they were entirely proper because they were "by private arrangement."[18] Yet von Glasenapp was using knowledge gained from his official position for private gain during his term of office. In most other countries this might be regarded as corruption.

Von Glasenapp, however, hoped to make even more money from Farago. On April 9, 1973, the judge reminded the writer:

> I wanted to let you know that I still have one of the largest collections of documents on euthanasia in the Third Reich. Before it disappears . . . into an archive, I thought I'd at least let you know I have it.[19]

Von Glasenapp and Farago had several discussions about prospects for film rights. On August 19, von Glasenapp again wrote to Farago informing him of his schedule for a forthcoming visit to the United States, adding:

> I am dying to know what the film people have to say. My situation is such that I could do at this moment with some additional income.[20]

It is clear therefore that von Glasenapp was depending on Farago to improve his financial state and that Farago needed von Glasenapp for information. Such a relationship between a serving judge and a commercial author peddling inadequately confirmed Nazi stories was unorthodox. But one tragic inadvertent consequence may have been the death of an innocent man.

Following Farago's claim in the London *Daily Express* that he had tracked Mengele to Pedro Juan Caballero, Simon Wiesenthal, in May 1973, claimed he too knew Mengele was living there. Then came Tuvia Friedman, who said that his $50,000 reward had also led to information that Mengele might be hiding in the same small border town. On October 17, 1973, the Polish War Crimes Commission said that their inquiries also suggested Mengele was there. On October 25, West German justice officials in Bonn were quoted in the *New*

York Times as saying that Mengele had indeed been located in Pedro Juan Caballero. The same report quoted Judge von Glasenapp as saying that he did not think Mengele would be caught, but that several witnesses he regarded as reliable had told him Mengele was in Paraguay and was willing to talk about his past. One of those "reliable" witnesses who had spoken to von Glasenapp was Ladislas Farago, who wrote in an early draft of his book:

> In actual fact I was assured by Judge von Glasenapp that my Mengele material proved extremely useful for his own investigation. He told me that the pinpointing of Mengele's place of residence by me, a third party, gave the German authorities an opportunity to raise the issue with President Stroessner of Paraguay during his semi-official visit to Germany in 1973.[21]

For one elderly farmer of German descent living near Pedro Juan Caballero, the cumulative effect of this amateur speculation, confirmed as it seemed to be with official statements from the Poles and West Germans, had the most disastrous result.

Late in November 1973, a group of men burst into the farmer's home during the middle of the night, beat him, and shot him dead. His wife, who tried to intervene, was beaten and suffered internal injuries. Their three children were left unharmed. According to Aldolfino Paralta, the local police chief, the dead man's name was Albert Fredrichi. He had lived on the outskirts of the town for nineteen years and was known as a recluse with eccentric ways. In the wake of the sustained publicity throughout 1973 about Pedro Juan Caballero being Mengele's hiding place, the press speculated that Fredrichi was the Auschwitz butcher. The man's widow, Endentran, described these reports as "absurd" as she packed her bags to leave for good. She said the murderers had not taken any valuables or goods and that they spoke a language she did not understand. She believed he was killed by a group of Jewish avengers.

Delving into Fredrichi's past, newspapers claimed that he had been in the German army and had a history of violence and Nazi sympathies. According to a CIA report on the inci-

dent, Mrs. Fredrichi's suspicion that her husband's killers
were Jews may well have been right:

> He [informant] did say that the former German sol-
> dier by the name of Fredrichi had been beaten to death
> last year by Israeli terrorists who thought he was Men-
> gele. Fredrichi's wife lost portions of one of her ears and
> her stomach was cut open as a result of her beating. She
> survived the attempt and apparently wrote a letter to
> the German ambassador requesting a pension as a result
> of her husband being a former soldier.[22]

Von Glasenapp said that he could not remember whether
he was the source of the *New York Times* story stating that
West German justice officials believed that Mengele was hiding in Pedro Juan Caballero. Despite the fact that he received
money from Farago and was discussing a possible film, von
Glasenapp denied that he had been unduly influenced by
Farago. "I know that Farago offered a list of rumors," he said,
"and I remember saying to him that I was not very satisfied
with his material. There were a lot of what I call 'information
brokers' in South America at the time."[23]

Despite his questionable relationship with Farago, von
Glasenapp did make one significant attempt to locate Mengele. When Alois died in February 1974, von Glasenapp authorized telephone intercepts on the Mengele family homes
in Günzburg. On the day of the funeral, a grand and stately
affair, von Glasenapp ordered the police to mingle with the
mourners on the off chance that Mengele might have returned to pay his last respects:

> We had the right to control telephones but there was
> no success at all, nothing happened. Nothing. Silence on
> the western front. All quiet on the western front![24]

Telephone taps on the Mengele family were never authorized again. Von Glasenapp had played a hunch and lost. Had
more hunches like that been pursued, the West Germans
might eventually have succeeded.

C H A P T E R
16

"Pedro," the Neighbor

Alone in his subtropical slum, Josef Mengele rapidly declined. He did what he could to enliven his cheerless bungalow with its cracked hardwood floor and leaking roof. He painted his bedroom dark green and laid a tile path. But nothing could compensate for the loneliness that now tormented him. "My cage becomes more comfortable," he wrote, "but it remains a cage."[1] "Mr. Pedro," as he was known to his neighbors, sought out new friends with pathetic eagerness. Two old French women became occasional conversational partners. But he craved intellectual stimulation, and they could not satisfy his particular needs. Even Wolfram Bossert was never quite regarded as a true friend. "It is comradeship," Mengele wrote to Hans Sedlmeier. "He [Bossert] does not seem to have had a friend in his life."[2] With his usual cynicism, Mengele said he was "willing to settle for this comradeship" because Bossert had helped him in his hour of need. But it was Bossert, said Mengele, who was fated to meet an intellect like him, not the other way around.

His financial worries had also worsened. After dining out at an expensive restaurant, he said, "More than one visit a year I cannot afford." Income from his rented apartment left him with $250 a month, not enough, he complained, to sustain his share of regular payments to Wolfgang Gerhard in Austria for his medical bills. "I have sent him $600 so far this year, which is more than I spend on myself; not only shall I discontinue my donation, but I'm asking you to do so too," he wrote to Sedl-meier. Mengele suspected that Gerhard had exaggerated the cost of cancer treatment for his wife and son. In a subsequent letter, he also told Karl Heinz to stop sending any money to Gerhard until Gerhard provided proof of the real costs:

> He shall report precisely, exactly what solutions he has in mind. To begin with, he shall take care of his sick wife. His further disposition will depend on the course of her disease, the end of which seems doubtful to me. . . . The first thing he got out of my plight was to turn it to his advantage and get something out of you . . . he wasn't satisfied with what I sent him. I do not intend to buy any help from him but I'm afraid the solution to the "dumb man" [false identity card] could become expensive.[3]

So anxious had Mengele become about his financial state that he was not sure he could afford the record player and tape deck he planned to buy to relieve his boredom. "I am more than ever dependent on your help," he wrote home. Gitta Stammer felt that his family could have done more for Mengele. "They were not very generous with him," she said.

His health was also deteriorating. His blood pressure was too high, his spinal problem caused him great pain, and he suffered migraines, allergies, and insomnia; a prostate operation was pending. He had rheumatism in his hands, and an area of one leg was permanently swollen, the result of a tropical-insect bite in Paraguay. Fear of being kidnapped by the Israelis had also returned, as had his old anxiety about his forehead giving him away. Once he ventured out alone to a sausage shop and thought that a customer "scrutinized me too closely." Terrified, he vowed never to go back again. Now living within reach of newspapers, he regularly read the coverage about him. "When there was a newspaper article about him he'd sit and think for hours," said Wolfram Bossert. "He wanted to know where the news had come from and if it was true or if it was a police plant."[4] At night he slept with an old Mauser pistol by his bed.

He consoled himself with the prospect of a visit from Rolf, though no definite plans had yet been made. In his acutely anxious state, Mengele beseeched his son to leave nothing to chance. "Before I start to look forward to that meeting," he wrote, "I want to know all the details about the planning." Mengele told Rolf:

A visit would be an adventure that would have to be planned very well in advance. A faultless passport, in a different name, would be a prerequisite. If one has that, then one doesn't need to make any great contortions. The preparatory work for this would be to make precise inquiries about all travel arrangements (visa, registration, etc.) and a watertight alibi. If all these requirements are met, then you have to plan this undertaking right down to the last detail and without self-deception. There must be no gap in the plan of operations and you must be able to have an overview from beginning to end, and it all has to be in your head.[5]

In another letter, Mengele told Rolf that the most important feature was the false passport—a "dumb man" as he called it:

If you aren't holding a "dumb man," we need not waste time thinking about it any more. If you don't know what I mean have it explained to you by Uncle H [Sedlmeier]. This is an irrevocable demand without which any undertaking means a frivolous challenge with unforeseeable and dangerous consequences.[6]

In that same letter, Mengele revealed that his late brother Alois's son, Dieter, now running the family firm with Karl Heinz, had rejected all his attempts at establishing a dialogue. "I do not know Dieter, and I have no information about him," Mengele lamented. "He hasn't answered my sympathy cards on the death of his father and his mother. He wants to avoid any contact with me." Again Mengele implored Rolf to re-establish ties with the Günzburgers, whose wealth and power his son mistrusted. And again, much to Rolf's irritation, he praised Karl Heinz:

> He has driven his ship these last two and a half years carefully and with insight and without any regard for himself. He uses his workmen's expertise well and uses the experience of his assistants and has a good relationship with his workers and employees, and he is critical, modest, indefatigable and he knows what he wants. That's the way it seems to me from here. . . . I do regret that you have left the Günzburg scene willingly.[7]

In his moments of deeper despair, Mengele resorted to splenetic outpourings of fascist rhetoric. He complained how "the selection, promotion and development of overaverage intelligence" was being "misconstrued, misrepresented and rejected" by what he called "supposedly democratic principles." He savaged a book by Hitler's armaments minister, Albert Speer, who confessed to having made a pact with the devil before he realized the implications. In *Inside the Third Reich*, written by Speer while serving his twenty-year jail sentence, he described Hitler as a megalomaniac. "To characterize him as the megalomaniacal architect of the nation is a useless attempt, and proves the inability of Speer, the 'expert,' to understand the intentions of the Order." Mengele went on:

> It's a pity that so little of the greatness of the time has stayed in the memory of a man who was allowed to play in the game in such a favored position. Speer hasn't heard either now, or in those days, the call of history. But his attempt to revise history cannot diminish the greatness of that time.

In Mengele's view, Speer's admission that he was wrong to follow Hitler was just an exercise in public self-flagellation:

> If Speer's confessions are real, he has to be accused of severe misuse of the friendship of his Führer, whom he has been trying to compromise. Speer lacked bravery and all the qualities that allow a great personality to be able to make more out of the friendship of his highest commander.
>
> [H]e accuses himself and he takes on guilt which at

times he isn't even accused of and then he believes, or so he hopes, that this can be atoned by sitting in prison for a few years, now that his head has been pulled out of the noose. . . . Perhaps the nightmare of having to stand in the shadow of the other [Hitler] has always tortured him and has now turned into revenge.[8]

More than ever, in the closing stages of his life, Mengele yearned for contact with his family back home. He asked Sedlmeier to rent another post office box "for the acceleration of post traffic." Mengele counseled Sedlmeier:

Picking up could be done by you or KH [Karl Heinz] or anybody else that is trustworthy. In order not to have only my mail in that box, you can send an envelope with a postcard from your occasional journeys to that box. This of course other people can do. That way the receiver stays out of the game except insofar as arranging for the p.o. box, a single effort that doesn't seem unacceptable to me.[9]

In this way, Mengele argued, more letters could be exchanged without risk of being discovered. Mengele suggested that renting the post box in a big town would be safer and draw no attention, whereas in a small village—presumably Günzburg —"it would be a sensation."

Mengele's only contact outside his neighborhood was Wolfram Bossert, who brought him recorded cassettes of his favorite classical music. Sometimes he would go for an outing with the Bossert children, Sabine and Andreas, to whom he became a favored "uncle" having built a wooden paddleboat for them. His links with the Stammers were now strictly business. Gitta and Geza visited only when they brought cash for the apartment rent and money sent from Günzburg. Mengele was hurt to learn in 1975 that for the first time in twelve years, Geza Stammer had not invited him to his birthday party.

His main companion for the first year of his new solitary life was a sixteen-year-old neighborhood gardener, Luis Rodrigues, who liked watching *The Wonderful World of Disney* and soap operas on TV. Mengele was so lonely that sometimes he asked him to stay the night. Rodrigues recalled how Mengele loved music and how he sometimes whirled clumsily around

the room to a waltz. Rodrigues recalled his early impressions
of Mengele:

> At first he was very serious with me and we only spoke
> about the job, work in the house or gardening. Then,
> after some time, he became friendlier with me, and he
> used to treat me very nicely, and he used to talk to me
> about what I liked, and how I was getting along, and
> how my family was. He once told me that I would one
> day be very proud I worked for him, and I would tell my
> children I had worked in his house.[10]

As the year's end approached, at Rodrigues's prompting
Mengele bought a $150 twenty-four-inch Telefunken black-
and-white television set. He told the boy that he wanted the
set to watch the Winter Olympics. He confided to Hans Sedlmeier he thought it might persuade "my new housemate to
stay."

But Mengele's television did little to relieve the pain of his
loneliness. It did not persuade the boy to spend more time.
And Mengele reported home that although it was a "break in
my monotonous life," he got no enjoyment from the set because "the channels hardly come through and the repeated
interruptions by commercials really do disturb me." Much of
the program content, in any case, infuriated Mengele. Television was like a "lightning conductor for his moods—it gives
him an opportunity to get worked up, to get angry, and to
curse," wrote Wolfram Bossert.[11]

Deep depression and anxiety had now set in as Mengele
bided his time alone in Alvarenga Road, his one attempt at
striking up a friendship having been rebuffed. He ended 1975
with a letter to Sedlmeier, noting that "nothing can improve
my mood." Mengele's spirits and health were sinking fast. He
talked about suicide, saying it would be a blessed relief from
his aches and pains and from a world that cared nothing for
him.

The beginning of the end came sooner than he expected. In
May 1976, Mengele spent a Sunday with the Stammers' elder
son, Miki, and a friend, Norberto Glawe. When they dropped
him off at his bungalow gate, Mengele felt quite dizzy and ill.
Inside the house, a "sudden pain" hit him in the right side of
his head. In Mengele's own words, "fluttering visions, vertigo,

tingling sensations in the left half of my face and my left arm (like ants running), and difficulties with my speech and increasing pain in my head were the major symptoms. Later, this barbaric pain in my head was accompanied by nausea."

As a doctor, Mengele knew from the symptoms that he had suffered a stroke. "I couldn't use either my left arm or my left leg, (paralyzing)," he wrote. Norberto Glawe went to a nearby clinic for advice about "Don Pedro," and was told to take him immediately to the hospital.[12]

Lying awake that night, Mengele spent many anxious hours. "I thought, my friends will wonder 'what to do with that old wreck.' "[13]* Early the next morning, Norberto Glawe and his mother arrived to take care of "Don Pedro." Then the Bosserts came to take him to the Santa Marta Hospital in the Santo Amaro suburb of São Paulo, where doctors diagnosed a mild cerebral hemorrhage.† What Mengele did not know then was that his admission to the hospital had brought him within a whisker of having his cover blown.

Mengele had been introduced to Norberto Glawe and his parents as "Don Pedro" by Wolfgang Gerhard earlier in the year. Norberto's father, Ernesto, was an Argentinean industrialist of German descent. The Glawes had moved to Brazil in 1959, where they met the Bosserts because Liselotte Bossert taught the Glawe children. The Bosserts introduced them to Gerhard.

Gerhard immediately struck Ernesto Glawe as "unbalanced." He said Gerhard "had a true adoration for Adolf Hitler, made a point of showing himself to be a real Nazi, and wanted the return of the Nazi regime." Both Gerhard and the Bosserts made a special point of asking the Glawes if they could help take care of their elderly friend, "Don Pedro," who

---

* Bossert was one friend who was not surprised that Mengele had suffered a stroke. He later wrote to Sedlmeier: "I am convinced that his stroke was due to an internal damming up because he has no professional life . . . his explosive nature is imposed on the people he lives with. The sudden isolation after ten years of relative security . . . together with the general stress and the worry about his existence . . . brought on the stroke."

† One of the main problems facing the forensic scientists who examined the bones exhumed from the grave at Embu, near São Paulo, in June 1985 was the absence of Mengele's recent medical records. The Santa Marta Hospital was unable to assist since they destroyed records after five years. All that was available was Mengele's entry card under the alias he used—Wolfgang Gerhard—the length of stay, the sickness, and the name of the doctor responsible for his treatment.

was in need of "spiritual and social help and friends." Ernesto explained:

> I thought it was a little strange since I didn't know Gerhard at all well. But I saw nothing wrong in it either. Once a month I went to the old man and brought him chocolate and helped take care of him. We brought him food and we visited him eight or ten times maybe.[14]

Just as Gerhard had not confided Mengele's secret to the Stammers when he first went to live with them, so he kept the Glawes in the dark. He asked the Glawes to take care of the old man because he had to return to Europe to care for his son Adolf, stricken with bone cancer. Gerhard's wife had died of cancer in 1975. Yet despite this family crisis, Gerhard had taken the trouble to visit Mengele for a very special reason.

At Mengele's expense, Gerhard flew back to São Paulo to renew his Brazilian identity card, which was about to expire, so that Mengele could continue to use his false identity. The laminated plastic card was opened up and Mengele's picture was withdrawn, revealing Gerhard's own picture underneath. It was then relaminated in a local shop so that Gerhard could present it for renewal at the Department of Public and Social Order. After it had been reissued, the plastic covering was reopened, Mengele's photograph placed squarely over Gerhard's, and then relaminated. As Mengele himself remarked, the new card—or "dumb man," as he called it—was far from perfect. The differences in Gerhard's age (fourteen years younger) and height (six inches taller) were glaring:

> The "Old Swiss" is out of duty but the new "dumb man" is naturally not so ideal as it seemed to look at first. Remarkable is the stature, not to mention his age. Nevertheless, I hope it will be of sufficient use for me.[15]

It was precisely these anomalies that alerted one already suspicious person to the fact that "Don Pedro" was hiding a murky past. As young Norberto Glawe accompanied "Don Pedro" to the Santa Marta Hospital on May 17, 1976, he noticed that he was using the identity card of Wolfgang Gerhard, the "unbalanced" Nazi who had introduced them earlier that year. He also noticed that "Don Pedro" paid his admission fee with a crisp $100 bill.

Norberto's father, Ernesto, said he had already begun to have doubts about Mengele's real identity because of his conflicting accounts about what he did in the war. At first "Don Pedro" told him that he had been a sergeant in the German army. Later he said that he had served as a doctor at the front. "I never knew for sure whether he was Pedro or not," said Ernesto Glawe.[16]

After two weeks in the hospital, "Don Pedro" was released. Norberto Glawe agreed to move in with him at his bungalow in Alvarenga Road while he convalesced. Cooped up together in such a confined space, "Don Pedro" began to get on the boy's nerves, as his father explained:

> My son spent two weeks with him. While Don Pedro recovered, he had a barbecue and invited several of his friends. But at the end of those two weeks, my son had an argument or disagreement with Don Pedro and he left. He was an egocentric and violent character. We never saw him again.[17]

By now the Glawes had a strong suspicion as to the real identity of this opinionated and self-righteous old man. "I found a catalogue from a company for agricultural machinery," said Ernesto Glawe. "It had the name 'Mengele' on it. I put two and two together."[18] Finally there was a break-in in which Mengele's mauser pistol was stolen. To Mengele's embarrassment, the gun, registered in Geza Stammer's name, was stolen while Norberto was there. The discovery of a pistol in Mengele's house confirmed to the Glawes that "Don Pedro" was not an ordinary senior citizen.[19]

But like the Stammers, the Glawes did not act on their suspicions even though the evidence was now quite strong. "My problem was that I wasn't positive and I was frightened," Ernesto Glawe later told the São Paulo police when they discovered the relationship in June 1985. He also told the police that they had no further contact with "Don Pedro" after Norberto Glawe left the bungalow in the summer of 1976.

That was patently untrue. In his diary Mengele allotted the Glawes a code name, as he did for all the key conspirators who helped him. He called them the "Santiagos," and his diary makes several references to meeting and exchanging gifts

with them after the summer of 1976. It was clear that they
were not the closest of friends, but neither were they enemies. For example, on January 14, 1977, Mengele wrote to his
friend Hans Sedlmeier:

> I visited the Santiagos shortly before Christmas and I
> gave a fruit press to the wife, who took good care of me
> in those days, a press which she asked for. They brought
> me a big decorated plate of Christmas cakes. It is going
> to stay at this level of contact and occasional visits and it
> is good this way.[20]

The following Christmas, 1977, Mengele told Sedlmeier that
he had seen the Santiagos again: "Mus [Bossert] and I spent
Christmas afternoon at the Santiagos."[21]

When the Glawes' relationship with Mengele was disclosed,
they tried to put some distance between themselves and Mengele. In June 1985, Ernesto Glawe told ABC News:

> Personally I never wanted to be an intimate friend of
> his. I have never avoided having Jewish friends and I
> have never been a Nazi. In fact I have two employees
> who are Jewish. I consider this idea of neo-Nazism to-
> tally passé. I feel very badly about it [the assistance to
> Mengele] now, because I helped someone who really
> did not deserve any assistance.[22]

But in his act of public contrition, Ernesto Glawe made one
important omission. He failed to mention that they had received hush money from Mengele. By the summer of 1976
the Glawes knew precisely who Mengele was. The false identity card, the "Mengele" catalogue, the conflicting war stories
—undoubtedly they confided their suspicions to their friends
the Bosserts, who felt they could trust the Glawes with the
secret. Despite his anger, Mengele felt obliged to pay the
Glawes for their silence, as this letter from Sedlmeier to Mengele revealed:

> In connection with the Santiago affair, you mentioned
> that you were disgusted that one had to pay friends for
> their services. Don't we do the same with the tall man
> [Wolfgang Gerhard]? If we had considered this neces-

sity with G + G [Gitta and Geza Stammer] you might still be together.[23]

Mengele's fees to "the tall man," which had risen since he acquired his identity card, were proving to be a considerable drain on his private funds. Marianne Huber, the Gerhards' landlady in Graz, Austria, said that one of the children told her that "Gerhard had sold his ID card for $7,000." In what currency, she did not know.[24]

To raise the extra cash, Mengele had to sell the São Paulo apartment he had bought in the Stammers' name. "By selling the apartment I am getting rid of a lot of difficulties and bother even though I had to lose some hair," he wrote.[25] Mengele complained in his diary that he did not get much from the sale:

> Ge [Geza Stammer] arrived in order to hand over the accounts for the apartment. That closing of accounts reveals the unimaginable misery with that property, on which I had worked so hard and in such drudgery! Alas, a part of my fate! When I deduct from the incoming 9000 US dollars the expenses of the last two years [around 1500], I get nothing more than just 7500 US dollars.[26]

Unknown to Mengele, his devoted nephew Karl Heinz had been paying a large share of Gerhard's medical expenses.* News of Karl Heinz's secret funding was revealed to Mengele only after he had his stroke. But Mengele did not like to be reminded of it:

> I did not appreciate reading in your letter that KH has often been helping and reached deeply into his pocket. Even though I know "the right hand shouldn't know what the left hand does," it would be useful for me to be informed of any support action. I did expressly indicate that this type of grant should not become a permanent habit. The sick Burli [Adolf] and Christmas are special occasions and only such occasions can be appropriate for

---

* As of August 1984, Karl Heinz was listed as a limited partner in Mengele & Sohne Maschinenfabrik & Eisengiesserei Gmbh & Co., with 3.5 million deutschemarks' worth of shares, worth approximately $1.25 million.

this. KH has written to me in a positive way and I would
like to thank him for his generosity in this matter.[27]

In another letter home Mengele complained:

Despite his undoubted generosity it upsets me to be a
financial burden to him. Everything comes out of his
private funds. . . . One can't ignore that these
amounts have over time become a considerable sum,
and even they were not enough . . .[28]

However, Mengele's embarrassment did not stop him from
begging Karl Heinz for more money after Gerhard told him
that the cost of his son Burli's treatment had escalated because
the child needed more surgery. In a letter to Sedlmeier, Mengele said:

After more than a year my friend has finally written to
me and naturally, not much good news . . . about Burli
[Adolf], he had to be operated on again for further medical care by the female cancer doctor, the doctor who the
neurologists think is having some success, and for this
medical care he did not have the means. He doesn't say
anything about how he intends to get those means, and
leaves it to my intelligence to guess it. I guessed it—as of
course you would have done. So we both know what he
probably thinks or expects. What I mean is this: once
you say "dumb man" [false identity card], then one
must take the consequences and the consequences in
this case are the sick son. How much, you want to know?
Last time it was between 4,000-5,000 DMs [deut-
schemarks, approximately $1600]. Most likely it has not
gotten any cheaper. Therefore I want you to explain
these facts to Karl Heinz and ask him for his assistance in
my name. When I wrote my letter to him it seemed
inappropriate to mention it. He will understand that.
This matter does not permit any delay.[29]

Mengele's concern about his finances and his health provoked another major crisis. Although he had recovered movement in his limbs within the first twenty-four hours of hospital
treatment, his stroke had left him in an acutely anxious state.
Bossert wrote to Sedlmeier that "his relentlessness comes out

in his physical disquiet; he can't sit still, he constantly taps his fingers and clips his fingernails." Mengele had become obsessed with his health. His letters home to Günzburg were marked with minutely detailed reports about his declining health and anxious state:

> I suffer from an unusual phenomenon which doesn't improve. It consists of a very strong reaction to a surprise stimulation (e.g., the noise of a car backfiring, not noticing a person is there, unexpectedly being spoken to). This exaggerated shock reaction embarrasses me so far as others noticing it is concerned; they laugh and wonder what's going on. I can't explain my "craziness" to everybody, who take me for an anxious fool. The trembling of my right hand during difficult work (e.g., handling a screwdriver) seems to have increased. Or do you think that these are general aspects of aging?[30]

Deprived of the ability to pursue his favorite pastime of making handicrafts, Mengele was reduced to aimlessly puttering about the house. His relationship with his neighbors had not advanced beyond a superficial state. They saw only a smiling facade, polite and self-contained. "If you asked what country he was from, he would always say, 'Europe,'" said Jaime de Santos, a local caretaker. "I liked him. He was nice. He never got angry or nervous." When de Santos was short of money and asked him for a loan, Mengele readily complied.[31] But beneath this neighborly veneer his failing health and financial worries had created a deeply disturbed old man. In his diary Mengele wrote, "My mood is as if burned out. All what one does seems so senseless! All is so empty." Mengele also wrote a letter to Sedlmeier in which he showed that he was again contemplating suicide:

> The fact that again and again I have to come to you asking this type of favor [money] embarrasses me, but it seems to be part of the game. Sometimes I think I should finally give up. It is so hopeless all alone. But then again this type of despair doesn't seem right to me. Everything in life that has special value is costly. Sometimes one gets these sudden passing phases, but you must not allow yourself to go crazy.[32]

As Mengele's pleas for money to pay Gerhard became more desperate, Sedlmeier began to suspect that Gerhard was inflating his son's medical expense claims for his own personal benefit:

> I cannot yet say how KH will respond to the requests of the tall man [Gerhard]. He was informed by a copy of one of your letters to me, and he must decide for himself. I'll keep my opinion about the tall man's behavior to myself, but I have to say that I fear that he uses Burli's [Adolf's] condition to improve his finances, because his medical expenses and necessary cures will be refunded for the most part. Since my last reported meeting with the tall man I haven't been back to him. I will let you know the decision that KH reaches in this matter as soon as I get a chance to talk with him.[33]

On the other hand, Mengele reminded Sedlmeier of just how valuable Gerhard had been in helping him evade capture:

> He has done me an unrepayable favor. . . . A favorable conclusion to this business is important for me. He really offered me friendship and services that no amount can pay off.[34]

But Sedlmeier's response did not give Mengele's spirits much of a boost:

> I don't have a resolution from KH on the matter. I have reminded him but he has left the matter in abeyance. How important you consider this is evident from your last and second to last letters, of which I have sent him copies. I count on talking to him about that during the next few days and if not I will remind him.[35]

It was during this crisis period that Mengele found strength and hope in only one thought—the possibility that after a twenty-one-year separation he might at last see his only child, Rolf.

C H A P T E R
17

———
———

"Now I Can Die in Peace"

———
———

Mengele's instructions for his son's secret visit resembled a set of military orders. From the moment he first suggested the idea in 1973, Mengele insisted that Rolf travel on a false passport and lay a series of false trails. "There must be no flaw in the plan," he warned his son. "We must not make the smallest mistake."

Rolf had taken four years to decide that he would make the long journey to Brazil—"an odyssey," as his father later called it. Father and son, joined by blood, separated by history, had different reasons for wanting this extraordinary reunion. Rolf, torn by doubts about his father's monstrous past, torn by loyalty to his own flesh and blood, could not postpone the confrontation any longer. "I was fed up with the written arguments," he said. "I wanted to talk to my father, confront him personally." Mengele awaited the moment with great anticipation, moved more by curiosity than by real affection, prepared for the only inquisition in his life. "You wish to have a dialogue," he said. "Very well . . ."

Yet a real dialogue was almost certainly out of the question. It was clear to Rolf from the self-righteous tone in one of his father's letters that he would not tolerate close scrutiny of the dark secrets of his past:

> On the one hand I cannot hope for your understanding and compassion for my life's course; on the other I do not have the minutest inner desire to justify or even excuse any decisions, actions or behavior regarding my life. . . . When it comes to indisputable traditional values, where I sense danger to those close to me or to the unity of my people, my tolerance has its limits.[1]

Nevertheless Mengele, lonelier than he had ever been in his life, hoped the visit would be a lengthy one:

> It is not going to be easy for me to express how much I look forward to that meeting. Perhaps with the confession that it represents the next goal in my life. Therefore I want you to reflect on not making the stay too short.[2]

Despite this earnest plea, Mengele could still not resist a taunting sting for Rolf. He would never let Rolf forget that he had ignored him for most of his life. In one breath he thanked Rolf for sending greetings on his sixty-sixth birthday; in the next, Mengele jibed: "I am pretty sure you will care more about your mother's birthday than mine." In the same letter, Mengele could not resist another dig. Irene had been badly injured in a car accident. "Let's stay with your mother and her bad luck," he wrote. "When I learned of that event two months later from Uncle Ha [Sedlmeier], besides my own deep inner feelings I was disappointed that I was not informed by you."[3]

With nothing else to do except fret about his health and financial problems, Mengele occupied himself with planning the trip down to the last detail. In May 1977, he wrote to Sedlmeier imploring him to ensure that Rolf use a false passport, or "dumb man," and gave detailed instructions for his arrival in São Paulo:

The final meeting place cannot yet be divulged. It should not be given directly, but rather by an intermediary in order to detect possible shadowing. Having successfully passed through the airport controls, he should first go to the hotel . . . then by taxi to the Estacao do Metro [subway station] Vila Mariana. From there he will go by underground to the San Bento station, directly in the center. If he feels he is being shadowed during these travels, then the only solution is to go back to the hotel, to hang around town for a few days, and then to travel back home again.[4]

Mengele need hardly have worried since the West Germans were not giving the slightest priority to following any members of his family. But since he did not know that, his elaborate instructions to Rolf continued, with an echo from the past. "Use the subway in an inconspicuous manner," he urged his son, advising him how to merge with the crowd on the platform just as he had done on his escape by train through Italy in 1949. He also told Rolf how to get to the Bosserts' house. From there, Wolfram Bossert would lead him to the ramshackle bungalow on Alvarenga Road:

The reason for all this traveling, apart from security, is that there is no one in Mu's [Bossert's] house between 6 a.m. and 1 p.m. Should the arrival not be between these times, then for security reasons it is still advisable to take the underground trip, only the traveler goes from San Bento back to Vila Mariana and takes a taxi there to Mu's house. If I am given the exact time of arrival including the hour, then I can prepare things much better.[5]

He also asked Rolf to bring presents for the Bosserts—"a few engravings of towns, little objets d'art, etc. It won't be very much." Mengele criticized his family for not paying more attention to those who had helped him. "Just a note of thanks and a token gift would suffice to keep them all happy," he complained to Sedlmeier. "I don't understand, after the Ge + Gi [Stammers] disaster, that this still hasn't dawned on you. Your response to my request, that you should send a few

kind words to the Mus [Bosserts], is typical of your attitude to
my friends."[6]

For himself, he asked Rolf to bring a Latin-English dictionary, parts for his German-made electric razor, some tape
recordings, and copies of Ovid's *Tristia (Elegies)* and *Epistu-
lae ex Ponto (Letters from the Black Sea).* He also asked Sedlmeier to buy Rolf and Karl Heinz a book just written by his
friend Hans Ulrich Rudel, in which the Luftwaffe ace reaf-
firmed his faith in Hitler, and featured pictures of his wartime
aerial exploits. "One day it will be of historical value," Mengele forecast. The German Bundestag had just been in an
uproar over the Luftwaffe's presentation of a special honor
guard for Rudel when he visited an air base to autograph
copies. Mengele was outraged at the political storm. "I only
read casual references to Uli's affair," he fumed. "Naturally,
the whole mob of characterless subservients which nowadays
tyrannizes Germany tear into him." Mengele said the ultimate irony was that Israel could now teach Germany a lesson
in national pride and military strength.

Sedlmeier promised to do his best to get the presents, but a
signed copy of Rudel's book was proving more difficult. "Most
bookshops don't carry his books," Sedlmeier wrote back.
"Getting his signature might be even more difficult. Since his
stroke he can hardly write with his left hand. If the young
[Rolf and Karl Heinz] are interested in these, I'll leave it to
them to buy."

At Mengele's request, Sedlmeier was in charge of checking
the security of Rolf's travel plans. On May 27, 1977, he wrote
to Mengele saying that Rolf intended to travel that September, by charter flight from Luxemburg to Rio de Janeiro, that
he had obtained a false passport, and that he would stay for
four weeks, three of them "at your disposal." Sedlmeier explained:

> On Monday I met Rolf. . . . We went through the
> plan in detail. . . . He won't be able to hire a car for
> various reasons. Perhaps Mu could rent one for him
> since he doesn't have a driver's license that fits his pass-
> port. He will have to show his normal license if he is
> checked, but this is something you must decide there. I
> don't need to go into detail about the plan. It's bound to

be a lot easier than you imagine. We both laughed at
your instructions. . . . As soon as the flight is confirmed
I will let you know the exact date. . . . Whether he is
going to do the Rio–São Paulo stretch by internal flight
or by train or bus, only he will decide at the time and
place.

He wants to move around like a tourist without any
constraints and make his decisions as and when the
mood takes him. Don't forget that he's much traveled,
speaks fluent English and is not afraid of hardship.[7]

Mengele was furious and alarmed that his instructions were
not being obeyed to the letter. He wrote back to Sedlmeier
and insisted that on no account should Rolf risk driving a car
unless he had an international driver's license that matched
his false passport. And he demanded to know more details
about the passport itself.

The first irrevocable demand is the perfect assistant
[false passport], about which I did not learn a thing in
your last letter. Recent information I got concerning
entry controls suggests there could be serious problems.
If all my conditions are respected, then, as you say,
"everything will be much easier" and I won't have to
"imagine anything!" I don't propose to signal my agreement until I know every detail about the assistant. I am
also totally confused by your remark about a "tourist
wanting to move around freely." I'd always thought he
was coming to see me![8]

In the midst of these angry exchanges, Rolf delayed his trip
a number of times. Sedlmeier began to lose patience with Rolf
as well as his father. In August he asked Rolf to make up his
mind: "You should have discussed things in more detail. . . .
For the time being I won't announce your new date, in order
not to cause any confusion, especially since I can't really give
an excuse for this new change."[9]

Two days later Sedlmeier was so exasperated that he wrote
to Mengele asking to be relieved of his role as middleman in
the travel plans. Mengele had accused him of inventing reasons for Rolf's continued delays. Sedlmeier had tired of
Mengele's idiosyncracies and paranoia:

Unfortunately you misinterpreted my statements about the tourist business and of [Rolf] having no fixed dates for the journey. He should write to you himself about this as I think it only right that all further details to do with the trip, the reporting, and all the correspondence should be left to Rolf.[10]

But Mengele and his son were not able to resolve the final details, and the ever faithful Sedlmeier stepped in to mediate again. Finally the travel date was fixed: October 10. As a bonus, Sedlmeier held out the prospect of a special visit by Mengele's old friend, Hans Rudel, who was convalescing after treatment for a stroke at the Mayo Clinic in the United States:

One week ago I was visiting Uli [Rudel] and spent a couple of hours there. . . . I have asked him to visit you in case he has time; he said he would see when it was possible. After he visits the U.S. he will visit La Paz, Paraguay and Brazil.[11]

To prepare Rolf for the meeting and to fully brief him about the background of his father's circumstances in Brazil, Sedlmeier arranged a meeting with Karl Heinz, who through regular correspondence was on more intimate terms with Mengele than was his own son. It took place in August, in Sedlmeier's garden in Günzburg. The trio also went over an outline travel plan and Karl Heinz gave Rolf $5000 to take to Mengele. "We spent many hours in my garden and had an opportunity to discuss the undertaking in all its details," Sedlmeier reported to Mengele. Finally, Sedlmeier had a word of warning for Mengele, locked as he was in a Nazi time warp. Rolf, he would find, represented a generation of German youth whose ideology and values were wholly different from his own:

The world, especially here with us, has changed tremendously and these changes have passed you by. . . . You have not been through these times with us. You have no right to criticize from afar. The preconditions that you take as a basis for all actions and thoughts simply no longer exist. You have stood still in the concepts of the old days, which unfortunately, yes, I use the word unfortunately, are no longer valid.[12]

Rolf departed for Rio de Janeiro from Frankfurt with a $600 charter ticket on Varig Airlines. He traveled on a passport which he had stolen from a friend, Wilfried Busse, when they were on holiday earlier that year.* Busse had left his passport in the car when he stopped to buy something from a shop. "I looked down and saw Wilfried's picture," said Rolf. "I thought to myself, 'That looks just like me.' My father had been going on and on about a foolproof passport. So I thought, 'That's the one.'"[13]

As his father had instructed, Rolf brought with him gifts for the Bosserts and for his father, a Latin-English dictionary, an attachment for his electric razor, and the $5000 cash from Karl Heinz. An hour or so into the flight, Rolf began to have last-minute doubts. He said: "I remember thinking to myself, 'Should I really be going? It won't change anything.' But these misgivings were just nerves. I knew that I wouldn't turn back once I got to Brazil. It was something I had to do. I'd been thinking about it for too long."

Rolf was accompanied by a second friend, whose name he will not disclose, the only person outside his family circle whom he completely trusted to keep the secret. This friend held Rolf's real passport in his pocket, to be produced in case Rolf was challenged by Brazilian immigration. Their plan was simple: once Rolf had safely entered Brazil, he would visit his father in São Paulo while his friend enjoyed the beaches in Rio. Rolf would return to Rio for the scheduled return charter flight to Germany, together with his friend.

"I wasn't at all nervous about entering Brazil," said Rolf. "My friend and I had traveled together before when we worked in the Middle East, and used to play games with each other's passports . . . to see if we could get through immigration. On this occasion the Brazilians didn't even give me a second look."

Rolf spent his first night in Brazil in Rio de Janeiro's poshest hotel, the Othon Palace, checking in as Wilfried Busse. The next day he boarded a commuter plane to São Paulo. Once there, in order to cover his trail and to ensure that he was not

---

* Although Busse was his friend, Rolf did not trust him with the knowledge of his secret journey. Months later, Busse mentioned to Rolf that he had mysteriously lost his passport. Rolf feigned ignorance, commiserating with him.

followed, he took three taxis in a circuitous route before arriving at the Bosserts' house at 7 Missouri Street.

The final leg of the journey was accomplished in Bossert's rickety old Volkswagen bus. As he pulled into Alvarenga, a dusty road full of potholes, Rolf Mengele experienced probably the strangest collection of emotions that any son has ever felt for his father. He was about to meet the most hated man in the world.

The Volkswagen stopped in front of Mengele's house. "It was actually more of a hut," said Rolf. "I was tired and suffering from nervous exhaustion."

It had been twenty-one years since Rolf last saw his father—in the Swiss Alps when he knew him as a long lost uncle who had held him spellbound with tales of daring wartime exploits. During those twenty-one years his father had been revealed as a monster.

The man standing at the gate now was a shadow of the hero of old. The pride had gone. So had the self-assurance. There was a pathetically eager look about his father, as he raised his arms for an awkward embrace. "The man who stood before me," said Rolf, "was a broken man, a scared creature."

Josef Mengele was trembling with excitement. There were actually tears in his eyes. Rolf felt as if he were in the presence of a stranger. "That's when I made a few gestures to overcome the unfamiliarity and the emotion," he said, and he responded to his father's offer of an embrace.

The bungalow his father was living in was small and simple. Mengele slept on the brick floor. Rolf had the bed.

And then the questioning began, cautiously at first, with Rolf affecting a conciliatory approach, getting his father to state his case, lulling him into a false sense of security so that Mengele might think that his son shared, after all, a sympathetic view. In fact, Rolf had adopted a lawyer's approach, calculating that only by patiently drawing his father out, could he spot the weaknesses and flaws in his case, which would allow him to prepare for a robust and probing cross-examination:

> I told my father I was interested in hearing about his time in Auschwitz. What was Auschwitz according to his version of events? What did he do there? Did he have a

role in the things he was charged with? For tactical and
psychological reasons I very cautiously touched upon
this subject, trying to analyze it and separate out the
more obscure and complex arguments my father was
trying to inject.[14]

Night after night the inquisition went on. Mengele's answers were so full of philosophical and pseudo-scientific verbi-
age that Rolf began to fear "my mind would be overrun." His
father kept straying off the essential points, justifying his racist
views, falling back at one stage on a detailed critique of pre-
historic evolution. When Mengele had finally exhausted his
hand, Rolf launched his counteroffensive. Why, Rolf asked
him, if he felt so sure of his ground, had he not turned himself
in? "My father replied, 'There are no judges, only avengers,' "
said Rolf. How could his father explain that many crippled and
deformed people had brilliant minds? "My father could not
give me a proper answer to that. He just waffled on and on."
What precisely was his evidence for asserting that some races
were superior to others? "Here most of his arguments were
sociological, historical and political," said Rolf. "They were
quite unscientific." Wasn't such an attempt to categorize races
in any case immoral and deeply inhuman? "My father knew
that this was my route into Auschwitz and what he did there,"
said Rolf. "He saw my approach and knew that I hadn't accepted what he'd been saying."

In the fourteen days and nights that Rolf spent with his
father, he learned a lot about his father's moods, his suicidal
tendencies, his depression, his temper. He learned nothing
about what his father did in the war. In a philosophical way,
Mengele tried to justify what he had done without saying
exactly what it was. But never once did he admit his guilt:

I proposed that whatever he or anyone else did or did
not do in Auschwitz, I deeply detested it, since I regard
Auschwitz as one of the most horrible examples of inhumanity and brutality. He said I did not understand. He
went there, had to do his duty, to carry out orders.

He said everybody had to do so in order to survive,
the basic instinct of self-preservation. He said he wasn't
able to think about it. From his point of view he was not

personally responsible for the incidents at the camp. He said he didn't "invent" Auschwitz. It already existed.

He said that he had wanted to help people in the camp but there had been a limit to what he could do. As far as selections were concerned, he said, the situation was analogous to a field hospital during time of war. If ten wounded soldiers are brought into the hospital in critical condition, the doctor must make almost instantaneous decisions about whom to operate on first. By choosing one, then necessarily another must die. My father asked me: "When people arrived at the railhead, what was I supposed to do? People were arriving infected with disease, half dead." He said it was beyond anyone's imagination to describe the circumstances there. His job had been to classify only those "able to work" and those "unable to work." He said he tried to grade as many people "able to work" as possible.

What my father was trying to do was to persuade me that in this manner, he had saved thousands of people from certain death. He said that he did not order and was not responsible for gassings. And he said that twins in the camp owed their lives to him. He said that he personally had never harmed anyone in his life.[15]

The more that Mengele perverted the truth, the angrier he seemed to become. Sensing Rolf's incredulity, he shouted at him: "Don't tell me you, my only son, believe what they write about me? On my mother's life I have never hurt anyone." It was at this point that father and son agreed no useful purpose would be served in pursuing the debate. As Rolf explained:

I realized that this man, my father, was just too rigid. Despite all his knowledge and intellect, he just did not want to see the basis and rules for the simplest humanity in Auschwitz. He didn't understand that his presence alone had made him an accessory within the deepest meaning of inhumanity. There was no point in going on. I had to resign myself to that fact. He did promise to write everything down. He kept saying that if I had time to study what he meant, I might see his point. But unfortunately he never did.[16]

In the end, said Rolf, it was impossible to discuss the concepts of evil or guilt because his father felt no guilt:

> I tried. These allegations, these facts left me speechless; I tried to tell him that his presence in Auschwitz alone was unacceptable to me. I was hoping he'd say, "I tried to get a transfer to the front. I did this, I did that." But it didn't come to this preliminary agreement. Unfortunately I realized that he would never express any remorse or feeling of guilt in my presence.[17]

The confrontation between father and son was not visible to the neighbors and rare visitors. To neighbors, the young man who was seen staying with "Pedro" was his "nephew." "A good-looking young man," recalled Mengele's housemaid, Elsa de Oliveira.

Despite the unbridgeable gap, Rolf found his father mentally alert. He spoke Latin and Greek and still had a lively and inquiring mind. They walked together and shopped together, buying a ceiling lamp to enliven the drab hallway. Rolf remembers that "everyone appreciated him and everyone liked him." Together they visited the Bosserts, and they traveled to Mengele's earlier homes in Serra Negra and Caieiras. Rolf recalls that owners at both farms were pleased at the visit and "proudly presented to us the well-done handwork of Señor Pedro."

A visit to the Stammers, however, was more strained:

> My visit to the Stammers was welcome on the one hand because they were very curious about me. On the other hand they had a bad conscience, of course, caused by the way they got rid of him in the end. They had a terrible fear that their future daughter-in-law, who was present, would hear the name "Mengele," the name under which I introduced myself to them. So I quickly changed to "Wilfried Busse" again.
>
> The Stammers were building a new house. My father told me that the Stammers had an economic advantage over him during all those years. He could do nothing since he was dependent on them. They "borrowed" money from him and were surprised, even angry, when

he wanted to have it back later. They were quite
pleased when we left.

But while the Stammers gave Rolf a cool reception, the
Bosserts were "completely different . . . extremely correct." They tried their best to make Rolf's stay a pleasurable
one. Yet they sensed there was difficulty between father and
son. Liselotte Bossert remembers the situation:

> I didn't think they got on very well, but there was
> some sort of respect between them. Because Rolf Men-
> gele is part of present-day Germany, and probably has
> feelings of guilt that he was looking for in his father but
> didn't find. Because his father didn't feel guilty. He was
> a scientist and thought to have acted properly—from his
> point of view—in his earlier days.[18]

While the Bosserts analyzed Rolf and his relationship with
his father, Rolf was drawing firsthand conclusions about the
psychological dependencies and weaknesses that had formed
between his father and his protectors, the Stammers and the
Bosserts. Rolf could see why his father had fallen out with the
former and had become friendly with the latter:

> He [Mengele] didn't realize how he had troubled the
> Stammers with his sharp intelligence, his pointed re-
> marks, his logic, and his arguing. They must have con-
> sidered him a senior schoolmaster and were certainly
> glad and relieved to finally get rid of him. At last they
> could live an illogical, disorderly, lazy, pleasure-seeking
> life again, their way of life, without a bad conscience
> and without playing the hypocrite of play-acting for
> him.
> As for the Bosserts, he was the connection with the
> past, a justification for their own past. He intellectually
> stimulated them, and he explained to them a lot of
> things, so they were able to understand new things.
> But mainly he was a person who needed their help
> and their devotion. A man who was also worth their
> devotion. A man who had been driven out, who was not
> understood. They helped him completely unselfishly.
> And, unlike the Stammers, when he got on their nerves,
> they simply said so to him or they just went away.

Since Rolf favored the Bosserts, he spent considerable time with them during his trip. They took his father to Bertioga, the beach where he was to die sixteen months later. At the Bosserts' suggestion, Mengele took Rolf to a small jewelry shop in Eldorado, where he bought a $500 emerald ring for Rolf's fiancée, Almuth.

As Rolf's visit stretched into the second week, the Bosserts thought the relationship between father and son seemed to be improving. However, Rolf knew the brick wall he had encountered on the subject of the Holocaust would never break down. After only two weeks, Rolf decided it was time to go.

Their farewell at the São Paulo airport was a brief and formal affair. Mengele was too preoccupied with his fear that someone might be watching to openly express any emotion. " 'We shall try to meet again very soon, all of us,' were his last words." But Rolf knew he would never see his father again.

After meeting with his friend in Rio for a few days of sightseeing, Rolf flew home to Frankfurt. He re-entered West Germany using his real passport; no questions were asked about the fact that the son of Josef Mengele had just returned from South America, his father's presumed sanctuary. The German customs officials even failed to notice that the passport lacked the required entry visa stamp for Brazil.

For Mengele, Rolf's journey home was another anxious time. "I felt enormous tension," he later wrote to him. "I didn't know whether you'd need help considering the stricter controls at German points of entry. You didn't confirm your arrival back in Germany so I was pretty nervous by the time your letter finally reached me four weeks later."[19]

In this letter Mengele thanked Rolf for the "many endearing and unforgettable days" they spent together, complaining about the shortness of Rolf's visit. But there had not been much left to say, he conceded, "facing the fact that you are not sensitive to my influence." Notwithstanding the complaints, Rolf recognized that his father had discovered a newfound respect for his son:

> He was proud of his son, like a soldier after a successful reconnaissance patrol. After all, he was like his son, even if different: pig-headed and spoiled by the postwar propaganda and by the stepfather's home and educa-

tion. All that will settle down. At least the son had found the right wife. Soon he would be a grandfather. That visit gave him a fresh impetus and new hope.

A month later Mengele wrote to Rolf again, this time to congratulate him and his second wife, Almuth, on their wedding. "If I had known how much you enjoyed precious stones, I would have sent you a bigger one," Mengele told his new daughter-in-law. Now that Rolf had a wife, he said, it might help him get closer to his son.[20] And then he expressed gratitude to Rolf for taking the trouble to see him after all those years apart: "Now I can die in peace."

CHAPTER
18

———
———

"My Life Is at an End"

———
———

Rolf Mengele's meeting with his father finally relieved the conflict between his obligations as a lawyer and his blood ties as a son. He would not hand over his father to the authorities. "In the end he was my father," said Rolf. "I couldn't report him to the police."[1]

But the fear that he might yet be discovered still preyed heavily on Mengele's mind. Even in the final miserable year of his life, he never once lifted his guard. The Bosserts suggested that he move to a more cheerful neighborhood, but for Mengele a change of scenery carried an unacceptable risk. "Any widening of the circle of people you get to know inherently brings unpredictable dangers," he said. "These have to be compared with the advantages to be expected."[2]

More than ever now, he craved friendship and company. He told Rolf he had hopes of getting to know an Austrian couple that had moved nearby. But his highest hopes were pinned on his new housemaid, nearly forty years his junior, a small, sharp-featured woman with bleached blond hair. Elsa Gulpian de Oliveira had gone to work for the old man she

knew only as "Don Pedro" in response to an advertisement.
Mengele came to depend heavily on her for company. When
she was there, he was happy. When she left, he moped.

Elsa grew fond of her boss. "He was well preserved, and
good looking," she said. "I admired his politeness, things that a
woman would admire."[3] While she cleaned his house and
cooked his food, Mengele wrote in his diary or went for long
walks. He tried to introduce her to classical music and the arts.
When her sister married, Mengele took Elsa's hand for a
dance. Soon there were expensive gifts—a gold bracelet, a
ring, a white woolen shawl. Although he never once tried to
kiss her, Elsa became the sole object of his emotional desire.
For the third time in his life, Josef Mengele had fallen in love.
Elsa recalls his possessiveness:

> He never liked my having boyfriends. He always used
> to say, "This one isn't going to work out," or "That one
> doesn't really care about you." He started to ask me why
> I made myself look good to go out with young men but
> not when I went out with him. One day he invited one
> of my boyfriends to the house and as we came down the
> stairs holding hands he stared at us. Later he told me he
> was jealous of me holding hands with the young man
> and he confessed that he loved me and asked me to
> move in with him.[4]

Elsa refused. "I told him that I would not live with him unless
he married me," she said. "I told him I wanted to get married
legally. If he had asked me, I would have married him." But
Mengele was distraught. "He started crying and said he
couldn't marry me, but he wouldn't tell me why," she said.[5]

Spurned so late in life, Mengele behaved like a lovesick boy.
He pestered Elsa's mother, promising he would give her
daughter a good and homely life. He broke down in front of
her and sobbed. "My mother and I used to get very nervous,"
said Elsa. "My mother would say, 'How crazy is that man?' He
even walked back and forth in front of our house, waiting for
me."[6]

Elsa had brought a new light into Mengele's life. But in
October 1978, she went out of it as quickly as she had come in
when she announced that she intended to get married. Mengele never quite recovered from the shock. "He cried and

said I must not marry my husband because he really didn't care for me," she said. "He cried and he said he was going to die soon."

From then on Mengele declined rapidly. "I had a bad time of it these past two months," he wrote to Sedlmeier, "barbaric pains, sleepless nights and disappointments." Once more, thoughts of suicide entered his head. "Long-lasting pain of this kind causes one to be very nervous and sick of living."[7]

Mengele was now plagued by high blood pressure, a severe inner ear infection, and a prostate condition. His degenerating spine was also very painful. Even his few friends had tired of his moaning. He complained that Wolfram Bossert had told him it was "a good thing that I lived alone because of all my moaning and sighing. I really wouldn't wish my pain on this insensitive man."[8] And he accused his family of virtually abandoning him. "No one told me about the birth of Rolf's baby," he wrote to Sedlmeier.[9] He was especially grieved by the silence from Rolf.

Amid the wretchedness of these last months came a sinister echo from his past. Rolf's wife, Almuth, had aroused Mengele's interest because she was a twin. "The nosiness of this old explorer of family heredity should be understandable," he wrote. "For the first time one of us has chosen his partner from the north," he said. "These incoming Nordic genes are to be appreciated and the best results are to be expected from this combination."[10] Mengele asked Almuth for more details of her family background. But he did not get a reply.

Life in Alvarenga Road now seemed empty and devoid of purpose. Mengele tried to fill the gaping hole left in his life by Elsa's departure. Inez Mehlich, a maid who had worked part-time for him before, agreed to live in, sleeping in a makeshift wooden hut in his back garden. Sometimes, she said, Mengele behaved like a small child. "He was so anxious that he once pounded on the door of my hut in the middle of the night," she said. "I opened it and he said, 'Oh, I'm sorry—I just wanted to make sure you were there. O.K. It's all right. Goodnight.'"

By Christmas 1978 Mengele had lost the will to live. He walked around in an absentminded daze, not seeming to care what might happen to him. Once he nearly fell down a well in

the backyard; another time he was almost killed when he
ventured outside. Neighbors, startled by the screech of
brakes, saw a bus straddling the road and amid the swirling
dust, Mengele, grazed yet shuffling out of sight as if oblivious
of his brush with death.

It was in this distracted frame of mind that Mengele left his
bungalow at 5555 Alvarenga Road for the last time. He
seemed to know that he might never return. After agonizing
for several days, he finally accepted an invitation from the
Bosserts to stay at their rented beach house at Bertioga,
twenty-five miles south of São Paulo. It was late January 1979,
the height of a sweltering Brazilian summer. "He kept wondering whether it would do his spirits any good," Inez recalled. "He said he was very tired but in the end agreed to
take the trip. 'I am going to the beach because my life is at an
end,' he told me."[11]

Alone, he took the two-hour bus ride to Bertioga, arriving
there on February 5. Lisolette Bossert remembers "he started
letting off steam right away. He seemed to be very irritated by
something." For most of the next two days, Mengele stayed
inside the tiny two-bedroom beach house. Its shutters were
closed despite the broiling heat. "It must have been like a
steam bath inside," said Arnaldo Santana, who lived behind
the summer house. "I was working close by and I could hear
talking, always in German."

At 3 p.m. on February 7, Mengele finally emerged. "We
thought a walk would soothe his mind, as he would see nature,
the beach and the water," said Liselotte. It was another hot
day, the sunshine blazing down. He and Wolfram Bossert
walked along the beach and then sat in the sun for a while.
Bossert recalls that Mengele was heartsick for Germany:

> I am convinced that he was longing to return to Ger-
> many. That was clear toward the end; on the last day he
> made it clear. I don't know whether he knew death was
> coming, but he was sitting on a large rock by the sea, all
> by himself, looking out across the sea to the east. And he
> said: "Over there is my country. . . . I would like to
> spend the last days of my life in my native town of
> Günzburg, somewhere at the top of a mountain, in a
> little house, and to write the history of my native town."

That was what he really wanted. . . . At the time, I didn't think anything of it, but knowing now what happened that day, I can remember it quite clearly.[12]

About 4:30 in the afternoon, to cool off from the burning sun, Mengele decided to chance the gentle Atlantic waves. Ten minutes later he was fighting for his life.

Young Andreas Bossert saw him first and shouted, "Uncle, come out, the current is too strong." Alerted by his son, Wolfram Bossert looked up and saw a thrashing movement in the sea. He called out and asked Mengele if he was all right. A grimace of pain was the only response. Plunging into the sea, Bossert swam as fast as he could to rescue his friend. By the time he reached him, there was scarcely any movement left. Paralysis had seized his body. Young Andreas Bossert remembers a lifeless body lying lopsided on the water, bobbing up and down with the swell of the sea. Mengele had had a second stroke. Bossert recalls the frantic few moments:

> I had to swim with one arm and drag him with the other, and the sea was dragging us both out. I fought and fought, trying to keep his head above water, never feeling any ground under my feet, so that I knew that we weren't getting any closer to shore. I got to a stage where I felt I couldn't hold on any longer. But then, somewhere in my subconscious I had a thought that I should use the force of the waves. So I dived, digging my heels into the sand and then holding the body above my head—he was still alive then.[13]

Suddenly and unexpectedly Mengele began to make a desperate last fight for life. His eyes now fixed earnestly ahead, he was trying to swim with one arm, his strokes getting stronger. For a moment it seemed that he had survived the worst. But then his face lost all its determination, his arm fell back, and there was no movement.

Bossert remembers his effort to just carry Mengele to shore:

> I was left with this deadweight. . . . I surfaced and let myself be carried forward by the waves, then I dived again, dug my heels into the ground and held him above me, before coming up again. And this is how we managed to get ashore.

As Wolfram Bossert got nearer to dry land, a group of rescuers waded out to meet him and grabbed Mengele by his legs and arms, carrying him to the beach. Bossert was quite exhausted from his rescue attempt. So hard had he struggled that he nearly drowned, and he had to go to the hospital himself.

A clutch of people had gathered as news of the drama spread, Mengele's now motionless body lying on the sand. A doctor who had seen it all massaged his heart and administered the kiss of life. For a few moments there was a flicker of response, but in the end the doctor's efforts were to no avail.

The body was left on the beach until late that night. Every few minutes it had to be dragged farther up the sand because of the incoming tide. "I nearly had a screaming fit," said Liselotte Bossert. "It was so undignified." Then a policeman, Expeditio Dias Romao, came to take charge of the body.

Accidents were not uncommon on this popular stretch of sand, but Romao said he would always remember this one. Darkness had fallen by the time he arrived. Kneeling in an almost reverential pose was Liselotte Bossert, holding a candle at the dead man's head and wailing, "The Uncle is dead. The Uncle is dead."[14]

C H A P T E R
19

———
———

"Keep Everything a
Secret"

———
———

Rolf Mengele's first reaction to the news of his father's death was one of enormous relief. "I basically had a conflict that could never be resolved," he said. "On the one hand he was my father; on the other hand there were these allegations, these horrific pictures of Auschwitz. I was very relieved that this solution came about and not another, like maybe a trial, as important as it might have been."[1]

Word of the "Uncle's" demise reached the Mengele family by letter from Wolfram Bossert to Sedlmeier:

> It is with deep sorrow that I fulfill the painful duty of informing you and the relatives of the death of our common friend. Right up to his last breath of air he fought heroically, just as he had done during his life full of turmoil.[2]

The funeral had been a rushed and traumatic affair. It was all over within twenty-four hours. Immediate disposal of the body was urgently required in that subtropical heat, yet formalities had to be completed. Liselotte Bossert had to cope with them alone because her husband was recovering in the hospital from his rescue attempt. He was so exhausted that the doctor told her she was lucky not to have lost him too.

Shortly before his death, Mengele had told the Bosserts he wished to be cremated. Given the time and regulations, that had not been possible to arrange. "In this mainly Catholic country there are still strict rules to follow concerning this," Bossert explained to Sedlmeier. The Brazilian authorities required a signature from a close relative guaranteeing that all the surviving members of the deceased's family agreed to cremation.

Anticipating this problem and unknown to Mengele, Wolfgang Gerhard had made provision for a burial plot next to his own mother's at Our Lady of the Rosary Cemetery, on a hillside at Embu, twelve miles west of São Paulo. On his brief visit in 1976, Gerhard had even taken the trouble to prepare the cemetery director, Gino Carita, for the arrival of a "sickly older relative."

But when Gerhard's plan was put into action, it almost backfired. The corpse had been put in a coffin at a first aid station and taken straight to the local coroner, Dr. Jaime Edson Andrade Mendonca, who just prodded the body. At 2 a.m. he was in no mood for a complete postmortem. Liselotte Bossert heard the man who had brought in the coffin say: "Well, it's obvious, the person has drowned." Mendonca then issued a death certificate in the name of Wolfgang Gerhard, aged fifty-three.

Confronted with a simple white coffin and a certificate showing the death of the man who had actually booked the burial plot, Gino Carita was very curious. Then came the most awkward moment of all. Carita said he wanted to open the coffin and see the body. Liselotte Bossert recalls the event:

> When he saw the name Wolfgang Gerhard, quite a rare name in these parts, he immediately remembered him and said: "It can't be possible—he mentioned an old uncle and now he is here himself!" He said to me that we should, perhaps, look at him now. And then I knew straightaway that this was the last thing I had to do, that

nobody should discover that it was the body of Mengele
—nobody must ever know this—and that's why I became hysterical and said, "No, I don't want to, I can't.
My husband is ill and I don't know how he is, and I am all
alone here and I want to get the whole thing over with
as quickly as possible." The man said he respected my
wishes, especially as a body pulled out of the water is
never a pretty sight . . . so he went along with my
wishes.[3]

Carita relented, not wishing to offend a grieving friend of the
deceased, and Mengele's secret was taken to the grave.

The irony is that had Mengele's wish for cremation been
carried out, his life in Brazil would probably have remained a
secret forever. It was the exhumation of his bones six years
later that provided scientific proof of his identity. Anything
less would undoubtedly not have satisfied his hunters, raised
on a diet of press fantasies about his superhuman powers of
escape. Certainly it had never been the intention of the Bosserts and the Mengele family to divulge the truth.

On the face of it, the Mengele family's decision not to announce Josef's death seems a surprising one. In strictly commercial terms, an announcement of Mengele's death could
only have benefited the family firm in Günzburg, vulnerable
as it was to accusations of complicity in his continuing freedom. At least that is what everyone assumed. "There is no
reason for the family not to announce his death," commented
a skeptical police superintendent, Menachem Russek, head of
the Nazi crimes section of Israel's police, when news first
broke of Mengele's hillside grave. "It's a trick. He's still alive."
In fact, the family had calculated that the financial benefits
from an announcement were far outweighed by the torrent of
questions that this would raise about their forty years of collaboration. As they had done in the past, the Mengele family
had placed their own financial interests as the top priority,
ignoring any moral obligation to Mengele's hunters or survivors to announce the death and end the case. "They [the
Mengele family] replied in a letter that naturally the case was
much too dangerous to be revealed and that much water
would have to flow under the bridge before this could be
expected," said Wolfram Bossert. Moreover, the final decision

rested with Mengele's next of kin, his son, Rolf. And Rolf decided "out of consideration to those who had helped my father" that the world should be left to go on guessing. At least, for a while.

Nondisclosure was certainly what the Bosserts desired, though for even more perverse reasons. "Not only does it avoid personal inconvenience but it also keeps the opposing side wasting money on something that is antiquated," Wolfram Bossert wrote to Sedlmeier.[4]

Since Wolfgang Gerhard had died of a cerebral hemorrhage two months before Mengele, Bossert suggested that Gerhard's children be paid a "settlement allowance" because the Günzburgers would need their collaboration for the paperwork if they decided to transport Mengele's body back to Germany for a proper funeral. The Mengeles preferred to leave matters as they were.

For the second time in two years, Rolf flew to São Paulo, this time to collect his father's effects and settle his affairs. He flew under his own name and passport, leaving Frankfurt on a regularly scheduled airliner. He spent Christmas with the Bosserts, not returning to West Germany until January 3, 1980. The Bosserts were rewarded handsomely for sheltering his father. Rolf gave them the $1000 cash left over from the $5000 he had brought his father during the 1977 trip. Rolf also gave the house at 5555 Alvarenga Road to be equally divided between the Bosserts and the Stammers. It may have been run-down, but it was worth $25,000. The Stammers eventually sold their share to the Bosserts, who took over the entire property. The Bosserts were grateful to Rolf for his generosity and thanked him in a subsequent letter "for allowing us to achieve a lifelong dream."

Rolf took his father's gold watch, letters, diaries, and pictures. "Emotionally, I believe, as you probably would, it is best to burn all of it," Bossert had written to Sedlmeier. "On the other hand his fate is too remarkable. The descendants do deserve an intellectual heritage, even if the current generation doesn't consider it important."[5] (These lofty ideals faded six years later when Mengele's corpse was discovered at Embu. Representatives of *Stern* magazine beat a path to the Bosserts' door and paid them a handsome fee for some unimportant remnants of Mengele's papers and photographs they had hidden from Rolf on his 1979 trip.)

After gathering his father's personal material, Rolf proceeded to Rio and checked in to the posh Othon Palace hotel, where he had stayed two years earlier under a false name. That caused one of the most awkward moments in his life. "Ah, Mengele," said the concierge. "Do you know you have a very famous name around here?" Rolf feigned a jolly laugh. Inside, he was shaking like jelly. He hid the duffle bag in the dropped ceiling of his hotel room. "Any professional search would have found the material in less than a minute," said Rolf, "but it was the best I could do."

Why did it take six years for the secret of Mengele's Brazilian exile and his death to emerge? Aside from a small circle of unrepentant Nazis like Hans Rudel, there were by now almost forty close friends and family who knew but never said a word. Among these were Rolf, his first wife, Irmi, and her parents; his second wife, Almuth, and her parents, the Jenckels; Mengele's first wife, Irene; her husband, Alfons Hackenjos; their son, Jens, and his wife, Sabine, who was Rolf's secretary; Mengele's nephews, Dieter and Karl Heinz, and their wives; his nieces, Ute and Monika, and their husbands; Mengele's second wife, Martha, and her son, Wolf Ensmann, from her first marriage; Rolf and Almuth's friend, Wilfried Busse; the pharmacist and his wife in Munich, Mengele's friends who had provided him safe shelter in 1945; the Stammers and their two children; the Bosserts and their two children; the Glawes and their son; and of course the dissembling Hans Sedlmeier, his wife, and their two children, one a doctor and the other a lawyer. It is extraordinary that such loyalty to a man so patently evil, and to his family, overrode any consideration of higher morality or public duty—stranger still that from somewhere in the supposedly enlightened ranks of the younger Mengeles not a word was leaked to the authorities, even after his death.

The truth had to be wrested from this arcane and amoral brotherhood, which was divided by bitter jealousies over money and power but united in the common goal of saving their necks and the neck of one of the nastiest men ever known to have inhabited the earth. In the end it was public pressure that forced the authorities to go on the offensive and flush out the facts.

That process began late in 1977, with the very people who had helped create the myth of Mengele's invincibility and his high-level protection in Paraguay—the Nazi-hunters and amateur sleuths. The idea of Paraguay as Mengele's permanent home had long been ingrained in the public consciousness. It was the frustrating lack of progress in confirming this established "fact" that persuaded the United States and Israel to resolve the Mengele mystery once and for all.

In August 1977, a dubious story in a glossy Argentine magazine reported that Josef Mengele had been seen driving a black sedan through the streets of Asunción. Simon Wiesenthal went a step further. In September he told *Time* magazine that Mengele had two posh houses and was always surrounded by armed bodyguards with walkie-talkies. Mengele wore dark glasses, he said, and was an active member of a "surviving network of Nazi bigwigs known as *Die Spinne* [The Spider]." According to Wiesenthal, Mengele was a frequent visitor to the German Club in Asunción, where he often made a spectacle of himself by slamming his pistol on the bar.[6]

Time also reported the claims of a recent visitor to Paraguay, Professor Richard Arens of the law faculty at Temple University in Philadelphia. Arens claimed that Paraguayan defense officials had told him that Mengele was in the country as President Stroessner's close advisor on torture techniques and that he had been experimenting on defenseless Ache Indians in the Chaco. Despite the best efforts of the American embassy in Asunción to persuade *Time* that the story was probably fictitious, the magazine went ahead and published it.

Inaccurate as it was, the *Time* article lit a slow-burning fuse on the Mengele hunt, which had been curiously absent from the front pages for three years. Those first wisps of smoke appeared with an inquiry to the state department from Senator Alan Cranston, Jr., in January 1978. The assistant secretary for congressional relations, Douglas J. Bennett, Jr., replied that although the state department could not confirm that Mengele was in Paraguay, it was "difficult for the United States Government to become directly involved in the Mengele case . . . because Mengele does not reside in the United

States and the crimes of which he is accused did not occur in United States territory."[7]

Just to be certain, the department cabled the U.S. embassy in Asunción, requesting any "hard information on Mengele's presence (past or now), in Paraguay and his activities, or at least detailed comments on the Mengele reference in the *Time* article."[8] The following day the embassy cabled back Paraguayan interior minister Sabino Montonaro's response. He said that Mengele "took out citizenship in 1959; lived in Paraguay for about two years, or until 1961–1962; Mengele has not re-entered Paraguay since that time; if you do not believe me I will be glad to show you the police record."[9] The trouble was that no one any longer believed a word the Paraguayans said. Their public denials during the 1960s of Mengele's Paraguayan citizenship and their refusal to actively assist in the hunt, coupled with their appalling record on human rights, had irreparably damaged their credibility.

The state department, however, had detected a shift in the Paraguayan government's attitude since President Jimmy Carter came to power in 1976. Now Paraguay was wrestling with an image problem caused by the Carter administration's highlighting of its record of torture and detention without trial. With *Time* magazine having resurrected the specter of Asunción as a haven for the world's most wanted man, the government faced a major public relations crisis. Paraguay was certainly a refuge for many wanted men. But even Montonaro bridled at what seemed to be a rerun of all the old allegations that Mengele and Stroessner were close friends.

The subject of Mengele soon became a regular topic of conversation for Ambassador Robert White when he took the Paraguayans to task over their repressive regime:

> When I got to Asunción, the Paraguayan government would say to me, "What can we do to improve our image abroad?" I would reply that one of the things they could do was cancel Mengele's citizenship. We discussed it quite a bit.[10]

In March 1979, the CBS *Sixty Minutes* program screened a shortened version of a British documentary on the hunt for Mengele. With the assistance of a resourceful German doctor, John Ware and Mike Beckham of Granada Television had obtained secretly filmed conversations with several of Mengele's former Paraguayan friends, including Alban Krug, Armando Raeynarts, a hotelier who had met him, and Werner Schubius, who knew him in Asunción. For the first time there was on the record evidence that Mengele had been sheltered, at least for a time, in Paraguay after the Eichmann kidnapping.

In the documentary, Krug evaded questions as to when exactly he had sheltered Mengele and muttered threats about "not advising anyone to come looking for him here." Granada had also obtained for the first time a copy of Mengele's Paraguayan citizenship document. When Israel's former ambassador in Asunción, Benjamin Varon, appeared in the film saying Mengele had "one of his homes in Paraguay at least until 1972," the overall effect of the program was to indicate that the government of Paraguay still had something to hide.[11] Seen by 20 million viewers, the program made a significant impact. Americans were outraged. Congress was petitioned with letters and telephone calls demanding that America take action to force Paraguay's hand.

Responding to the public outcry, in June 1979, Senator Jesse Helms submitted Senate resolution number 184:

> . . . it is the sense of the Senate that the President of the United States should immediately call upon Paraguay to apprehend and extradite Josef Mengele to stand trial in the Federal Republic of Germany.[12]

In the debate that followed, Senator Helms referred to Mengele's "work in genetic engineering" as the "Frankenstein project of the century." Helms expressed a view that seemed to shake the United States out of its postwar apathy:

> The fact that Josef Mengele should remain today in freedom, never having been brought to trial, makes him a living symbol of the Holocaust we cannot continue to tolerate. To forgive or forget the crimes of Josef Mengele would require the amputation of our conscience and the dismemberment of our memory.

The Senate unanimously passed the resolution urging the president to demand that Paraguay act to arrest and extradite Mengele. In the House of Representatives, fifty-seven congressmen signed a petition that was delivered to the Paraguayan ambassador to Washington, Mario Lopez Escobar, demanding the same action.

Paraguayan government-inspired demonstrations against President Carter's tough new approach on human rights had already strained relations between Asunción and Washington. But there was never any doubt about who held the whip. Aid was held back and defense cuts were threatened. Now Ambassador White pressed home the congressional demands about Mengele: "Eventually the Paraguayans responded to my suggestion that his citizenship be revoked. They said, 'What a great idea.' "[13]

On August 5, 1979, Interior Minister Montonaro held a press conference and laid the groundwork for the revocation of Mengele's citizenship. He denied that Mengele was in the country and said truthfully that he had left Paraguay "a long time ago." On August 8, Montonaro directed the Paraguayan attorney general, Clotildo Gimenez Benitez, to ask the supreme court to revoke the citizenship, which it did that same day. The court stated that it had reached its decision because Mengele had been "absent from the country since 1960."

When Mengele's citizenship was revoked, Ambassador White assumed Mengele must have died. "I must say that up until that time I always believed that actually he was in Paraguay," he said.[14] The ambassador was right, of course, about Mengele's death, though he did not know what had happened in Brazil. The question is, did President Stroessner know?

According to Ambassador White, it is inconceivable that Montonaro would have revoked Mengele's citizenship without the president's authority, since he views the status of Paraguayan nationality as sacrosanct. "Stroessner must have been consulted," said Ambassador White. If he is right, it suggests that Stroessner was privy to Mengele's death in Brazil within six months of its occurrence but nonetheless allowed the world to go on guessing for another six years.

No doubt that this is the kind of game that Stroessner would have enjoyed, if only to avenge the false accusations that his country had harbored Mengele for twenty years. But almost certainly Stroessner did not know Mengele had died.

The president's close friend, Hans Rudel, was privy to the secret, although according to Rolf, he did not know exactly where Mengele had been buried. And just as the Mengele family had reached a pact with the Bosserts never to disclose the death, Rudel too was bound by that oath of silence. Had Stroessner known the exact details, no amount of allegiance to Hans Rudel would have prevented him from laying to rest once and for all the Auschwitz ghost that had haunted his country for so long.

The Nazi-hunters were certain that Mengele was still alive and that Stroessner's decision to revoke his citizenship was an elaborate plot to extend him even greater presidential protection. The first of their salvos aimed at exposing this sinister move was fired by Simon Wiesenthal. Scornful of Montonaro and the Paraguayan supreme court's decision, Wiesenthal said it "meant nothing" and offered a new $50,000 reward for Mengele's capture. He also urged Paraguay to issue another arrest warrant and offered to pay the police $10,000 for his arrest.

Wiesenthal's skepticism about the Paraguayan action was shared by a group of Jewish industrialists in New York, who with the help of a prominent local Jewish spokesman, actually hatched an elaborate plot to kidnap Mengele. Word reached the group, which included one survivor of Auschwitz, that two Paraguayan intelligence officers were prepared to betray Mengele for $500,000. After several weeks' negotiations, the Paraguayans agreed to arrest Mengele when he arrived at a bank in Asunción where he was said to come regularly. Mengele would then be taken to the Brazilian border town of Foz de Iguaçu. When his identity had been confirmed, he would be handed over to the authorities. On receipt of a telephone call from one of the industrialists, $500,000 would be transferred from a Bahamian bank to a special account for the Paraguayans.

Early in November 1979, $500,000 was deposited in the Bahamian bank. When the Paraguayans were satisfied the money was there, they signaled to the New Yorkers that they were ready to move in. Two American bounty hunters, one a Vietnam veteran, traveled to Foz de Iguaçu, where they waited for news of the arrest. On November 22 the Americans were told by the Paraguayans that Mengele would be picked up at the bank the following day. On November 23 there was no sign of Mengele or the Paraguayans. Although their money was safe, the Americans had been the victims of a crude shakedown by two corrupt Paraguayan policemen. The incident showed how seriously reports of Mengele hiding in Paraguay were taken even after his citizenship was revoked. The New York industrialists were not men given to precipitate action.[15]

Meanwhile Wiesenthal's claims became more extreme. Mengele was hiding in a special Nazi colony in Chile; he had gone to Bolivia but the police would not cooperate; no, he was in Uruguay; he had heart trouble and was about to give himself up to a West German embassy; he had been seen "five times recently . . . his capture could happen in the next several weeks."

But even Wiesenthal's vivid imagination could not match the best of the stories claiming Mengele was still alive. Early in 1981, the hunt switched to a wealthy suburb in the United States. Billboards advertising Rupert Murdoch's *New York Post* screamed: "Angel of Death in Westchester County." The paper was reporting the *Life* magazine claim that from 1978 to 1979 Mengele had lived in a private house near the Ohel Shmuel Yeshiva on Haines Road in Bedford Hills, about thirty miles north of New York City. "It's the first I've heard of it," was the laconic reaction of Allan Ryan, Jr., chief of the Justice Department's Office of Special Investigations.

He was not the only skeptic. But the *Life* story did contain several genuinely interesting facts about the Mengele family's financial interests in the United States, and this brought the U.S. closer to launching its final hunt. *Life* reported that Mengele's nephew, Dieter, was a part owner in an American corporation, KMN International Farm Equipment, Inc., a distributor of farm machinery. Incorporated in October 1973, the company listed Dieter as its legal representative. KMN stands for three equal partners: "K" is for Bernard Krona GmbH; "M" is for Mengele & Sons; and "N" is for H. Niemayer and Sons. Subsequent inquiries showed outlets in Arkansas and Wisconsin. Although Dieter said he sold his interest in this firm in 1982, further investigations show he retained an ownership share in another U.S. company, the BSD Farm Corporation of Delaware, founded in November 1979. The Mengele family also reportedly bought four hundred acres of farmland in Greencastle, Indiana, in December 1979, valued at $1.2 million.[16]

In April 1984, there seemed to be another Mengele skeleton in America's closet. There was a report that he would have been caught by the FBI on a flying visit to Miami in 1979 but for a last minute tip-off. This time the source appeared to be reliable. An assistant United States attorney in Miami, Jerry Sandford, claimed he had been given the secret task of arresting Mengele at the airport after the FBI received word that he would be flying in from Asunción on board Braniff flight 974, arriving at 6:30 a.m. on August 29, 1979.

Since Sandford was running for local political office in 1984, it seemed an opportune moment to tell the electorate how close he had come to catching Mengele and how he had persisted with the hunt ever since. He chose the *Jewish Floridian* to break his story:

> On a Friday afternoon I got a call from the justice department in Washington telling me that I had been selected to handle a matter of extreme delicacy. They refused to give me a name. They told me to tell no one, not even my boss, about this assignment.[17]

At 8 p.m. that night two FBI agents arrived at Sandford's house to explain the mission. Sandford went on:

> I was stunned. Suddenly it seemed as if I had lived just for this night. Then an hour later I got a call from Washington telling me Mengele had apparently been tipped off and wouldn't be arriving. My disappointment was bitter.[18]

In fact there had been a tip to the FBI that Mengele was flying into Miami, but it was all an elaborate hoax. Members of Paraguay's opposition political parties had made a reservation under the name "Josef Mengele," in the hope that the recurring image of the "Angel of Death" would compromise the Stroessner government. Not knowing the source of the reservation, the West Germans had picked it up and asked the FBI to check.*

---

* Dieter Mengele visited Miami several times in the late 1970s; he claimed he had a Jewish girlfriend there. He told John Martin of ABC News that when he came back in 1983 with his wife and Rudi, an elderly Günzburg friend, the FBI mistook Rudi for his fugitive uncle. The

Afterward Sandford became convinced that Mengele might be tied up in a drug smuggling racket. As a former chief of the drug trafficking prosecution unit for the U.S. attorney's office in Miami, Sandford put together a chart of what he called "possible links among anti-communist groups, terrorists, narcotics people, and pro-Nazi groups." Although only conjecture, his suspicion was shared by the CIA. As early as 1972, CIA reports suggested that Mengele was using the name Dr. Henrique Wollman, and lived near Encarnacion and "that [he] and others [are] heavily involved in narcotics traffic."[19] In November 1979, the CIA again speculated that Mengele might have been involved in drug dealing. An internal memorandum was drawn up in collaboration with the Drug Enforcement Administration, but it was never made public. A CIA officer coordinating foreign narcotics intelligence said that the article, "though a tantalizing bit of information, is based on very circumstantial and unsubstantiated evidence and does not warrant publication as finished intelligence."[20]

Speculative as these reports were, their effect when they were disclosed early in 1985 added to mounting congressional pressure on the United States to throw its formidable resources into the Mengele hunt. The CIA, said Senator Alfonse d'Amato, had just let "the information hang there. No one pursued this."

One premise never seemed to be in doubt: Mengele was alive, of that everyone was sure. In Frankfurt, Hans-Eberhard Klein, the prosecutor in charge of the West German investigation, said he had no reason to think Mengele was dead—but in view of the Bonn government's inaction over the years, it is difficult to know the basis for Klein's assertion. The West Germans had never inspired much confidence in their determination to exhaust all possible leads.

Six months before Mengele's death was discovered, Serge Klarsfeld, the Paris-based Nazi-hunter, told Klein he believed Rolf Mengele had made a secret trip to Brazil using a false

---

FBI had been alerted by a middle-aged couple the Mengeles had met on the beach. Dieter had told the couple his real name and during the conversation spoke about the firm in Germany. The next day the FBI arrived at Dieter's hotel room and questioned him about his friend Rudi. The beach couple were Jewish and told the FBI they thought Rudi might be Mengele himself.

passport. Rolf's Berlin apartment had been searched by one of Klarsfeld's supporters, and Wilfried Busse's passport was found.* It was stamped with a Brazilian visa. As it turned out, this was the passport that Rolf used on the first leg of his journey to Brazil in October 1977 to meet his father. But according to Klarsfeld, prosecutor Klein showed little interest in the lead. "We gave all the information to Klein," said Klarsfeld. "But we couldn't find out what he did with it because he always told us that anything to do with Mengele was an official secret."[21]

The Israelis were certainly convinced that Mengele was alive. A respected member of New York's Jewish community traveled to Jerusalem in late 1984 with information that suggested Mengele owned a large farm in Uruguay. There were several high-level government meetings over what seemed to be a new and decisive lead. What neither the New Yorker nor the Israeli government knew was that the two men who were the source of the information had a history of trying to sell invariably false stories about Nazis for large sums of money.

These two story brokers, Saul Stenzburg, a former Argentine policeman, and Herbert John, a West German journalist with shady contacts in the Nazi information business, also persuaded *Paris Match* and the *New York Post* to spend more than $50,000 on investigating the old man in Uruguay they said was Mengele. The *Post* sent an advance party of sleuths who returned with pictures of the suspect on his large hacienda, which was registered in the name of "Branaa." For the *Post,* the most persuasive feature of the story was the evidence of a prostitute who Stenzburg said visited Branaa once a month. From such intimate contact, the girl had learned that "Señor Branaa" was German and that his friends called him "Doctor."

A team of United States photo-identification experts were asked if they thought the photographs were of Mengele. The experts were among the most eminent in their field: Dr. Ellis R. Kerley, a forensic scientist who had been a consultant on the Warren Commission investigating the death of President John Kennedy (and was to be a member of the 1985 U.S.

---

* Klarsfeld's agent may have found the Busse passport, but he missed a much larger trophy. In Rolf's apartment were two bags filled with more than thirty pounds of Mengele's personal writings. They were overlooked in the supposedly thorough search.

forensics team sent to Brazil to determine whether the bones at Embu were Mengele's); Peggy C. Caldwell, consultant forensic anthropologist for the office of the medical examiner in New York City and a teacher at the prestigous Smithsonian Institution in Washington, D.C.; and Dr. Lawrence Angel, curator of physical anthropology at the Smithsonian Institution.

All three experts conducted a series of independent experiments on the photographs, comparing them with verified pictures of Mengele. They made precise measurements and evaluated characteristics such as "adherence of ear auricle to skull," "lobular appearance and shape of forehead," "obliquity of palpebral slit." Measurements and comparisons were made of the length of the nose, the nose root diameter, the length of the face, the nasal "breadth of the alae," the base of the nose to the lip closure, and many other features.

The results of all three independently tested samples were remarkably similar. Phony pictures had been deliberately placed in each set of pictures. Each expert rejected these. Each expert also concluded that the Branaa photographs and the known pictures of Mengele were one and the same man. And they did not fudge their answers.

Dr. Kerley said, "The 1937 photographs [Mengele's SS pictures] and the 1985 photograph are very probably the same individual. The conclusion is based on the compatibility of most of indices as indicated by the analysis of variance and on the high probability of .9505 [95 percent] that they are all from the same population." Dr. Angel said that in his judgment the likeness was "pretty much like seeing an automobile coming down the street at about 50 feet away and saying, 'That is a Mercedes.' It is of that order. We ordinarily act on that kind of thing. On this comparison I would be willing to go to court if necessary." Peggy Caldwell concluded that the 1937 and 1985 photographs were of "the same individual regardless of the difference in his age at the time the photographs were taken." She said that the "dental data" clinched the verdict for her. "Yes, I would sentence a man to the electric chair on the basis of this," she said.[22]

When the Israelis heard these verdicts, they sent their own men to Uruguay to check the story. At the same time, the TV networks learned of the new Mengele suspect. Fearing they might be scooped by NBC, which had shot several thousand feet of videotape of the old man washing his car, ABC approached Señor Branaa directly and asked, "Are you Dr. Mengele?" The poor man spent the rest of the day trying to convince the reporter that he was not the Auschwitz doctor. After Branaa introduced them to business colleagues and old friends and showed them school records, ABC was satisfied that the forensic scientists had made an enormous blunder.

Nevertheless, it was West German prosecutor Klein's view that prevailed: Mengele was still alive. And reports from Europe seemed to bear this out. Two young British psychologists, Simon Jones and Kirn Rattan, researching a psychological profile of Mengele, thought they had made a breakthrough in contacting the elusive fugitive. Fritz Steinacker, the Frankfurt lawyer who acted for Mengele when he was divorced as well as when he was stripped of his medical and anthropological doctorates, had agreed to forward their written questions through an unidentified intermediary to Mengele. Steinacker promised that in three months they would receive an answer directly from the doctor himself. In hindsight it appears to be Steinacker's perverse way of having some fun with serious Mengele researchers. "You could say that on that basis we believed Mengele was probably alive," said Jones. "Steinacker was Mengele's lawyer, after all."

The U.S. government also believed Mengele was alive. They gave some credence to intelligence reports in 1984 that he had been seen in Paraguay. Slowly but inexorably, the momentum for American involvement in the Mengele hunt was gathering pace. In June 1984, in an uncharacteristically defeatist mood, Simon Wiesenthal complained that perhaps the time had passed for the hunt for Mengele. "After all, when you bring an old man to court, there is natural sympathy for him," he sighed.

But congressional sympathy for that argument still had some distance to run. Two crucial events at the beginning of 1985 persuaded Congress that the Josef Mengele mystery had to be cleared up once and for all. Dead or alive.

C H A P T E R
20

———
———

"Dust to Dust"

———
———

The wind howled across the flat ice fields of southern Poland, rattling an eerie tune on the strands of wire surrounding Auschwitz before it battered the camp's gray stone blocks. Bracing themselves against the penetrating cold, a hardy group of camp survivors, some disfigured by Josef Mengele's cruel knife, held candles and retraced their steps of exactly forty years ago to the day. It was January 27, 1985, the fortieth anniversary of the camp's liberation by Soviet troops. It was also the start of a campaign, by the twin survivors of Mengele's experiments, to stir the conscience of governments to find Mengele at any cost.

It was such a cold day that Marc Berkowitz, Mengele's former errand boy who had been injected with unknown substances so many times he lost count, was shivering despite his double sweaters and thick coat. "I don't know how we stood in roll call for hours on end," he said. "But we did, in the same weather, sometimes colder, I guess, with only a tattered shirt and a thin pair of pants."

Berkowitz pointed out to his son the crematorium where

the grandmother the boy never knew had been gassed. Dor Shielanski, a member of Israel's parliament and an Auschwitz survivor, said, "We know that Mengele is still alive. He must be made to pay."

The event was reported on TV stations around the world. A week later the TV crews were in Jerusalem at one of the most macabre gatherings ever held. A mock trial of Josef Mengele would hear evidence from his guinea-pig survivors before a distinguished panel chaired by Gideon Hausner, Israel's chief prosecutor at the Adolf Eichmann trial, Telford Taylor, chief American prosecutor at Nuremberg, and Simon Wiesenthal.

Wiesenthal and some Israeli colleagues had resorted to this well-publicized "trial" in a last desperate attempt to highlight the failure of governments to run Mengele to ground. There had been some last-minute in-fighting between Wiesenthal and the Klarsfelds, who had wanted to be there. According to Serge Klarsfeld, Wiesenthal wanted the Nazi-hunting stage to himself. "He's an egomaniac," said a slighted Klarsfeld.[1]

The event was an enormous success. For four consecutive nights, TV screens showed victims—midgets, Jewish women, twins—telling the most gruesome tales, all testifying to Mengele's unspeakable crimes. Altogether 106 known survivors of his grotesque research were ready to take the stand.

The groundwork for this new and final push had been laid the previous month when the Los Angeles-based Simon Wiesenthal Center, in a fanfare of publicity, released declassified American army intelligence documents showing that Mengele may have been in U.S. hands in April 1947.* In fact, the documents had been declassified eighteen months before, but the timing of the release, the pilgrimage to Auschwitz, and the mock trial at Jerusalem was a masterly stroke of public relations planning, especially coming after the buildup of speculative stories the previous summer suggesting that Mengele might have tried to enter the U.S. and indicating the extent of Dieter Mengele's business interests there. Pressure on the U.S. government to act became irresistible.

On February 6, 1985, the day the Jerusalem "trial" drew to a close, U.S. attorney general William French Smith directed

---

* Inquiries showed that Mengele was not in U.S. custody in April 1947. But he was in American hands, under his own name, during the summer of 1945. See Chapter 3.

the justice department to examine every aspect of the Mengele case—and to find him. As Smith told reporters that day:

> The allegations have been such, and the public interest has been such, and the notoriety of the individual has been such, that it seemed appropriate to open the investigation. We intend to be thorough. We also intend to be speedy.[2]

The scope of the inquiry was later spelled out in detail by Stephen Trott, chief attorney for the criminal division of the justice department:

> It is intentionally broad and all-encompassing. It is designed to allow us to determine what if any contacts this government had with Mengele following the end of the war; whether he ever entered the United States, and, if so, under what circumstances; how Mengele left Europe and made his way to South America; and, finally, to locate him and bring him to justice.[3]

The department that was to coordinate the entire project was the Office of Special Investigations, which had been established by the Carter administration to hunt down and deport the hundreds of Nazi criminals who lied about their wartime crimes in order to gain entry into the United States at the end of the war and had hidden there ever since. The task of conducting the search for Mengele was assigned to the U.S. Marshal's Service. Both the OSI and the marshal's were to draw on the extensive services of the CIA, the FBI, the National Security Agency, and the defense and state departments. In short, it was to be one of the biggest international manhunts the United States had ever undertaken.*

Shamed into action, the Israeli government announced two days later that a new attempt would be made to find Mengele. The Israeli justice minister, Moshe Nissim, said that a special panel composed of police, foreign affairs, and justice ministry officials would be set up to coordinate the effort. It was a tacit admission that the Mossad file on Mengele was bare, despite

---

* The marshals believed the best way to find Mengele was to employ a group of shady informers throughout South America. At U.S. taxpayers' expense, they even employed, as a consultant, the German correspondent who six months earlier had been the chief advocate of the contention that Mengele was alive and well in Uruguay.

the request in 1976 by Prime Minister Menachem Begin for
the Mossad to give Nazi-hunting a higher priority than it had
enjoyed since Isser Harel resigned as its chief in 1963. Begin's
former press spokesman, Dan Patir, said:

> I remember the Prime Minister saying this kind of
> criminal should be brought to justice. He did refer to
> Mengele in particular and he certainly wanted his case
> looked into. His view was that major criminals like this
> should not only not be free, but that younger genera-
> tions should be educated by a trial not to forget.[4]

In fact, one Mossad case officer had been keeping no more
than a watching brief on the Mengele case since 1980. Some
abortive inquiries were made that year in Günzburg, but that
was the extent of the Israeli intelligence activity. A former
senior Mossad agent who knows the Mengele case officer said:
"He's a nice boy but he only speaks Hebrew. Without German
and Spanish one can't get far on the Mengele case. He hasn't
learned a thing. Mengele was treated like five hundred other
jobs, no more."[5]

The Israeli announcement was followed by unprecedented
reward offers from both the Jerusalem and Bonn governments. West Germany increased its bounty from 25,000 to 1
million marks ($330,000); the Israeli government offered a
staggering $1 million. The private Nazi-hunters followed on
an equally grand scale. The Simon Wiesenthal Center offered
$1 million from anonymous contributors, the Washington
Times, owned by the Reverend Sun Myung Moon, matched it
with $1 million; Tuvia Friedman of the Haifa Nazi Crimes
Documentation Center offered $100,000, and Serge and
Beate Klarsfeld pledged $25,000.

The terms of Sun Myung Moon's reward were so strict as to
make it seem a publicity stunt. The successful applicant had to
send in a coded six-number, double-copied letter, giving the
story to the paper first with very precise information that
would lead directly to Mengele's capture. Then Mengele had
to be tried and convicted of a war crime before any money
was paid. The Wiesenthal Center reward only appeared to be
$1 million: if anyone successfully pinpointed Mengele and
gave the information first to the Center, they would receive
only $333,000, the other $666,000 being split between the

Center itself and outlets for Jewish education. The German and Israeli offers were restricted: Mengele had to be tried only in the country offering the reward. Tuvia Friedman's offer was valid only if he received the information before anyone else. Apparently only the Klarsfelds were offering a no-strings-attached grant for the fugitive, dead or alive.

Suddenly the Mengele story seemed to have a life of its own. From this point until long after Mengele's bones were found, scarcely a day passed without one of the three American TV networks presenting a progress report on the hunt for the Angel of Death. The networks spent vast sums of money dispatching crews to Paraguay and Europe. Magazines and newspapers followed in their wake. The *New York Times* assigned Ralph Blumenthal, one of their most respected investigative journalists, to the story full time. The resourceful John Martin of ABC News also made several important news breaks.

Though he could not know it then, one of Martin's most significant contributions was an interview with Mengele's nephew, Dieter. It was the first time any member of the Mengele family had agreed to be interviewed. Owning approximately $3.5 million worth of shares in Mengele & Sons in Günzburg, Dieter is the wealthiest of all the clan. And although he and Karl Heinz jointly run the firm, Dieter has the final say in all the important decisions because he controls a clear majority of the voting shares.

Dieter had watched with alarm as the new surge of activity put the family secret in greater danger of exposure than ever before. With such vast sums offered, he could no longer be sure that one of the dozens of people privy to the secret in Günzburg and São Paulo might not break ranks and try to claim some of the reward, even if information about a dead man did not fall strictly within most of the reward conditions. Business was also suffering from association with the name. Dieter persuaded Karl Heinz that the time had come to leak the news of their uncle's death. The question was, how?

They decided that the news had to be delivered in a way that would leave it unclear that the family had certain knowledge of Mengele's fate. At the same time it had to have enough authority to be believed. The leak had to be controlled. Information had to seem informed but speculative. The two cousins hoped the result would be to curtail the search, on the assumption that Mengele was indeed dead, while avoiding a detailed inquisition of where he had lived and exactly who had protected him. This time they hoped, the story would fade away forever.

Of the two cousins, Dieter was the obvious partner to give the interview. Having lived as a teenager with his fugitive uncle in Buenos Aires for three years, Karl Heinz was vulnerable to some embarrassing questions that might detract from the purpose of persuading the world that Mengele was dead. But the cousins' strategy was flawed from the start. They failed to understand that for Mengele's victims, as for most civilized people, nothing less than absolute proof of his death would be satisfactory.

The interview was conducted in the Mengele company boardroom, directly under the large oil portraits of Karl Sr., Alois, and Karl Jr. When John Martin asked if he could interview Karl Heinz too, Dieter replied:

> Well, first of all he's not here today . . . second thing is he doesn't speak English . . . and third, this is the main point, he . . . because he was living with . . . for a couple of years . . . with the man . . . he . . . he doesn't know what his feelings are. So, his main feelings are the same as mine. But for him, it's very difficult for him to express himself on this special matter.[6]

The "controlled" leak about his uncle's death emerged like this:

Martin: Do you think he's survived?

Mengele: I think 'til now. I think he's dead.

Martin: You think he's dead?

Mengele: He's dead.

Martin: Why . . . why do you think that?

Mengele: First of all, he's seventy-four.

Martin: Seventy-four on Saturday.

Mengele: Okay. And there are so many people looking for him. I don't think that . . . If it's true what I'm reading, that everybody's looking after him, they would have found him if he's still alive. And for instance, my . . . my grandfather, he was seventy-five and he died. My uncle was forty-nine when he died.* And my father was sixty. So, you see, we are not so very healthy.

Martin: But . . .

Mengele: But I think this could be taken out.

Martin: Okay. I'll take that part out. But don't you think you would know, someone would tell you? They know you. They know the family. Wouldn't they tell you if they found he was dead?

Mengele: I . . . I've . . . you see, we have no connection. We have no connection after 1960 with him. So we don't know who, with whom he's in contact.[7]

Sensing Martin's disbelief, Dieter tried to make his point a second time:

I really must say once more, I think he's dead. If people want to know this or not . . . that is my feeling.

Dieter dissembled throughout the interview. He denied that Mengele ever received financial or other assistance from the company or the family. But his most blatant lie came in answer to a question about whether he or Karl Heinz had ever received letters from Mengele. Mengele had, of course, sent many letters to Karl Heinz and in a letter he sent to Rolf in 1974, he complained that Dieter had not "answered my sympathy cards on the death of his father and his mother." All these details were naturally unknown to Martin at the time. But he correctly guessed that there must have been some correspondence and pressed home the point:

Martin: In all this time, never a postcard? Never a letter? Never . . . any contact from him to you?

Mengele: Not that I know of.

---

* Dieter was referring to Karl Jr. In fact he died when he was thirty-nine.

Martin: Or to Karl Heinz? To his former stepson?

Mengele: No. Probably to my father [Alois] or . . . or
. . . I have no idea. But not to Karl Heinz and not to
me.[8]

The interview raised more questions than it answered.
There was a clear conflict between Dieter's hint that his uncle
was dead and prosecutor Hans-Eberhard Klein's assertion
that he was alive. The American OSI also believed he was
alive. Since the Mengeles had an inherent credibility problem
accrued over four decades of silence, the verdict swung behind the West Germans and the Americans. For Dieter and
Karl Heinz, it was back to square one.

On March 23, Rolf was asked to join Dieter and Karl Heinz
for a meeting in Günzburg to discuss the next move. Dieter
apologized to Rolf, who was angry at not being consulted or
even notified before Dieter's ABC interview. "I tried to get
you before the interview," Dieter lied, "but I could not reach
you. I had to make a quick decision because it was very bad
here, they had television cameras at the factory and all. But
don't worry, I have kept our little secret." The little secret
referred to the Mengele family agreement not to disclose
Josef's death. This time Dieter did not beat about the bush,
however, as Rolf explained:

> He said he didn't want to live with this any more. It
> was bad for business and we should get it over with. He
> said that it would come up again in ten years time when
> there was the fiftieth anniversary of Auschwitz. He was
> also worried about the safety of his daughter in that
> someone might try to hurt her. Dieter wanted the story
> leaked out but he didn't want an announcement or any-
> thing that would tie the family into having helped my
> father.[9]

At the Günzburg meeting, Karl Heinz favored another attempt at a controlled leak, but he was worried about the
Bosserts, Stammers, and Sedlmeier being compromised. Dieter's solution was a macabre and harebrained scheme. He suggested that Mengele's bones should be collected from São
Paulo and dumped at the door of prosecutor Klein's office in
Frankfurt with an anonymous note saying, "These are the

remains of Josef Mengele." Rolf ruled that out straightaway. "I said, 'And who's going to go and get the bones? Me, I suppose, because it was my father. No thanks.' " Rolf was opposed to any leak, arguing that protecting the security of those who had helped his father was paramount. "After the Bosserts and Sedlmeier die, then we can disclose it," he told his cousins. As Mengele's son, it was Rolf's view that ultimately prevailed.[10]

In Bonn, meanwhile, three clues to Mengele's death were buried in the files of prosecutor Hans-Eberhard Klein's office. The first was the lead that Klarsfeld had given him late in 1984 suggesting that Rolf had made a trip to Brazil on a false passport in 1977. The second was an intercepted letter from a German identified as Gert Luk, in Paraguay, to a prisoner in West Germany, Manfred Röder, leader of a neo-Nazi movement called the "German Action Group." Röder was serving a thirteen-year sentence for bomb attacks on immigrants.[11]

Letters to prisoners are read by the authorities as a matter of course. Luk's letter reported that "the Uncle" had died on a Brazilian beach. Suspecting that this might be a reference to Mengele, the West Germans contacted their Brazilian counterparts and asked if they could shed any light on the message. The Brazilian response was not very helpful. "Which beach," an official was said to have replied. "We've got ten thousand miles of beach."[12] Since the West Germans did not pursue their hunch by trying to locate Luk in Paraguay, the clue was not given the significance it deserved. Nothing was done for several months.

The third clue was the evidence of a West German university professor. While on holiday at Munenstertal in the late autumn of 1984, he had joined Sedlmeier and his wife, Renate, for dinner at the Spielweg Hotel. During the course of an animated conversation, oiled by brandy and wine, Sedlmeier let slip that he had sent Mengele money over the years. The professor, from Giessen, passed the information to the police. "I guess he [Sedlmeier] felt that since my father had been dead for five years, it didn't really matter any more," said Rolf. "He just let his guard drop."[13]

Of the three clues, it was the professor's that was clearly the most significant. Klein had always suspected Sedlmeier to be intimately involved in sheltering Mengele, but this had never been proved, though how hard the West Germans tried is open to doubt. A police raid in 1964 on Sedlmeier's Günzburg house had drawn a blank. A statement from Sedlmeier in 1971 had been a stream of falsehoods. On both those occasions, Sedlmeier had been well prepared, having been tipped off by a policeman friend. As a result of the professor's tip, Sedlmeier had been questioned a third time, in December 1984. But again he had given away nothing except an admission that he had seen Mengele in Brazil in 1962. He certainly did not tell Klein that Mengele had died. In the absence of harder evidence, Klein said that he had been impotent to move against Sedlmeier.

By the end of 1984, the West Germans were no nearer to solving the Mengele mystery than they had ever been. It was at this point the investigation received the important boost it so desperately needed. At the instigation of the Americans, the Israelis and the West Germans agreed to share their intelligence on the hunt. This unique arrangement gave new hope to those who were afraid that Mengele was either dead or never would be caught. It moved the normally cautious Klein to say, "I'm sure he's alive and I'm confident he'll be caught." Neal Sher, director of the Office of Special Investigations, the most senior American actively engaged in the hunt, echoed Klein's optimism. "Yes, I think we'll get him," he said. "I'm 99 percent sure of that."[14]

On May 10, 1985, fifteen representatives from the three governments convened in Frankfurt for a conference to formalize their new joint effort. The meeting was more symbolic than substantive, since all the major details had been agreed upon before. The teams included some high-powered figures: assistant attorney generals from Washington and Jerusalem, the assistant director of the U.S. marshals, and the commissioner of the West German criminal police.

Klein chaired the meeting since the search for Mengele had been principally a West German responsibility. He was anxious to take the lead. In that sense, the new coordinated effort and the fear of being outflanked by the Americans had given Bonn a much needed prod. Although Klein chose not to disclose the professor's tip about Sedlmeier's drunken indiscretion, he did announce that a warrant would be sought to search his house. With the Americans new to the Mengele hunt and the Israelis' total commitment represented by the agreeable but part-time police superintendent Menachem Russek, it had not been difficult for the West Germans to seize the initiative.

The prosecutors' attempt to persuade a judge to issue a search warrant on the basis of the professor's evidence failed at first. But when they returned a second time with the intercepted letter from Gert Luk, they succeeded.

Six thousand miles away the trail was getting warmer too. From Paraguay came the first hint that Mengele may indeed have died. The irony was that it occurred right under the noses of Beate Klarsfeld and an American TV crew while they were trying to pick up Mengele's lost trail. On May 24, CBS's crew for their *Sixty Minutes* program came across an old man named Alfonz Diercks in southern Paraguay. What this sixty-five-year-old photographer and farmer told producer Barry Lando would have given him his biggest scoop ever had he believed it. Diercks said that several years before, Alban Krug had told him that Mengele had died in a swimming accident in Brazil. Diercks also said he had taken many photographs of Mengele while he lived briefly with Krug in Paraguay. After Krug heard of Mengele's death, he asked Diercks to destroy the photographs and negatives. This Diercks dutifully did. To Lando and his crew it was just one more uncheckable but probably dubious story, like many then rampant in that part of Paraguay. Nevertheless, the following day Diercks's claim was reported in the pro-government newspaper, *Hoy*, as Beate Klarsfeld prepared to leave after publicly accusing President Stroessner of shielding Mengele. Like Lando, she also believed the story was simply untrue.

At the same time, back in Frankfurt, armed with their new search warrant, the federal police were about to raid Sedlmeier's house at number 3 Nordstrasse, in Günzburg. On Friday, May 31, when they were sure that he and his wife were at home, the police moved in. On this occasion Sedlmeier had no advance warning from his police informant friend, and the search party had the advantage of surprise. "This time it had gone too high in the police—no one could help Sedlmeier," commented Rolf. "I don't think the local police even knew about the raid." The police conducted a thorough and businesslike search. At one stage Sedlmeier tried to make a dash for a jacket hanging in a closet, but an officer got there first and found an address book containing some telephone numbers and addresses in code.

A further search uncovered photocopies of letters to and from Mengele that Sedlmeier thought had been destroyed. To Sedlmeier's anguish and astonishment, his wife, a close friend of Mengele's before the war, had hidden them in her wardrobe. "How could you do that?!" came Sedlmeier's anguished cry. "Oh, my God, what an idiot!"

Sedlmeier was placed under house arrest while the police tried to decode the addresses and telephone numbers. He refused to talk or give any information. But already the police suspected that Mengele was dead because one of the letters they found was the one from Wolfram Bossert announcing "with deep sorrow the death of our common friend." Although some telephone numbers had no country or city dialing code, within hours the police established that other entries related to São Paulo. The Brazilian authorities were immediately notified.

The man who took charge of the investigation in São Paulo was the city's police chief, Romeu Tuma, a stocky fifty-three-year-old law graduate of Arab extraction. He had risen quickly through the ranks to become the feared chief of the secret service in 1972. In March 1983, he was appointed superintendent of the São Paulo police. Tuma had run one previous big Nazi fugitive case. In 1978 he arrested Gustav Wagner, the Austrian deputy commandant of the Sobibór extermination camp, who had lived peacefully in São Paulo since 1952. Wagner had organized the construction of a crude but efficient killing center utilizing carbon monoxide fumes from a captured Soviet tank. It claimed 250,000 victims over a fifteen-month period. Wagner was also reported to have taken special pleasure in killing people brutally with his own hands.* The capture of Wagner was prestigious and attracted media interest. Tuma, an engaging and approachable man, enjoyed the attention. This time the message from Bonn presaged an even bigger event.

Tuma's inquiries centered on two addresses. One was listed as "Guararapes 650." There was no such number for that

---

* Bonn's request for Wagner's extradition was rejected by the Brazilian supreme court after Wagner successfully pleaded that he was protected by the statute of limitations. He committed suicide in 1980 while in custody.

street. But the point where it would have been was directly intersected by Missouri Street. The residents of number 7 were an Austrian couple, Wolfram and Liselotte Bossert. Finding the Stammers was easier. Sedlmeier's address book listed what looked like a post office box, "C. P. 7448." It was registered in the name of Geza and Gitta Stammer.

Tuma immediately dispatched surveillance units to the homes of the Bosserts and the Stammers. For four days his men maintained a twenty-four-hour watch on both houses. When no one resembling Mengele's description was seen, the Bosserts' house was raided. Inside they found Wolfram and Liselotte Bossert, their two children, and a Mengele shrine. Remnants of his personal effects, some writings, and dozens of photographs were perfectly preserved in one cupboard. All had been held back from Rolf on his 1979 trip to collect his father's personal estate. Among the papers was a semiautobiographical essay with a Latin title, *Fiat Lux*, or "Let There Be Light,"* written by Mengele when he lived on the Fischers' farm near Rosenheim after the war. Another essay was headed *Verbum Compositum*, or "Collected Work," aptly described by the *New York Times* as a collection of "harebrained scribblings on evolution."[15] The police also found a 1983 Christmas card addressed to the Bosserts from Rolf, with a picture of him with his wife, Almuth, and their young daughter.

The West German authorities dispatched two German officers from the federal criminal police, the LKA, to assist in the investigation.† At first the Bosserts claimed they did not know that their friend's name was Mengele. They maintained that he was Peter Hochbichler from Switzerland. The couple was interviewed together by non-German interrogators. Liselotte constantly interrupted her husband in German when she thought he was about to give any compromising answers. But after two hours they ended the charade. The Bosserts told the Brazilian police that Mengele's remains

---

* Mengele's ego is evident in the choice of a title for this autobiographical book. "Let There Be Light" is also the name of the first book of Genesis in the Bible.

† Although the police found a substantial quantity of Mengele papers at the Bosserts' they missed some diary pages, more pictures, and two sound recordings of Mengele, Wolfram Bossert, and Wolfgang Gerhard, which were secreted at the Bosserts' weekend farm. Reporters from *Stern* magazine persuaded the Bosserts to part with this material for a reported 80,000 deutschemarks, about $30,000, before the police learned of its existence.

could be found in a hillside cemetery, at Embu, twenty-five miles from São Paulo. "I didn't think you could find us so quickly," admitted Wolfram.

The following day Gitta Stammer was brought in for questioning. Her husband, Geza, was heading for Singapore on board a tanker captained by one of his sons, an officer in the Brazilian merchant marine. Gitta Stammer proved to be much tougher to crack than either of the Bosserts. She claimed total ignorance of Mengele. Tuma's men did not get one truthful word out of her during her day in custody.

Word of the breakthrough had by now leaked out to the German newspaper *Die Welt*. On Thursday, June 6, the paper reported that the body of Mengele had almost certainly been found in Brazil. The Americans and Israelis, who had pledged total cooperation just three weeks earlier in Frankfurt, were furious when they learned of this sensational news from early morning broadcasts reporting the *Die Welt* story. What further angered the Americans was Bonn's relaxed response to the whole affair. Quickly brought up to date by telephone, the Americans urged their German colleagues to interview Gert Luk, the Paraguayan who was the original source of information that the "Uncle" had died. Klein's office said there was no hurry—Luk was due to arrive from Paraguay in four weeks and could be interviewed then.

Neal Sher, the American OSI chief, returned to his Washington office from a Boston awards ceremony, the great fanfare that had launched the U.S. hunt three months earlier still ringing in his ears. "If we were the ones who had made the breakthrough, we would have shared it with the other countries before going public," said a chagrined Sher.[16] It had begun to look as if the West Germans had stolen the show. Senator Alfonse d'Amato who had been so vocal in getting the hunt started certainly felt it looked that way. He asked Sher rhetorically when he was planning to join his German colleagues in Brazil. That night Sher boarded a jet at Kennedy Airport. "We're going with a healthy degree of skepticism," he said. Off the record, his staff was highly skeptical. "Our intelligence reports suggest he's still alive," said an OSI official. "There's every sign that he was seen recently."[17]

Simon Wiesenthal, who coincidentally flew into New York's Kennedy Airport for a lecture tour commencing that Thursday afternoon, said the story was a hoax: "99 percent it's not him" was his seasoned view. It was vintage Wiesenthal:

> This is Mengele's seventh death. Only in Paraguay has he been dead three times, always with witnesses who say it is him. On one of these occasions, we found the body of a woman. If Mengele really died, then the whole world would have been informed five minutes after, not five years. His wife, children, relatives, besides friends and sympathizers, would have done everything to announce the death of Mengele, so they could spend the rest of their lives in peace.[18]

In hindsight, the statement shows just how little Wiesenthal ever really knew about the inner machinations of the Günzburg clan. But Wiesenthal was by no means alone. Most Mengele experts agreed initially, the authors included. Beate Klarsfeld, who had just returned from Paraguay where only days before she had accused Stroessner of shielding Mengele, said:

> Alfredo Stroessner's government had every interest in informing the world of Mengele's death if it was true. This way the country would be free of the image of a sanctuary for Nazis. It's strange that this would come to light when there is a record of $3.4 million to whoever gives information leading to Mengele's capture. Moreover Stroessner has a trip prepared for July [to West Germany]. It's understandable that he's trying to rid himself of Mengele before this visit.[19]

Unknown to Beate Klarsfeld, Stroessner had already canceled his trip. No public explanation was offered. The information was passed on in a confidential diplomatic note to the West German ambassador in Asunción, Konrad Gacher. But it was obvious that as long as the fate of Mengele remained a mystery, any Stroessner trip to West Germany would be transformed from a state visit into a television inquisition about Mengele.

Meanwhile, at the hillside cemetery in Embu, a circus of TV cameras, photographers, onlookers, policemen, and ghouls had gathered. Wolfram and Liselotte Bossert stood stonily by the side of police chief Tuma, whose shiny black suit shim-

mered in the bright autumn sun. The Bosserts were there to
ensure that the right grave was opened. For nearly an hour
three gravediggers with picks and shovels burrowed four feet
down before they struck the coffin. Its top was stuck, and the
police ordered one of the gravediggers to smash it open. His
pick shattered the wooden lid, revealing shreds of clothing
and mud-colored bones. Mengele's arms had been placed at
his side, the traditional burial pose for SS men, instead of with
hands crossed over the breast, as is the Brazilian custom.
Bending down over the open grave, Dr. Jose Antonio de
Mello, assistant director of the police forensic laboratory,
picked up the skull, then held it high for what surely was one
of the world's most grisly photographs. Glancing at the teeth,
he observed that they had been recently treated, and he said
the body was quite well preserved. "We should be able to
identify the race, height, and color without much difficulty,"
he said. Then the bones were haphazardly dumped into a
white plastic tub, and taken to a laboratory where they were
placed under armed guard.

The interrogation of Gitta Stammer continued after the
exhumation, and slowly she began to break. "We had to pull it
out hair by hair," said one official. She told the police that
Wolfgang Gerhard had introduced Mengele to them and that
he had admitted his identity two years later. Slowly the pieces
were coming together, though the Israelis remained skeptical. A spokesman for the Israeli consulate in São Paulo said his
government had decided not to send a representative. Police
superintendent Menachem Russek, heading the Israeli hunt,
said he thought the incident was an elaborate smoke screen
put up by Mengele's family to allow him to live the last few
years of his life in peace. "He must be feeling himself cornered now," said Russek. "He knows the American, German,
and Israeli police are cooperating and the circle around him is
closing." Isser Harel, former Mossad chief whose two efforts to
kidnap Mengele had failed, was blunter still: "I view all stories
from Brazil with great skepticism."[20]

Only forensic science could rule out a hoax, and there were
doubts that even that would produce a definitive answer.
Identification techniques had advanced to an ultra-sophisti-
cated state, but in Mengele's case one vital clue for identifying

skeletons was absent. Dental X-rays, as reliable as fingerprints, did not exist.

A formidable team of experts was being assembled. Three forensic scientists were sent to São Paulo on behalf of the Simon Wiesenthal Center: Dr. John Fitzpatrick, acting chairman of the department of radiology, Cook County Hospital, Chicago; Dr. Leslie Lukash, chief medical examiner, Nassau County, New York; and Dr. Clyde Colling Snow, forensic anthropological consultant, Oklahoma state medical examiner's office, Oklahoma City. Three more were sent on behalf of the department of justice and the U.S. marshal's office: Dr. Ali Hameli, chief medical examiner of the forensic science laboratory, State of Delaware; Dr. Ellis Kerley, department of anthropology, University of Maryland; and Dr. Lowell Levine, forensic odontology consultant, Huntington Station, New York.

Their task was to see how known physical characteristics and verified photographs of Mengele compared with the remains found at Embu. For the skull comparison, a process called "electronic supraposition" was used. It involved the use of two video cameras and a video mixer to superimpose what was left of the skull on a full-scale verified photograph of Mengele's head. The team also managed to find a partial fingerprint and graying hairs from the back of the head from which they hoped to be able to discover the skeleton's blood type. A few clues could also be salvaged from Mengele's medical records in his SS file. He had broken a finger bone in his left hand and also suffered from osteomyelitis as a boy. None of the individual clues would be decisive in itself. Collectively, however, they could be significant.*

For one brief weekend, the skeptics held their ground. A São Paulo dentist, Maria Helena Bueno Viera de Castro, said that according to her records she treated the old man whose photograph appeared in the Brazilian newspapers during March or April 1979—two or three months after Mengele was supposed to have died. Moreover, Arnaldo Santana, the

---

* The experts worked on the assumption that Mengele had broken his hip. This information came from Simon Wiesenthal, who said that Mengele had fractured his hip during a motorcycle accident at Auschwitz. His SS record showed he had an accident and that he was injured, but there was no record of a fracture. Coincidentally the scientists did find an old hip fracture that had healed. Rolf Mengele and his mother said Josef Mengele did not break a hip in Auschwitz, and must have broken it after he left Europe in 1949.

housekeeper who worked at the back of the Bosserts' beach house, said that when he saw the body on the beach there was no moustache. No one who knew Mengele in São Paulo could remember him ever without a moustache. Then there was the coroner, Dr. Jaime Edson Mendonca, who had signed the death certificate. How could such an experienced man fail to have noticed that the body he examined under the name of "Wolfgang Gerhard" was six inches shorter and much older than the fifty-three years listed on the identity card? Finally a leading plastic surgeon, Roberto Farina, told the Associated Press that the archive shots of Mengele showed "substantial differences" from those that the police had released for publication in the newspapers. There was even a rumor that the gravedigger, Gino Carita, had seen the body in the coffin after all, and he had recognized it as the real Wolfgang Gerhard from his previous visit.

One by one, these arguments were broken down. The dentist was not certain of her facts when questioned by the police. There had been a mixup in her records. Santana was wrong, since moustache hairs were found on the corpse. The coroner, on his own admission, had not given the corpse a very thorough examination. The plastic surgeon had simply made a mistake. The gravedigger was challenged by Liselotte Bossert, who said that her fake crying fit ensured that nobody would open the coffin. She had seen it covered in the grave. Within a week, even Wiesenthal had changed his tune. "I think it's fifty-fifty it's him," he said.

One person in a position to provide proof of Mengele's death was his son, Rolf. But Rolf had no idea of what had been happening. He was on holiday with his wife and child, touring in Spain in a motor home, cut off from newspapers and TV for nearly two weeks. Without a set itinerary, the Mengele family had no way to contact him.

On Friday evening, June 7, Rolf returned to his home in Freiburg, switched on the television, and saw the late news. From the reports coming out of Brazil, he knew that his father's secret was out:

> I thought to myself, "This is serious." I thought that Dieter must have leaked the story. We had all had an agreement that none of us would act without consulting

the others, so I was a little surprised. The last time we met in March, Dieter had been very anxious to get the story out but without involving the Stammers or the Bosserts or the family at this end. So I thought not only had Dieter leaked it but that it had all gone wrong.[21]

A message on Rolf's dining table from the housekeeper said that Dieter had been telephoning repeatedly. A telephone call quickly established that Dieter was not the source of the break. With the story quickly disseminating, the question was how best to repair the damage. A crew from NBC had camped outside Rolf's house, and newspaper reporters were knocking on his door and telephoning his office nonstop. Rolf proposed to Dieter and Karl Heinz that the family make a statement. "I didn't see how we could avoid it anymore," said Rolf. "The Stammers were talking, the Bosserts were talking. It would all come out sooner or later." But Dieter and Karl Heinz refused to make a statement, in a final but vain attempt to conceal their past links with their uncle. "Everyone in Günzburg was just paralyzed. No one had known what to do," said Rolf. "They had been so paralyzed that no one had even telephoned the Bosserts or the Stammers after the raid on Sedlmeier's house to warn them that the police might raid their houses."

For advice on how to handle the press, Rolf turned to a journalist friend of his secretary, Sabine Hackenjos, who had just married his stepbrother, Jens. He was Herbert Bauermeister, a freelance reporter who had known Sabine from her days as a Munich socialite. Bauermeister advised Rolf to clear the air. Rolf agreed that some explanation was needed. But he also saw the chance to make a handsome sum of money. On Sunday, June 9, he telephoned *Stern* magazine, pretending to be his stepbrother, Jens, and offered letters, diaries, and photographs of Mengele. Rolf got nowhere because he was asked to phone several senior editors at home. Since none was there that night, he gave up trying.

Bauermeister then advised Rolf to try *Bunte* magazine in Munich. He knew some of its staff and vouched for their integrity. Bauermeister also advised Mengele to forget about trying to make money. Instead he should donate the material to *Bunte* on condition that profits and magazine rights from

their vastly increased circulation would be donated to the
victims of concentration camps. That night, Monday, June 10,
Rolf met with senior *Bunte* executives in the Black Forest and
agreed to terms. The following day he issued a statement
admitting that he had gone to Brazil in 1979 to confirm "the
circumstances of my father's death," and that he had stayed
silent until then "out of consideration for the people who
were in contact with my father for the last thirty years."[22]

Rolf's decision to disclose details of the family's contact with
Mengele throughout his fugitive life opened a wound between his mother's side of the family and the Günzburgers
that has yet to heal. Rolf explained:

> Dieter and Karl Heinz were totally opposed to an
> announcement, and they particularly objected to me
> going public with *Bunte*. Their position still was that the
> family should not be tied to this in any way. In the end
> they said, "Okay, do it your way. But whatever you do,
> do not involve us and the firm." So at that stage, particu-
> larly because I respected what Karl Heinz and Sedl-
> meier had done for my father, I did not then disclose the
> extent of their involvement.[23]

Thus no mention was made of the five round-trip plane trips
Sedlmeier had made at the company's expense, disguised on
the accounts.

Sedlmeier was furious with Rolf for his decision to go public.
Only once did he speak about his involvement in the Mengele
affair. Interviewed by a reporter from the *New York Times*
who had spent all day outside his home, Sedlmeier was at his
intemperate worst:

> Well, naturally I knew because I got a letter from the
> Bosserts. My wife stupidly kept it. Stupid. I don't know
> why she did, but that's what got us in the end. They
> came here and found it. I could tell you what Mengele
> did, what he did during Auschwitz, what he did after
> Auschwitz. But you wouldn't believe me. The newspa-
> per won't print the truth because it's not in the interests
> of the Jews. . . . I'm sorry you came all this way for
> nothing. But I refuse to talk about the Mengele affair.

Journalists have already written so many lies and what
the Jewish press has asserted . . .[24]

As the *Times* reported, Sedlmeier did not finish the sentence, apparently out of exasperation. Many Günzburg residents seemed to share his sentiments. A British camera crew
was ordered by the police to move away from Dieter's home.
"Leave us in peace," another man shouted at them. The local
paper gave precisely two paragraphs on an inside page to its
most notorious native son.

As for the Mengeles, they remain skeptical of the more
horrendous charges against Josef.

Rolf, his late brother Alois, and Sedlmeier had offered Mengele the chance to prove that he had been badly wronged.
"Write down all that happened at Auschwitz," they told him.
But Mengele's answer was always the same: if found by the
police, the manuscript would give his identity away.

Dissatisfied with these evasive replies, Karl Heinz had
sought out the answer for himself, three years after Mengele
died. At Sedlmeier's suggestion, in December 1982, Karl
Heinz visited Dr. Hans Münch, one of his uncle's former
friends at Auschwitz, to ask him for his version of what went
on there. Dr. Münch was a young SS lieutenant at a biological
research station in an Auschwitz subcamp when he met Mengele. He told Karl Heinz that, yes, his uncle had been involved
with gas chamber selections. But had he ever killed anyone
with his bare hands? Unlikely, said Dr. Münch, since camp
discipline was so strict. Had he ever conducted experiments?
That depended on what kind of experiments. The odd spinal
tap or injection, his uncle could very well have performed.
But autopsies on purposely killed twins, electric shock experiments, connecting the blood supplies of twins? Unlikely, said
Dr. Münch, and at any rate, he never saw for himself.

And so some rationalization had been going on among the
Günzburgers. It was important to be, in their view, "objec-
tive" about an extermination camp. That is why Dieter told
John Martin in his ABC interview that he thought some of the
allegations against Mengele had been "exaggerated." Rolf explained:

It was important to the family that my father had not
been involved in the act of killing with his own hands.

> They were not so concerned about him being a little cog
> in a big machine like Auschwitz because it was the war
> and in their view those things happened.[25]

To Rolf, just his father's presence at Auschwitz was un-
forgivable. To the rest of the Mengeles, it was a distasteful
function that he could not avoid. Today the two Mengele
factions do not speak, irreconcilably divided over their judgments of Josef's crimes.

But what of Rolf himself? He has never quite resolved his
feelings for his father. For there are still many inconsistencies
in Rolf's role. He said he regards Auschwitz as "abhorrent"
but kept silent about his father because of "the damage to the
family that a trial would have caused." And yet the lasting
damage to his family, now that the truth about their collaboration is out, has been greater still.

"If he was guilty, I advised my father to give himself up,"
said Rolf. "Not at the beginning, because he wouldn't have
gotten a fair trial. But later, he should have." But a trial was
what Rolf by his silence had worked so hard to avoid.

History will correctly judge as morally obscene the
Günzburgers' attempts to rationalize their uncle's presence at
Auschwitz. But Rolf somehow cannot yet bring himself to
believe his father was a fiend. He never even considered
changing his name. "It didn't matter that much to me, but I
will probably change it for the sake of my children," he said.
And that is puzzling, too. For although the West German
prosecutor's office compiled an arrest warrant setting forth his
crimes in all their grotesque and minute detail, Rolf, the lawyer, demands yet more proof. He still wants the debate his
father refused to engage in. That is why Rolf has been beating
his breast in a public way—a subconscious penance, perhaps,
for what his father did, its magnitude only dawning on him
with the revelation of his death.

The life, times, and death of Josef Mengele were a squalid
business from beginning to end. And what an ignominious
end it was. On June 21, 1985, his bones, his skull, his bits and
pieces, were paraded before an eager audience on the twentieth floor of the São Paulo police headquarters. It all matched
up: the broken left finger, the height—174 centimeters—a
telltale gap between his two upper front teeth. In one corner

of the room his skull was displayed; in another a discussion was taking place about his degenerating spine. "This was present in the lower part of the column," said one specialist, pointing to his crumbling vertebrae. Elsewhere a doctor was trying to make a point about Mengele's hip. "We see here a montage of the hip bones," he said. "I want to show you what we found . . ." And so on.

"Is there any doubt at all, Dr. Levine, that this is Josef Mengele?" asked John Martin of ABC News.

"Absolutely not," replied the forensic odontologist from New York.

For the sake of the civilized world's peace of mind, these scientists had performed one worthwhile experiment on an unworthy life.

Notes

_____

_____

CHAPTER 1
The Formative Years

1. *Mengele-Post* (Mengele & Sons newsletter), No. 3/72, #5, November 1972.
2. Judge Horst von Glasenapp, interviewed by John Ware for "The Hunt for Dr. Mengele," *World in Action* program, Granada Television (London), November 1978.
3. Julius Diesbach, interviewed in *Siete Dias* (Buenos Aires), March 26, 1980, p. 24.
4. Dr. Norman Stone, personal interview by authors, June 1985.
5. Josef Mengele autobiography, in possession of Mengele family.
6. Ibid.
7. Rolf Mengele, personal interview by authors, August 1985.
8. *Kommunistische Arbeiterzeitung* (Communist Worker's Paper), No. 203–204, Oct. 23, 1985, p. 14.
9. *Mengele-Post* (see n. 1).
10. Prof. Hans Grebe, personal interview by S. Jones and K. Rattan, May 1985.
11. Arthur Gutt, Ernst Rudin, and Falk Ruttke, *Gesetz zur Verhutung erbkranken Nachwuchses* (The Law for the Prevention of the Spread of Congenital Illness) (Munich: Lehmann Publishing, 1936), p. 60.
12. Heinz Höhne, *The Order of the Death's Head* (New York: Ballantine, 1971), p. 742.
13. Letter: Mengele to Rolf and Almuth Mengele, 1978.
14. Ulrich Volkstein, in *Stern* magazine (Hamburg), June 20, 1985, p. 16.
15. Benno Müller-Hill, *Todliche Wissenschaft: Die Aussonderung*

von Juden, Zigunern und Geisteskranken 1933–1945 (The Deadly Science: The Selection of Jews, Gypsies and the Mentally Ill) (Hamburg: Rowohlt, 1984), p. 39.

16. Helmut von Verschuer, personal interview by the authors, June 1985.

17. Flora Schreiber, "The Satanic Dr. Mengele," *The New York Times Syndication Service*, May 4, 1975.

18. Berlin Document Center file: *SS Ahnentafel* (SS Family Tree Evaluation).

19. Book review by Josef Mengele in *Der Erbarzt 1940* of *Grundzuge der Erbkunde und Rassenpflege* (Fundamentals of Genetic and Racial Hygiene) by L. Stenel–von Rutkowski.

20. Book review by Josef Mengele in *Der Erbarzt 1940* of *Ueber Vererbung angeborener Herzfehler* (Hereditary Heart Defects), published from *Vererbungs- und Konstitutionslehre* (Principles of Heredity and Constitution), Bd. 23, S.695. by G. v. Knorre.

21. Andreas Hillgruber, interviewed in *Bunte* magazine (Munich), June 20, 1985.

22. Letter: Irene Mengele to Herrn Wahl, August 15, 1941, in possession of S. Jones and K. Rattan.

23. Robert L. Koehl, *RKFDV: German Resettlement and Population Policy 1939–1945* (Cambridge: Harvard University Press, 1957), pp. 64–65.

24. Berlin Document Center file on Josef Mengele.

25. Müller-Hill, *Todliche Wissenschaft*, pp. 112–113.

26. Ibid.

CHAPTER 2
Auschwitz: May 1943–January 1945

1. Miklos Nyiszli, *Auschwitz, A Doctor's Eyewitness Account* (London: Granada Books, 1973), p. 23.

2. Rudolf Hoess, *Commandant of Auschwitz* (London: Pan Books, 1961), p. 126.

3. Nyiszli, *Auschwitz*, p. 36.

4. Hoess, *Commandant*, p. 216.

5. Ibid., p. 218.

6. Benjamin B. Ferencz, *Less Than Slaves* (Cambridge: Harvard University Press, 1979), p. 24.

7. *KL Auschwitz, Seen by the SS*, 2nd ed., (Poland: Panstwowe Museum in Oswiecimin, 1978), pp. 215, 218.

8. Hoess, *Commandant*, pp. 175–176.

9. Berlin Document Center file on Josef Mengele: *Einstellungsverfugung, SS-und Polizeigericht XV Breslau* (Order of Suspension of the Judicial Proceedings by the SS Court in Breslau), September 28, 1943.

10. Arrest warrant and indictment issued in Frankfurt am Main on January 19, 1981, by the *Landgericht 22. Strafkammer* (State Court Number 22), file number (22)50/L Js340/68.

11. Berlin Document Center file on Josef Mengele: *Rasse- und Siedlungshauptamp, Aerztlicher Untersuchungsbogen* (Questionnaire of the Race and Resettlement Office).

12. Dr. Ella Lingens, personal interview by S. Jones and K. Rattan, February 14, 1984.

13. Berlin Document Center file on Josef Mengele: *Beurteioung des Standortarztes* (Assessment of the SS District Doctor).

14. Nyiszli, *Auschwitz*, p. 111.

15. Olga Lengyel, *Five Chimneys* (London: Granada, 1972), p. 152.

16. Nyiszli, *Auschwitz*, p. 52.

17. Flora Schreiber, "The Satanic Dr. Mengele," *The New York Times Syndication*, May 4, 1975.

18. Ibid.

19. Lengyel, *Five Chimneys*, p. 153.

20. Michael Bar-Zohar, *The Avengers* (London: A Baker, 1968), p. 234.

21. Ella Lingens, *Prisoners of Fear* (London: Gollancz, 1948), p. 77.

22. West German indictment (see n. 10).

23. Rolf Mengele, personal interview by the authors, August 1985.

24. Dr. Hans Münch, personal interview by the authors, June 1985.

25. Irene Hizme, interviewed in *People* magazine, June 24, 1985, p. 65.

26. René Slotkin, interviewed in *People* magazine, June 24, 1985, p. 65.

27. Dr. Martina Puzyna, personal interview by the authors, June 1985.

28. International War Crimes Group, Sworn Statements, Volume IV, file number 000–50–37708, October 2, 1947, maintained in National Archives, Washington, D.C.

29. Bernd Naumann, *Auschwitz* (London: Pall Mall Press, 1966), p. 272.

30. Rolf Mengele interview (see n. 23).

31. West German indictment (see n. 10).

32. Münch interview (see n. 24).

33. West German indictment (see n. 10).

34. Benno Müller-Hill, *Todliche Wissenschaft: Die Aussonderung von Juden, Zigunern und Geisteskranken 1933–1945* (The Deadly Science: The Selection of Jews, Gypsies and the Mentally Ill 1933–1945) (Hamburg: Rowohlt, 1984), p. 23.

35. Nyiszli, *Auschwitz*, p. 28.

36. Ibid., p. 37.

37. Vexler Jancu, sworn statement given to Judge Horst von

Glasenapp, Frankfurt prosecutor's file on Josef Mengele, March 13, 1973.

38. Vera Kriegel, personal interview by the authors, November 16, 1985.

39. Müller-Hill, *Todliche Wissenschaft*, p. 164.

40. Vera Alexander, interviewed by Central Television (London) for Home Box Office production "The Search for Mengele," October 1985.

41. West German indictment (see n. 10).

42. Puzyna interview (see n. 27).

43. Ibid.

44. Vera Alexander interview (see n. 40).

45. Testimony of unidentified survivor before six-person tribunal/ mock trial of Josef Mengele, Jerusalem, February 1985.

46. Ibid.

47. Nyiszli, *Auschwitz*, p. 53.

48. Prof. Yehuda Bauer, interviewed by Central Television (London) for Home Box Office production "The Search for Mengele," October 1985.

49. Nyiszli, *Auschwitz*, p. 54.

50. Robert Jay Lifton, "What Made This Man Mengele," *New York Times Magazine*, July 21, 1985, p. 22.

51. Nyiszli, *Auschwitz*, p. 55.

52. Müller-Hill, *Todliche Wissenschaft*, p. 114.

53. Nyiszli, *Auschwitz*, p. 132.

54. Müller-Hill, *Todliche Wissenschaft*, p. 83.

55. Nyiszli, *Auschwitz*, p. 126.

56. Münch interview (see n. 24).

57. Lengyel, *Five Chimneys*, p. 152.

58. Eva Kor, interviewed by Central Television (London) for Home Box Office production "The Search for Mengele," February 1985.

59. Puzyna interview (see n. 27).

60. Ernest Michel, interviewed in *People* magazine, June 24, 1985, p. 68.

61. West German indictment (see n. 10).

62. Puzyna interview (see n. 27).

63. Schreiber, "The Satanic Dr. Mengele" (see n. 17).

64. Annani Silovich Pet'ko, sworn statement to the State Prosecutor, Moscow, September 1973.

65. Gisella Perl, *I Was a Doctor in Auschwitz* (New York: International Universities Press, 1948), pp. 110–111.

66. Ibid., p. 122.

67. West German indictment (see n. 10).

68. Lifton, "What Made This Man Mengele," p. 23.

69. Transcript of Session 68 of the trial of Adolf Eichmann, Jerusalem, July 6, 1961.
70. West German indictment (see n. 10).
71. Rolf Mengele, personal interview by authors, July 1985.
72. *KL Auschwitz*, pp. 278–279.
73. Evaluation Report on Josef Mengele, Garrison Commander's Office, Auschwitz, August 19, 1944, maintained as part of the Berlin Document Center file on Josef Mengele, West Berlin.
74. Nyiszli, *Auschwitz*, p. 75.
75. Evaluation Report (see n. 73).
76. Irene Mengele, written statement to authors, September 1985.
77. West German indictment (see n. 10).

CHAPTER 3
Arrested and Freed

1. Letter from Chief SS Officer of the SS Garrison at Gross Rosen, to Department III, Economic and Administration Section of SS, stating that Mengele is in Gross Rosen as of February 7, 1945; maintained in Bundesarchivs, Koblenz, Federal Republic of Germany.
2. Benno Müller-Hill, *Todliche Wissenschaft: Die Aussonderung von Juden, Zigunern und Geisteskranken 1933–1945* (The Deadly Science: The Selection of Jews, Gypsies and the Mentally Ill) (Hamburg: Rowohlt, 1984), pp. 24–25.
3. Josef Mengele autobiography, in possession of Mengele family.
4. Ibid.
5. Ibid.
6. Ibid.
7. Rolf Mengele, personal interview by the authors, July 1985.
8. United Nations War Crimes List, Number 8, maintained by Office of Special Investigations, Washington, D.C.
9. Josef Mengele television documentary, broadcast on WDR-TV, Cologne, Federal Republic of Germany, June 27, 1985.
10. Target Detail, Minimum Briefing Chart for Günzburg, Allied war records, January 13, 1945; maintained in National Archives, Washington, D.C.
11. Munich pharmacist, personal interview by Rolf Mengele, June 1985.
12. Ibid.
13. Mengele autobiography (see n. 3).
14. Alois Fischer, personal interview by Dr. Günther Deschner, July 1985.
15. Maria Fischer, personal interview by Dr. Günther Deschner, July 1985.
16. Alois Fischer interview (see n. 14).
17. Mengele autobiography (see n. 3).

18. Maria Fischer interview (see n. 15).

19. Mengele autobiography (see n. 3).

20. Alois Fischer interview (see n. 14).

21. Mengele autobiography (see n. 3).

22. Irene Mengele diary, entry of October 7, 1945, in possession of Irene Mengele.

23. Rolf Mengele, personal interview by the authors, August 1985.

24. Ibid.

25. Letter: Irene Mengele to S. Jones and K. Rattan, April 14, 1984.

26. Louis B. Snyder, *Encyclopedia of the Third Reich* (New York: McGraw-Hill, 1976), p. 167.

27. International Military Tribunal, Nuremberg, morning session, Volume XI, 1946, maintained in National Archives, Washington, D.C.

28. Müller-Hill, *Todliche Wissenschaft*, p. 83.

29. Ibid.

30. Helmut von Verschuer, personal interview by the authors, June 1985.

31. Snyder, *Encyclopedia*, p. 70.

32. Prosecution closing statement against defendant Gebhardt, "Trials of the Criminals before the Nuremberg Military Tribunals," Volume I.

33. Robert E. Conot, *Justice at Nuremberg* (New York: Carroll & Graf, 1983), p. 291.

34. Mengele autobiography (see n. 3).

35. Letter: Gisella Perl to Colonel Damon M. Gunn, War Crimes Branch, Civil Affairs Division, Washington, D.C., November 1947.

36. Letter: Colonel Edward H. Young, Chief of the War Crimes Branch, to Gisella Perl, December 8, 1947.

37. Letter: Telford Taylor to Colonel Edward Young, January 19, 1948.

38. Letter: Colonel Edward Young, Chief of the War Crimes Branch, to Gisella Perl, February 12, 1948.

39. Letter: Special Agent Benjamin J. Gorby to the Commanding Officer, 430th Counter-Intelligence Corps Detachment, Vienna, April 1947.

40. David Marwell, historian, U.S. Department of Justice, Office of Special Investigations, in prepared statement before the C.A.N.D.L.E.S. (Children of Auschwitz Nazi Deadly Lab Experiment Survivors) International Tribunal of the Truth about Mengele, Terre Haute, Indiana, November 15, 1985.

CHAPTER 4
Flight from Europe

1. *Mengele-Post* (Mengele & Sons newsletter), No. 3/72, #5, November 1972.
2. Julius Diesbach, personal interview by Ricardo Rivas, February 1980.
3. Alois Fischer, personal interview by Dr. Günther Deschner, July 1985.
4. Rolf Mengele, personal interview by the authors, August 1985.
5. Inge Byhan, "This is Josef Mengele," *Bunte* magazine (Munich), June 27, 1985, p. 32.
6. Ibid.
7. Josef Mengele autobiography, in possession of Mengele family.
8. Ibid.
9. Josef Mengele's International Red Cross passport file, Number 100501; maintained by International Red Cross Headquarters in Geneva, Switzerland.
10. Mengele autobiography (see n. 7).
11. Ibid.
12. Inge Byhan, personal interview by the authors, June 1985.
13. Mengele autobiography (see n. 7).
14. Ibid.

CHAPTER 5
Argentina:
Lull before the Storm

1. Rolf Mengele, personal interview by Professor Norman Stone, June 1985.
2. Josef Mengele autobiography, in possession of Mengele family.
3. *Comision Investigadora de Actividades Antiargentinas* (The Investigating Commission into Anti-Argentine Activities), Report Number 5, Buenos Aires, November 28, 1941.
4. John Gunther, *Inside South America* (New York: Harper & Row, 1966), p. 181.
5. *Buenos Aires Herald,* December 1945.
6. International Military Tribunal, Nuremberg, Volume XIII, p. 581, maintained in National Archives, Washington, D.C.
7. *Seguridad Federal* (Federal Security), *Direccion Coordinacion Federal* (Argentine Internal Intelligence), "Foreign Consignment," Internal Memorandum, Buenos Aires, April 1946.
8. Memorandum from Niceforo Alarcon to the Minister of the Navy, "German Disembarkation at San Clemente del Tuyu," April 18, 1946, file number CF-OP-2315, Federal Coordinancion archives, Buenos Aires.

9. Willem Sassen, interviewed by John Ware for "The Hunt for Dr. Mengele," *World in Action* program, Granada Television (London), November 1978.

10. Ibid.

11. Werner Jung, personal interview by the authors, July 1985.

12. U.S. Counter-Intelligence Corps files on Hans Ulrich Rudel, internal memorandum, August 1950.

13. Central Intelligence Agency file on Josef Mengele, internal memorandum, July 18, 1972.

14. Dieter Mengele, interview by John Martin for ABC "World News Tonight," March 13, 1985.

15. Werner Jung, personal interview by the authors, July 1985; Colonel Alejandro von Eckstein, personal interview by the authors, December 1984.

16. Jung interview (see n. 15).

17. Von Eckstein interview (see n. 15).

18. Ibid.

19. Jung interview (see n. 15).

20. Margaret Jung, personal interview by the authors, July 1985.

21. Elsa Haverich, background interview by Central Television (London), for Home Box Office production "The Search for Mengele," August 1985.

22. José Stroher, personal interview by the authors, November 1984.

23. Rolf Mengele, personal interview by the authors, July 1985.

24. Hans Sedlmeier, sworn statement to West German Judge Horst von Glasenapp, December 9, 1971.

25. Jewish businessman, personal interview by John Ware, *World in Action* program, Granada Television (London), June 1978.

26. West German Prosecutor's Office, Summary Fact Sheet, Frankfurt.

27. Rolf Mengele, personal interview by Dr. Günther Deschner, June 1985.

28. Rolf Mengele, personal interview by the authors, August 1985.

29. Ibid.

30. Wolfram Bossert, background interview by Central Television (London), for Home Box Office production "The Search for Mengele," August 1985.

31. Letter: Marc Turkow to World Jewish Congress, New York, August 12, 1960.

32. Serge Klarsfeld, personal interview by the authors, July 1985.

33. Werner Junkers, personal interview by the authors, July 1985.

34. Werner Schattman, personal interview by the authors, July 1985.

35. "Josef Mengele" documentary, AOR-Television (Cologne, Federal Republic of Germany), June 27, 1985.

36. Simon Wiesenthal, personal interview by the authors, June 1984.

37. Heinz Truppel, background interview by Central Television (London), for Home Box Office production "The Search for Mengele," August 1985.
38. Elsa Haverich, Central Television interview (see n. 21).

CHAPTER 6
Flight to Paraguay

1. International Military Tribunal, Nuremberg, Volume 5, p. 412.
2. Hermann Langbein, personal interview by the authors, April 1985.
3. Ibid.
4. West German indictment fact sheet, attached to arrest warrant dated June 5, 1959, file number 22GS 77/59, Frankfurt.
5. Werner Jung, personal interview by the authors, July 1985.
6. Hans Sedlmeier, sworn statement to Judge Horst von Glasenapp, December 9, 1971.
7. Margaret Jung, personal interview by the authors, July 1985.
8. Langbein interview (see n. 2).
9. Ibid.
10. West German indictment fact sheet (see n. 4).
11. Elsa Haverich, background interview by Central Television (London) for Home Box Office production "The Search for Mengele," October 1985.
12. Jeff B. Harmon, "Bowling with Dr. Mengele," *Harper's*, July 1982.
13. Colonel Alejandro von Eckstein, personal interview by the authors, December 1984.
14. Josef Mengele diary, entry for March 12, 1960, in possession of Mengele family.
15. Von Eckstein interview (see n. 13).
16. West German arrest warrant for Josef Mengele, dated June 5, 1959, Court Number 22, issued by Judge Robert Müller.
17. Central Intelligence Agency report on Josef Mengele, internal memorandum, July 18, 1972.
18. Cesar Augusto Sanabria, personal interview by the authors, December 1984.
19. Von Eckstein interview (see n. 13).
20. Werner Jung interview (see n. 5).
21. Michael Bar-Zohar, *The Avengers* (London: A. Baker, 1968), p. 248.
22. Dr. Otto Biss, personal interview by the authors, December 1984.
23. Werner Jung interview (see n. 5).
24. Review by the authors of Paraguayan Interpol file on Josef Mengele, Asunción, December 1984.
25. Review by the authors of Argentine Federal Police files on Josef Mengele, Buenos Aires, November 1984.

26. Paraguayan Interpol file (see n. 24).
27. The Secretary of the Treasury's Report on Interpol, compiled for Senator Joseph Montoya, April 10, 1975, p. 12.
28. Naturalization Certificate for José Mengele, Number 809, Asunción police files.

CHAPTER 7
Operation Mengele

1. Isser Harel, *The House on Garibaldi Street* (London: Andre Deutsche, 1975), p. 19.
2. Ibid., p. 9.
3. Ibid., p. 219.
4. Isser Harel, personal interview by the authors, August 1985.
5. Ibid.
6. Harel, *Garibaldi Street*, p. 41.
7. Ibid., p. 46.
8. Ibid., p. 219.
9. Ibid., pp. 219–220.
10. Harel interview (see n. 4).
11. Zvi Aharoni, personal interview by the authors, August 1985.
12. Harel, *Garibaldi Street*, p. 220.
13. Ibid., p. 221.
14. Ibid., p. 223.
15. Ibid., p. 224.
16. Ibid., p. 225.
17. Harel interview (see n. 4).
18. Harel, *Garibaldi Street*, p. 252.
19. Ibid., p. 288.
20. Historical archives of *La Nación*, *El Clarín*, and *La Prensa*, reviewed by the authors, Buenos Aires, November 1984.

CHAPTER 8
One Step Ahead

1. Nicholas Eichmann, interviewed in *La Razón* (Buenos Aires), December 27, 1965, p. 2.
2. Josef Mengele diary, entry for June 10, 1960, in possession of Mengele family.
3. Flora Schreiber, "The Satanic Dr. Mengele," *New York Times Syndication Service*, May 4, 1975.
4. "Josef Mengele" documentary, ZDF Television, Federal Republic of Germany, June 28, 1985.
5. Archives of Federal Judge Jorge Luque, relating to West German extradition request of Josef Mengele, certified copies from Court Number 1, Buenos Aires, in possession of the authors.

6. Ibid.
7. *International Herald Tribune*, Paris edition, June 30, 1960, quoted by the World Jewish Congress (London) Survey number 2253.
8. Ibid.
9. Colonel Alejandro von Eckstein, personal interview by the authors, December 1984.
10. Margaret Jung, personal interview by the authors, December 1984.
11. Werner Schubius, interviewed by John Ware for "The Hunt for Dr. Mengele," *World in Action* program, Granada Television (London), November 1978.
12. Jewish businessman, personal interview by John Ware for "The Hunt for Dr. Mengele," *World in Action* program, Granada Television (London), June 1978.
13. Josef Mengele diary, entry for July 31, 1961, in possession of Mengele family.
14. Peter Bensch, personal interview by the authors, May 1985.
15. Archives of Judge Luque (see n. 5); Letter sent to West German embassy in Buenos Aires from the Argentine foreign office, November 1970.
16. Judge Jorge Luque, personal interview by the authors, November 1984.
17. Ibid.
18. Archives of Judge Luque (see n. 5); Memorandum from Carlos Guillermo Daneri, secretary in the Federal Police, to Judge Jorge Luque, July 2, 1960.
19. Argentine Federal Police communiqué, July 19, 1960, Federal Police archives, Buenos Aires.
20. Josef Mengele diary, entry for September 18, 1960, in possession of Mengele family.
21. Former Israeli intelligence informant, name withheld upon request, personal interview by the authors, July 1985.
22. Josef Mengele diary, entry for November 23, 1960, in possession of Mengele family.
23. Inge Byhan, "Joseph Mengele," *Bunte* (Munich), July 11, 1985, p. 33.

CHAPTER 9
The Man in the Watchtower

1. "In His Last Days in Austria, Gerhard Was on Public Charity," *Estado de São Paulo*, June 11, 1985, p. 13.
2. Gitta Stammer, personal interview by the authors, June 1985.
3. Gitta Stammer, background interview by Central Television

(London) for Home Box Office production "The Search for Mengele," August 1985.

4. Josef Mengele diary, entry for January 15, 1961, in possession of Mengele family.
5. Ibid.
6. Ibid.
7. Gitta Stammer, Central Television interview (see n. 3).
8. "Employees Witnessed the Operation," *Jornal do Brasil* (Rio de Janeiro), June 11, 1985, p. 5.
9. Ibid.
10. Ibid.
11. Gitta Stammer interview (see n. 2).
12. "Operation," *Jornal do Brasil.*
13. Zvi Aharoni, personal interview by the authors, August 1985.
14. Letter: Hans Ulrich Rudel to Wolfgang Gerhard, February 3, 1961, in possession of Gerhard family.
15. Isser Harel, personal interview by the authors, July 1985.
16. Central Intelligence Agency file on Josef Mengele, internal memorandum, 1961.
17. Peter Bensch, personal interview by the authors, May 1985.
18. "Secret Agent Hunting Nazi Mengele, Assassinated in Argentina," *La Razón* (Buenos Aires), March 13, 1961, p. 12.
19. Archives of Federal Judge Jorge Luque, relating to West German extradition request for Josef Mengele, certified copies from Court Number 1, Buenos Aires, in possession of the authors; Memorandum from Vincente Victor Fimiani, Police Commissioner of the Federal Police Delegation in La Plata, Argentina, to Federal Judge Horacio Raul Rios Centeno, Court Number 3, Buenos Aires, May 11, 1961.
20. Archives of Judge Luque (see n. 19); Letter from Embassy of the Federal Republic of Germany to the Minister of Foreign Relations and Culture, Foreign Office of Argentina, July 24, 1961, West German embassy file number DAJ 1263/28521/959.
21. Archives of Judge Luque (see n. 19); Memorandum from central headquarters of the Federal Police, Buenos Aires, to Federal Judge Jorge Luque, Court Number 1, San Martin, Buenos Aires, December 15, 1961.
22. Rolf Mengele, personal interview by the authors, August 1985.
23. Josef Mengele diary, entry for August 19, 1962, in possession of Mengele family.
24. Gitta Stammer, Central Television interview (see n. 3).
25. Ibid.
26. Gitta Stammer interview (see n. 2).
27. Gitta Stammer, Central Television interview (see n. 3).
28. Ibid.

29. Josef Mengele diary, entry for April 1962, in possession of Mengele family.

30. Ibid.

31. Professor Norman Stone, personal interview by the authors, June 1985.

32. Letter: Hans Sedlmeier to Josef Mengele, August 10, 1977, in possession of Mengele family.

33. "A Romance in Serra Negra," *O Estado de São Paulo*, June 12, 1985, p. 16.

34. Gitta Stammer interview (see n. 2).

35. Wolfram Bossert, background interview by Central Television (London) for Home Box Office production "The Search for Mengele," August 1985.

36. Josef Mengele diary, entry for June 1, 1962, in possession of Mengele family.

37. "Exhumation of the Enigma," *VEJA* (São Paulo), June 12, 1985, p. 22.

38. Review by the authors of Paraguayan Interpol file on Josef Mengele, Asunción, December 1984.

39. Former Israeli intelligence informant, name withheld upon request, personal interview by the authors, July 1985.

CHAPTER 10
"We Could Have Had Him"

1. Adolf Eichmann, recorded and transcribed by Willem Sassen, 1959; transcripts in possession of *Time-Life, Inc.*

2. Zvi Aharoni, personal interview by the authors, August 1985.

3. Ibid.

4. Ibid.

5. Ibid.

6. Stewart Steven, *Spymasters of Israel* (New York: Ballantine Books, 1980), p. 144.

7. Isser Harel, personal interview by the authors, July 1985.

8. Ibid.

9. Aharoni interview (see n. 2).

10. Ibid.

11. Ibid.

12. Harel interview (see n. 7).

13. Steven, *Spymasters*, p. 159.

14. Harel interview (see n. 7).

15. Steven, *Spymasters*, p. 178.

16. Harel interview (see n. 7).

17. Ibid.

18. General Meir Amit, personal interview by the authors, July 1985.

19. Former Israeli intelligence officer, name withheld upon request, personal interview by the authors, July 1985.

CHAPTER 11
Chasing Shadows

1. Alan Riding, "Nazi Hunter, In a Protest in Paraguay, Demands Mengele's Arrest," *New York Times*, May 25, 1985, p. 23.
2. Philip S. Gutis, "Bonn Said to Have Tried to Buy Mengele Extradition," *New York Times*, June 10, 1985, p. 3; "Paraguay Keeps Mengele," *La Nación* (Buenos Aires), November 26, 1970, p. 34.
3. "Mengele in Paraguay, Say Germans," *La Prensa* (Buenos Aires), February 8, 1964.
4. Ambassador Benno Weiser Varon, personal interview by the authors, May 1978; Colonel Alejandro von Eckstein, personal interview by the authors, December 1984.
5. "An Offer for the Capture of Mengele, Who Is Hiding in Paraguay," *El Clarín* (Buenos Aires), July 7, 1964.
6. Bernd Naumann, *Auschwitz* (London: Pall Mall Press, 1966), p. 93.
7. "Mengele Reward," *O'Globo* (Rio de Janeiro), July 9, 1964.
8. "The German Prosecutor Insists that Mengele Is Hiding in Paraguay, and that the Authorities of That Country Are Not Doing Anything to Find Him," *La Razón* (Buenos Aires), July 10, 1964, p. 2.
9. "German Prosecutor Says Mengele Hiding in Paraguay," *El Clarín* (Buenos Aires), July 1, 1964.
10. "The Story that Israeli Commandos Are Trailing Mengele Is Fantasy, Says Paraguay," *La Razón* (Buenos Aires), September 23, 1964.
11. *Der Spiegel*, Letters to the Editor, August 19, 1964.
12. Letter: Record Department, Johann Wolfgang Goethe University (Frankfurt) to the authors, June 7, 1985.
13. Letter: Josef Mengele to Rolf Mengele, 1974, in possession of Mengele family.
14. "Paraguayans Consistent—Mengele Not Here," *El Clarín* (Buenos Aires), June 1, 1966.
15. Hubert Krier, interviewed by Felix Kuballa for ADR Television documentary, "Mengele," Federal Republic of Germany, June 27, 1985.
16. Colonel Alejandro von Eckstein, interviewed by John Martin for ABC Television "World News Tonight," April 2, 1985.
17. *New York Times*, Obituaries, July 2, 1968, p. 26.
18. Varon interview (see n. 4).
19. Benno Weiser Varon, "Living with Mengele," *Midstream*, December 1983, p. 28.

20. Ibid., pp. 25–26.
21. Ibid., p. 27.
22. Benno Weiser Varon, interviewed by John Ware for "The Hunt for Dr. Mengele," *World in Action* program, Granada Television (London), November 1978.
23. Varon, "Living with Mengele," pp. 27–28.
24. Ibid., p. 28.
25. Ibid., p. 26.

CHAPTER 12
"I've Seen Mengele"

1. "Wiesenthal's Last Hunt," *Time*, September 26, 1977, pp. 36–38.
2. Simon Wiesenthal, *The Murderers Among Us* (London: Heinemann, 1967), p. 151; (New York: McGraw-Hill, 1967).
3. Ibid., p. 152.
4. Ottmar Katz, personal interview by the authors, July 1985.
5. Simon Wiesenthal Bulletin, Item 13, 1978 edition.
6. Benno Weiser Varon, "Living with Mengele," *Midstream*, December 1983, p. 24.
7. *Midstream*, Letters to the Editor, May 1984.
8. Ibid., June 1984.
9. Tom Bower, "What Next for the Mengele Industry," *Times* (London), June 14, 1985, p. 14.
10. Michael Bar-Zohar, *The Avengers* (London: A. Baker, 1968), pp. 200–201.
11. Varon, "Living with Mengele," pp. 26–27.
12. Ibid., p. 26.
13. William Orbello, personal interview by the authors, October 1984.
14. "Nazi Murder Investigation Heats Up," *La Razón* (Buenos Aires), March 12, 1965, p. 1.
15. Jack Anderson, "How Search for Mengele Uncovered Herbert Cukurs," *United Feature Syndicate*, August 28, 1977.
16. Former Israeli intelligence officer, name withheld upon request, personal interview by the authors, December 1985.
17. Wiesenthal, *Murderers*, pp. 158–159.
18. Bar-Zohar, *Avengers*, p. 246.
19. Colonel Alejandro von Eckstein, personal interview by the authors, November 1984.
20. "Nazi Mengele Caught on Film," *Crónica* (Buenos Aires), October 1, 1966; "Brazilian Takes Mengele Picture," *La Razón* (Buenos Aires), January 20, 1967.
21. "The Trail of Mengele," *Gente* (Buenos Aires), August 25, 1967, p. 34.

22. "Ex-Nazi Pinpoints Bormann and Mengele," *Crónica* (Buenos Aires), January 2, 1967, p. 1.
23. "Mengele Not in Cascavel," *La Prensa* (Buenos Aires), July 6, 1967.
24. Ibid.
25. "Mengele Captured in Brazil," *La Razón* (Buenos Aires), May 7, 1966.
26. "Bormann Alive Says Ex-Nazi," *New York Times*, January 1, 1968, p. 31.
27. Erich Erdstein, personal interview by the authors, September 1984.
28. Ibid.
29. Ibid.
30. Central Intelligence Agency file on Josef Mengele, internal memorandum, November 1970.
31. Ibid.

CHAPTER 13
"He Was an Impossible Man"

1. Josef Mengele diary, entry for June 7, 1962, in possession of Mengele family.
2. Gitta Stammer, background interview by Central Television (London), for Home Box Office production "The Search for Mengele," August 1985.
3. Rolf Mengele, personal interview by the authors, August 1985.
4. Josef Mengele diary, entry for February 6, 1961, in possession of Mengele family.
5. "Employees Witnessed the Operation," *Jornal do Brasil* (Rio de Janeiro), June 11, 1985, p. 5.
6. Gitta Stammer, personal interview by the authors, June 1985.
7. Rolf Mengele interview (see n. 3).
8. "Mengele Remembered by Employees," *Jornal do Brasil* (Rio de Janeiro), June 11, 1985, p. 5.
9. Ibid.
10. Wolfram Bossert, background interview by Central Television (London), for Home Box Office production "The Search for Mengele," August 1985.
11. Liselotte Bossert, background interview by Central Television (London), for Home Box Office production "The Search for Mengele," August 1985.
12. Wolfram Bossert, Central Television interview (see n. 10).
13. Ibid.
14. Manfred von Conta and Hans-Werner Hübner, "The Complication," *Stern* (Hamburg), June 27, 1985, p. 55.
15. Ibid., p. 58.

16. Josef Mengele diary, entry for August 18, 1969, in possession of Mengele family.
17. Gitta Stammer, Central Television interview (see n. 2).
18. Liselotte Bossert, Central Television interview (see n. 11).

CHAPTER 14
Greetings from Afar

1. Letter: Hans Sedlmeier to Josef Mengele, August 10, 1977, in possession of Mengele family.
2. Letter: Josef Mengele to Hans Sedlmeier, January 6, 1978, in possession of Mengele family.
3. Letter: Josef Mengele to Hans Sedlmeier, August 4, 1978, in possession of Mengele family.
4. Rolf Mengele, personal interview by the authors, February 1986.
5. Letter: Josef Mengele to Rolf Mengele, circa early 1973, in possession of Mengele family.
6. Ibid.
7. Ibid.
8. Letter: Wolfram Bossert to Wolfgang Gerhard, quoting Mengele, August 17, 1972, in possession of Gerhard family.
9. Letter: Josef Mengele to Rolf Mengele, circa mid-1973, in possession of Mengele family.
10. Ibid.
11. Manfred von Conta and Hans-Werner Hübner, "The Complication," *Stern* (Hamburg), June 27, 1985, p. 54.
12. Letter: Josef Mengele to Rolf Mengele, March 1974, in possession of Mengele family.
13. Letter: Josef Mengele to Rolf Mengele, circa early 1974, in possession of Mengele family.
14. Letter: Josef Mengele to Rolf Mengele, circa mid-1974, in possession of Mengele family.
15. Ibid.
16. Letter: Josef Mengele to Rolf Mengele, autumn 1974, in possession of Mengele family.
17. Gitta Stammer, background interview by Central Television (London) for Home Box Office production "The Search for Mengele," August 1985.
18. Letter: Josef Mengele to Rolf Mengele (see n. 16).
19. Wolfram Bossert, background interview by Central Television (London) for Home Box Office production "The Search for Mengele," August 1985.

CHAPTER 15
"We Don't Know Where Mengele Is"

1. "German President Says Mengele in Paraguay," *El Clarín* (Buenos Aires), November 10, 1970; "Extradition Difficult in Mengele Matter," *La Opinión* (Buenos Aires), February 3, 1976.
2. "Paraguayan Ambassador Denies Reports on Mengele," *Jornal do Brasil* (Rio de Janeiro), November 19, 1970.
3. "Reward for Capture of Mengele," *La Nación* (Buenos Aires), January 21, 1971.
4. Zvi Zamir, personal interview by the authors, April 1978.
5. "Mengele's Wife Prefers Silence," *Novella* (Buenos Aires), February 11, 1971.
6. Hans Sedlmeier, sworn statement to West German Judge Horst von Glasenapp, December 9, 1971.
7. Ibid.
8. Horst von Glasenapp, personal interview by the authors, May 1985.
9. Ibid.
10. Ibid.
11. Letter: Ian McColl to Ladislas Farago, April 27, 1973, in possession of Special Collections, Boston University.
12. Ibid.
13. Letter: Ladislas Farago to Ian McColl, May 3, 1973, in possession of Special Collections, Boston University.
14. Ladislas Farago, *Aftermath: Martin Bormann and the Fourth Reich* (New York: Simon & Schuster, 1974), p. 10.
15. Letter: Hugh Trevor-Roper to Ladislas Farago, January 3, 1973, in possession of Special Collections, Boston University.
16. Letter: Hugh Trevor-Roper to Ladislas Farago, April 1, 1974, in possession of Special Collections, Boston University.
17. Photocopy of personal check of Ladislas Farago, dated January 18, 1973; Memorandum from Ladislas Farago to Joel Weinberg, Esq., January 1973, in possession of Special Collections, Boston University.
18. Von Glasenapp interview (see n. 8).
19. Letter: Horst von Glasenapp to Ladislas Farago, April 9, 1973, in possession of Special Collections, Boston University.
20. Letter: Horst von Glasenapp to Ladislas Farago, August 19, 1973, in possession of Special Collections, Boston University.
21. Draft of manuscript for *Aftermath: Martin Bormann and the Fourth Reich*, p. 520, in possession of Special Collections, Boston University.
22. Central Intelligence Agency file on Josef Mengele, internal memorandum, June 7, 1974.

23. Horst von Glasenapp, personal interview by the authors, August 1985.

24. Horst von Glasenapp, interviewed by John Ware for "The Hunt for Dr. Mengele," *World in Action* program, Granada Television (London), November 1978.

CHAPTER 16
"Pedro," the Neighbor

1. Letter: Josef Mengele to Wolfgang Gerhard, circa 1976, in possession of Gerhard family.

2. Letter: Josef Mengele to Hans Sedlmeier, circa February 1975, in possession of Mengele family.

3. Ibid.

4. "Mengele on the Run: Two Protectors Speak," *International Herald Tribune*, June 11, 1985, p. 1.

5. Letter: Josef Mengele to Rolf Mengele, early 1975, in possession of Mengele family.

6. Letter: Josef Mengele to Rolf Mengele, mid-1975, in possession of Mengele family.

7. Ibid.

8. Letter: Josef Mengele to Rolf Mengele, circa August 17, 1975, in possession of Mengele family.

9. Letter: Josef Mengele to Hans Sedlmeier, circa September 1975, in possession of Mengele family.

10. Luis Rodrigues, personal interview by the authors, June 1985.

11. Letter: Wolfram Bossert to Wolfgang Gerhard, circa 1976, in possession of Gerhard family.

12. " 'Santiago' Identified as Mengele Helper," *Folha de São Paulo*, June 12, 1985, p. 15.

13. Letter: Josef Mengele to Hans Sedlmeier, May 28, 1976, in possession of Mengele family.

14. "Santiago," *Folha de São Paulo*.

15. Letter: Josef Mengele to Hans Sedlmeier, January 14, 1977, in possession of Mengele family.

16. Ernesto Glawe, interviewed by John Quinnones for ABC Television "World News Tonight," June 1985.

17. Ibid.

18. "Santiago," *Folha de São Paulo*.

19. Letter: Josef Mengele to Wolfgang Gerhard, circa 1976, in possession of Gerhard family.

20. Letter: Mengele to Sedlmeier (see n. 15).

21. Letter: Josef Mengele to Hans Sedlmeier, January 6, 1978, in possession of Mengele family.

22. Ernesto Glawe, ABC interview (see n. 16).

23. Letter: Hans Sedlmeier to Josef Mengele, August 10, 1977, in possession of Mengele family.
24. James M. Markham, "Mengele 'Double' Called Fervid Nazi," *New York Times*, June 13, 1985, p. 5.
25. Letter: Mengele to Sedlmeier (see n. 13).
26. Letter: Josef Mengele to Hans Sedlmeier, circa 1976, in possession of Mengele family.
27. Letter: Josef Mengele to Hans Sedlmeier, June 14, 1977, in possession of Mengele family.
28. Inge Byhan, "No Regrets," *Bunte* (Munich), July 18, 1985, p. 114.
29. Letter: Josef Mengele to Hans Sedlmeier, July 8, 1977, in possession of Mengele family.
30. Letter: Mengele to Sedlmeier (see n. 15).
31. Jaime de Santos, personal interview by the authors, June 1985.
32. Letter: Mengele to Sedlmeier (see n. 29).
33. Letter: Hans Sedlmeier to Josef Mengele, August 10, 1978, in possession of Mengele family.
34. Letter: Josef Mengele to Hans Sedlmeier, August 18, 1977, in possession of Mengele family.
35. Letter: Hans Sedlmeier to Josef Mengele, September 1, 1977, in possession of Mengele family.

CHAPTER 17
"Now I Can Die in Peace"

1. Letter: Josef Mengele to Rolf Mengele, circa mid-1975, in possession of Mengele family.
2. Letter: Josef Mengele to Rolf Mengele, April 1977, in possession of Mengele family.
3. Ibid.
4. Letter: Josef Mengele to Hans Sedlmeier, May 4, 1977, in possession of Mengele family.
5. Ibid.
6. Ibid.
7. Letter: Hans Sedlmeier to Josef Mengele, May 27, 1977, in possession of Mengele family.
8. Letter: Josef Mengele to Hans Sedlmeier, June 30, 1977, in possession of Mengele family.
9. Letter: Hans Sedlmeier to Rolf Mengele, August 8, 1977, in possession of Mengele family.
10. Letter: Hans Sedlmeier to Josef Mengele, August 10, 1977, in possession of Mengele family.
11. Letter: Hans Sedlmeier to Josef Mengele, September 1, 1977, in possession of Mengele family.
12. Letter: Sedlmeier to Mengele (see n. 10).
13. Rolf Mengele, personal interview by the authors, August 1985.

14. Ibid.
15. Ibid.
16. Ibid.
17. Ibid.
18. Liselotte Bossert, background interview by Central Television (London) for Home Box Office production "The Search for Mengele," August 1985.
19. Letter: Josef Mengele to Rolf Mengele, circa late 1977, in possession of Mengele family.
20. Letter: Josef Mengele to Rolf and Almuth Mengele, January 6, 1978, in possession of Mengele family.

CHAPTER 18
"My Life Is at an End"

1. Rolf Mengele, personal interview by the authors, August 1985.
2. Letter: Josef Mengele to Rolf Mengele, circa late 1977, in possession of Mengele family.
3. Elsa Gulpian de Oliveira, personal interview by the authors, June 1985.
4. Ibid.
5. Ibid.
6. Ibid.
7. Letter: Josef Mengele to Hans Sedlmeier, October 3, 1978, in possession of Mengele family.
8. Ibid.
9. Ibid.
10. Letter: Josef Mengele to Rolf and Almuth Mengele, June 23, 1978, in possession of Mengele family.
11. Inez Mehlich, personal interview by the authors, June 1985.
12. Wolfram Bossert, background interview by Central Television (London) for Home Box Office production "The Search for Mengele," August 1985.
13. Ibid.
14. "Anonymous Tourist at the Beaches of Bertioga," *O Estado de São Paulo,* June 12, 1985, p. 16.

CHAPTER 19
"Keep Everything a Secret"

1. Rolf Mengele, interviewed by ZDF Television for documentary "Mengele," Federal Republic of Germany, June 27, 1985.
2. Letter: Wolfram Bossert to Hans Sedlmeier, February 1979, in possession of Mengele family.
3. Liselotte Bossert, interviewed by Central Television (London) for

Home Box Office production "The Search for Mengele," August 1985.

4. Letter: Bossert to Sedlmeier (see n. 2).
5. Ibid.
6. "Wiesenthal's Last Hunt," *Time*, September 26, 1977, pp. 36–38.
7. Letter: Douglas J. Bennett, Jr., to Senator Alan Cranston, January 19, 1978; State Department file on Josef Mengele.
8. State Department cable to United States embassy, Asunción, April 25, 1978; State Department file on Josef Mengele.
9. United States embassy, Asunción, cable to State Department, Washington, D.C., April 26, 1978; State Department file on Josef Mengele.
10. Robert White, personal interview by the authors, April 1985.
11. "The Hunt for Dr. Mengele," *World in Action* program, Granada Television (London), November 1978.
12. United States Senate Resolution #184, June 19, 1979.
13. White interview (see n. 10).
14. Ibid.
15. New York businessman, name withheld upon request, personal interview by the authors, October 1984.
16. Legal memorandum, in possession of Mrs. Sheila Dekel.
17. Jerome Sanford, "How Close Was Mengele to Being Nabbed in Miami," *Jewish Floridian*, April 27, 1984, p. 1.
18. Ibid.
19. Central Intelligence Agency file on Josef Mengele, internal memorandum, July 31, 1972.
20. Central Intelligence Agency memorandum to Louis Bachrach, Chief of Operations for Intelligence for the Drug Enforcement Agency, November 30, 1973; Central Intelligence Agency file on Josef Mengele.
21. Serge Klarsfeld, personal interview by the authors, April 1985.
22. Peggy Caldwell, written report concerning photo comparison of possible Mengele suspects, March 1985, in possession of authors.

CHAPTER 20
"Dust to Dust"

1. Serge Klarsfeld, personal interview by the authors, April 1985.
2. William French Smith, quoted by Associated Press, February 6, 1985.
3. Stephen Trott, prepared statement before the United States Senate, Subcommittee on Juvenile Justice, March 19, 1985.
4. Dan Patir, personal interview by the authors, April 1985.
5. Former Israeli intelligence officer, name withheld upon request, personal interview by the authors, July 1985.

6. Dieter Mengele, interviewed by John Martin for ABC Television "World News Tonight," March 13, 1985.

7. Ibid.

8. Ibid.

9. Rolf Mengele, personal interview by the authors, August 1985.

10. Ibid.

11. Ralph Blumenthal, "Mengele Trail: Clues of Paper, Then of People," *New York Times*, June 23, 1985, p. 16.

12. Ibid.

13. Rolf Mengele interview (see n. 9).

14. Neil Sher, quoted by Associated Press, April 22, 1985.

15. Blumenthal, "Mengele Trail."

16. Neil Sher, personal interview by the authors, November 1985.

17. Office of Special Investigations analyst, name withheld upon request, June 1985.

18. Simon Wiesenthal, interviewed on ABC Television "Nightline," June 7, 1985.

19. Beate Klarsfeld, interviewed on ABC Television "Nightline," June 7, 1985.

20. Isser Harel, quoted by Associated Press, June 9, 1985.

21. Rolf Mengele interview (see n. 9).

22. James K. Markham, "Mengele's Son Asserts Body Is His Father's," *New York Times*, June 12, 1985, p. 1.

23. Rolf Mengele interview (see n. 9).

24. "Go-Between Tells of Trips to Brazil," quoting Hans Sedlmeier, *New York Times*, June 13, 1985, p. 1.

25. Rolf Mengele interview (see n. 9).

Bibliography

——

——

Books and Articles

Appleman, John Alan. *Military Tribunals and International Crimes*. New York: Bobbs-Merrill Co., 1954.

Arendt, Hannah. *Eichmann in Jerusalem*. New York: Viking, 1963.

Bar-Zohar, Michael. *The Avengers*. Translated by Len Ortzen. London: A. Baker, 1968.

———. *The Hunt for German Scientists*. London: Barker, 1967.

Bower, Tom. *Blind Eye to Murder*. London: Granada, 1983.

———. *Klaus Barbie*. London: Michael Joseph, 1984.

Brand, Joel. *Adolf Eichmann*. Munich: Ner-Tamid Verlag, 1961.

Brockdorff, Werner. *Flucht vor Nurnburg*. Munich: Verlag Welsermuhl, 1969.

Byhan, Inge. "Keiner fragte nach seinen Taten," *Bunte* (Munich), July 4, 1985.

———. "So Entkam mein Vater," *Bunte* (Munich), June 20, 1985.

———. "So viele halfen ihm," *Bunte* (Munich), June 27, 1985.

Cecil, Robert. *The Myth of the Master Race: Alfred Rosenberg and the Nazi Ideology*. New York: Dodd, Mead, 1972.

Clarke, Comer. *Eichmann: The Man and His Crimes*. New York: Ballantine, 1960.

Cohen, Elie. *Human Behavior in the Concentration Camp*. Translated by M. H. Braaksma. New York: Norton, 1953.

Cohn, Norman. *Warrant for Genocide: The Myth of the Jewish World Conspiracy and the Protocols of Zion.* London: Eyre & Spottiswoods, 1967.

Conot, Robert E. *Justice at Nuremberg.* New York: Carroll & Graf, 1983.

Conway, John S. *The Nazi Persecution of the Churches, 1933–45.* London: Weidenfeld & Nicolson, 1968.

Davidson, Eugene. *The Trial of the Germans: An Account of the Twenty-Two Defendants Before the International Military Tribunal.* New York: Macmillan, 1966.

Dawidowicz, Lucy. *The War Against the Jews.* New York: Holt, Rinehart & Winston, 1975.

Deutschkron, Inge. *Bonn and Jerusalem: The Strange Coalition.* Philadelphia: Chilton Books, 1970.

Dicks, Henry V. *Licensed Mass Murder: a socio-psychological study of some SS killers.* London: Routledge & Kegan Paul, 1972.

Donat, Alexander. *The Holocaust Kingdom: A Memoir.* New York: Holt, Rinehart & Winston, 1965.

Eban, Abba. *The Final Solution: Reflections on the Tragedy of European Jewry.* London: Council of Christians and Jews, 1961.

Farago, Ladislas. *Aftermath: Martin Bormann and the Fourth Reich.* New York: Simon & Schuster, 1974.

Ferencz, Benjamin B. *Less Than Slaves.* Cambridge: Harvard University Press, 1979.

Friedman, Filip. *To jest Oświęcim?* Warsaw: Panstwowe, 1945.

Friedman, Tuviah. *The Hunter.* London: Gibbs & Phillips, 1961.

Friedrich, Otto. "The Kingdom of Auschwitz," *The Atlantic Monthly,* September 1981.

Frye, Alton. *Nazi Germany and the American Hemisphere 1933–1941.* New Haven: Yale University Press, 1961.

Gollancz, Victor. *The Case of Adolf Eichmann.* London: V. Gollancz, 1961.

Gunther, John. *Inside South America.* New York: Harper & Row, 1966.

Harel, Isser. *The House on Garibaldi Street.* London: Andre Deutsche, 1975.

Harmon, Jeff B. "Bowling with Dr. Mengele," *Harper's*, July 1982.

Hart, Kitty. *I Am Alive*. London: Abelard-Schuman, 1962.

——. *Return to Auschwitz*. New York: Atheneum, 1983.

Hausner, Gideon. *Justice in Jerusalem*. New York: Harper & Row, 1966.

Higham, Charles. *Trading with the Enemy*. New York: Dell Books, 1983.

Hilberg, Raul. *The Destruction of the European Jews*. Chicago: Quadrangle Books, 1961.

Hoess, Rudolf. *Commandant of Auschwitz*. Translated by Constantine Fitzgibbon. London: Pan Books, 1961.

Höhne, Heinz. *The Order of the Death's Head*. Translated by Richard Barry. New York: Ballantine, 1971.

Hudal, Alois. *Die Grundlagen des Nationalsozialismus*. Leipzig: Günther Press, 1937.

Irving, David. *Hitler's War 1939–1942*. London: Macmillan, 1977.

——. *Hitler's War 1942–1945*. London: Macmillan, 1977.

——. *The War Path, Hitler's Germany 1933–1939*. London: Macmillan, 1977.

Kahn, David. *Hitler's Spies: German Military Intelligence in World War II*. New York: Macmillan, 1978.

Kanfer, Stefan, with Carlson, Peter. "I Knew Josef Mengele," *People*, June 24, 1985.

Kempner, Robert M. W. *Eichmann und Komplizern*. Zurich: Stuttgart/Wein, 1961.

Kent, George O. "Pius XII and Germany. Some Aspects of German-Vatican Relations, 1933–43," *American Historical Review*, 1964.

Kessel, Sim. *Hanged at Auschwitz*. Translated by Melville and Delight Wallace. New York: Stein & Day, 1972.

Klarsfeld, Serge, ed. *The Holocaust and the Neo-Nazi Mythomania*. Paris: Beate Klarsfeld Foundation, 1978.

Knieriem, August von. *The Nuremberg Trial*. Translated by Elizabeth D. Schmidt. Chicago: H. Regnery Co., 1959.

Koehl, Robert L. *RKFDV: German Resettlement and Population Policy 1939–1945*. Cambridge: Harvard University Press, 1957.

Kraus, Ota, and Kulka, Erich. *The Death Factory: Document on Auschwitz*. Translated by Stephen Jolly. Oxford, N. Y.: Pergamon Press, 1966.

Langbein, Hermann. *Auschwitz und die junge Generation: Zusammengassung von Vorträgen an deutschen Schulen*. Vienna: Europa Verlag, 1966.

———. *Die Stärkeren: Ein Erblebsnisbericht aus Auschwitz*. Vienna: Europa Verlag, 1962.

———, with Adler, H. G. and Lingens-Reiner, Dr. Ella. *Auschwitz— Zeugnisse und Berichte*. Vienna: Verlag, 1962.

Leiber, Robert, S. J. "Pius XII and the Third Reich," *Look*, May 17, 1966.

Lengyel, Olga. *Five Chimneys*. Translated by Paul Weiss. London: Granada Books, 1972.

Levi, Primo. *The Reawakening*. Translated by Stuart Woolf. Boston: Little, Brown, 1965.

———. *Survival in Auschwitz*. Translated by Stuart Woolf. New York: Collier, 1969.

Lewinska, Pelagia. *Twenty Months at Auschwitz*. Translated by Albert Teichner. New York: Lyle Stuart, 1968.

Lifton, Robert J. "What Made This Man Mengele," *New York Times Magazine*, July 21, 1985.

Lingens-Reiner, Ella. *Prisoners of Fear*. London: Victor Gollancz, 1948.

Linklater, Magnus; Hilton, Isabel; and Ascherson, Neal. *The Nazi Legacy*. New York: Holt, Rinehart & Winston, 1984.

Luna, Felix. *Dialogis con Frondizi*. Buenos Aires: Editoriale Desarollo, 1963.

Mengele, Josef. *Rassenmorphologiche Untersuchung des vordern unterkiefabschnittes bei vier rassichen grupen*. Leipzig: Hedrich, 1937.

———. *Sippenuntersuchungen bei Lippen-Kiefer-Gaumenspalte*. Frankfurt: Würsberg, 1938.

———. Book review on "Grundzuge der Erbkunde und Rassenpflege," in *Der Erbarzt* (Frankfurt), 1940.

———. Book review on "Ueber Vererbung angeborener Herzfehler," in *Der Erbarzt* (Frankfurt), 1940.

Mengele, Karl. *Die Voelkerrechtilche Stellung des Fürstentums Liechtenstein; Zugliech ein Beitrag zur Lehre von der Völkerrechtspersönlichkeit.* Leipzig: R. Noste, 1928.

Mitscherlich, Alexander, and Mielke, Fred. *Doctors of Infamy: The Story of the Nazi Medical Crimes.* Translated by Heinz Norden. New York: Henry Schuman, 1949.

Mollo, Andrew. *To the Death's Head True; the story of the SS.* London: Thames/Methuen, 1982.

Müller-Hill, Benno, *Todliche Wissenschaft: Die Aussonderung von Junden, Zigunern und Geisteskranken 1933–1945.* Hamburg: Rowohlt, 1984.

Naumann, Bernd. *Auschwitz.* London: Pall Mall Press, 1966.

Newman, Judith Sternberg. *In the Hell of Auschwitz.* New York: Exposition, 1964.

Nyiszli, Miklos. *Auschwitz: A Doctor's Eyewitness Account.* Translated by Tibere Kremer and Richard Seaver. London: Granada Books, 1973.

Parker, John J. "The Nuremberg Trial," *Journal of the American Judicature Society* 30 (December 1946).

Perl, Gisella. *I Was a Doctor in Auschwitz.* New York: International Universities Press, 1948.

Perlman, Moshe. *The Capture and Trial of Adolf Eichmann.* New York: Simon & Schuster, 1963.

Perón, Eva. *Historia del Peronismo.* Buenos Aires: Ediciones Mundo Peronista, 1952.

Perón, Juan Domingo. *The Perón Doctrine of Political and Social Philosophy.* Buenos Aires: Editorial Fidelius, 1947.

Przewoznik, Enrique. *Yo Sobrevivi Mis 789 Dias Con Joseph Mengele.* Buenos Aires: Editorial Galerna, 1980.

Reitlinger, Gerald. *The Final Solution.* London: Valentine Mitchell, 1953.

———. *The SS: Alibi of a Nation.* New York: Viking, 1968.

Samuels, Getrude. "Wanted: 1000 Nazis Still at Large," *New York Times Magazine,* February 28, 1965.

Sassen, Willem Antonius Maria. Interview in *La Razón,* September 12, 1960.

Schreiber, Flora. "The Satanic Dr. Mengele," *New York Times Syndication Service*, May 4, 1975.

Sereny, Gitta. *Into That Darkness*. New York: Vintage Books, 1974.

Shirer, William L. *The Rise and Fall of the Third Reich*. New York: Fawcett Crest, 1960.

Snyder, Louis B. *Encyclopedia of the Third Reich*. New York: McGraw-Hill, 1976.

Stein, George H. *The Wafen-SS*. Ithaca, N.Y.: Cornell University Press, 1966.

Steven, Stewart. *Spymasters of Israel*. New York: Ballantine Books, 1980.

Szmaglewska, Seweryna. *Smoke over Birkenau*. Translated by Jadwiga Rynas. New York: Henry Holt, 1947.

Tettens, T. H. *The New Germany and the Old Nazis*. New York: Random House, 1961.

Turkow, Jonas. *In the Struggle for Life*. Buenos Aires: Editorial Galerna, 1949.

Varon, Benno Weiser. "Living With Mengele," *Midstream*, December 1983.

Weiss, Reska. *Journey Through Hell*. London: Vallentine, Mitchell, 1961.

Wiesenthal, Simon. *Ich Jagte Eichmann: Tatsachenbericht*. Munich: S. Mohn, 1961.

————, with Wechsberg, Joseph. *The Murderers Among Us*. London: Heinemann, 1967; New York: McGraw-Hill, 1967.

Published Government Reports and Studies

Cole, Hugh M., and McDonald, Charles E. *The U.S. Army in World War II, Europe: The Last Offensive*. Washington, D.C.: Office of the Chief of Military History, Department of the Army, 1963.

Comision Investigadora de Actividades Antiargentinas. Information Volume Number 5, Buenos Aires, 1941.

Ellis, Maj. L. F. *The Defeat of Germany*. London: Her Majesty's Stationery Office, 1968.

Informe Confidencial de Actividades Nazis en la Argentina. Buenos Aires: Comite Contra el Racismo y el Antisemitismo de la Argentina, 1941.

Jackson, Robert H. (prepared by). *Report of the United States Representative to the International Conference on Military Tribunals.* Washington, D.C.: Department of State, 1949.

Murphy, Raymond; Stevens, Francis B.; Triners, Howard; and Roland, Joseph M. *National Socialism Basic Principles, Their Application by the Nazi Party's Foreign Organization and the Use of Germans Abroad for Nazi Aims.* Washington, D.C.: United States Government Printing Office, 1943.

Nazi Conspiracy and Aggression. 10 vols. Washington, D.C.: United States Government Printing Office, 1947.

Taylor, Telford. *Final Report to the Secretary of the Army.* Washington, D.C.: United States Government Printing Office, 1949.

Unpublished Government Reports and Studies
Report of the forensic experts concerning the remains discovered at Embu, Brazil, June 1985, in possession of Office of Special Investigations, United States Department of Justice, Washington, D.C.

Archive Sources
Berlin Document Center, West Berlin; Biblioteca Nacional, Asunción; British Library, London; Bundesarchiv, Koblenz; *El Clarín,* Buenos Aires; *La Nación,* Buenos Aires; *Gazete de Povo,* Curitiba, Brazil; Hoover Institution of War, Revolution and Peace, Stanford, California; Interpol file, Asunción; *Jornal do Brasil,* Rio de Janeiro; *La Prensa,* Buenos Aires; *La Razón,* Buenos Aires; Latin American Reuters, Buenos Aires; *Manchete,* Rio de Janeiro; Ministerio del Interior, Archivo General de la Nación, Buenos Aires; *O'Globo,* Rio de Janeiro; Policia Federale file, Buenos Aires; Seguridad Federale file, Buenos Aires; Special Collections, Boston University; Yad Vashem, Jerusalem; WAST Records Center, West Berlin; Wiener Library, London; Zentralstelle der Landesjustizverwaltungen, Ludwigsburg, West Germany.

Freedom of Information Act
Requests were made to United States government agencies for documents relating to "Josef Mengele." Documents were received from: Central Intelligence Agency, Washington, D.C.; Defense Intelligence Agency, Washington, D.C.; Department of the Army, Military Intelligence files, Ft. Meade, Maryland; Federal Bureau of Investigation, Washington, D.C. and field office Miami, Florida; Federal Records Center, Suitland, Maryland; National Archives and Records Services, Modern Military Branch, Washington, D.C.; Na-

tional Personnel Records Center, Military Branch, St. Louis; Office of Special Investigations, Department of Justice, Washington, D.C.

Unpublished Diaries and Personal Writings

Diaries of Josef Mengele (May 1960–January 1979), in possession of Mengele family.

Diaries of Irene Mengele (1944), in possession of Irene Mengele.

Autobiography of Josef Mengele, in possession of Mengele family.

Letters (1973–1982) of Josef Mengele, Hans Sedlmeier, Rolf Mengele, Wolfram Bossert, in possession of Mengele family.

Letters (1975–1982) of Wolfgang Gerhard, Hans-Ulrich Rudel, in possession of Gerhard family.

Trial Transcripts

Trials of War Criminals before the Nuremberg Military Tribunal, under Control Council Law No. 10, Vol. V. Washington, D.C.: United States Government Printing Office, 1950.

International Military Tribunal, Trial of the Major War Criminals, published transcript of trial, Volumes I, IV, V, VI, VII, XI.

Transcripts of the Trial of Adolf Eichmann, Jerusalem, 1961.

Transcripts of the State of Hesse prosecution of defendants from the Auschwitz concentration camp, Frankfurt, 1964–1965.

Index

The National Bestseller!

GOODBYE, DARKNESS

by WILLIAM MANCHESTER

author of *American Caesar*

The riveting, factual memoir of WW II battle in the Pacific—
and of an idealistic ex-marine's personal struggle to understand
its significance 35 years later.

"A strong and honest account, and it ends with a clash of
cymbals."—*The New York Times Book Review*

"The most moving memoir of combat in World War II that I
have read. A testimony to the fortitude of man. A gripping,
haunting book."—William L. Shirer

A Laurel Book   **$5.95**   **32907-8**